D0084791

The Buddhist Experience in America

The Buddhist Experience in America

Diane Morgan

The American Religious Experience
Philip Goff, Series Editor

Greenwood Press
Westport, Connecticut • London

Library of Congress Cataloging-in-Publication Data

Morgan, Diane, 1947–
The Buddhist experience in America / Diane Morgan.
p, cm. — (The American religious experience)
Includes bibliographical references and index.
ISBN 0-313-32491-3 (alk. paper)
1. Buddhism—United States. 2. Spiritual life—Buddhism. I. Title. II. American religious experience (Greenwood Press (Westport, Conn.))
BQ722.M67 2004
294.3'0973—dc22 2004052655

British Library Cataloguing in Publication Data is available.

Library of Congress Catalog Card Number: 2004052655
ISBN: 0-313-32491-3

First published in 2004

Greenwood Press, 88 Post Road West, Westport, CT 06881
An imprint of Greenwood Publishing Group, Inc.
www.greenwood.com

Printed in the United States of America

The paper used in this book complies with the Permanent Paper Standard issued by the National Information Standards Organization (Z39.48-1984).

10 9 8 7 6 5 4 3 2 1

Contents

Series Introduction

Philip Goff

Some years ago, Winthrop Hudson, a leading religious historian, began his survey book on religion in America with a description of a London street. "When Americans walk down the street of an English city," he wrote, "they will be reminded of home."[1]

Few would dispute that for many years this was the case. Multiple faith traditions in today's United States trace their roots to English lineage, most notably the Episcopal, Methodist, and Baptist Churches. But that sort of literary device would not hold up under the pressure of today's diversity. Lutherans, Presbyterians, and Dutch Reformed adherents would balk at such oversimplification—and those are just a few among only the Protestant Christians. Add the voices of Jews, Eastern Orthodox, Muslims, Buddhists, and Irish, Italian, and Polish Catholics, and we would have a powerful chorus demanding their stories be told. And their stories do not begin on the streets of London.

Of course, Hudson knew that was the case. His point was not that all significant American religions began in England, but that, "with only a few exceptions, the varied religious groups of America have their roots abroad."[2] But clearly the "abroad" Hudson worked with was predominantly European, even if not entirely English. Today's scholarship has broadened that focus to include African, Asian, Central and South American, as well as Canadian and some "homegrown" traditions that are on their way to becoming worldwide faiths. If ever scholarship in American religion has reflected the lineage of its people, it is in the recent writings

1. Winthrop Hudson, *Religion in America*, 4th ed. (New York: Macmillan, 1987), 11.

2. Ibid., 11–12.

that have moved beyond conventional ideas of faith traditions to include non-Anglo peoples who, while often existing off the radar screen of the establishment, have nonetheless formed much of the marrow of American religious life.

Although our studies of American religion have expanded to include more migrating faith groups from more areas of the world, the basic question that divided historians early in the twentieth century remained: namely, are traditions of American life (religion, politics, economics, etc.) transplants from the Old World, or did something entirely new and unique form in the New World? This is, should we seek to comprehend America's present religious scene by understanding its roots? Or should we try to understand it by looking at its transformations?

Of course, the truth lies somewhere in between. One cannot understand present-day Methodists or Buddhists by knowing their Old World beginnings in England and China or Japan. Nor can one determine the transformations those faith traditions underwent in America without knowing a good deal about their Old World forms. The American experience, then, is one of constancy of tradition from one angle and continual revision from another. The fact that they may look, think, and sound different than their Old World forms does not negate the fact that they are still recognizably Methodist and Buddhist in their new contexts.

This series is meant to introduce readers to the basic faith traditions that characterize religious life today by employing that continuum of constancy and change. Each volume traces its topic from its Old World beginnings (when it applies) to its present realities. In doing so, readers will see how many of the original beliefs and practices came to be, as well as how they transformed, remained nearly the same, or were complemented by new ones in the American environment. In some cases—African Americans and Mormons most clearly—the Old World proved important either implicitly or imaginatively rather than explicitly and literally. But even in these cases, development within the context of American culture is still central to the story.

To be sure, each author in this series employed various approaches in writing these books. History, sociology, even anthropology, all play their parts. Each volume, then, may have its idiosyncrasies, as the authors chose which approaches worked best at which moments for their respective topics. These variations of approach resemble the diversity of the groups themselves, as each interacted in various ways at different stages with American society.

Not only do these volumes introduce us to the roots and development of each faith group, they also provide helpful guides to readers who wish to know more about them. By supplying timelines and glossaries, the books give a deeper sense of beliefs, behaviors, and significant figures and moments in those religions. By offering resources for research, including published primary and secondary sources as well as helpful websites, the series presents a wealth of helpful information for formal and informal students of religion in America.

Clearly, this is a series conceived and published with the curious reader in mind. It is our hope that it will spur both a deeper understanding of the varieties of religious experience in the United States and better research in the country's many and always changing traditions.

Preface

> Buddhism has the characteristics of what would be expected in a cosmic religion for the future: it transcends a personal God, avoids dogmas and theology; it covers both the natural & spiritual, and it is based on a religious sense aspiring from the experience of all things, natural and spiritual, as a meaningful unity.
> —Albert Einstein

Although Buddhism is now entering its third century in the United States, students still tend to think of Buddhism as an Asian religion whose roots in America, if they exist at all, are few and shallow. And even while they acknowledge its philosophical depth and ethical heights, Buddhism is too often considered exotic or even (more troublingly) vaguely "un-American." In addition, most students are unaware that there is not one Buddhism, but many Buddhisms. Just as the teachings of Jesus have given birth to Orthodoxy, Catholicism, and hundreds of different Protestant sects, the teachings of the historical Buddha have developed in Theravada, Pure Land, Nichiren, Zen, Tibetan, and many other traditions, each with a different way of interpreting those teachings. And each of these branches, in turn, is undergoing development as it becomes part of the American landscape. Only time will reveal its final fruit, but we are privileged to witness its first flowering now. And although the percentage of Buddhists in America will probably always remain low, Buddhism has always had a greater impact on culture than its small numbers might indicate. Concepts such as Nirvana and practices such as meditation have entered the mainstream of American life. "Zen" has turned into a commonplace adjective, and everybody likes the Dalai Lama. But Buddhism is a much more complex and powerful phenomenon than may be indicated by a catchy phrase, a political cause, or devotion to a charismatic personality.

Buddhism is the fourth largest religion in the world, exceeded numerically only by Christianity, Islam, and Hinduism. It is also the fastest-growing religion in the United States—if it is a religion at all. One of the great problems in discussing Buddhism as a religion is that neither term, Buddhism or religion, was known to the first Buddhists. Indian languages do not have an exact equivalent of the term, which implies that their understanding of religion was different from that of Westerners. Buddhism itself was and is objectionable to many "Buddhists" because the term suggests that the Buddha in Buddhism plays a role similar to the one Jesus plays in Christianity. This is not the case. Buddhists themselves often prefer to use the Sanskrit word "Dharma" (or, for Theravadins, its Pali cognate, "Dhamma"), whose intricate meanings include cosmic law, teaching of the historical Buddha, normative ethics, righteousness, manifestation of reality, mental content, and the factors of existence. However, most Buddhists have acquiesced to the term "Buddhism" to describe their practice.

No single introductory text can provide more than a hint about this rich tradition. We hope the hints will be intriguing enough to encourage further study.

Chapter 1 is a brief introduction to the phenomenon of Buddhism as it appeared in America during the nineteenth century, those first encounters that set the stage for its later development. Chapter 2 is devoted to the biography of the Buddha, and a discussion of the general tenets of Buddhism. This critical chapter is the basis for understanding not only the basics of Buddhism, but also the bases from which different schools of Buddhism arose. Chapter 3 discusses Theravada Buddhism, which while the oldest of Buddhist sects, was the last to have a substantial presence in the United States. The chapter includes a separate consideration of Vipassana meditation, which is its most visible aspect. Chapter 4 deals with various schools in the vast Mahayana tradition, with particular attention to Pure Land Buddhism, the Buddhism of most Japanese and Chinese Americans, and to Nichiren and Soka Gakkai. Both these traditions have been overlooked or ignored in the past. Chapter 5 explores the special case of Zen Buddhism, which, while a distinctly minority religion in Japan, has been historically the greatest Buddhist influence in America. Chapter 6 discusses Vajrayana, or Tibetan Buddhism, currently the fastest-growing school of Buddhism, due partly to the extraordinary popularity of the Dalai Lama among all classes of Buddhists and Americans in general, as well as because of its exotic interest. Chapter 7 considers how Buddhism has acclimated itself to the West and includes a discussion of how Buddhism responds to contemporary issues such as the environmental crisis.

In telling the stories of some of the founders such as Shakyamuni, Bodhidharma, Milarepa, Nichiren, and others, I have perforce relied upon the myths that surround the characters. It is impossible to know exactly how much is "true" from a purely historical point of view. Therefore, I have generally told the stories from the context of a believer, although I have occasionally indulged in speculation about certain points.

The book includes a bibliography and resource section that lists major Buddhist institutions, meditation groups, and monasteries, as well as sources where practitioners may purchase Buddhist supplies. I also include a list of research questions students may find useful in developing ideas for research papers. In addition, there is a glossary and a Who's Who in Buddhism.

A Note about Transliteration: I avoid diacritical marks on foreign words that have already entered general usage frequently enough to be recognized without them, such as vipassana (rather than *vipassanā*). Words in normal type do not include diacritical marks.

Dating: This book uses the now-normative B.C.E. and C.E. instead of B.C. and A.D. The term B.C.E. means "before the Common" (or Christian) Era while C.E. stands for Common Era. The numerals of the dates are exactly equivalent to B.C. and A.D.

Timeline

1844	Thoreau translates the Lotus Sutra from French.
1849	Chinese Buddhists arrive in America as workers.
1853	Chinese temples built in San Francisco.
1868	Japanese Buddhists arrive in Hawaii.
1875	Theosophical Society founded in New York.
1876	Charles D. B. Mills publishes *The Indian Saint.*
1879	Edwin Arnold publishes *Light of Asia.*
1880	Olcott and Blavatsky take *pansil* vows in Sri Lanka.
1881	Pali Text Society founded.
	Olcott publishes *Buddhist Catechism.*
1884	Olcott receives permission to administer the Triple Gem.
1891	Dharmapala founds the Maha Bodhi Society.
1893	World Parliament of Religions in Chicago.
1894	Carus publishes *Gospel of Buddha According to Old Records.*
1897	Dharamapala celebrates the first Vaisakha/Wesak in United States.
	Marie deSouza Canavarro converts to Buddhism—first woman to do so on U.S. soil.
1907	Soyen Shaku returns to United States to teach Russells.
1908	Nyogen Senzaki and Sokei-an Sasaki join Soen Shaku.
	Shaku publishes *Sermons of a Buddhist Abbot.*
1917	D. T. Suzuki publishes *Essays in Zen Buddhism.*
1919	Soyen Shaku dies.
1927	Evabs-Wentz publishes translation of the *Tibetan Book of the Dead.*
1928	Goddard practices at a Zen monastery in Japan.
1929	Salanave practices at a Zen monastery in Japan.
1930	Sokei-an Sasaki founds the First Zen Institute of America in New York.

1931	Goddard publishes *The Buddha's Golden Path: A Manual of Practical Dhyana Buddhism.*
1931	Goddard publishes *A Buddhist Bible.*
1933	Dharmapala dies.
	Suzuki publishes second series of *Essays in Zen Buddhism.*
1934	Goddard founds the Followers of the Buddha.
1936	Alan Watts publishes *The Spirit of Zen.*
1938	Ruth Fuller Everett teaches Zen at the First Zen Institute in New York.
1944	Ruth Fuller Everett and Sokei-an Sasaki marry.
	Robert Aitken meets Blyth.
1945	Sokei-an Sasaki dies.
1950	Robet Aitken enters a monastery in Japan.
1951	Christmas Humphreys publishes *Buddhism.*
1953	Philip Kapleau goes to Japan, and remains there twelve years.
1954	Yasutani founds the Sanbo Kyodan school.
1956	Maezumi arrives at the Soto Zenshuji Temple in Los Angeles.
	Ruth Fuller Sasaki opens her own *zendo* in Japan, the first Westerner to do so.
1957	Aitken practices in Japan with Yasutani.
	Watts publishes *The Way of Zen.*
1958	Ruth Fuller Sasaki is made a priest in Kyoto.
	Nyogen Senzaki dies.
1959	Dalai Lama leaves Tibet for India.
1960	Kwong meets Shunryo Suzuki at the Soto Center in San Francisco.
1961	Philip Kapleau ordained as a monk by Yasutani Roshi.
1962	Peggy Kennett goes to Sojiji Temple.
	San Francisco Zen Center founded by Shunryu Suzuki.
1963	Kennett installed as abbot of her own temple in Japan.
	Buddhist monk immolates himself in Vietnam as a protest against war.
1965	Kapleau returns to United States.
	Hart-Celler Act lifts immigration restrictions.
1966	Richard Baker ordained by Suzuki.
	Tassajara Mountain Center opens.
	Kapleau founds the Zen Center in Rochester, New York.
1967	Ruth Sasaki dies in Kyoto.
	Kapleau breaks with Yasutani.

1968	Glassman begins studying with Maezumi.
1969	Kennett founds the Zen Mission Society in San Francisco.
	Maezumi founds the Zen Center of Los Angeles.
1970	Shunryo Suzuki recognizes Richard Baker as his Dharma heir in Japan.
	Thien-an founds the International Buddhist Meditation Center in Los Angeles.
	Maezumi receives Dharma transmission from Yasutani Roshi.
1971	Shunryu Suzuki dies in San Francisco.
	Richard Baker succeeds Suzuki as abbot of San Francisco Zen Center.
	Maezumi founds Zen Center of Los Angeles.
1972	Kennett publishes *Selling Water by the River.*
1973	Alan Watts dies.
	Yasutani dies.
	Don Gilbert receives Dharma transmission in the Chogye school of Korean Zen from Seo Kyung Bo.
1974	Aitken receives Dharma transmission.
	Trungpa founds Naropa Institute.
1976	Salzberg, Goldstein, and Kornfield found Insight Meditation Society in Barre, Massachusetts.
	Karuna Dharma takes ordination from Thien-an.
	Osel Tendzin empowered as Vajra Regent for Trungpa.
1977	Ruth Denison founds Dhamma Dena Desert Vipassana Center.
	Bill Kwong receives Dharma transmission from Hoichi Suzuki in Japan.
	Bernard Glassman receives Dharma transmission from Maezumi in Los Angeles.
	Barbara Rhodes made Master Dharma teacher by Seung Sahn.
	Peggy Kennett publishes *The Wild White Goose.*
1978	Buddhist Peace Fellowship formed.
1979	Glassman founds Zen Community of New York.
1980	John Daido Loori founds Zen Mountain Monastery in New York.
	Karuna Dharma succeeds Thien-an as head of International Buddhist Meditation Center.
1981	Maurine Stuart receives Dharma transmission from Nakagawa Soen.

1983	Richard Baker resigns as abbot of SFZC. Seung Sahn founds Kwan Un Zen school. Reb Anderson installed as abbot of SFZC.
1987	Chogyam Trungpa dies.
1988	Alyce Zeoli enthroned as a *tulku*, renamed Jetsunma Ahkon Norbu Lhamo.
1989	Issan Dorsey receives Dharma transmission from Richard Baker. Kalu Rinpoche dies.
1990	Issan Dorsey dies. Maurine Stuart dies. Osel Tendzin dies.
1995	Glassman receives *inka* from Maezumi. Maezumi dies.
1996	Kennett dies.
1999	Glassman establishes the Order of Dis-Order.

Chapter 1

Introduction

> Go forth, and walk for the welfare of many, for the happiness of many, out of compassion for the world . . . let not two of you go by the same path. Expound the Dharma which is beneficent in the beginning, beneficent in the middle, beneficent in the end; teach its spirit and letter. —The Buddha

> The coming of Buddhism to the West may well prove to be the most important event of the Twentieth Century. —Arnold Toynbee

Buddhism was born in India, at the foot of a fig tree, over 2,500 years ago. Like a tree, Buddhism has sunk its roots deep, raised its branches high, flowered gloriously, and scattered its seeds far and wide: first to Southeast Asia—to China, Japan, Korea, and Tibet, then to the West—to Europe, Australia, and America. Like the living thing it is, Buddhism has grown with, changed with, and, in its turn, influenced every culture it has met. There is no one true Buddhism, just as there is no one true fig tree. Each grows and flowers in a way true to the soil in which it finds itself.

Buddhism is a religion, a philosophy, and a way of life. As a religion, it abounds in compassion. As a philosophy, it is rich in wisdom. As a way of life, it unites wisdom and compassion in an immensely practical way that leads to peace, freedom, and bliss. In fact, it is this aspect of Buddhism that leads its adherents to call it a "practice" rather than a "faith." It is the oldest worldwide religion—500 years older than Christianity and 1,200 years older than Islam.

Although Rudyard Kipling declared poetically that "East is East and West is West, and never the twain shall meet," he was quite wrong. For in Buddhism, East and West have not only met, but have fallen in love, gotten married, and produced offspring—most notably Theosophy, which, while not quite Buddhism, is not quite anything else either.

For those who understand only a little bit about Buddhism, or only a little bit about Western culture, this union may seem shocking. Western life seems obviously outer-directed, goods-oriented, and ego-centered. The fantasy of the West is to fulfill all desires. By contrast, Buddhism seems inner-directed, spiritually oriented, and dedicated to the idea that there is no self. How could such opposing views be reconciled so fruitfully? One answer is that the gulf is partly imaginary. Many elements of Buddhist philosophy accord perfectly with the American tenor of thought, including emphasis on experience over tradition, a results-oriented outlook, a belief in the equality of all persons, and tolerance for divergent beliefs. These are all "givens" both in Buddhist religion and in American political philosophy.

But another gulf separates classical Buddhism from the religious heritage of most Americans. Christianity, Judaism, and Islam, religions that claim the allegiance of the vast majority of Americans who have any religious affiliation at all, are monotheistic and mutually exclusive. Buddhism, on the other hand, is a "secular" religion, which many people deny (most of whom, but not all, are non-Buddhists) has any spiritual dimension whatever. It is an atheistic philosophy, not in that it explicitly denies the existence of an ultimate creator, but because it makes do without recourse to one. Its religious practice, which may include repetitive bowing, chanting, long periods of meditation, or working on koans (paradoxes or riddles), is quite different from that of normative Christianity, Judaism, or Islam, which rely on petitionary prayer, revelation, and reliance on an outside authority.

Nor do most members of the monotheistic traditions accept the total worldview of Buddhism, which assumes reincarnation and karma, the immutable law of cause and effect. On the other hand, Buddhist metaphysics, which emphasizes impermanence and ceaseless flux, seems in tune with discoveries in contemporary physics, as does the Buddhist concept of *anatta,* or un-selfness, a key idea in Buddhism long before David Hume rediscovered the idea several hundreds of years later. It is probably safe to say that while Buddhism as a religion is out of sync with the major monotheistic religions, Buddhism as a philosophy is right in line with contemporary scientific, metalinguistic, and philosophic thinking. Existentialism and the work of Ludwig Wittgenstein (1889–1951), a noted British (but Austrian-born) philosopher, have well-documented affinities to Buddhism.

One of Buddhism's great advantages, as both a religion and a philosophy, is that it is goal-oriented and practical. Pragmatic Americans like Buddhism because it works, whether they understand its finer points or not. They are attracted, seemingly in equal numbers, to its exotic origins, elegant philosophy, practical nature, and peaceful practices.

Another key feature of both classical American and traditional Buddhist thought is the concept of happiness as a worthwhile goal. Americans have taken the "pursuit of happiness" (a phrase that Thomas Jefferson, in the Declaration of Independence, used to replace John Locke's rather feeble and mercenary "property") as an unofficial national motto. The idea of happiness as a goal equal in value to "liberty" and "equality" is an essential one in American life, but Americans didn't invent it. Twenty-five hundred years ago, the Buddha, too, held up "happiness" as a goal worthy to be sought, right along with liberation and equality. As Robert Thurman, a noted American Buddhist scholar, said in a fall 1992 interview with *Tricycle,* "America was founded on many enlightened principles, such as universal liberty, individual equality, intellectual creativity, social fraternity, and personal power, so it's natural that Buddhism should harmonize with many of the more noble ideals of American political parties." Today, many people turn to Buddhism simply because it offers them what they believe to be their best opportunity to achieve happiness. It does so by offering a unique way to the goal—not by fulfilling every desire, but by eliminating the desire in the first place. This is a difficult demand, but then Americans have always liked a challenge.

Even today, however, Buddhism is not a universally admired religion. Theists oppose its atheistic basis, while others dislike its detached, nonemotional stance. Some feel that the core of Buddhism, meditation, can distance its practitioners from real life, family relationships, and action in the world. These people unite in calling Buddhism "escapist." And of course, there are those who object to Buddhism merely on the grounds that it seems foreign and exotic—the same reason that others are drawn to it.

Like every other religion, Buddhism succeeds where it does because it serves a spiritual need. People who delight in being Presbyterians, or Quakers, or Catholics, or Jews, or Muslims retain those identifications. Others, who find these traditions unfulfilling, turn elsewhere. And some of these become Buddhists.

Today, there exist at least two "Buddhisms" (and possibly more) in the United States. First there is the so-called ethnic Buddhism of immigrant communities from Burma, China, Japan, Korea, Sri Lanka, Tibet, and Vietnam. Most of these Buddhists are born, or cradle, Buddhists, although some have rediscovered their roots or converted to a different brand of Buddhism, such as Soka Gakkai, from the one they were born into. Another group of Buddhists are the "converted" Buddhists, still largely well-educated white Americans, who either through reading or personal encounters have chosen Buddhism as a religion. These two large classes by no means exhaust the possibilities of Buddhist identity (and each has subgroups), but they do, at least at the present time, account for most Buddhists. (Soka Gakkai is a partial exception.)

First Encounters (American and Otherwise)

Buddhism was the first missionary religion in the world. The Buddha commanded his monks to go abroad and spread the news of the Dharma far and wide, to continue the work to which he had devoted his life. Buddhists were among the first people ever to consider the possibility that religious belief could ever be anything other than a birthright. The success of each missionary effort depended partly upon the quality of the missionary, and partly upon the readiness of people to receive the message.

Relying on reports from missionaries to Japan and East Asia, many Americans understood Buddhism to be a kind of exotic paganism. Others tried to find parallels with Hinduism or Christianity, especially Catholicism, where observers noted intriguing outward similarities, such as rosary beads, chanting, and a strong monastic tradition. Whether these similarities were praised or not often depended on the denomination of the missionary. Later writers often saw Buddhism as a completely nihilistic and pessimistic religion. The German pessimistic philosopher Arthur Schopenhauer (1788–1860) claimed that Buddhism was exactly in tune with his own line of thinking.

Early reaction to Buddhism was generally hostile, although there were a few notable exceptions. Thomas A. Tweed, whose *The American Encounter with Buddhism 1844–1912,* is essential for anyone wishing to understand first reactions, suggests that the agnostic tendencies in Buddhism, and its attendant doctrine of "no-soul," were deeply alienating in a culture that cherished the idea of a loving Creator God and the concept of a unified self or soul enduring throughout eternity. However, there were always a few scientific-minded people who accepted the notion of "soul-less-ness" with apparent relish. Others, like activist Unitarian minister James Freeman Clarke (1810–88), who published *Ten Great Religions* in 1871, rejected Buddhism as too passive for social regeneration, although he praised its moral virtues. Even some academics and scholarly writers seemed constrained to show that Buddhism was inherently inferior to Christianity, largely on the basis of its perceived negativity, passivity, and pessimism. Since very few original texts had been translated into English or any other European language at the time, most people had only the foggiest notion of what Buddhism was really about. This is still true, although people no longer have the excuse of unavailable material.

In addition, the Buddhist concept of Nirvana, although complex and subtle, certainly seemed to have little in common with Christian ideas of Paradise. And then, of course, there is the matter of the First Noble Truth of Buddhism: the idea that all life is *dukkha*, a Pali term commonly translated as "suffering." The strenuous optimism of Victorian America was not at first disposed to accept such a belief, although it appreciated the related concept of "struggle" or challenge. Victorians, however, were of the opinion that struggles could be won and challenges overcome by "playing the game," a notion that Buddhists reject as superficial and naïve. In addition, the idea that suffering is caused by "grasping" or desire rather than its being a result of original sin also may have struck a sour note with Americans of Calvinist heritage. However, the Buddhist notion that each being was capable of ultimately achieving liberation struck a deep chord with the Victorians, whose faith in salvation was more loudly proclaimed than firmly believed.

Buddhism also challenged American lifestyles in another way. The Buddhist paradigm, a life free of ambition, greed, and self-indulgence, was one to which Victorian America paid a good deal of lip service, but little more. Although Christianity held many of the same ideals, Christian Americans were well used to "adjusting" these familiar values to a life of capitalism and material gain. Thus, while both Buddhism and secular American culture honored many of the same ideals (self-discipline, hard work, and self-reliance) aimed at the same goal—happiness, for most Americans happiness comes from *achieving* desires rather than divesting oneself of them. It is an immense, almost unbridgeable gulf. (Interestingly, the dismissal of Buddhism as a worthy religion was often coupled with praise for its founder. The liberal wing of the Transcendentalists frequently saw the Buddha as a moral reformer much like themselves. Some of them, especially those with an anti-Catholic bent, were fond of comparing Buddha to Martin Luther.)

The great popularity of Buddhism in Asia and its apparent imperviousness to Christianization remained largely a puzzle to most American Christians. Most people were also shocked at the occasional American convert. (It was bad enough that Asian Buddhists failed to convert to Christianity. It was worse when the occasional Christian fled the fold and turned Buddhist.)

However, initial hostility to Buddhism was rather quickly replaced by an eager interest, if not widespread acceptance. Not everyone who converted to Buddhism, of course, was serious about it, and not all who were serious converted to an "orthodox" style of Buddhism. Many freely mingled Hinduism, Theosophy, Buddhism, Spiritualism, mysticism, Swedenborgianism, and Transcendentalism in a heady eclecticism. People converted for many reasons, both private and social. Some had undergone a spiritual crisis, while others had had negative experiences within their own religious traditions. Some people were mainly drawn to the cultural or aesthetic aspect of Buddhism rather than its religious message. And of course many people were sympathetic to certain Buddhist ideas, doctrines, or lifestyles, but never actually became Buddhists themselves.

Others felt the appeal of Buddhist tolerance, peacefulness, scientific spirit, high ethical demands, and comparative egalitarianism. And while most converts were drawn to Buddhism as an alternative to Christianity, they often found enough parallels between the two religions (real or imagined) that kept them attached to Buddhism without feeling completely out of place. (Various writers attempted to show that Buddhism had influenced early Christianity—or vice versa. Most contemporary scholars reject both ideas.)

While most early American Buddhist converts lived in urban areas in the Northeast and California, there were a few in areas as isolated as Maine and South Dakota. The New England Transcendentalists, who flourished in the period between 1830 and 1860, became interested in Buddhism, although most of them were actually more drawn to Hinduism and in fact often confused the two religions. (Islam and Confucianism came in for a fair share of attention, as well.) Henry David Thoreau (1817–62) is credited with being the first translator of the Lotus Sutra into English; however, his 1844 translation was not from the original but from the French version done by the well-known Orientalist Eugène Burnouf.

In the same year Edward Elbridge Salisbury published "Memoir on the History of Buddhism," which was read at the first meeting of the American Oriental Society.

Lydia Maria Child (1802–80), a prolific writer in the cause of African Americans, Native Americans, and women, wrote the three-volume *The Progress of Religious Ideas Through Successive Ages*. Child was favorably impressed by Buddhism (and with Eastern religions in general). In fact, her main theme was that all the major religious traditions of the world held similar ideas about ultimate matters. Even more insistent was Samuel Johnson, who like Child, wrote a three-volume work on the same subject: *Oriental Religions and Their Relation to Universal Religion*. Johnson was of the opinion that there was a "higher plane of unity" that included the special claims of every religion.

The first American book-length treatment devoted exclusively to Buddhism was Charles D. B. Mills's *The Indian Saint: Or, Buddha and Buddhism* (1876). It was generally sympathetic, but like many people of his time, Mills criticized Buddhism for being too negative in its philosophy. The greatest puzzle to many Americans was how such a "negative" and "pessimistic" and "life-denying" religion should have been adopted by nearly half the world's population. While fascinated with the mystique of Buddhism, most early American observers, like the Reverend Edward Hungerford, found it to be pessimistic or even hopeless, with "no great glowing future . . . no eternal progress . . . No God, no soul, no Saviour from sin, no love, no heaven!" (Tweed 13). Despite the many attractive qualities of Buddhism, what Americans perceived as its pessimism may have prevented its taking strong early root here. (Of course, Christianity, as reflected in the predestinarian Puritan faith, has a pessimistic side as well.)

The most influential English-language work on Buddhism, however, was not written by an American but by an Englishman, Edwin Arnold (1832–1904). In 1879 he published his best-selling *The Light of Asia*, a free-verse biography of the Buddha. (The book sold about a million copies and went through eighty editions; one of its greatest boosters was bibliophile Andrew Carnegie.) Arnold's goal, as he stated in the book's preface, was "to depict the life and character and indicate the philosophy of that noble hero and reformer, Prince Gautama of India, the founder of Buddhism."

The Buddha as "hero" and "reformer" was certainly calculated to appeal to Victorian tastes, and whatever most people thought of Buddhism, the Buddha himself always remained a positive image in the minds of the European and American populace. In addition, Arnold drew important parallels between the Buddha and Jesus, which also attracted readers. To get a flavor of the elaborate diction and style of this epic, here is the first sentence.

> Below the highest sphere four Regents sit
> Who rule our world, and under them are zones
> Nearer, but high, where saintliest spirits dead
> Wait thrice ten thousand years, then Eve again;
> And on Lord Buddha, waiting in that sky,
> Came for our sakes the five sure signs of birth
> So that the Devas knew the signs, and said
> "Buddha will go again to help the World."

Intertwined with the newfound fascination in Eastern religions was Theosophy, a homegrown combination of Buddhism and Hinduism, founded in the 1870s. Its founders, Madame Helena Blavatsky and Henry Steel Olcott, claimed that ancient (and discarnate) spiritual masters held powerful truths that were secretly passed on to the major religious traditions (although mostly Eastern ones). These truths were revealed to Madame Blavatsky, who disclosed them to the rest of us. Her partner, Henry Steel Olcott, went on to found the somewhat more orthodox Bodhgaya Maha Bodhi Society in Sri Lanka in 1891, which actually served to increase interest in Buddhism in that country. Since Blavatsky and Olcott had both taken American citizenship, it can be said that these two, when they knelt before a temple priest in Ceylon (Sri Lanka) on May 25, 1880, and recited the Five Precepts and Triple Refuge, were the first Americans to become Buddhists. (The first Englishman to be ordained as a practicing Buddhist, rather than merely a scholar of Buddhism, was Allan Bennett, who received ordination in Burma in 1901, after which he took the name Ananda Metteya.)

Marie deSouza Canavarro, later known as Sister Sanghamitta, was the first woman to convert to Buddhism on American soil (1897). She left her husband and children and lived in Sri Lanka (Ceylon) for three years (1897–1900), running an orphanage. (Sri Lanka was at the time a British colony and attracted many Europeans.) Of uncertain background—even her country of birth is disputed—she lectured throughout the United States. She also experimented with Baha'i and Theosophy.

Inevitably, some people, mostly missionaries, drew too sharply delineated differences between Christianity and Buddhism, while others, notably Transcendentalists and some Theosophists, made it out that all religions were really the same. In some cases, early writers on Buddhism were more interested in advancing their own theories about what Buddhism was (or was not) than in trying to discover the truth.

Both adherents and opponents of Buddhism, moreover, typically oversimplified the complex nature of its various traditions. Most assumed that there was only one Buddhism rather than many. Samuel Johnson was one of the few early American writers on Buddhism who understood that it was not a monolithic religion, but included a number of sects. However, most of those who recognized different forms of Buddhism often mistakenly or willfully misinterpreted the tenets of branches with which they disagreed (or thought they did). Discussion about what Buddhism meant when it referred to no-soul (*anatta*), Nirvana, and other complex terms was rampant. (It still is, and the differences among American Buddhists are no sharper than those of Asian Buddhists. In fact, there has been little cross-denominational or ecumenical contact among Buddhists.)

Confusion about the different varieties of Buddhism is understandable, considering that different varieties of Buddhism developed in different countries. Today, the division between Korean and Japanese Zen Buddhism, for example, remains sharp in the United States, even if most of the adherents of these traditions are neither Korean nor Japanese, but Western. There are Jewish Buddhists, Christian Zen Buddhists, vegetarian Buddhists, Wiccan Buddhists, upper-Middle Path Buddhists, tantric Crazy Wisdom Buddhists, Buddhist economics, and health and healing Buddhists. However, as Lama Surya Das has pointed out, while important, perhaps insurmountable, differences exist among different Buddhist traditions, there are also many commonalities. In general, all schools of American Buddhism tend to be democratic, community- and lay-oriented, egalitarian (including gender-equal), ecologically and socially active, fairly nonsectarian, and exploratory—whether these qualities are evident "back home" or not.

During the late nineteenth and early twentieth centuries, many popular magazines as well as Protestant and Catholic journals discussed Buddhism and its relationship to Christianity. The first English-language Buddhist magazine published in the United States was *The Buddhist Ray*, which ran from 1888 to 1894 in Santa Cruz, California. Its editor was Herman Carl Vetterling (Philangi Dasa). It contained mystical and occult material as well as more orthodox Buddhist teaching.

Some, like German-born Paul Carus's (1859–1919) *Open Court*, even ran a debate between prominent Buddhists and Christians. Another of his periodicals, *The Monist,* also presented Buddhism in a positive light. German-born, rationalistic Carus, who had a Ph.D. in philology from Tübingen University, wrote his own best-selling *The Gospel of Buddha* in 1894, a popular anthology of major Buddhist writings. He penned a collection of Buddhist "hymns" set to contemporary music. Coming face to face with Buddhism at the World Parliament of Religions, Carus became a protégé of Soyen Shaku, the Rinzai Zen Master who spoke at the convention, although he never took formal vows himself.

Carus thought that Buddhism was far better equipped to handle societal problems than was Christianity; he also thought that Buddhism was the perfect bridge between religion and science. Carus believed that one reason Buddhism was not more widely accepted by Americans was that its pictorial representations were too passive for American taste. He thought the Buddhist "cause" would be better served by presenting the Buddha as more of a Greek god type, with classical lines and presumably a more "Western" look.

The most important event in the nineteenth century for Asian religions was the famous World Parliament of Religions, held in Chicago in September 1893, in conjunction with the World's Fair. Carus was convinced that the World Parliament of Religions was just the first step to global unity and peace. Buddhist attendees included the Sri Lankan Anagarika Dharmapala of the Theravada tradition (although he was not a monk) and Soyen Shaku (1859–1919), a Japanese Rinzai Zen Master of the Engaku Temple in Japan. In his turn Soyen Shaku regarded Carus as a "second Columbus." Nichiren, Tendai, Shingon, and Jodo Shinshu Buddhism were represented as well. (A hundred years later, the World Parliament of Religions was honored by a centennial gathering, also held in Chicago.)

Although the first World Parliament of Religions sparked an interest in Buddhism among native-born Americans, that interest was transitory. Another half-century would pass before Buddhism took firm root in the United States. (One partial exception was Miriam Salanave's Western Women's Bureau of California and East-West Buddhist Mission, a Zen organization established in San Francisco in 1935. It was short-lived. Although she had studied in Japan, Salanave probably did not receive sufficient training to become a real Zen Master.)

Other early Buddhologists in the United States were Henry Clarke Warren and his teacher, Charles Rockwell Lanman. Both these men were Sanskrit scholars who worked together at Harvard on the famous Harvard

Oriental Series. Another Harvard scholar was Eugene Watson Burlingame, who in 1921 published a three-volume translation of the Dhammapada in the series. Other early scholars included W. Y. Evans-Wentz and Kazi Dawa-Sandup.

America Mid-Century: Years of Buddhist Expansion

American Buddhism grew vastly during the 1950s and 1960s. There are many reasons. During the aftermath of World War II, Americans, many of whom had been stationed in Japan, became more interested in and tolerant of Japanese ideas. At least one future American Buddhist, Robert Aitken, actually became interested in Buddhism while imprisoned in a Japanese POW camp. The first Westerner to receive Dharma transmission in the Rinzai Zen tradition, however, was not a well-known figure, but the reclusive Walter Nowick, who began practicing in Japan with Zuigan Goto Roshi. Little is known about him, although he did return to the United States with some Japanese disciples and established a monastery in Maine. Unlike the leaders of the later, well-known centers in San Francisco, Los Angeles, and New York, Nowick remained outside the mainstream of Zen events and eventually stopped teaching.

American society also grew more diverse due to expanded immigration from Buddhist countries, and as Charles S. Prebish has pointed out, the more tolerant atmosphere in the wake of Vatican II may also have spurred many to research new religious philosophies. In addition, while the economy boomed as never before, it was accompanied by a sometimes vague, but no less deep for all that, spiritual dissatisfaction. The most visible of the new disaffected members of society was the so-called Beat Generation, represented by Jack Kerouac, Allen Ginsberg, and others, but they were not alone. And while their understanding of Buddhism was shallow, it was well-publicized. Buddhism had arrived.

It continues to arrive. More Buddhist Zen Masters, lamas, abbots, and other teachers appear daily. One nagging question, which can never be answered to everyone's satisfaction, concerns how representative of their separate traditions these teachers are. A case can be made that maverick and other atypical and unorthodox types may be the ones most drawn to leave their native country to establish their own particular interpretations of Buddhism as the norm. Of course, this has always been the case. Bodhidharma's strange brand of Buddhism never took root in his native India, but flowered into Ch'an Buddhism in China. The Pilgrims were persecuted in their native England for the strange views of Christianity they held. Shia Muslims were not allowed to stay in Arabia. The bottom line, whether orthodox or not, is that the teachers who came to the United States were the founders of American Buddhism, which developed largely under their tutelage.

What Is a Buddhist?

Although defining Buddhism can be complex, defining a Buddhist can be simply maddening. Is a Buddhist someone who was born of Buddhist parents? Must a Buddhist be exclusively Buddhist? (Many people of Chinese cultures identify themselves as Buddhist, Taoist, and Confucian all at once.) Is a Buddhist one who formally takes the vow of the Triple Gem (the "three refuges")? Or can one be a Buddhist simply by adhering to Buddhist beliefs? Are some beliefs more essential than others? Must one be a card-holding member of a Buddhist organization? Does it count if that group exists only on the Internet? Must a Buddhist be an actual practitioner? Is one a Buddhist if one attends Buddhist meditation practice but does not assent to some or all of Buddhist ideology? Must one congregate with other Buddhists, or is a lone Buddhist a true Buddhist? If one does practice, how often and how deeply? Can one be a true Buddhist if one does not believe that the Buddha was more than human being? Can one be a true Buddhist if one *does* believe the Buddha was more than a human being?

The best solution to this thorny problem is that used by the U.S. Census Bureau to identify members of racial groups: "self-identification." Anyone who claims to be a Buddhist is a Buddhist. Whether such a person is *really* a Buddhist can lead to the same sorts of quibbles that one encounters in every religion. Buddhism, in this respect, is no different from others. For example, is someone who believes in the teachings of Jesus but denies his divinity *really* a Christian? Yet this approach may seriously undercount the number of Buddhists. Many people, for reasons of their own, who would appear to be Buddhist by almost any criteria one cares to name, may *deny* actually being Buddhist. (In fact, this trait might almost be said to be rather Buddhist in itself.) Buddhists themselves don't always agree about who is and who is not a Buddhist, and who is the right kind of Buddhist. As a result, there are as many different kinds of Buddhists and kinds of Buddhism in the United States as there are in Asia, and possibly more.

This is a meditation hall or *zendo*. The only sounds may be those of the bell and wooden clapper. *Zazen* (sitting meditation) can last from ten minutes to a week or longer. Some Zen Buddhists maintain the entire world is a *zendo*. Don Farber Photography.

Who Are American Buddhists?

It is estimated that there are currently between 3 million and 4 million Buddhists in the United States, depending on who is doing the counting and what criteria the counter is using. (In any case, this is more than in any other Western country.) No one is sure exactly how many, since the U.S. Census Bureau no longer tracks religion, and many Buddhist groups don't keep numbers.

In a 1997 article of the *Journal of Buddhist Ethics*, Martin Baumann estimated that about 800,000 of these are Euro-Americans, while the rest are "ethnic" Buddhists. Most "convert" Buddhists are white and middle- or upper-class. They are sophisticated, and politically and socially liberal, probably more so than any other religious group (although Unitarians might give them a run for their money, at least on social issues). Buddhists also tend to be the most highly educated of any religious group by a wide margin. Statistics show that Jews tend to be drawn to Buddhism in greater proportions than are Catholics or Protestants, although this is probably less a function of their ethnicity or religious background than the fact that

Jews also tend to be in that highly educated, high-income bracket demographic group from which Buddhism draws most deeply.

Even though only about 2 percent of the American population is Jewish, Jews comprise more than 30 percent of non-Asian Buddhists. Half of all American-born teachers of Buddhism are women, a vastly different situation from the one in Asia, but one firmly rooted in true Buddhist egalitarianism. In fact, the current editor of the Buddhist journal *Tricycle,* is Helen Tworkov, who was born Jewish.

Today, most converts are first introduced to Buddhism through reading about it. This reading encourages them to begin meditation, and possibly to join meditation groups, many of which are associated with a particular school of Buddhism. Thus is born a new Buddhist. However, the first true Buddhists in America were not converts at all. They were Chinese immigrants. Although some writers have attempted to show that a Chinese Buddhist monk landed on the coast of Mexico in 458, this theory is discounted by most, but not all, investigators. The evidence consists largely of a memorial discovered in the Chinese imperial archives that describes the journey (in rather coded language) as well as various Aztec legends about a light-skinned visitor. One nineteenth-century writer on the topic, Edward P. Vining, suggested that the name "Guatemala" was really "Gautamatlan," the land of Gautama Buddha. No one today agrees with this idea.

Most scholars on this topic make a distinction between Asian American immigrants and their offspring, who are "born Buddhists," and those people who have converted to Buddhism. Until recently, most of the Buddhists in this country have been Asian immigrants or children of such immigrants. The relatively large numbers of such people on the West Coast probably explains why the West Coast Beat Generation adopted Buddhism so quickly in comparison with those on the East Coast.

The first on-record Chinese, nearly all males, came to California in 1849, in the wake of the 1848 Gold Rush at Sutter's Mill. Others came later to work on the railroads. These early immigrants practiced a religion that was by and large an exotic stew of Buddhism, Taoism, and Confucianism, although some purely Buddhist practices existed as well, especially Pure Land and Ch'an. By 1860, 10 percent of Californians were Chinese; that number peaked during the 1880s, reaching about 100,000. It would undoubtedly have grown even higher were it not for the Chinese Immigration Exclusion Act of 1882. After this act was passed, the number of Chinese in this country fell; by 1920 fewer than 65,000 remained, mostly old men. However, the few young people left tended to have large families, so the numbers eventually began to rise again. Still, the second-generation Chinese felt little connection with their ancestral religion, and Buddhism started a long, slow decline.

The first Chinese temples on the continent were the Kong Chow Temple and the Tin Hou Temple, both built in San Francisco around 1853. Others followed quickly. (The common phrase for temple was "joss house," which in the Chinese tradition is simply house of prayer or worship.) However, in obedience to the long-standing Chinese tradition of religious accommodation, these temples were not strictly Buddhist; they also reflected elements of Taoism and folk religions. As stated above, because of the decline in numbers over time and low interest in Buddhism by second-generation Chinese, most of the temples were abandoned. Currently, nearly all Chinese Buddhist temples in the United States are very young, most having been established within the past twenty-five years in response to the increased interest in Buddhism among Chinese Americans.

While the first Buddhist immigrants were Chinese, later, during the 1890s, Buddhists arrived from Japan and Korea. The first Japanese Buddhists actually arrived in Hawaii in June 1868, as contract workers on the sugar plantations; more arrived in California a year later, establishing the Watamastsu Tea and Silk Colony at Gold Hill in Eldorado County. By 1900, there were over 10,000 Japanese in the United States. Because of a series of increasingly restrictive quotas, however, fewer and fewer Asians of any nationality were allowed to enter U.S. borders, with the result that Buddhist immigration also slowed to a trickle. However, since the Hart-Celler Immigration Act lifted these immigration restrictions in 1965, four out of every ten people entering the United States have come from a Buddhist country, not only from China, but also Vietnam, Cambodia, Thailand, Laos, Burma, and Sri Lanka. There are now nearly 11 million Asian Americans in the United States—and most of them were born Buddhists. There are now about a million Chinese Americans, but since the Census Bureau no longer collects religious statistics, it is not possible to say how many of them are Buddhists; Stuart Chandler, in his essay "Chinese Buddhism in America" (printed in *The Faces of American Buddhism*), suggests that more of them may be Christian than Buddhist. It has been estimated that there are about 125 Chinese Buddhist organizations in the United States, but most of them have only a small active membership. Today, the largest Chinese temples, Hsi Lai in California and the Chuang Yen Monastery in New York, are geared more toward Euro-Americans than to Chinese.

For a long time, many writers on the topic of American Buddhism tended to ignore these "born Buddhists." This dismissal stemmed largely from the fact that the early Asian immigrants, especially the Chinese, tended to be insular and did not attempt to share their faith with outsiders. Some writers on the subject, such as Charles S. Prebish, used the term "two Buddhisms" to describe the disconnect between Asian American "born Buddhists" and middle-class, intellectual converts.

The religion of the "born Buddhists" has also been categorized as a "little tradition" consisting of community groups and popular or family-oriented practice as opposed to the "great tradition" of scholarly work. "Ethnic" Buddhism is another term that is frequently applied. Rick Fields, in the first edition of *How the Swans Came to the Lake*, actually used the term "white Buddhists" to describe converts, while others preferred "elite Buddhists" to describe the same people. Both kinds of Buddhists are equally "Buddhist," of course. Terms like "great" versus "little," "ethnic" versus "white," or "elite" seem pejorative and do an injustice to the great Buddhist tradition of inclusiveness. And most of the great Buddhist teachers of the world have been both Asian and born Buddhists.

Native-born non-Asians are more likely to be classified as "seekers," frequently searching out different Buddhist traditions until they find one in harmony with their personal spiritual goals. Of course, this is a very American characteristic. While people from other cultures can and do change religious affiliations, it is practically the norm in the United States. Converts may also tend to be drawn to contemplative rather than to devotional practices, although this may be changing. Most convert Buddhists are white and upper-class, although a growing number of African Americans and Hispanics are drawn to the Soka Gakkai school. All ages are represented.

Buddhism thus expands comfortably to fit those born Buddhist, whether in the United States or elsewhere, and those who have embraced it, between (for example) the "Tibetan-American Buddhists" and the "American-Tibetan Buddhists." After all, the very first Buddhists, including the Buddha himself, were all converts! The differences between converts and native-born Buddhists may be vast—or nearly nonexistent. The same may be said of the many varieties of Buddhism itself: Theravada, Pure Land, Zen. Following the Dharma is not dependent on language, skin color, or accident of birth. Nor is Buddhism merely a matter of sitting correctly for meditation, or worshiping at an altar, or studying ancient texts. Buddhism is a religion of rigorous ethical demands, which embrace everything from healthy ways of thinking to good ways of making a living and even of dying and beyond.

Models of Buddhism

Although traditional Buddhism, by which I am referring to Buddhism in its native cultures, was largely a rural phenomenon, American "convert" Buddhism has mostly flourished in urban cultural and intellectual centers. This pattern, however, is changing, with the development of the Internet and correspondingly easy communication between centers.

Today, there are more than 1,500 Buddhist temples in the United States, and millions of Buddhists. Popular films like *Kundun* and *Seven Years in Tibet,* and TV shows such as *Dharma and Greg* highlight Buddhist themes. *Time* magazine featured Buddhism on its cover in a 1997 story. The list of Americans who have embraced Buddhism (or at least some of its aspects) is long and impressive: Jerry Brown, Ellen Burstyn, Willem Dafoe, Steven Seagal, Lawrence Ferlinghetti, Richard Gere, Milton Glaser, Phil Jackson, Mitchell Kapor (Lotus Development Coroporation), Roy Lichtenstein, Robert Moscowitz, Robert Rauschenberg, Gary Snyder, and Oliver Stone.

Dr. V. A. Gunasekara, who comes from the conservative Theravada tradition, has made an examination of the institutional forms of Buddhism in the West for the Buddhist Society of Queensland, and shows that Western Buddhist institutions tend to be of four types:

1. *The Secular Buddhist Society Model* (model A). This model is concerned with the intense study of the Dharma in its original formulation as given in the Pali canon, the development of norms of living in substantial conformity to the requirements of the Dharma, and the encouragement of the observance of the Dharma generally.
2. *The Original London Vihara Model* (model B). This model encompasses the objectives of the secular societies, but places greater emphasis on the necessity to accommodate ordained monks to expound the Dharma. In its interpretation of the canon it tends to place greater emphasis on Buddhaghosa's exegesis whereas the secular societies tend to go to the original canon itself.
3. *The Lankarama Model* (model C). This is the ethnic Buddhist model par excellence. Its main objective appears to be to cater to the spiritual needs of expatriate groups using the particular national models of Buddhism as practiced in their home countries without any consideration of its relevance to the universality of the Buddha's teaching or the external conditions in the host country.
4. *The Meditation Center Model* (model D). Here the Buddhist institution is transformed into a center for "meditation" under the

> guidance of a self-proclaimed "teacher." The meditation practiced is a simplified form of the first foundation of *satipatthana* ignoring all the preconditions that the Buddha was careful to lay down for the correct practice of this technique of mindfulness.

Gunasekara goes on to note that many organizations fall somewhere betwixt or between the pure models that he presents here. Until the 1960s he believes that Buddhism in the West used models A and B, which he thinks are the most authentic, as the primary means of institutional expression of the Dharma. From the 1970s there was an unprecedented migration of Buddhists from Asian countries to the West. This resulted in a proliferation of model C institutions, whose main value seems to be community support, not missionary activity or true Dharma living. Gunesekara has little sympathy for this brand of Buddhism, which he thinks can be perceived as a "ghetto religion."

According to Gunasekara, model D Buddhism was spread by Western teachers who had learned it either from certain teachers in the Asian Buddhist countries (Thailand, Sri Lanka, and to a lesser extent Burma) or the disciples of Western Buddhists who had undergone this kind of training. Gunaskara has little sympathy for this model of Buddhism, believing that while the meditative techniques touted by many adherents may actually cure minor neuroses, they do nothing to help attain the great Enlightenment that lies at the heart of Buddhism.

However, institutional models are ultimately only institutional models, and they do little to answer the central question: What kind of Buddhists are Americans? The answer cannot be found in institutions, but in the spirit of its millions of followers, for that is the true Sangha.

So although some Americans follow the traditional Buddhist path of our ancestors, many more are converts, and in a happy coincidence of independent Buddhist and American thoughtways, have chosen to follow an eclectic path, choosing those Buddhist elements that suit the national psyche and lifestyle while ignoring or modifying others. Others move freely from one tradition to another (a process derisively termed "Dharma-hopping" by some). Thus many Americans practice a little Soto Zen, a little Rinzai Zen, and also borrow freely from other Buddhist traditions like Tibetan or Theravada Buddhism. This has been the way of Buddhism from its inception, and accounts for its remarkable resiliency and growth. As a living tradition, it grows and changes with those who love it.

Chapter 2

The Buddha and His Teaching

Buddhism without the Buddha is an absurdity. A study of Buddhism without reference to the Buddha is impossible. The Buddhist experience in America cannot be understood without exploring, at least to some extent, the Buddha's long life, deep teaching, and wide influence. (It should be noted that the word "Buddha" is not a name, but a title meaning "the Awakened One" and so is properly preceded by "the.")

The Life of the Buddha

No authorized life of the Buddha exists. The first biographies of him were pieced together between 200 B.C.E. and 200 C.E. from fragments of the earliest scriptures and from the oral tradition. There are five biographies, the Mahavastu, the Lalitavistara, the Nidanakatha, the Abhiniskramanasutra, and Buddhacarita, the last a poem by Asvaghosa. While these biographies are in general agreement, different Buddhist schools rely on different biographies for certain details.

While much of the material in the early biographies is clearly historically based, many myths and legends accumulated around the Buddha's life and works. It is even uncertain which sayings and teachings may be unequivocally attributed to him. In the account of his life that follows, I am including some material that, to a historian, must be regarded as legendary, but which to some Buddhists forms part of the framework of their belief. In fact, the legendary material, even more than the historical facts, reveals the meaning of Buddhism to its practitioners. It therefore deserves to be included.

The one the world knows as the Buddha was born along the modern Indian-Nepal border about 563 B.C.E., during a period of religious, economic, and social turmoil. (Traditional accounts inform us that the Buddha's story as a human being really begins 100,000 eons ago when he was an ascetic named Sumedha, but the Buddha's past lives are largely out of the scope of this book.) Ancient tribal kingdoms were battling expanding mini-empires, creating a climate of confusion. Common people were repressed not only by a rigid caste system but also by a religion that sanctioned it. The only path for religious rebels seemed to be that of the *sramanas,* the wandering ascetics who, with their disciples, could be seen making their dogged way across the country in search of spiritual liberation—the only kind available to most people.

The exact place of the future Buddha's birth was Lumbini, right at the foot of the Himalayas. It is said that his was a miraculous birth; he descended from the Tushita heaven in the form of a white elephant, which entered the right side of his mother, Maya. The pregnancy lasted for ten months, and Maya gave birth to her baby standing up, holding on to a Sal tree (the Buddha is said also to have died under such a tree). When he emerged he was "stainless," and was able to walk as soon as he was born. The legends say that as he walked, the gods held a white parasol over his head. He took seven long steps, surveyed all directions of the Earth, and announced, "I am the world-honored one. This is my last birth."

Despite this auspicious start, he was not always called the "Buddha." His birth name was Siddhartha Gautama, and he and his family were members of the aristocratic Kshatriya caste. Their tribe was Shakya. (Later on, especially in Japan, he would also be known as Skakyamuni, which means "Sage of the Skakya clan.") His father, Suddhodana, was a chieftain or prince of this clan. His mother died only a few days after giving birth to him, and her place was taken by her younger sister, also probably a wife of Suddhodana.

Legend tells us that at his birth, a wise sage named Asita recognized thirty-two special marks on his body that distinguished him as a Buddha, a teacher of men and gods. These marks include long ear lobes, a long tongue, and long arms. (In early times, long ear lobes indicated that he was of wealthy parentage; his heavy golden earrings pulled down the ear lobes with their great weight. Only later did they come to symbolize wisdom.) A radiant curl danced between his eyebrows, and the palms of his hands and soles of his feet bore Dharma wheels. Hard to miss also was the protuberance on top of the head. (Some sources claim that the topknot is a remnant of what the early sutras called a "turban head." It was a matter of disagreement as to whether this meant that the Buddha's head was actually

Legend tells us that the Buddha's mother, Maya, gave birth to him standing up, holding onto a Sal tree with her right hand. Immediately after birth he took seven steps to the north and uttered his "lion's roar." The oval halo around his head and the lotus petals (which appeared under every footstep) are traditional. Photographer Helen Rogers. © TRIP.

shaped like a turban, or whether the expression referred to the fact that one could see a royal turban on his head if one had sufficient spiritual vision.)

Asita prophesied that the young prince would become either a universal king or a great religious teacher. His father, naturally, preferred that his son become a king, and asked how it would be possible to ensure that fate for his son. He learned that in order to save his son from entering a religious life, he would have to shield him from all signs of suffering. To that end, his father surrounded his son with beautiful women, music, and lily ponds, and dressed him in luxurious silk. Thus the future Buddha grew up enjoying a life of utmost ease and unimagined luxury. He owned three marble palaces, for instance—one for each season, hot, cool, and rainy. Red, white, and yellow lotuses floated on the palace ponds. He married his beautiful cousin Princess Yasodhara when he was merely sixteen, and she eventually bore him a son, Rahula. Yet ultimately the plan failed. Despite his wealth, young Siddhartha was never satisfied, and said later that he felt like an elephant in a cage. If this is true, there was a good reason for it. Siddhartha Gautama was indeed a prisoner—of his own father.

When he was twenty-nine years old, Siddhartha surreptitiously left his pleasure garden "by the eastern gate," accompanied by his servant, Channa. On four separate trips, he encountered the now-famous Four Sights: an old man, a sick man, a dead man, and a happy religious mendicant, or *saddhu*. The first three sights tore the veil from his eyes about the truth of suffering inherent in all life, and the fourth encouraged him to believe that it was possible to find liberation from the ceaseless round of suffering through religion. He resolved to find out the truth for himself. This wasn't an easy task—legend tells us that there were ninety-six different philosophical traditions in India at the time, all of which claimed to hold the key to ultimate truth.

The story goes on to say that one midnight, the future Buddha left behind his sleeping wife Yasodhara and his baby son, Rahula. (The name "Rahula" means "fetters," which is a hint that even at the boy's birth, Siddhartha felt that the baby was another earthly tie.) According to some accounts, the Buddha left the very night the child was born. Others say that he had stayed only long enough to fulfill his obligation to his kingdom by siring a son. Siddhartha reportedly kissed his wife gently on her toe as he departed—so as not to wake her. It is uncertain whether he was merely being considerate or just wanted to avoid a scene. (The Buddha's wife and son both later joined his order.)

He asked Channa to saddle his favorite steed, Kanthaka. They rode until they reached the Anoma River, which marked the boundary of the Shakya Kingdom. When he crossed the river, Siddhartha cut off his long black hair, and exchanged his robes of Benares silk for the yellow rags of a mendicant. (Some sources claim that he changed clothes with a hunter.) He gave his jewelry to Channa along with his horse, instructing him to take them back to his former home. Siddhartha's life of wandering had begun.

For six years he wandered. First he sought learning from two famous teachers, Alara Kalama and Udakka Ramaputta. Alara taught him to enter the "sphere of nothingness," a kind of mystical trance, while from Uddaka he learned to enter the "sphere of neither-cognition-nor-noncognition." However, the knowledge he obtained from these exercises was merely intellectual and did not satisfy his deep hunger for truth. (He later incorporated both these states into his own meditational system, but recognized that they alone did not bring Enlightenment, only calmness and peace of mind.)

He then joined five other seekers and wandered about the countryside, undergoing tremendous ascetic ordeals. It is said that he ate only one grain of rice a day and got so thin that when he touched his abdomen, he could feel his spine. He slept on a bed of thorns. He had constant headaches and stomach pains. He held his breath until he became unconscious. His hair fell out. Eventually he realized that Enlightenment would not be born from pain and starvation, and he decided to accept a meal of rice and sweet milk. At this point, he decided to withdraw from the company of the five ascetics who had shared his path. They were furious with him, because his accomplishments in austerities had far surpassed their own, and they felt he was quitting just when he was near to succeeding. But Siddhartha had had enough.

He sat down under a fig tree (called the Bo tree, which means "awakening") and resolved to meditate without ceasing until he found Enlightenment. During his deep meditation (*dhyana*), all his past lives and their lessons revealed themselves to him. His meditation was not without interruption. It is said that at dawn on the day of the May full moon, he glanced up at the planet Venus, the morning and evening star, and had his great Awakening. This great event is celebrated throughout the Buddhist world even today.

But even then, his ordeal was not finished. Mara the Tempter, a kind of Buddhist "Satan" who represents both desire and death, challenged him with all kinds of distractions, including his three beautiful daughters, Discontent, Delight, and Desire, as well as an army of demons. Mara was deemed a tempter not because he tempted people to "sin," but rather because he presented them with a delusional view of reality. However, his strategy of distraction failed. Finally Mara asked in desperation by what authority the Buddha was acting. The Buddha answered by a simple gesture, placing his hand upon the Earth. That was his authority, and the scriptures tell us that the very Earth roared in response.

During his meditation, it is said that the Buddha came to many kinds of knowledge. He learned, for example, about all his previous existences, and who he had been in former lives. He also learned about the working of karma, which is the law of cause and effect, and how it affects rebirth. Finally he saw how to destroy the polluting states of minds, especially that of clinging, or desire, which serve to keep the mind unenlightened.

Siddhartha, now the Buddha, saw immediately that the way to Nirvana, or liberation, lay neither in sensual indulgence (the way he had spent his first twenty-nine years) nor in abject asceticism (the way he had spent the following six). Instead, he found that the way to Nirvana, to the extinction of the fires of greed, anger, and hatred, was through the Middle Way. The

Middle Way is a lifestyle that shuns both indulgence and asceticism, a lifestyle based on common sense and reasonable choices. Today the Middle Way remains a keystone of Buddhist thought and action. It is the road of moderation, of reasonable restraint. The body must be controlled, yet sustained.

The Buddha's next step was to teach his doctrine, which he called Dharma (not Buddhism). Dharma is a Sanskrit term, notoriously difficult to define. Since the earliest scriptures of Buddhism were written in Pali, the Pali equivalent for Dharma, "Dhamma," is sometimes used instead. The Buddha probably spoke a language closely related to Pali, but no one knows for sure. (To make things worse, the meaning of Dharma for Buddhists is somewhat different than for Hindus. Most commonly, however, it is a general term for the Buddha's teachings, and refers to the laws of the cosmos.) Legend tells us that the Buddha didn't commit himself to teaching right away, and in fact wandered around for three weeks (or one week, or one month, or seven weeks, depending on the source), rejoicing in his Enlightenment and wondering if he should enter Nirvana immediately. He thought that perhaps the Dharma was going to be too difficult to teach and learn, and that he might be wasting his time.

Luckily for the Buddhist world, however, he decided, out of compassion for the millions of remaining unenlightened beings, to show them the path to liberation. He was aided in this decision by the Vedic god Brahma Sahampati, who told him that there were indeed some people who had, as he put it, "only a little dust in their eyes." These people would be liberated, even in this life.

The first disciples were the five ascetics who had at first scorned the Buddha's rejection of their severe lifestyle, but who later understood that he had chosen a better path than theirs. The Buddha gave his first sermon at the Deer Park (it is still there, deer included) at Sarnath, a few miles outside Varanasi. In this sermon, the Buddha expounded his doctrine of the Four Noble Truths, which even today are the heart of Buddhism. Perhaps to his surprise, one of the five ascetics, Kondanna, immediately grasped his point. As the scriptures say, he attained the stainless "Dharma-eye." The Buddha had made his first disciple. That was the high point of the sermon, and because the Dharma had been set in motion at that point, the sermon itself is called "Setting in Motion of the Dharma Wheel." The other four ascetics soon followed the path of Kondanna, and also became enlightenened.

Others joined too, and the group, comprising sixty-one monks, including the Buddha, became the first Sangha, or community of monks. The

Sangha has been an integral part of most Buddhist traditions ever since, especially in the Theravada branches. Buddhist monks are known in that tradition as *bhikkhus*. Nuns (*bhikkunis*) were originally part of the Theravada Buddhism, but for a long time the tradition of nuns had been allowed to die out. It is now resurfacing all over the world. Devout laymen (*upasakas*) and laywomen (*upasikas*) did their part by donating money, food, and other gifts to the monks.

The Buddha continued to teach for forty-five years after his awakening. He traveled throughout the northeastern part of India, collecting disciples as he went, much as the *sramanas* had done, although his doctrine was different from theirs. He taught everyone who would listen to him, with no regard for caste or gender. His followers included members of the elite such as Yasa and his clique, ascetics such as Kassapa and his 500 followers, and Moggallana and Sariputta, who had first been students of another guru. Sariputta is famous in Buddhist circles for uttering the "lion's roar" that proclaimed the Buddha to be the greatest teacher ever. When he did so, the Buddha looked at him in amazement and asked him how he could possibly know such a thing—did he have direct experience of every teacher the world has ever produced? With that admonishment, Sariputta was silent. Sariputta himself became known for his own ability to teach. Moggallana was famous in his own right for his great meditative powers.

Eventually, the Buddha's own half-brother Nanda, his son Rahula, and even his own father became his disciples. But no women were ordained until the Buddha's aunt (who was also his stepmother) begged to be ordained. The Buddha refused again and again, even when she cut off her hair, donned saffron robes, and trailed after him weeping, along with other women who wished to join the Sangha.

The Buddha's reasons for this exclusion are not entirely clear, although he is recorded as having remarked that a Sangha that included women would last only 500 years, while one without them would endure for 1,000. The most reasonable explanation for the Buddha's attitude is probably the simplest historical one: the Buddha was the product of a patriarchal society, and even if he himself were enlightened about the capabilities of women, he had judged it too difficult for them to attain Enlightenment while in the form of a subjected sex. Some Hindus and even a few Buddhists continue to believe this. He did, however, allow himself to think better on this when Ananda, the Buddha's cousin and personal attendant, begged the Buddha to ordain them. The Buddha relented, but very reluctantly. According to tradition, it was the Buddha himself who imposed extra, severe strictures for nuns, and insisted that nuns always remain junior to monks in rank regardless of length of service. Even so, he bitterly complained that admitting women to the Sangha would cut its life in half. Despite this, the Buddha's own wife also joined his order.

In some cases, scriptures tell us, he used his supranormal powers to reach people who lived too far away to visit by normal means. He also dealt with demons, not by killing them or even driving them away, but by teaching them the Dharma. One particularly evil demoness was Haraiti, who devoured children every day in the city of Rajagaha. The Buddha kidnapped her own favorite child (out of 500!) and hid him in his begging bowl. He then patiently explained to the distraught demoness that she was causing the same kind of pain that she felt to the mothers of Rajagaha. Knowing that even demons need to eat, however, the Buddha made arrangements with the local officials to keep her and her children well supplied with offerings of a less deadly kind. For the most part, however, the Buddha eschewed using his psychic powers, feeling that they were dangerous. He declined Mara's suggestion that he turn the Himalayas into gold, for instance. On one famous occasion, he spoke with an ascetic who proudly informed him that due to his many years of meditation, he was now able to levitate himself across a river. The Buddha answered in surprise, "Why did you go to all that bother? You can pay a ferryman two cents to accomplish the same thing."

The only time when the new Buddhists did not walk abroad was during the rainy season (*vassa*). Partly this was because it is simply not practical, but it also had to do with respect for the green-springing earth. The Buddha and his disciples had no desire to smash tender new growth by trampling on it. So they stayed put.

At first they lived in makeshift, miserable huts (sometimes located in dumping grounds and graveyards), but King Bimbisara of Magadha was so impressed with the doctrine of the Dharma that he gave the new Sangha an entire pleasure-garden, called the Bamboo Grove, lying just outside the capital city, Rajagaya. A wealthy businessman provided snug dwellings. Thus the monastery was born, perhaps the first one in the world. Similar gifts of land were soon forthcoming. This set an important precedent—the close, symbiotic connection between the monastery and the laity. Forever after, the monasteries were dependent upon the lay community for money and sustenance, while the lay community looked to the monastery for spiritual direction and education. These roles remain unchanged even today in predominantly Buddhist countries, where the laity expect to develop good karma by giving to the monks, in the hope that in a later existence they themselves will be reborn with the spiritual toughness to enable them to become monks also.

While the first followers apparently did nothing to indicate their new status except to follow the Buddha, eventually a procedure for entering the fellowship developed. This included shaving the head, garbing oneself in a saffron robe, and reciting the Three Refuges or Triple Gem (*triratana*) of Buddhism: "I take refuge in the Buddha, I take refuge in the Dharma, I take refuge in the Sangha." (The saffron robe is still an important part of Buddhist garb. It serves multiple purposes besides clothing: it is a blanket, seat covering, groundsheet, headcovering, and windbreak.) One ancient commentary, the Theragatha, examines the cultural background of 328 of the first monks. Two-thirds of them came from cities; 41 percent were Brahmins (the highest caste); 23 percent were Ksatryia (the warrior/ruling caste); 30 percent Vaishya (the merchant caste). Only 6 percent were Shudra (laborers) or Untouchables. (Interestingly, this same kind of demographic holds true today for American "convert" Buddhists. Most are urban and upper-class. The very poorest classes usually don't have much time for religious experimentation.) Once they joined the Sangha, however, social distinctions ceased to exist among them.

Today, Buddhists all over the world pay tribute to the Buddha, his doctrine, and the community of monks by reciting the Triple Gem. The words, which are the same for all Buddhists, can take on multiple meanings, depending upon the specific tradition of the practitioner. For example, the word "Buddha" might refer to the historical personage Siddhartha Gautama, to any of a number of enlightened beings, or to an almost godlike, divine Buddha. "Dharma" specifically refers to the doctrines of Buddhism, but this doctrine is not precisely the same in various traditions. And the word "Sangha," while traditionally referring to the community of monks, can in a wide sense, be taken to mean all Buddhists.

Just like Jesus of Nazareth, with whom he has often been compared, the Buddha had a traitor among the ranks. This was another one of his cousins, Devadatta. Perhaps out of jealousy, Devadatta tried to subvert the Buddha's mission by several acts of sabotage, including pushing boulders onto him from above while he was preaching and setting a rogue elephant after him. These plans failed. The rocks stopped just short of the Buddha's feet, and the elephant became his friend. (The Buddha had spent some time earlier in the forest with a bull elephant for a companion and knew their ways.)

The Buddha forgave his cousin all his transgressions, however, proclaiming that even he, black-hearted as he was, would one day achieve Buddhahood.

The Buddha taught others not merely by his words, but by his deeds and spiritual authority, again much like Jesus. Two examples suffice to illustrate. On the first occasion, one of the Buddha's monks was lying ill with dysentery. No one would touch him, and the poor man lay in his own soiled garments. When the Buddha arrived, he and his faithful Ananda washed the man themselves, and made a comfortable bed for him. "Truly," he said to the rest of his shame-faced disciples, "you monks have no one to care for you but one another. If you wish to care for me, look after your own community." Jesus of Nazareth said much the same thing 500 years later, in Matthew 25:35–43, when he adjured his disciples to feed the hungry and clothe the naked.

But on a second occasion, the Buddha chose a different way from the one Jesus sometimes employed to bring people to understanding. A woman whose son had died approached the Buddha and begged for a miracle—that he would restore the boy to life. The Buddha looked at her gently for a moment and responded that he would perform the deed if she would bring him a special ingredient, some mustard seed from a house in which no one had ever died. She darted off and searched high and low. Of course, she found no such house. She then returned to the Buddha with the painfully true knowledge that death is ubiquitous among all sentient beings, and that special dispensations were not to be granted. All beings are part of the great cycle.

When he was eighty years old, the Buddha died, apparently from food poisoning, but perhaps from poisoning of a more deliberate kind. The fatal meal, *sukaramaddava* (either poisonous mushrooms or tainted pork or both), was served by a blacksmith named Kunda, and the Buddha, always aware, told him not to serve anyone else. The Buddha then consumed the meal, contracted dysentery, and lay down on his right side to die. He chose a grove of Sala trees for this occasion, and it is said that they rained blossoms upon him, even though it was out of season.

His 500 monks, many laypersons, gods, and animals surrounded him. Before he died, he asked if any of them had any last questions or doubts. No one did, although it is said that faithful Ananda had to turn away to weep, and the Buddha thereupon entered into four successive states of meditation (*jhanas*) until he passed into ultimate peace (Parinirvana). The last elements of the conditioned world and body passed away, and the Buddha entered into the illimitable. This scene, by the way, is one of the most frequently depicted in all Buddhist art. Some of the attendants are pictured as serene; those are the ones who will attain Nirvana themselves in this life.

Others are distraught, thus exemplifying the fact that they have not yet attained a complete understanding of the Dharma.

The Buddha's reported final words to his disciples were: "All compounded things are impermanent. Seek out your own salvation with diligence." This became a cornerstone of Buddhist teaching, and is partly responsible for the proliferation of a great many "kinds" or schools of Buddhism all over the world. The last words reinforced his consistent teaching. Over and over he adjured his listeners not to be satisfied with tradition, hearsay, legend, scripture, or teachings (including his own). Even logic and evidence-weighing had its limits. He also recognized the power that our own emotions or "likings" have on our judgments. Only when we *know* in ourselves what is true should we believe it. Buddhist knowing is a matter of experience, not book learning, but it is not some drifting, vague mysticism. It is a knowledge that takes effort, ethical living, and concentration to attain, and Buddhism always defines itself as a "practice," something that is done rather than simply believed. Even the Triple Gem speaks of a series of *actions*: "I take Refuge in the Buddha, I take refuge in the Dharma, I take refuge in the Sangha." Thus it is not a dogma or creed. While Buddhism does have beliefs, they are not its defining characteristic.

The Buddha had directed his body to be cremated, but it lay in a coffin for seven days, because no one except Mahakashyapa, his greatest disciple, was able to light the funeral pyre, and Mahakashyapa had been absent at the time of the Buddha's passing. His relics were later collected and distributed to stupas (moundlike ceremonial structures) all over India and neighboring lands. Since there can be only a limited supply of funerary relics, in later times copies of these relics, hair, possessions, or even Buddhist texts came to stand in their place in the stupa. These relics are believed to contain great power, and have been fought over, stolen, and worshiped throughout the centuries.

Stupas are undoubtedly pre-Buddhist structures, perhaps even prehistorical. Once they were the burial mounds of kings. It is believed that walking clockwise around a stupa brings blessings. In India these stupas are generally constructed of mud hardened into brick, but in the United States they are made of concrete.

Teachings of the Buddha

While Buddhists often refer to the life of the Buddha as a model of behavior, it is his teachings that are the core of Buddhism. The Buddhist experience in

America (or anywhere else) cannot be understood apart from the central truths that he taught. Although Buddhists come in many styles—Theravadin, Tibetan, Pure Land, Zen, Nichiren, Soka Gakkai—all follow the same basic principles of Buddhism. All Buddhists all over the world subscribe (at least in theory) to these key ideas.

It should be borne in mind, however, that it is no simple matter to encapsulate the Buddha's vast teachings in just a few pages. For one thing, the Buddha taught for forty-five years (compared to only three years at the most for Jesus). For another, none of the Buddha's words were committed to writing until many years after he had died; this makes it impossible to be sure precisely what he said. Third, it appears that the Buddha varied his teaching somewhat according to his audience. In fact, this last tendency has been called the "doctrine of skillful means," and is a hallmark of much Buddhist teaching even today. Yet another factor must be considered. As a product of his culture, the Buddha believed firmly in the doctrine of rebirth and karma, and these ideas are discussed below. The Buddha did not invent them, and he assumed that his listeners believed and accepted them as well. This creates somewhat of a stumbling block to many American "convert" Buddhists, who have not been brought up to accept these notions. For them, karma and rebirth are sometimes understood metaphorically. Others, however, accept them as literal truth.

As far as method goes, the Buddha generally taught the way Socrates did, through dialogue and skillful questioning, although he also made use of sermons and pronouncements. Above all, however, he valued experience, and counseled his hearers again and again to test and experiment and prove his doctrines for themselves.

The Four Noble Truths (Samudaya)

The central aspects of Buddhist doctrine are expounded in the Four Noble Truths. These truths are the fundamentals of Buddhist understanding and practice.

The First Noble Truth

"All life is *dukkha.*" The word *dukkha,* like most words peculiar to the vocabulary of a specific religion, is notoriously hard to translate. The most commonly used equivalent is "suffering," but that can be a bit too strong. *Dukkha* includes not only genuine anguish, like being burned at the stake, but milder and more chronic forms of discomfort: unease, worry, headaches and heartaches, regret, sorrow, apprehension, dissatisfaction, illness, desire, hatred, ignorance, envy, and anger. When the word is understood to include such a catalogue of woes, it seems very true to say that indeed life is characterized by *dukkha*.

However, even (and perhaps especially) the most pleasant things in existence are the sources of *dukkha*. While it is tempting to identify *dukkha* with experiences such as illness or physical pain, it is a fact that much suffering and unease spring from envious or desirous contemplation of pleasant feelings or things. "What a great computer. I wish I had it. It's a lot more powerful than that dinosaur I have at home." "I really like my special parking place under the maple tree. I hope no one else gets it." "Terry is the best thing that ever happened to me. I hope nothing goes wrong with this relationship." "I pray nobody ate the last of the chocolate almond ice-cream. I'm really looking forward to that." "It took me four hours to clean this house. It looks perfect. Now I just hope the slobs around here won't track mud across the floor." As we can see, worrisome thoughts can spring even from activities or objects that first brought happiness.

This doesn't mean that there is no pleasure or happiness (*sukha*) in life; there is a great deal. But the Buddha doesn't talk about it much because in the first place, happiness doesn't present a problem for us; only suffering does. In the second place, while happiness is certainly present in most lives, it is very transient. It appears to be possible to be in real pain for a lot longer than it is to be perfectly happy.

The concept of *dukkha* is closely connected with another teaching metaphor the Buddha used frequently: that of sickness. He often compared himself to a doctor and the Four Noble Truths to medicine. (Again, Jesus of Nazareth used a similar metaphor.) In this light, we can see that the First Noble Truth involves the recognition of sickness. If we don't acknowledge the pervasiveness of suffering in the world, if we don't understand that we ourselves are in pain, we won't take the medicine we need to make us truly whole.

The Second Noble Truth

If the First Noble Truth involves the recognition of ill, the Second Noble Truth is its diagnosis. *Dukkha* is caused by *tanha*. *Tanha* is best translated as "grasping," "clinging," or "craving." It means an inordinate desire to get, to keep, and to cling to things. From morning until night, from birth to death, we are driven by *tanha*. At the root of *tanha* lies the natural wish for happiness and the mistaken notion that happiness is something that can be gotten or achieved. Another reason why desire never leads to satisfactory results is that it is essentially useless. According to Buddhist philosophy, we already have everything we need (nothing) and are already everything we aspire to be (a Buddha). So desire, by its nature, leads us away from our goal—not toward it. And if, by some miracle, we did manage to achieve our every desire, the result would not be happiness; it would merely be boredom.

Tanha applies first of all to pleasant experiences (desire for sense-pleasures, or *kama-tanha*), such as the desire for sex, food, and even subtler joys like music and art, just as *dukkha* applies first of all to unpleasant experiences. But just as *dukkha* can spring from pleasure, *tanha* can also apply to unpleasant things (desire to get rid of, or *vibhava-tanha*). This even includes wanting to rid ourselves of negative things like pain and jealousy. In its most severe form it can lead to suicide, to the desire to rid oneself of life.

Human beings cling not only to love and glad times, but also to anger, hatred, desire, and delusion. We hold our opinions (*ditthi*) and emotions so dear that we are loath to give them up, even when they are obviously unproductive, wrong, and painful to ourselves and others. This is part of our conceit, or *mana*. Thus *tanha* is not limited to clinging to material things. In fact, the Buddha said that mental grasping was even less satisfactory than grasping after things of the body, since the mind changes even more quickly than the body does. Equally dangerous is the desire to "become" (*bhava-tanha*), to fulfill the needs of a vaulting ambition—even the ambition to become enlightened.

Tanha causes suffering because it is impossible to satisfy, the nature of the world and the nature of the person, being what they are. Both are always changing (often at different rates) so even if one could possibly attain one's desire one could not keep it; it would change. Or the grasping person would change and no longer be satisfied. Nothing in the universe is static; all moves on a ceaseless round of birth, suffering, death, rebirth, and redeath called *samsara*. Our desire, grasping, and clinging bind us ever tighter to the endless wheel while making it impossible for us ever to attain our goal. And even for those who disbelieve in a future existence or existences, it is plain at the moment of death that we lose everything we have gained and clung to, making death that much more tragic. How much more freely could we approach death if we took away its power to deprive us of anything.

If the teaching of the Buddha contained only two Noble Truths rather than four, we might be justified in declaring it, as some early observers did, a pessimistic religion. But Buddhism does not stop with the recognition and diagnosis of illness. It proceeds directly to its treatment and cure.

The Third Noble Truth

The Third Noble Truth opens a door. There is an off wheel of suffering, a way to be free from the grasping of desire, a way to let go. Although it seems hopeless, it is within the power of every human to extract himself or herself from the agonies of *samsara.* The first two Noble Truths are not complete without the third. Happiness is truly possible, but it comes not from grasping and desiring, but from letting them go. It is a veiled reference to Nirvana itself. But how is this possible? The Buddha is about to teach us—follow the Eightfold Path.

The Fourth Noble Truth

The way to liberation and Enlightenment is the Eightfold Path, which provides the guidelines for an ethical, wise, and peaceful life. Since the Sanskrit can be translated in a number or ways, I am providing a couple of "choices" for some of the more disputed or variously translated terms. The Pali word usually translated as "right" is *samma,* which more precisely indicates wholeness or completion. Some authorities prefer to use "perfect" instead of "right."

- Right View or Right Understanding (*samma ditthi*)
- Right Resolve or Right Thought (*samma sankappa*)
- Right Speech (*samma vaca*)
- Right Action (*samma kammanta*)
- Right Livelihood (*samma ajiva*)
- Right Effort (*samma vayama*)
- Right Mindfulness (*samma sati*)
- Right Concentration (*samma samadhi*)

The Eightfold Path can be divided into three elements: *prajna* (wisdom), *sila* (ethical behavior), and *dhyana* (meditation). *Sila* guides our interactions with other beings, *dhyana* brings peace of mind and lays the foundation for Enlightenment, and *prajna* is the transcendental wisdom that links Buddhist mind with truth. While some branches of Buddhism seem to emphasize one or another of these paths, they are all equal and all necessary.

The wisdom or *prajna* element encompasses Right Understanding and Right Thought. One must first have heard of the Buddha's teaching (Right Understanding) and be motivated (Right Effort) to learn more. This is not a mere intellectual understanding, but a personal realization of the truth.

The ethical element of *sila* encompasses the Middle Section of the Eightfold Path: Right Speech, Right Action, and Right Livelihood. Right Speech means more than not lying. (Lying in itself is very serious, of course. In Zen Buddhism, it is said that if a teacher teaches false Dharma, his eyebrows will fall off. Although, if one must lose a body part, it might as well be the eyebrows as anything else.) Right Action refers primarily to the Five Grave Precepts of *panca sila:*

1. No killing humans or animals. Some Buddhists extend this precept, recognizing that all is made up of nonliving elements, to the "lives of minerals" and thus use the First Precept as a basis for environmental activism.
2. No stealing. This injunction includes exploitation and social injustice, both of which steal the spirit of others.
3. No sexual misconduct or gluttony (it all comes under the rubric of "misuse of the senses"). In fact, the Buddha ordered strict celibacy for his monks, informing them that it would be better if "your member entered the mouth of an enraged cobra or viper than the organ of a woman." In modern terms, this precept is generally used to endorse sexual chastity for monastics and responsible sexual behavior toward others, saving sex for marriage or at the very least for one person with whom one has a committed, permanent relationship.
4. No telling lies. This component of the Five Precepts includes open-minded listening, and joyful speech—speech that is not frivolous and that is intended to heal, enlighten, and bring joy. It means no gossiping, no slandering, no swearing, no using harsh or hurtful language, and no wasting other people's time with idle chitchat.
5. No drinking or drugs. They cloud the senses and injure the body. As the Vietnamese monk and peace activist Thich Nhat Hanh has reminded us, "Mindful consumption is the object of this precept. We are what we consume."

Right Livelihood means to live in such a way that the Five Precepts are not violated. Certain jobs, such as that of slaughterer, violate the First Precept. But other occupations, such as that of being a teacher, lawyer, or merchant, can leave one vulnerable to violating other of the precepts. It is not forbidden to choose such a profession, but one must keep the precepts constantly in mind so as not to violate them.

These precepts are phrased negatively, which serves to open a much wider field of action than positively phrased injunctions. For example, one may say to a child, "Don't walk down Maple Street," which gives him or her an opportunity to walk down any number of other streets. If, however, one says, "Walk down Elm Street," the obedient child has no choice in the matter but to walk down Elm Street. Of course, negative precepts allow people a lot of maneuvering room as well, so Buddhist teachers are careful to inculcate the spirit as well as the letter of each precept to students.

Each of the Five Grave Precepts is of course open to interpretation. Different traditions, cultures, and even individuals disagree about whether or not it is ever permissible to kill animals or even human beings. Is it ever permissible to tell a lie, perhaps to save a life or to make someone feel better? As in other religious traditions, an endless number of Buddhist books on ethics have been written dealing with these complicated issues.

To show how culture plays a part, Robert Aitken uses the example of terminal illness. In Japanese culture, it is considered compassionate to lie to the patient about the seriousness of his or her disease. In the United States, it is considered better to be "truthful." What constitutes a "lie" is not universally agreed upon. Culture and circumstance play a part. For example, a person is usually not considered to lie when she is playing poker, even when she is, by her betting, intending to deceive other players. That's because the other players know the rules and expect her to attempt to deceive them. Perhaps in the same way, members of certain cultures expect to be deceived about matters like terminal illnesses. As a worldwide religion, Buddhism makes allowance for differences in culture and expects people to follow the precepts in culturally acceptable ways.

In addition to the Five Grave Precepts, monks were to adhere to five additional ones: (1) no eating more than one meal a day, and that must be consumed by noon; (2) no attending the theater or other worldly entertainments; (3) no using perfumes or jewelry; (4) no sleeping on luxurious beds; and (5) no handling of money, gold, or silver. Monks who were fully professed had to follow the 227 rules of the Sangha as well.

The last step on the Eightfold Path is Right Meditation, or *samadhi*. It encompasses Right Effort, Right Mindfulness, and Right Concentration. In Right Effort, one purifies the mind from unwholesome thoughts. In Right Mindfulness, one becomes consciously aware of all aspects of existence. And in Right Meditation, one enters into progressively higher states of consciousness.

Central Buddhist Concepts

Central Buddhist beliefs are not like the dogmas of religion—all are subject to investigation. The Buddha taught that one should not believe a thing merely because it is preached, and invited his listeners to look and see for themselves whether or not what he was saying was true.

A-theism

There is no personal creator-God in Buddhism. While the Buddha did not formally deny that such a being could exist, he treated it as of no importance and impossible to know in any case. For this reason, many Western critics denied that Buddhism could even be called a proper religion, although there is no "legal" definition of the term, and, like most religions, Buddhism contains a highly evolved ethical system and a concern for ultimate truths about the world.

The Buddha also taught that the gods were irrelevant, or perhaps nonexistent. If they did exist, they existed on their own plane, far from human events. They were not enlightened or ethically superior to human beings, only longer-lived, more powerful, and probably happier. These qualities, however, did not make them worthy of prayer, and if prayed to, they would be unable or unwilling to answer. (Hindus later got their revenge on the Buddha's atheism by claiming that the Buddha himself was an avatar of the great god Vishnu.)

The word "agnostic" might be the perfect one to apply to the Buddha, except that like "atheist" without the hyphen, it has taken on connotations that may not apply to the Buddha's thought. Buddha never spent time vehemently *denying* the existence of gods. It was something he just didn't want to talk about. The important element for Buddhists is that early, classical Buddhism does not have recourse to a supreme being. Things are more complex in the Mahayana tradition of Buddhism, which developed the concept of bodhisattvas, who indeed have many godlike properties.

Anatta: The Doctrine of No-Self

Buddhism maintains quite simply that no construct such as the "self" exists. Nearly all religions pay tribute to the idea of "selflessness," and in its Christian formulation, the idea is a familiar concept to Americans. Selflessness means charitable giving, consideration for others, and sacrifice for the greater good. It is an ethical concept. Buddhism has a similar ethical concept, expressed in the word *dana,* or generosity. *Dana* is based upon compassion (*karuna*) for the sufferings of all beings. In Buddhism, however, the idea of *selflessness* is not an ethical ideal at all; it's a profound metaphysical truth. There is no self.

This doesn't mean that the word "I" can never be spoke by Buddhists, of course. It does mean that we should know what we really mean when we say it. That which we call "self" is a mere convention, a name, a figure of speech, a shorthand way of expressing a process. The "self" is an event. It is not a substantial metaphysical reality. This difficult concept of *anatta* lies at the heart of Buddhism, and while the notion that there is no enduring self may seem a dark and pessimistic idea to Westerners, to Buddhists it is liberating. As long as we cling to the idea of a self, we are bound to the ever-turning wheel of birth and rebirth. When we let go of the idea of self, we let go of that world and enter Nirvana, the state beyond life and death. (When asked if a person continues to exist after death, the Buddha maintained a "noble silence." There is obviously no answer to such a question.) If there is no self, then even suffering is *ultimately* an illusion, a mistaken notion, for there is no being who can suffer. Thus, the idea of a "self" is not only metaphysically mistaken, it also leads to existential suffering. It is an example of *avidya,* or the ignorance that lies at the root of so many wrong ideas and painful lives.

For the human being is, like every other being on earth, not a thing, but a process, an event, an ever-changing condition. Since we cannot remain entirely the *same* from moment to moment, it follows that we are different, and then different again the next moment. Even if the difference is very slight, it nonetheless *is* a difference. We see, therefore, that what we call a "self" is a compendium, a bundle of disparate physical components, feelings, sensations, ideas, likes, aversions, pains, and fancies. None of these fleeting features constitutes a "self." To put it more bluntly, the "self" is merely a hypothesis, a mistaken reification, or "thing-making." Buddhism regards the self as subject, not as a thing or object. As a subject, it is growing, changing, expanding, and capable of liberation. On the deepest philosophical level, it simply isn't there at all; it's just a convenient way of talking about a curious phenomenon.

The Buddha's insistence upon this doctrine was a response to what he saw as a fatal flaw in classical Hindu philosophy, expounded in the sacred scriptures called Vedanta, which insists upon an eternal self or Atman. The Atman was unconditioned, meaning that it was unlimited by physical, mental, or psychological phenomena. The Buddha's problem with this apparently optimistic notion was that it encouraged people to identify themselves with this eternal but invisible substance. This in turn led people to think of themselves as something separate and apart from the world of *samsara,* as essentially having nothing ultimately to do with it. In fact, many classical Hindu thinkers maintain that *samsara* is not truly real, since it partakes of ceaseless material change. In their metaphysic, only the Atman and its universal counterpart, the Brahman, is real. When people separate themselves from the world in this way, the Buddha felt, they divorced themselves from the ability to live fruitfully in the world or to exhibit compassion. (There is no point in being compassionate to beings who are not real.) In the Buddhist view, this dehumanizes us.

For the Buddha, only by maintaining that "selfhood" is an artificial construct can we free ourselves to act authentically, and perhaps, according to some Buddhist thinkers, radically reconstruct an idea of self that stretches beyond the subject individual to include all beings. Curiously, this idea is also found in Hinduism, so it is an idea that serves to unite Buddhism and its mother religion more closely than either would sometimes care to admit. Having no fixed self is, to Buddhists, a concept that sets us free by relieving us of a burdensome attachment. This brings us to another point. The Buddhist (and Hindu) ideal of nonattachment is not easily accepted by Westerners. What about love, they ask? Isn't love an important value? How can there be love if there is no attachment? This is precisely the Buddhist point. Real love has nothing to do with attachment and grasping. It has everything to do with freedom. Nonattachment makes real love possible.

In Buddhist philosophy, the "self" is merely a conventional way of referring to a temporary and always changing collection of attributes, perceptions, and consciousness. It is like the wind, dwelling nowhere, being in itself nothing, yet manifesting itself through its very vicissitudes and changefulness. When the wind stops blowing, it disappears; its "substance" is in its movement, which is by definition, change. Other analogies could include a cloud, fire, a rainbow, or a mirage. The idea is that the self is a collection of attributes which themselves are ever changing. This is why clinging to the concept of self is a futile endeavor; one cannot cling to the wind.

What human beings perceive as the self, the Buddha called the "Five Aggregates" or "Five Heaps." The Sanskrit word is *skandha,* while the cognate Pali word is *khandha.* The Buddha used the analogy of a chariot, which is made up of wheels, axle, body, and so forth. None of them is separately a chariot; only the aggregate can be so called. Here are the Five Aggregates:

1. Matter or form (*rupa*). This includes the physical body (gender, size, and age, for example) and its four elements:

- Earth element, or solidity, by which a material body has some degree of hardness or softness, roughness or smoothness.
- Water element, or fluidity, which represents the property of cohesion.
- Heat or fire element, possessed by all bodies. In contemporary terms, this is called energy.
- Air or wind element—the principle of distention and vibration, by which all material particles are in a state of vibration. By reason of the air element, material bodies exhibit movement.

All material phenomena, including bodies, possess these four elements in varying degrees. What distinguishes each body from another is the proportion in which the primary elements are combined. We discriminate the types of matter on the basis of the dominant element as well as their derivatives, the sense organs and their respective functions. These include the five sensory receptors, or faculties of the eyes, ears, nose, tongue, and body. It also includes sense data, and what is called the life faculty, which keeps the body alive.

The other four components relate to the mental, rather than the physical life.

2. Sensation or feeling (*vedana*). This refers to the impression or "taste" that accompanies our contact with an object with one or more of the senses. These sensations can be physical or mental. Sensations can be pleasant, unpleasant, or neutral. The simplest example might be what happens when one slams one's head into a wall. It is the mind, of course, that decides how to assess the sensation. This can vary from mind to mind. Some persons, for instance, like to be tickled and others don't. This a primitive, preconscious recognition, not sharp enough to be called "awareness"

or even "perception." Altogether, the Buddha analyzed eighteen types of feeling, three kinds each through six sense faculties, the sensory receptors plus the mind. When there is a pleasant object or feeling, attachment is bound to arise, and when there is an unpleasant object, aversion will arise. Both attachment and aversion are hindrances to Enlightenment.

3. Perception (*samjna*). Although perception may seem to be identical to sensation, there is a difference. In perception, the mind intellectually recognizes the object. For example, one can have one's head slammed into a wall and feel a sensation, but might not actually know what one's head was slammed into. In perception, the person recognizes that object as a wall. It is a "processing mechanism."

4. Mental formations (*samskara*). These include all volitional or willed activities of the mind, including emotions. It includes the process of naming and identifying phenomena.

5. Consciousness (*vijnana*). Consciousness or discrimination arises along with a suitable set of conditions. There are six types of consciousness, all arising from contact of an object with its bodily organ. So there is a consciousness of seeing, hearing, smelling, tasting, touch, and mental consciousness.

Together the Five Aggregates are called the "aggregates of attachment" and are subject to birth, old age, and death.

Dukkha: The Inevitability of Suffering

As the First Noble Truth explains, *dukkha* is an inherent part of existence. It cannot be avoided. Along with the doctrines of *anicca* and *anatta,* it is one of the Three Marks of Existence.

Anicca: The Doctrine of Impermanence

Nothing is permanent; all things are constantly in flux. Boulders wear down, stars die, and even the solid little atom is not so solid as we used to think. *Anicca,* along with no-selfness and suffering, is one of the three characteristics of existence. In most Buddhist thinking, only Nirvana is exempt from *anicca* and some thinkers aren't too certain about that, either.

Karma

Karma refers to action and the fruits of action, and has been properly likened to a law of physics. No one can escape it or change it. Prayers, sacrifice, mortifications, bribery, trickery, even the gods are powerless over this purely mechanical process. If it were otherwise, the laws of the universe would be in abeyance, and nothing would be certain. Karma is part of Dharma. It determines one's status in this life and the next. Our destiny in the next world is the result of choices and actions in this life and the lives previous to this one. However, once we are placed in this life, we are free to make of it what we will. Our next birth can be better than this one. Because existence entails suffering, the goal is to remove oneself from the endless round of existence. This can be done by eliminating ignorance and craving. When we are liberated from this cycle, we achieve Nirvana.

Karma should not be confused with blind fate. In Buddhist philosophy, all thoughts and actions leave a "track"; in other words, they have an effect that reverberates throughout the life (and beyond) of the person who is responsible for them. If disaster befalls one, however, it should not be seen as a punishment, for in Buddhism there is no one to punish us. Instead, disaster is a natural result of some earlier act. We create our own destiny.

Having said this, however, it is important to understand that not every misfortune that falls upon us is necessarily the result of some immoral act or weakness, in either this life or a previous one. We can also suffer from the immoral acts or weaknesses of others, and the cycle can go on indefinitely until all reach Enlightenment. Furthermore, each action carries two effects. One is a manifest effect, which may not appear until a certain period of time has passed. The second effect is an inward one, which is impressed immediately upon the heart, whether it shows itself outwardly right away or not. For example, if a person sticks a pin into his or her hand, it may take a while before the infection manifests itself. However, the instant the pin enters the body, it carries the germs of that infection, even though the injured person may be unaware of the true hurt, and felt only the momentary annoyance of the pinprick.

In a like manner, there are two causes for each effect, internal and external. External causes impinge upon us from without. For instance, let's say a brick falls on one's head. That is certainly a cause for pain and anger. But the falling brick does not *compel* us to respond with anger. Our response is the second cause, and that is our choice. Instead of responding with fury to the person who dropped or threw the brick, we can respond with loving concern to make sure that no else gets hit with a brick in a like manner, either by working to make sure better safety precautions are put into play or by having the person who threw the brick get the psychological care she or he needs. We are responsible for our own actions, and by our choices we can turn disaster into good. Obviously it is not always possible to find much good in a disaster. One simply has to do the best one can, and then "let it go."

The result (or, in colloquial parlance, "comeupance") of karma is called *vipaka,* a Pali word that literally means "ripening." Karma itself means "deed " or "action." *Vipaka* is the ripening of action. While some may see this concept as fatalistic, it appears otherwise to Buddhists. For while we must by the inexorable laws of logic bear the effects of our actions, at every moment in our lives we are in a sense reborn and able to make our lives anew. New lives mean new choices, and new karma. (In addition, everyone also has pieces of seemingly undeserved luck, too. These lucky moments are likewise the results of accrued karma, for which we may congratulate ourselves. We earned them.) The doctrine of karma also explains why some people seem to have everything—wealth, power, position—but then suffer a serious health problem or some other catastrophe.

Thus it is possible for humans to be reborn into the animal world, or that of demons, hungry ghosts, or even hell-beings. Good karma can bring us to the world of gods. But all worlds are limited by time. Only by achieving Nirvana can one triumph over the conditioned cosmos.

It is also possible, according to some practitioners, to disperse bad karma in this lifetime by certain kinds of mindfulness practice, in which karmic formations are permitted to rise in the mind, be recognized, and then pass away into oblivion. Other Buddhists welcome misfortune, believing that they are having an opportunity to burn off bad karma in this life, thus freeing them for advancement in the next.

Rebirth and *Samsara*

Samsara is the world of ceaseless birth and rebirth. It has no true beginning or end. All beings have led an infinite number of past lives. Only our ignorance and delusion keep us from being aware of them. Rebirth can occur in both the animal and human spheres. This notion helps explain the population explosion. Although more people exist on earth than ever before, the total number of sentient life-forms remains constant.

Samsara means that one can be reborn again and again into the realms of the hell-beings, hungry ghosts, animals, humans, or worlds of the gods. No one can escape rebirth, which is considered a bad thing, for the world is full of *dukkha*.

In the Buddhist idea of rebirth, what passes from one life to the next is not a substance, not a "thing," not even a soul. Rather, it is the continuation of a process. There is causal connection between one birth (and thus one life) and the next. Karma accumulated in one life influences the new birth. It is not the same "person" who is reborn, but it's not precisely someone else either. The classical explanation for this procedure is the example of a candle flame that is passed to another. The new flame is not the old flame, but it's not a totally different one either.

Another way of looking at it is that there is birth and death (or generation and extinction) at each moment. This ceaseless birth and death is common to all sentient beings, not just human beings. This makes the candle flame analogy complete, for just as the candle flame is constantly dying and being renewed by burning the wax, so each of us is constantly dying and being reborn, even in the midst of life.

In the classical Buddhist scheme of things, all beings are subject to birth, death, and rebirth (*samsara*), at least until one has attained Enlightenment. One may be born into any of the six realms: that of the gods, humans, spirits, hungry ghosts, demons, or animals. True Enlightenment is possible only for those born into human form, which is thus considered the most fortunate birth. It is worth noting that the gods themselves will also eventually die and be reborn. And even though they are gods, they cannot achieve Enlightenment in their deity-form.

It is said that if one wants to know what one will be in the next life, one merely has to look at one's behavior in this one. One's karma is entirely under one's own power. It can't be affected by prayer or ritual, as the Hindu Brahmins taught. This idea is both a great freedom and a great responsibility. It's good to know that a minor mistake in the saying of a chant won't result in being reborn a donkey, but it places additional burden on thinking right thoughts, which can be even more difficult. One charmingly subtle way in which the Buddha appeals to our vanity about good looks, and how they can be related to moral behavior is found in the Pali canon, the Cula-Kammavibhanga Sutta, or "Shorter Analysis of Action" (Majjhima Nikaya 135, translated by Thanissaro Bhikku):

> There is the case, where a woman or man is ill-tempered & easily upset; even when lightly criticized, he/she grows offended, provoked, malicious, & resentful; shows annoyance, aversion, & bitterness. Through

> having adopted & carried out such actions, on the break-up of the body, after death, he/she reappears in the plane of deprivation . . . If instead he/she comes to the human state, then he/she is ugly wherever reborn. This is the way leading to ugliness: to be ill-tempered & easily upset; even when lightly criticized, to grow offended, provoked, malicious, & resentful; to show annoyance, aversion, & bitterness.

In other words, poor reaction to correction will make one ugly in the next life. Surely the Buddha meant this as a simple cause-and-effect relationship, but it does make people think.

Buddhism acknowledges the deep fear of death that lies at the heart of all living beings. Its doctrine of rebirth may comfort some, but even rebirth is a "temporary fix" until one achieves Enlightenment. What happens then? The Buddha kept his "noble silence" on the matter, and as for the Zen Masters, many would concur with Zen Master Dogo: "I won't say! I won't say!"

Along the same lines, a samurai soldier once asked Zen Master Hakuin what would happen after he died. "How should I know?" responded the Zen Master.

"You should know. After all, you're a Zen Master," countered the samurai.

"Yes, but not a dead one."

Interdependent Co-Arising, or Dependent Origination (*Paticca Samuppada*)

All beings are tied together in a vast, interdependent network. It is a condition of life. In John Dunne's simple language, "No man is an island." Buddhism reaches further and establishes the fact that no being whatever is an island. This is not a philosophical position or a matter of faith. It is a statement of fact, based upon observation. Nothing in the world has independent existence. Each being and each phenomenon is built upon previous ones. As each individual being undergoes change, all beings change. Enlightenment is not possible until this concept is clearly realized. Buddhist philosophy is built upon this fact. Western science rediscovered this principle of physics on its own, in the so-called butterfly effect, but failed to derive from it an ethical principle, as the Buddhists did.

The Pali text (Samyutta Nikaya II 28;65) in which the Buddha expounded this doctrine reads:

> This being, that becomes;
> From the arising of this, that arises;

This not being, that becomes not;
From the ceasing of this, that ceases.

To clarify this simple but apparently enigmatic doctrine, Buddhist philosophers (if not the Buddha himself) developed an elaborate schematic that all phenomena develop from those that precede them. Although one can "begin" anywhere on this circular path, it conventionally starts with ignorance or delusion. All components of the personality, the *skandhas,* are also involved in this chain of events. The *avijja* spoken of is the deep, primal *avijja* of "selfhood," the mistaken notion that we are or have some eternal, abiding "self," rather than a dynamic, ever changing collection of elements. *Avijja* is not just "unknowing" (which can be a good thing), but "mis-knowing," or being in error about an important truth. This is not merely wrong, but also dangerous.

- spiritual ignorance (*avijja*) produces
- willed action, constructing activities, or mental formations (*sankhara*), which produces
- conditioned, discriminative, or normal consciousness or life force (*vinnana*), which produces
- name, mind, and body (*namarupa*), which produce
- the six sense bases (*salayatana,* the five traditional senses, plus the mind), which produce
- contact or sense impressions or stimulation (*phassa*), which produce
- feelings or sensations (*vedana*), which produce
- desire, thirst, or craving (*tanha*), which produces
- attachment, grasping, or clinging (*upadana*), which produces
- becoming or coming-to-be, or existence (*bhava*), which produces
- birth or rebirth (*jati*), which produces
- old age, pain, lamentation, and death (*jara-marana*) with all the suffering associated with it.

Each link in this chain of causation is called a *nidana.* This is just another way of talking about *samsara,* but it is stripping it to its roots. For easier comprehension, the doctrine of dependent origination is often shown as a great Wheel of Becoming, which is clutched by Yama, the traditional god of death. It can also be called the "Wheel of Life" or the Chain of Causation (having twelve "links"). Each of the twelve links has an image that symbolizes it:

- ignorance: blind man
- willed action: potter
- consciousness: monkey
- name, mind, and body: three people in a boat
- the six senses: house with doors and windows
- sense impressions: two lovers
- feelings: man whose eye is pierced by an arrow
- desire (thirst): man drinking
- clinging: monkey climbing a tree
- becoming: pregnant woman
- birth: woman giving birth
- old age, sorrow, pain, and death: burdened old man walking toward a lake

The complex diagram representing the wheel has three animals at its center: a rooster representing greed, a pig representing ignorance, and a snake representing hatred. (Of course, in Western symbolism, pigs are more frequently associated with greed than roosters are, but differences in cultures must be taken into account.) In Buddhism, ignorance, greed, and anger or hatred are called the "Three Poisons." The animals are depicted as either swallowing or vomiting one another, depending on how one looks at it.

Nagarjuna, a Buddhist philosopher of the second century C.E., proposed a simpler formulation of the same concept. Clinging to existence means clinging to the self. Clinging to the self entails karma. Karma plays out in the endless cycle of rebirth and redeath. And why do we cling to existence in the first place? Ignorance. Or, as Nagarjuna calls it, *avidya,* its Sanskrit equivalent.

Compassion (*Karuna*)

Since all beings are joined together in *samsara,* all share its characteristics of change, suffering, and un-selfness. Buddhist compassion is directed specifically to the characteristic of suffering, which is all-pervading. Because we are all ultimately one and share all characteristics, compassion is not only virtuous, but practical. Not showing compassion to other beings is like not caring for one's own body or mind. *Karuna* is a term used primarily by Mahayana Buddhists; Theravadins use the word *metta,* or lovingkindness, which works to very much the same end.

Wisdom (*Prajna*)

Buddhist wisdom has nothing to do with book-knowledge. It refers instead to a transcendental, overwhelming consciousness of truth and Dharma. For many Buddhists it is intimately paired with compassion, and it is said that wisdom and compassion are the two wings of Enlightenment.

Tolerance

Buddhism advocates tolerance of all religions. Because the Buddha himself had urged his followers to find out for themselves, one is not permitted to prevent others from their own explorations. Buddhism shares this admirable characteristic with its parent religion, Hinduism.

Nirvana

Nirvana is one of the key terms in Buddhism, and one of the most complex, ambiguous, and difficult concepts for Westerners (or anyone else, for that matter) to grasp. Literally, this Sanskrit word means "blowing out" or "cooling off" or even "extinguishing," but most Buddhist scholars would deny that it means utter extinction. (Since Buddhist philosophy maintains there is no self to begin with, it is hard to say what might be extinguished, anyway. It originally referred to putting out a fire.) Some say what is extinguished is the ego-self, or the self that is prey to greed, anger, and ignorance. However, nearly all Buddhists agree that Nirvana does not equal "nothingness," or "nonexistence," since such a designation would put Nirvana squarely back into the world of duality, which it is supposed to unite. However, one should not make the opposite mistake either, and claim that Nirvana involves some sort of otherworldly existence. It can be "here" as well as "there" (or both or neither).

In typical Indian fashion, it is most often described in negative terms—neither life nor death, existence nor nonexistence. Whatever it is, it cannot be distinguished by the senses or described adequately by language. The only thing we can say for sure about it is that it is a state (or nonstate) of supreme bliss and utter value, although it probably does not mean heaven or paradise. The Buddha himself has this to say about Nirvana:

> Monks, there is an unborn, unoriginated, unmade, and unconditioned. If there were not, there would be no escape from the born, originated, made, and conditioned. Since there is the unborn, unoriginated, unmade, and unconditioned, there is escape from the born, originated, made, and conditioned.

There seems to be a bit of circular reasoning here, but given the subject, perhaps that is inevitable.

Some Buddhists categorize Nirvana into two types: (1) Nirvana that has a residual basis and (2) Nirvana that does not have a residual basis. The first kind, that with a residual basis, is what occurred when the Buddha reached Enlightenment. The "residue" in this case was the earthly Buddha who was then able to conduct his teaching mission. The second kind of Nirvana, Nirvana without residue, or Parinirvana, occurred when the Buddha passed away.

Another way of looking at it is as a release from the suffering that is inherent in the world and one of the marks of existence. Since Buddhism looks upon existence as suffering, the end of existence is equated with freedom from suffering. But since Buddhism also holds to the ancient Indian doctrine of rebirth, it explains Nirvana as freedom from the wheel of ceaseless rebirth (and consequent redeath). Since most Westerners don't believe in rebirth anyway, the idea of Nirvana also holds a somewhat different meaning for them. It is often called a state (or event, especially in its Japanese version, *satori*) that is beyond both permanence and impermanence, or that can be described as the ultimate manifestation or destruction of these conditions.

Its ultimate meaning remains a mystery to those who have not experienced it. What happens to a flame that has been extinguished or passed on to another candle? These questions reveal why most discussions of Nirvana begin and end with talking about what it is not, or simply refer to it as "bliss" and leave it at that.

It is said that the Buddha could have chosen to enter Nirvana permanently when he was Enlightened, but chose instead to teach the Dharma, the path to Enlightenment. In other words, the Buddha began to show the way to Nirvana for the rest of humankind. This act of selfless compassion became characteristic of Buddhism in general.

Enlightenment

Enlightenment is also called liberation, release, Awakening, and, in Zen, *satori*. For some Buddhists, Enlightenment is a gradual, step-by-step process. For others, it comes suddenly (although usually only after years of preparation). Enlightenment is possible for every single person. To receive Enlightenment, it is not necessary to be a saint, mystic, or intellectual. It is only necessary to seek it diligently.

A less "loaded" term than Enlightenment, but one that explains the same phenomenon, is "Awareness." Awareness is the understanding of things as they are now and things as they are in the processing of becoming. It means to see clearly, without prejudice. It means, as the Japanese Zen Master Dogen said, to see mountains as mountains and water as water. This is not as easy as it seems. In Buddhist symbolic language, for example, those in the realm of the hungry ghosts see water not as water but as raging fire or as pus or blood. Their lust and anger and desire delude them about the true nature of reality.

But what do any of us, in our normal state of awareness, know of water, nature's chameleon? It is comprised of oxygen and hydrogen, but it is not like either of them. It can be hot or cold, soothing or tormenting. It can evaporate as steam or solidify as ice. It can be a gentle rain, a mysterious fog, or a raging storm. It can take shape in a swamp, a pond, a bubbling spring, or the mighty ocean. It can be a snowflake or a diamond of dew. It can be a friend or an enemy. It is blue or green or white or gray or clear. Quietly, it reflects the sky and trees; quietly, it reshapes the mountains. In this way, water is the exemplar for all reality, which is never one thing with one meaning, but a complex net of relationships and a myriad of forms, none of which reveal themselves except to the mind of awareness, the mind that, like water, reflects and shapes its world.

The Five Hindrances and the Ten Fetters

Those who have not obtained Enlightenment may be impeded by the Five Hindrances or bound by the Ten Fetters. The Five Hindrances are: (1) sensual desire; (2) aversion; (3) sloth; (4) restlessness or worry; and (5) doubt. Sensual desire and aversion are mirror images of each other, as are sloth and restlessness. Both avoid the Middle Way. Doubt, by which is meant a constant plaguing, irresolvable doubt, not the earnest questioning which is recommended, can lead the mind to circulate endlessly and worriedly over the same matter, thus combining the worst aspects of restlessness and sloth.

Many of the same states of mind are listed among the Ten Fetters, which chain us to this existence: (1) belief in the existence of personality; (2) doubt; (3) attachment to rulers and rituals; (4) sensuous craving; (5) aversion; (6) craving for material things; (7) craving for formless existence; (8) conceit; (9) restlessness; and (10) ignorance. When the fetters and hindrances have been overcome, one can progress to the state of the arhat, a worthy one, which in Theravada Buddhism is the ideal to which all humans ought to aspire.

Quietism

To the outsider, Buddhism, with its emphasis on finding peace within, seems unduly passive and quietist. But viewing it in this way is to misunderstand the nature of the tradition. It has long been a Buddhist axiom that one cannot liberate others until one has freed oneself. It is just as if two people are tied up at opposite ends of the room. One person has to free himself before he can free the other person. It isn't a matter of oneself being more important than others. It is a purely practical wisdom. Even Buddhist activism is "quietist" in this respect.

The Buddhist Cosmology

Although it is not necessary to agree with or even understand the complex (and to a scientist, primitive) cosmology of Buddhism to be a Buddhist, it is interesting, not only from an academic point of view, but also because the entire Buddhist cosmology can be interpreted metaphorically in such a way as to enrich one's understanding of everything Buddhism teaches.

According to Buddhist thinking, the universe has no perceptible beginning, no creator, and no real purpose. The universe we seem to know is just the lowest of many planes of existence. The dimension of the entire cosmos is incalculable, in both space and time. There is an infinity of world systems (each world system is a planet in ordinary thinking) scattered through limitless space; each one of them comes into being and then decays through endless time.

The universe is multileveled, containing pure mental states, heavenly realms, and underworlds. The underworlds include that of humans, animals, hungry ghosts (*petas*), and the hell-realm (*niraya*). Human beings are in the most fortunate position in all the world, for it is only from the human realm that one can eventually attain Enlightenment. While the human realm is often considered part of the four lower realms, it is also sometimes linked with the world of the *devas,* or gods.

The world of the gods is sometimes divided again into two realms, that of the *evas,* or true gods, and the less exalted world of the titans, or *asuras,* who are proud and power-hungry. The gods proper live in the twenty-six heavens. Everyone dwelling in the worlds of hell-beings, animals, humans, gods, titans, or the six lowest heavens is said to live in the realm of sense-desire. (Mara the Tempter lives in the highest of the lowest heavens.) The world we inhabit is part of the world of sense-desire.

In this realm of sense-desire beings are aware of the qualities of things, and attracted or repelled by them. Above this realm is the realm of pure form, in which beings are aware of objects but devoid of sensuous desire for them. In the highest four realms, the so-called formless realms, beings live in states of higher consciousness, but there are no physical objects. Even those beings in the highest heaven, who live for 84,000 eons, eventually die. (The Theravada scriptures hasten to inform us, however, that the time seems to pass quickly.) The good news here is that Mara the Tempter will therefore eventually die; the bad news is that his job of tempting will be taken by someone else.

At the center of the world rises the mythical Mt. Meru, the axis of the world. Here the gods dwell or, in a different schema, just meet and discuss matters. Seven golden ranges of mountains encircle Mt. Meru, each separated from the next by a vast sea. (Both Hinduism and Buddhism share the idea of Mt. Meru; however, only Buddhism has the mountains and oceans.) On the last ocean float four continents, one at each point of the compass. The southern continent is Jambudvipa, usually identified with India. A solid wall of iron mountains (*Chakravala*) forms a boundary around everything. (As Buddhism developed, spiritual geographers decided to place the continents somewhat closer to Mt. Meru, to depict a closer relationship between the gods and human beings.)

Above Mt. Meru exist three realms into which beings may be brought to birth. These realms, from the lowest to the highest are (1) the Realm of Desire (*kamadhatu*); (2) the Realm of Form (*rupadhatu*); and (3) the Realm of No-Form (*arupadhatu*). In these realms six types of beings may be born: (1) gods; (2) human beings; (3) animals; (4) titans or demons (*asuras*); (5) hungry ghosts (*petas*); and (6) hell-beings.

To illustrate the essentially metaphorical nature of these conceptions, we can take the example of the hungry ghost, a being whose counterpart does not specifically appear in Western mythology. The hungry ghost is depicted as having an enormous belly and a miniscule mouth. Thus a hungry ghost is perpetually full of desire, desire that can never be satisfied.

Below Mt. Meru lie the horrible hells (usually depicted as eight in number), each lower and nastier than the last. The hell-realm is a bad one to be born into. One is continually frozen or burned or sliced—and constantly being revived to reexperience the sufferings. The most terrible is the Avici Hell, but even from here, beings can eventually be released and ultimately attain Nirvana. (It will take an unutterably long time, though, thus satisfying the human need for both revenge and hope.) At the base of Mt. Meru, right at the level of the ground, are the caves in which dwell the perennially bad-tempered demons. Every once in a while they creep out of their caves to fight the *devas* for control of the Wish-Fulfilling tree that grows halfway up Mt. Meru.

Mt. Meru has four terraces. The first three are inhabited by *yaksha,* supernatural creatures who sometimes plague Buddhist monks and nuns by disturbing their meditations. On the fourth level live the Guardian Kings of the Four Quarters, who are accorded godlike status. They keep a careful eye on what is happening on Earth and send reports up to the summit where the gods (*devas*) proper dwell.

The gods live lives of 1,000 years. This is longer than it sounds, however, since each deity-day equals 100 human years. This means a life span of 36,500,000 years. Their lives are truly delightful, filled with wine, goddesses, and song, but in the end they too are mortal. (For gods who are poor in arithmetic, the day of doom is signaled by awful body odor.) Of the heavens, the fourth, or Tushita Heaven is the most wonderful, being the one in which the bodhisattvas live.

Above the gods are the four aerial heavens, and above them are further realms, the Realm of Form and the Realm of No-Form. Most can be explored through deep meditation.

The most important region to us is the Realm of Desire, or *kamaloka,* where human beings dwell. In fact, nearly all beings, including hell-beings and most gods, live here. It is only from this world that a person may achieve Enlightenment and be free of the ceaseless round of birth and rebirth.

In summary, there exist three major realms. They are from lowest to highest: the Realm of Desire (six heavens and the lower worlds of humans, animals, hungry ghosts, and hell-beings); the Realm of Pure Form (five pure abodes and eleven other heavens); and the Formless Realm (four mental states). That makes thirty worlds in all.

Time

However endless, time is conveniently divided into periods called *kalpas.* The biggest *kalpa* is the *maha-kalpa,* which is divided into four shorter periods, each of which is still so long that it cannot be measured even in thousands of years. During the first period of a *kalpa,* the previously existing world system is either annihilated or reduced to its constituent elements.

At that time, most beings are reborn into the Brahma realm, the highest and most subtle plane of phenomenal existence. When the second period begins, the leftover energy of matter (objective existence) and the Brahma world and its inhabitants (subjective existence) become isolated from each other. The world of duality is born, and subject and object are unable to interact. During the third period, the universe re-forms, and most beings return from the Brahma world to be reborn on a dark and water-covered earth. They are not like us, however, for they are self-luminous, fed by rapture, and not differentiated by sex or species.

After a very long time, something that appears suspiciously like rice appears on the earth, and the denizens of Earth taste it, like it, grow gross with it, and depend upon it. Craving is born. Sexes and species appear. We are now in the fourth period—and waiting for it all to begin again.

This world is subject to vast, sweeping cycles of growth and decay. At the beginning of each new age, or *kalpa,* we have immensely long life spans (80,000 years), which declines down to ten years at the end. Fortunately, the current age is the Bhadra Kalpa, which will last 320,000,000 years and into which 1,000 Buddhas will be born. Each Buddha will discover the Dharma and teach it, so that for a while after the birth of each Buddha, the Dharma will be readily available to all who seek it. Afterward, things will inevitably take a downward turn, and the Dharma will be obscured due to corruption of the teaching. The Buddha of our current time is Sakyamuni, although the Dharma is now obviously obscured. The previous Buddha was Dipankara, and the next will be Maitreya. Buddhism is one of the only religions, which, while accepting the final truths of its founder, does not deny that other equally enlightened beings will appear to instruct future ages.

Buddhist Practice

Buddhism has always been more than a system of belief. It is a way of life, characterized by specific practice. In most cases, the belief directs the practice. For example, the Buddhist concept of compassion is useless as a mere concept. Since compassion, by its very nature, involves relationship with others, it must be translated into action, must reach across the artificial boundaries that separate one being from another.

No Sacrifice

One important innovation the Buddha made to religious practice was his doing away with the idea of sacrifice, which was the very heart of the ancient Aryan and Vedic religion, as indeed it is of many others. The famous horse sacrifice, for instance, involved the shedding of blood of literally thousands of animals. The Buddha taught that no sacrifices should ever be made. There are two extremely good reasons. In the first place, the Buddhist virtue of compassion absolutely forbids it. It goes totally against the First Precept. Second, sacrifice is a waste of time and money. It does not work, because there is no one or nothing to take heed of the sacrifice. Therefore, the Buddhist virtue of wisdom proscribes it.

Meditation

Meditation is deeply characteristic of modern Western Buddhism. It has largely replaced the academic study of Buddhist texts and doctrines, and perhaps more disturbingly, even the practice of the Dharma. For most Western Buddhists, meditation is viewed primarily as a path to Awakening, and is also the path to the deepest levels of being. The purpose of meditation is to put the meditator in touch with himself or herself. It is to awaken the heart within one. The Buddha himself achieved his Enlightenment through meditation. By sitting straight, positioning oneself in the natural order of things between Earth and Heaven, one learns to recognize one's position in the universe. By steady, mindful breathing, one recognizes that the spirit (literally "breath") of the cosmos is flowing through one. Another important element in meditation is proper breathing—"breath sweeps mind," as Zen Master Jakusho Kwong says, referring to the breath's ability to cleanse the mind.

In meditation, the meditator learns to see objects for what they truly are, neither adding nor subtracting in a frenzy of trying to make meaning or to simplify without basis. This is not an easy task. Human beings by nature are "meaning-making creatures," and it takes a great deal of training and discipline to learn to focus one's attention rather than let it escape, dissipate, and eventually drain away.

The Buddha also used meditation as a teaching technique. In one famous story, a Brahmin, disenchanted with previous schools, approaches the Buddha. He is even brave enough to challenge him. "I do not ask for words. I do not ask for no-words," he reportedly said. The Buddha's answer was to "sit." Sitting in this sense does not mean lounging about. It is an intense, powerful, meditative activity that creates a whole universe of energy. The Brahmin understood the lesson immediately, even if Ananda, the Buddha's loveable but none too bright disciple, did not. The Brahmin experienced the Dharma in action, which oddly is very much like the Dharma in stillness. Meditation is the dynamic in-between state, neither here nor there, beyond sleep and waking, encompassing the cosmos.

Correct posture is extremely important in most, but not all, forms of Buddhist meditation. In Zen it's called "acquiring a seat," and is said to take three years of daily work to achieve. Although this posture may differ somewhat from culture to culture, most Buddhists believe that the classic full-lotus position is most conducive to insight. In the full-lotus position, each foot rests upon the opposite thigh. Knees are dropped to the ground. This creates a solid foundation and is supposed to reduce strain on the neck and back, although the strain on the knees and legs is considerable. The back is unsupported, and the eyes are half-closed and lowered. Many Buddhists place their hands in the so-called cosmic *mudra,* with the left hand resting on the right palm. The thumbs touch slightly. The hands are placed about three inches below the navel, an area known as the *tanden,* or power-spot, of the body. It is also known as *hara.*

Meditation is very difficult, especially at first, when practitioners must fight off sleepiness, boredom, anxiety, or the feeling that the purpose of meditation is simply to escape the concerns of ordinary living. Indeed, not everyone is capable of the long sitting required for proper *zazen,* the Zen term for sitting meditation. (In Japan, practitioners who fall asleep or abandon proper sitting practice are hit with sticks, while in China, monks often placed rocks on their heads. Neither of these methods works well in the United States. Students object strenuously.) So in addition to sitting, many Buddhists practice walking meditation, ceremonial bowing, and chanting mantras as further ways to practice.

It is apparent that meditation, both seated and walking, can take many forms. Some kinds of Buddhist meditation, notably Tibetan and *samatha* meditation in the Theravada tradition, involve visualizations, while others, notably Zen, do not. Some people count their breaths; others follow their breaths without counting; still others use meditation to label and dismiss feelings, others use meditation time to work on a koan, say a mantra, or practice a visualization. For many Buddhists, meditation is a form of action. It purifies the mind and subtly but deeply influences others. In Zen Master Philip Kapleau's phrase, it denies the distinction between "being and doing."

Here the Buddha sits in a lotus posture beneath the Bodhi Tree. The left hand lies in the lap symbolizing both meditation and wisdom. The right hand reaches toward the ground, calling upon the Earth to witness the truth of the Enlightenment. It is slightly unusual to show the palm reaching outward here but it probably represents benevolence and charity. The curled ring finger is the mark of the solitary finder of the Enlightenment. Photographer Helen Rogers. © TRIP.

While it may seem that meditation is a way to avoid action, Buddhists regard it as a way to learn to act without reacting. The steady breathing exercises put one in touch with one's center, so that one can act authentically from the heart, not react from a chaos of emotional or mental responses.

In Zen Buddhism, meditation frequently takes an extended form known as *sesshin,* in which meditators sit in silence for anywhere from two to seven days. Brief periods are allotted for sleep and meals. The practice supposedly originated during the Buddha's lifetime, when the monks were holed up during the rainy season.

Bowing

Ceremonial bowing is important in many kinds of Buddhist practice, and for some Buddhists serves the same function as meditation. Zen Master Jakusho Kwong recommends it especially for those who are angry or withdrawn. Bowing practices differ from tradition to tradition. In the Japanese full bow, one stands with hands folded together at the chest, and then kneels, placing the head on the floor. Hands are open and raised up on each side, a gesture of both supplication and vulnerability. In Tibetan

Buddhism, the formal bow ends with the bower flat on the floor, hands stretched in front of the body in a full prostration.

Mantras

A mantra is a ritualized chant of power-laden syllables, and is very important in most forms of Buddhism. The scriptures stipulate that the chant should be neither too loud nor too soft, too fast nor too slow. It is not a speaking voice, yet should not be distracting. This is another practice Buddhism inherited from Hinduism.

Begging and Work

Religious mendicants, or wandering beggars, were accepted and quite common in classical India. In fact, the Buddha specifically forbade his early followers to engage in productive work. It is also currently the practice in Southeast Asia. In Japan, the custom of religious begging, or *takahatsu,* is common, although in some cases it is a mere formality. The Chinese monk Pai-chang Huai-hai (Hyakujo in Japanese), however, required his monks to labor in the field and support the monastery. (The begging tradition never caught hold in China as an honorable way for religious persons to get by.) Pai-chang Huai-hai also felt that physical work actually helped mental acuity. In the United States, of course, begging is simply not an option for Buddhist monks; it is not culturally acceptable.

In modern times, Buddhism teaches that work is an honorable activity, one that has two aspects. In the first place, work, especially quiet, repetitive work, can be a form of meditation. This aspect of work helps develop wisdom, one of the two great virtues of Buddhism. Second, work can be a freewill offering to others. This kind of work helps develop compassion, the second great Buddhist virtue. Thus work is never segmented off from the rest of life, as is often the case in the contemporary world. Instead, work is integrated with religious practice, thus sanctifying work and making religious practice a vital part of day-to-day existence.

In monasteries, work is often begun with a bow and burning of incense to remind the worker of the true nature of work—which is to reveal one's humanity. Work is part of the human condition and indeed of human nature, and should be performed lovingly and with joy, even when the work seems hard. Since we ourselves are an event rather than a substance or entity, in work and action we fully express our purpose and ourselves. When we think of work as *labor,* a mindless, oppressive series of motions, we feel burdened and exhausted. But when we understand work as opportunity, we use the

This is an example of a full prostration to the image of the Buddha. The worshiper may have begun with a kneeling gesture. The hands, palms down, are four to six inches apart with just enough room for the forehead to be brought to the ground between them. The feet are about a foot apart. This is called the prostration with the five limbs—the forehead, the forearms, and the knees. Photographer Fiona Good. © TRIP.

term in the same way as we do when we say that a computer or a toaster or a car "works"; we see that work defines our purpose. Those who do not work are deprived of an essential component of living.

Even distasteful work performed in a giving and meditative spirit takes on religious meaning, and serves to uplift, fulfill, and focus the worker. Physical work is never regarded as degrading. That kind of attitude only develops in cultures that regard the mind as a separate entity from the body. In Buddhism, however, both mind and body are part of the cycle of beings (*samsara*) and both are subject to change. One is not above or beneath another.

Temple Attire

Although many customs in Buddhism are different from culture to culture, one that has remained relatively intact upon entrance into the United States is the Asian one of removing one's shoes before entering a temple or monastery. This is not a religious requirement, and Buddhist scriptures nowhere insist upon it. Some people feel that they should remove their socks as well, while others think it more polite to leave their socks on. Considering that Buddhism was born in a country where many people did not even own shoes, let alone socks (or would even have recognized socks if they saw them), American Buddhists have been free to make up their own rules in this regard.

The Role of the Teacher

The Buddha officially taught that each follower should seek his or her own salvation with diligence; in fact, these were his last words. As a practical matter, however, Buddhism has developed a system in which teachers are essential, or at least useful, in the attainment of Enlightenment. And as the Buddha himself was a teacher, this seems like a reasonable assumption. This is a role that is vastly different in contemporary America from what it was in ancient China or medieval Japan. Traditional teachers were almost always male, conservative, and authoritarian, and the setting was nearly always a monastery. Today American teachers are frequently female, and the student/teacher relationship is freer and more egalitarian. The setting may still be a monastery, but it is more likely to be in the secular world.

Some traditionalists worry that the current free and easy style of passing on the Dharma to others will lead to a break in centuries-long lineage records (although many of those are rather suspect in themselves). Since the whole concept of lineage was to preserve a pure teaching, the worry is that unauthorized teachers are now polluting the Dharma. If this is so, the problem can be traced (at least in Zen) at least as far back as D. T. Suzuki and Nyogen Senzaki, neither of whom received formal Dharma transmission from their own master, Soyen Shaku. The same situation held true with the first Tibetan missionaries to the United States, most of whom were young, untried, and without high standing in the land of their birth. One problem this lack of tradition has caused is that in America there is simply no cultural context, no expectation as to how a teacher is supposed to behave or what he or she is supposed to teach. Thus deviant teachers may not be recognized as quickly in this country as in traditional Buddhist ones.

Finding the right teacher has always been one of the most difficult parts of being a Buddhist, and the records are rife with many false starts among famous-to-be Masters. Zen Master Bernard Glassman has stated that all teacher/student relationships contain moments of doubt.

Having the right teacher is regarded as a shortcut to Enlightenment, and classical Buddhist teaching places the teacher in a powerful authoritarian role. This makes the selection of a teacher even more important. One Zen saying has it, "While looking for a teacher, eyes wide open. Once you find the teacher, eyes shut." This means not only shutting one's eyes to other teachings and ways, but also shutting one's eyes to foibles (or seeming foibles) in the Master. The teacher represents the Buddha himself, the object of one's devotion. Yet the Buddha cautioned, "Rely on the doctrine, not on the person." This advice suits Americans well. In the United States, respect for individual freedom and choice has placed most of the responsibility for finding the right teacher (and leaving when it is time) on the student. Common sense, intuition, and careful study should always remain unfailing guides.

Buddhist Vows and the Monastic Community

As stated earlier, all Buddhists take the Five Vows (*panca sila*)—to refrain from killing, stealing, sexual impropriety, lying, and taking intoxicants. Monks and nuns make further promises, including not to handle money, not to sleep on luxurious beds, and not to entertain themselves with theatrics. They have traditionally been expected to be celibate as well, although that is changing in some groups. The rules of discipline for monks and nuns are known as Vinaya, and traditionally those for nuns were more numerous than those for monks. (This was the Buddha's idea.)

The Expansion of Buddhism

Buddhism, unlike its parent faith Hinduism, did not remain stranded on the Indian subcontinent. Because of its extreme flexibility and adaptability, it was destined to be a world faith almost from its beginning—never by conquest, but always through the powerful persuasion of its ideas. For Buddhists, it was a jewel too precious to remain long hidden.

One of the earliest documents in Buddhist history, the Samyutta Nikaaya, gives an account of the Buddha's command to his disciples:

> Go ye, O monks, wander around for the good of the many, for the happiness of the many, out of compassion for the world, for the benefit, good, and happiness of humans and *devas*. Let not any two go in the same way.

From the very beginning, then, the Buddha intended the Dharma to be spread far and wide over the face of the Earth.

Soon after the cremation of the Buddha and the dispersal of his bones as relics to various places, the First Council, comprised of 500 senior monks, met at Rajagaha to discuss the future of the new religion. One of the monks, Upali, recited the Rules of Discipline, or Vinaya, while Ananda recited the teachings themselves. Ananda began each recitation with the words, "Thus I have heard," and these words have remained part of the sutras to this day. By using the words "Thus I have heard," Ananda makes it clear that he was not inventing the words, but reciting directly from his memory of the Buddha's teachings. The teachings were then discussed, and an authorized version of them was created, although the teachings were not written down for about 400 years. This was common practice in India. Not only was the rate of literacy low, but many felt that sacred words were *too* sacred to be revealed in writing; their truth could only be justly handed down from teacher to student.

As Buddhism grew, other councils were convened. The Second Council was held 100 years after the Buddha's death, the Third 100 years after that, and the Fourth, which is not recognized by Theravadin Buddhists, about 100 C.E. In the Theravadin view, a Fourth Council was held in Sri Lanka sometime during the first century B.C.E. Theravadins also hold that a council was held in Ashoka's capital Patapaliputta about 250 B.C.E., which resulted in the publication of a book of discourses that opposed the views of the other schools.

At the Fourth Council, the canon, or collection of sacred writings, was committed to writing, being inscribed in the Pali language on palm leaves. (Properly prepared palm leaves are an extremely durable medium, much more so than paper or parchment.) This Pali canon is also known as the Tipitaka, or "Three Baskets." (The palm leaf scriptures were originally stored in baskets.) The three baskets include the Vinaya Pitaka, or Rules of Discipline, which explains the 227 rules for monks; the Sutta Pitaka, which contains collected sutras or discourses of the Buddha; and the Abhidhamma, which consists largely of commentary and analyses of the Sutta Pitaka. The Abhidhamma was a later addition, reaching fruition about the fourth century C.E. Today the Pali canon forms the scriptures of Theravada Buddhism. And, as often happens with any organized religion, Buddhism began to separate into different schools and branches. Eventually eighteen were recognized.

Emperor Ashoka Maurya of Magadha

The most important figure in the spread of Buddhism throughout India and beyond was Emperor Ashoka (ruled c. 272–236 B.C.E.), whose kingdom stretched from the Persian border to the Ganges and as far south as Goa.

Ashoka endorsed this peaceful religion (perhaps from feelings of guilt, considering the carnage for which he himself had been responsible in earlier years). He dispensed with torture, and perhaps even abolished the death penalty. He gave up hunting, preferring pilgrimages instead, and forbade animal sacrifice in the capital. In keeping with a long-established tolerant Indian tradition, Ashoka also supported other peaceful movements, including Jainism and ascetics of all religions.

Ashoka sent out the good news of Buddhism to Syria, Egypt, and Macedonia. No one is sure that the messages ever got to where they were sent, however, since the annals of those countries contain no word of them. We do know that many of his missions had only a temporary impact. However, his daughter Sanghamitta and his son Mahinda (or Malinda) became famous missionaries to the island of Sri Lanka, and it was there that the Buddhist canon was first written down on palm leaves and preserved. (Sri Lanka also has two important relics of the Buddha—a tooth and a collarbone.)

Today Sri Lanka still has a strong Buddhist presence, and many Western Buddhists have received ordination in that country. Sri Lanka has sent Buddhist missionaries to the West in fairly impressive numbers. Sri Lanka is also home to the modern Sarvodaya movement ("Awakening and Benefit of All") in which Buddhist principles are applied to economic and social growth. It is a kind of engaged Buddhism more fully considered in chapter 7.

During Ashoka's time, a permanent split developed in the Buddhist community. Although the reasons behind the division are multiple, it can be summed up this way. One group, the Sthaviras, wished to maintain monastic control over Buddhism, while the other group, the Mahasamghikas, wanted more authority to rest with the laity. This is the root of the present-day split between the Theravada and the Mahayana Buddhist communities. Other disputes rested upon philosophical grounds. One school, the Puggalavadins or Personalists, never accepted the doctrine of *anatta*. Another group, the Sarvastivadins, believed that the past and future, and not just the present, were real constituents of reality. (Certain elements of the Sarvastivadin philosophy were later incorporated in Tibetan Buddhism.) The Vibhajjavadins maintained that there is ultimately no difference between Nirvana and *dukkha*. Similar "minority-report" groups rose and fell. Theravada remained the strongest, but it withdrew from India and set up its headquarters in Sri Lanka, where even today it remains strong.

After Ashoka's death, his empire declined, and eventually King Demetrius of Bactria (now Afghanistan) and his general Menander conquered much of the old empire. Demetrius was killed in a counterattack, but Menander maintained control of northwest India. He became a Buddhist, although he was Greek by culture and ancestry. When he died, his ashes were split among several of the cities he ruled, and his relics were likewise divided, an action, which in Buddhist tradition, is reserved for the Buddhas and Universal Kings (*Chakravartin*).

Although the Hellenistic influence in India was relatively brief, it did leave a lasting monument: the depiction of the Buddha as a human being. Before this time, the Buddha had only been suggested by images like an eight-spoked wheel, a tree, or, at most, footprints. The Greeks gave the Buddha a face and figure, as was customary in their own culture. So the Buddha became reborn in the Greek image—not the chubby, smiling Buddha of Chinese conception, but a young and graceful man, fully human yet godlike in beauty. This was the Greek ideal.

Another famous proponent of Buddhist doctrine was Bodhidharma (c. 470–543 C.E.), the Twenty-eighth Patriarch after Shakyamuni Buddha; he is also considered the First Patriarch of Ch'an (Zen) Buddhism. He is most famous for his answer to Emperor Wu, who asked what the basic principles of holiness were. "Vast emptiness. No holiness." Bodhidharma is most famous for undergoing immoveable meditation facing a wall for nine years. He reputedly accepted a disciple only after the latter cut off his arm to prove his sincerity. (This disciple, Hui-k'o, became the Second Patriarch.) This may seem extreme, but another legend tells us that Bodhidharma cut off his own eyelids to help him stay awake during meditation. Perhaps as a result, he is always pictured with a fierce look.

Curiously, Buddhism was essentially wiped out of the land of its birth, partly because of foreign invasions and consequent persecutions and partly because the native religion of India, Hinduism, in a reform movement, addressed many of the criticisms that Buddhists had leveled at it.

The Buddhist Canon or Sacred Writings

Most of the sacred works in the Buddhist tradition are known as sutras or *suttas,* which means "thread." (We get the English world "suture" from them.) *Sutra* is the Sanskrit term, and is used by most Mahayana schools. *Sutta* is a Pali term and is used by the Theravada tradition. The sacred works of the Tibetan tradition are called the Tantras. The earliest ones were written on palm leaves, an amazingly durable substance, much tougher than paper. Most of these works are written not as philosophical treatises, but as poetry. In fact, some appear to have been written for recitation, not silent study. This makes them easier to read, but perhaps no less easy to understand.

Buddhist Observances and Festivals

The most important holiday in honor of the Buddha is his birthday celebration. Most Buddhists observe this event on the day of the full moon in May. In leap years, this holiday is held in June. However, Japanese Buddhists celebrate it on April 8. In addition, while some Buddhists celebrate the Buddha's birth, Enlightenment, and Parinirvana on one day, other traditions use three different dates. The dates often depend on a lunar calendar, and so occur at different times in the Gregorian calendar used in the United States.

The date of the Buddhist New Year depends on the country of origin or ethnic background of the people. For example, in many Theravada countries, such as Thailand, Burma, Sri Lanka, Cambodia, and Laos, the New Year is celebrated in a three-day celebration beginning on the first full-moon day in April. In most Mahayana countries the New Year begins on the first full-moon day in January. However, Chinese, Koreans, and Vietnamese celebrate the New Year in late January or early February according to the lunar calendar, and the Tibetans usually celebrate about one month later.

In the United States, celebrations often reflect the ethnic heritage of the believers as well as the school of Buddhism involved. For example, Abhidhamma Day, in the Burmese tradition, celebrates the occasion when the Buddha is said to have gone to the Tushita Heaven to teach his mother the Abhidhamma. It is held on the full moon of the seventh month of the Burmese lunar year.

The Buddhist Calendar

Unfortunately, there is no single Buddhist calendar to which all Buddhists adhere. Dates are calculated differently in different parts of the world. However, the most common type of Buddhist calendar is lunar; it begins roughly in December or January. Each month lasts approximately twenty-nine or thirty days, depending upon the length of the lunar cycle. Every once in a while an extra intercalary or leap day is added after the seventh month. Every few years, an extra month is also inserted.

Buddhist Teachings and the West

Westerners have a comparatively easy time understanding some of the basic aspects of Buddhism, precisely because they accord with their modern sensibility and scientific view of the world. Although they are not brought up with the concept of multiple existences, Westerners understand the doctrine of interdependent origination well. The idea that all phenomena are tied together by conditioned causal relationships, and that all phenomena are constantly passing into new forms (*anicca*) is a familiar one.

Much more difficult for many is the part that depends upon commitment, taking refuge in the Triple Jewel: the Buddha, the Dharma, and the Sangha. Understanding Buddhist ideas intellectually, especially if that understanding is shallow, may not be enough to make one a Buddhist, at least according to some experts.

Author Stephen Prothero, scholar of Buddhism, has noted most Americans get their knowledge of Buddhism merely from books, not from traditional practice. In a favorable book review of fellow scholar James William Coleman's *The New Buddhism: The Western Transformation of an Ancient Tradition* for Salon.com, he continues rather acidly, "The Dalai Lama and Thich Nhat Hanh are the Coke and Pepsi of this Buddhist generation, but homegrown brands such as Jack Kornfield and Lama Surya Das can also move 100,000 tomes without getting off their zafus." For many writers, being a Buddhist means being a complete Buddhist, and it is tempting for many of them to discount Buddhists who, in one way or another, don't fit the picture they themselves have drawn. Buddhists who chant, Buddhists who don't chant, Buddhists who are socially active, Buddhists who are not socially active, Buddhists who believe the Buddha to be more than human or less than human, and so on—all have been discredited sooner or later by one expert or another as not being sufficiently "Buddhist." Disputes about the nature of Buddhism are certainly nothing new.

Chapter 3

Theravada: The Way of the Elders

Theravada (the Way of the Elders) Buddhism considers its form and doctrine to be closest to that taught by the Buddha, and it is the most conservative of all Buddhist traditions. Originally Theravada was one of a number (usually reckoned as eighteen) of such ancient, orthodox schools collectively (and somewhat derisively) called Hinayana ("lesser vehicle") by the Mahayana ("greater vehicle") Buddhists. The other schools of that tradition have since died out, however, leaving only Theravada as representative of this traditional brand of Buddhism. While Theravadin teachings are probably very close to that of the original Buddha, Theravada itself has undergone some changes over the years. The formative voice of Theravada was Buddhaghosa, a Brahmin scholar of the fourth century. He converted to Buddhism and is the author of the Visuddhimagga ("Way of Purity") as well as commentaries on the Vinaya, the "book of discipline" and one of the major texts in Theravada.

Theravada was the most monastic of all the early schools of Buddhism. The word *sangha* means merely "society" in Sanskrit, but it came to refer primarily to the monastic community. Indeed, the monastic way of life remains the ideal for this group of Buddhists. Interestingly, the word is now once again being used in its original, broader sense, although primarily by the non-Theravadin Buddhist community. In fact, writer Gary Ray coined the term "cybersangha" back in 1991 to denote the Buddhist groups who engage one another mainly on-line. And Andrew Rawlinson has revived the ancient term "Arya Sangha," the "noble Sangha," to include teachers of all Buddhist traditions, including Westerners.

It was the Theravadins who preserved the earliest canonical writings of Buddhism, and the path of the scholar, or *gantha-dhura,* was considered a higher calling than that of the meditator, or *vipassana-dhura.* These monks played an important role in the education of village youngsters. This particular model has been difficult to follow in the United States. While many American Buddhists are highly educated in their field, few of them lead monastic lives. Indeed, most of the "scholar-practitioners" of Buddhism, as Charles S. Prebish calls them, are academics and other laypeople.

Currently Theravada has about 100 million adherents worldwide, primarily in Burma, Cambodia, Laos, Sri Lanka, Thailand, and part of Vietnam. Despite these numbers, Theravada was the last great Buddhist school to gain a foothold in the United States. Mostly this has been because the countries in which Theravada is dominant have had the fewest contacts with the United States until recently. Theravada has always been less popular with potential Buddhist converts than has Zen or Tibetan Buddhism, largely because of its emphasis on the monastic tradition, and Buddhism in America has generally been a lay movement. A career as a monk has very little appeal to most Americans. Thus, most Americans drawn to Theravada have confined their interest to the uniquely Theravada Vipassana meditation, described below.

Although it is most widespread in Southeast Asia, Theravada has shown, at least on the surface, a surprising vitality in the United States; there are now approximately 150 Theravada temples throughout the country, all (except one) built after 1970. However, a closer analysis, such as the studies done by Paul David Numrich, show that most of these monasteries have only three or four monks, almost all of whom were born in a Theravada country. In fact, there appear to be no new monks from second-generation ethnic groups, although there are a few Caucasian (and even an African American) monks.

The Theravada Canon

Theravada Buddhism is based on the Pali canon of scripture. Pali is a literary Middle Indo-Aryan language of north Indian origin allied to Sanskrit, and, like Sanskrit, not used as ordinary parlance. It is unclear whether the Buddha spoke this language; it certainly would not have been his mother tongue, although he may have known the language and used it. Most of the Buddha's work occurred in Magadha, where the dominant language was Magadhan, not Pali. Some scholars believe that Pali was spoken in one region of Magadha, Ujjain; unfortunately, the Buddha is not recorded as ever having visited there. Most scholars now maintain that Pali is an artificial language, like Esperanto, designed specifically to record the Dharma and was never the spoken language of anyone. At any rate, the earliest discourses of the Buddha now extant are written in Pali.

Although some Theravadin scholars maintain that only those who can read the Buddha's words in Pali can discover their deepest levels of meaning, the Vinaya itself records that the Buddha commanded his disciples to spread the word using local languages. This is in great contrast to Islam, for example, where the only authorized version of the Qu'ran is the accepted Arabic text. This being said, however, it remains a fact that Theravadin monks have shown no interest whatever in translating their own texts into other languages. Until very recently, the job was undertaken solely by Westerners. At the present time, the Theravada canon in both the Pali language and Roman script has been published by the London-based Pali Text Society, but its circulation has been limited. So far, the only European language into which the Theravada idea of the Dharma has been translated substantially is English.

Theravada scripture consists of the Tipitaka, or "Three Baskets," discussed in chapter 2. Although it can never be known for sure, the Pali canon is *probably* the best record we have of the Buddha's teachings. It was written down in Sri Lanka about 80 B.C.E. Bits of other early Buddhist canons have been found, with a few deviations from the Pali canon in their wording, although not in their fundamental doctrines. Some scholars believe that the near unanimity in text and doctrine is evidence that all come from the Buddha himself.

Theravadins make the point that the *suttas* (sacred text—*sutras* in Sanskrit) themselves are the best guide to the true interpretation of the Buddha's doctrine. In one well-known passage from the Pali canon, known as the "Charter for Inquiry," the Buddha is quoted as saying to the Kalama people (who had asked him how they were to know the truth):

> Kalamas, don't go by reports, by legends, by traditions, by scripture, by logical conjecture, by inference, by analogies, by agreement through pondering views, by probability, or by the thought, "This contemplative is our teacher." When you know for yourselves that, "These dhammas are unskillful; these dhammas are blameworthy; these dhammas are criticized by the wise; these dhammas, when adopted and carried out, lead to harm and to suffering"—then you should abandon them . . . When you know for yourselves that, "These dhammas are skillful; these dhammas are blameless; these dhammas are praised by the wise; these dhammas,

> when adopted and carried out, lead to welfare and to happiness"—then you should enter and remain in them." (AN III.65)

In other words, the truth is known by experience alone. Despite this stricture, Theravadins have plenty of *suttas* to choose from. In the Pali canon, the *suttas* are divided into five Nikayas, or "collections," with the first four generally considered the oldest. Not all important Pali literature is included in the canon, however. A chief example is the Milindapanha, which reportedly records a conversation between a certain Buddhist monk and Milinda, a king of Greek ancestry (whose Greek name is Menander). Buddhaghosa also wrote an important compendium of meditation practices in the fifth century C.E.

Theravada Beliefs and Practices

While all Buddhists maintain the same basic beliefs, each tradition has its own emphases. The following are particularly characteristic of Buddhism.

The Buddha

A Buddha may appear at any time, in any *kalpa,* but not necessarily. (A so-called empty *kalpa* is one in which no Buddha appears.) Our Earth has been blessed by twenty-eight Buddhas, including Shakyamuni, over the course of many *kalpas*. The *kalpa* in which we are now living has hosted no less than five Buddhas: Kusanda, Konagamana, Kasyapsa, Sakyamuni, and Maitreya, who is yet to come.

For Theravada Buddhists, the Buddha is a man, not a divine figure, and there exist more than one of them. However, the statement that the Buddha was a human being should not be taken to imply that the Buddha is "just" a human being. Although Theravadins maintain that the Buddha was born a human being, he, by his assiduous efforts and the merit he had gained in previous lives, eventually transcended simple humanity when he attained Enlightenment. A common metaphor to explain this is that of the lotus. The lotus rises from the muddy earth, grows through water, and rises in the air. It has transcended its original condition, but it is still a lotus, a lotus revealed in its true glory. This is the case with the Buddha.

Because the Buddha has achieved Nirvana, he is beyond life and death and time. He is wholly other, and cannot be reached by prayers, although something of his power remains in this world. This fact explains the veneration of the relics of the Buddha. One text says that 5,000 years after the death of the Buddha, his "age" will have passed away. At that time, all his remaining relics will magically gather at the foot of the Bo tree, where the Buddha was Enlightened, and will disappear in a flash of light. This future phenomenon is referred to as the "Parinirvana of the Relics."

Death and Rebirth

The Theravada school holds that the moment of death is followed immediately by a rebirth (unless one has attained Enlightenment). Only about half the Mahayana schools that developed over the centuries agreed, the rest positing some kind of heaven or, in the case of Vajrayana, a kind of intermediary state.

Gathering Merit

The main purpose in the life of a Theravadin is to gather merit (or good karma) to ensure a better birth in the next life. (Some people even carry "merit books" to keep tabs on their progress.) The main way to accomplish this is by following the Five Precepts (against killing, stealing, lying, sexual misconduct, and intoxicants). However, practicing the virtues of giving (*dana*), friendliness (*metta*), ritual chanting (*paritta*), and supporting a monk or monastery also helps.

Generosity (Dana)

Dana means "giving" and giving has been elevated in the Theravada tradition to a religious act of great importance and symbolism. It is enjoined upon all followers of the Buddha to give in order to help alleviate suffering. For laypeople, *dana* is absolutely essential to rebirth in a better life. However, *dana* has deeper implications than that of simply giving. The philosophical basis for it is the utter impermanence and substantial unreality of all beings. Giving, in Buddhism, is merely the realization that "clinging" or "grasping" entails great suffering. Giving is an acknowledgment of the fleeting and flowing nature of all "selves" and all existences. It is the enactment of life itself. If there is no self, there is nothing to hoard and no one to do the hoarding.

It is beneficial to give donations to monks at any time; there is even a special verse said along with the donation that transfers the merit of the gifts to the gods, so that they too can possibly be reborn into a realm in which they can obtain salvation. Likewise, when a boy enters the monkhood, his mother shares the merit, since she is giving something just as he is.

One particularly meritorious form of giving is related to the rite of the dead. Feeding monks seven days after the death of a loved one and also in yearly memorial services may benefit ancestors who may have become hungry ghosts.

While many Westerners question the efficacy of giving on the behalf of others, Buddhists often use the metaphor of lamp lighting. One lamp can light many, and then all give light.

Lovingkindness or Friendliness (Metta)

The virtue of *metta,* or "lovingkindness," is essential to Theravadins. It is to be put into action to ensure a better rebirth. This is accomplished by a meditative process called "sending and taking" in which the meditator takes in the pain and suffering of others with each intake of breath, and sends out lovingkindness with each exhalation.

Chanting (Paritta)

Paritta is ritual chanting. Theravada rites generally begin with three chants. The first is the *namo tasso* ("praise to the blessed one"). The second is the *tisarana* ("threefold refuge"—Buddha, Dharma, Sangha or monastic community). The practitioner recites in Pali "*Buddham saranam gachchami, dhamman saranam gachchami, sangham saranam gachchami,*" which means "I take refuge in the Buddha; I take refuge in the Dharma; I take refuge in the Sangha." The third chant is the *panca sila* ("recitation of the Five Precepts or ethical rules"). *Panca sila* is sometimes abbreviated as *pancil.* In certain cases, some of the chanting is performed in the living language of the practitioner, including English. Chanting may be followed by a brief period of meditation.

Ethics (Sila)

Sila means "morality" and refers primarily to the great Buddhist precepts: no killing, no stealing, no sexual misconduct, and so on. Buddhists believe that it is impossible to control the mind without refraining from nonvirtuous actions. This restraint helps build good karma. It is also a part of ethics to encourage others to behave likewise.

Worship (Puja)

This custom, and the word itself, is derived from Hinduism. In Hinduism *puja* is an act of worship of a deity, but in Buddhism it is more properly considered to be a mark of respect. It includes an offering of food, flowers, and incense before an image of the Buddha. It may include a recitation of the *tisarana* and a brief meditation. A *puja* is performed on special days such as *uposatha,* or fasting days, that occur on quarter-moon days. One kind of *puja, bodhi puja,* has traditionally been performed before Bodhi trees, in honor of their role in the Buddha's Enlightenment.

Related to worship are relics. Relics of the Buddha have great significance in Theravada Buddhism. Legitimate relics may be physical remains of the Buddha, his possessions, or symbolic objects. The theory is that body parts or objects associated with an enlightened being are infused with some of the goodness and power of that individual. They bring blessings to devout persons who practice near them. Because such objects are scarce, Buddhist texts or copies of the objects are often used instead.

Prostrations

Theravada Buddhists prostrate themselves before an image of the Buddha, first by kneeling with the palms together at heart or head level, then by bowing forward to the floor three times. Laypeople also prostrate themselves before monks, who are thought to embody the Triple Gem of Buddhism.

Offerings to the Monastery (Sanghika Dana)

Monastery gifts can include food, robes, razors, medicine, toothpaste, and other simple necessities. Monks are permitted three robes: a single undergarment, a double waistcloth, and a single upper robe. The major occasion for such gift giving is *kathin,* which traditionally occurs after the rainy season in October or November. *Kathin* is usually a communal event, but gifts may also be given by individual donors.

Meditation

In Theravada Buddhism, meditation has two successive goals, *samatha,* or tranquility, and *vipassana,* or insight. In *samatha,* meditators concentrate upon a single object, such as the breath, a candle, or a circle of color. Many Theravada texts contain a list of traditional objects. As concentration improves, meditators become more and more calm. As they grow calmer, they pass through eight *dhyanas,* or deep states of absorption. These states are said to correspond to the states of the blissful gods, but they in themselves are not permanent and do not lead to Enlightenment. In fact, these are the same states that the Buddha reached while studying with his two teachers but abandoned when he found that they did not bring Awakening.

Meditators move on to Vipassana meditation, in which the mind is fully opened to the complete realization that all existence rises and constantly passes away. Vipassana has become a rapidly growing field, and as such is treated separately below.

The Monastic *Sangha*

Of all the terms associated with Theravada Buddhism, the one that resonates most strongly is *sangha,* meaning literally "comprising" and referring to an assembly or community. Unlike Zen Buddhism, which organizes itself primarily around a teacher, classical Thervada Buddhism is centered in the sangha itself. And while some monks may emerge as teachers, the emphasis is always on the monastic community. In common Theravada usage, the term *sangha* means "monks" (a *sangha-bhukkhu*) but other, related uses have also applied. Ancient texts often specify certain other kinds of *sangha,* for example, the *sangha-savaka,* or the *sangha* of disciples, or the *sangha-ariya,* the *sangha* of noble or enlightened ones. However, beginning about the third century B.C.E., the term became more and more narrowly defined, so that today, when Theravadins recite the Three Refuges, the third specifically refers to the "monastic community." (Mahayana Buddhists often apply the word *sangha* to refer to the entire Buddhist community, both laity and monks, but this usage has never been applied by Theravadins, who often regard it as a distortion of the word's original intent.)

The early monks were all homeless wanderers, and did not develop settled communities until later. They first met only during the rainy season, since it was too difficult to walk abroad during that time. Because they were forced to stay in one place, the rainy season became the traditional season for intensive study and practice. (Since the United States does not have a "rainy season" as such, American monastic communities have had to make their own adjustments in this regard. Many believe it is a distinct advantage not to have study periods based upon the weather conditions.)

Meditation, while very important in the Theravada tradition, is not the over-riding occupation in many monasteries. Most of the more rigorous meditators are the so-called forest monks, who have also established a tradition in the United States.

Food Gathering (Pindapata)

Theravada monastic rules forbade the occupants to work, insisting they make their living from begging. The mendicants were recognized on their travels by their shaved heads, saffron robes, and begging bowls. Monks are also allowed to eat in the homes of the laypeople who invite them. This was not only to ensure they remembered that they are of one weft and weave with the rest of the community, but also to allow them time for study. Giving to a begging monk is an excellent way for a layperson to acquire merit.

Ordination (Upasampada)

Ordination is a spiritual rite of passage in which ten monks act as witnesses. The Buddha prescribed two levels of ordination, the novice level (*samanera*) and the higher level (*upasampada*). The candidates for the first level must be at least fifteen, while the aspirants for the second level must usually be at least twenty years old, have permission from parents or wives, be exempt from military service, and be free of certain diseases and debt. The rules also stipulate that the candidate must be a human being. (It is said that one time a snake attempted to join the Sangha and was forbidden by the Buddha.) The new monk has his head shaved and is draped in a saffron robe. The candidate asks the assembly three times if he may be ordained. If the monks agree, they remain silent. If anyone objects, he speaks and gives his reason. The exact time of the ordination is recorded, since seniority is measured by the length of time the person has spent as a monk. In traditional Theravada countries, all males were expected to become monks, at least for a short time.

Ordination of Women

While the Theravada tradition originally included convents as well as monasteries, no convents have existed since the eleventh century in Sri Lanka and the twelfth century in Burma. (There were never any women monastics in Thailand.) For women, the Vinaya requires that ten monks *and* ten nuns (the so-called twofold assembly, or *ubhato-sangha*) act as witnesses to the ordination, which must be performed by a *bhikkhuni,* or nun. This requirement has held back the rebirth of women monastics in Theravadin countries, since, after the order of nuns died out, there were no nuns left to act as witnesses.

Despite this apparently insuperable obstacle, the orders are being reestablished (with help from women monastics in other traditions). However, a great deal of controversy surrounds the project, mainly centering on how the lineage can be refounded. In the Buddhist tradition, Dharma passes directly from teacher to student. If the teachers have died "without heir" (or, as often happened, been killed) it is difficult to say by what authority one can begin a new doctrinal lineage. However, it is true that apparently the lineage of nuns was transferred to China before it died out in Theravada countries. However, since the Chinese version has distinct Mahayana overtones, some purists deny that there is any valid way to create a new order of nuns.

In any case, nuns had a more difficult time of this than did monks, and were subjected to eight additional rules (*attha garudhamma*). These rules mainly ensured that nuns remain subservient to monks. Menstruation was considered "polluting" and was a major obstacle to women's achieving full equality. It was easier for women to join a Sangha after menopause. However, thanks to the *attha garudhamma,* even the most senior woman was considered junior to the most junior of monks, although women were entitled to full arhatship.

Today many devout Theravada women lead a nunlike lifestyle, but because there is no official Sangha for them, they are not considered officially nuns. (Considering the difficulties nuns had in the old Sanghas, perhaps this is not altogether a bad thing.) They are known as "precept-holders." In America, there is an openness to the admittance of women monastics, and two Theravada monasteries, the Dharma Vijaya Buddhist Vihara of Los Angeles and the Bhavana Society in Highview, West Virginia, have ordained women as *samaneri,* novices who keep the precepts (sometimes eight and sometimes ten) but who have not achieved full ordination to the rank of monk by the *upasampada* ceremony. This halfway measure, begun about 100 years ago in Theravada countries, is not likely to encourage female interest in the Theravada monastic tradition, at least not in America. However, the International Association for Buddhist Women does address the question of nuns' ordination, including the development of the full (*bhikshuni*) ordination in countries where it has died out. At the 1987 Conference on World Buddhism in North America,

Vihara Temple. Photographer Spencer Grant. © TRIP.

which met in Ann Arbor, the matter was a subject of hot debate, as it is even today.

Some American Theravadin women live as nuns in meditation centers or temples. However, unless their compatriots are extremely enlightened, they do not receive full privileges in the community, and must bow before the monks, even if they are senior to them in practice. A few women are able to see this as an exercise in self-discipline, and simply try to ignore it. Others feel oppressed by it.

Since orthodox Theravada Buddhists consider the Sangha as the bearer of the Buddhist heritage, if Theravada is to flourish in America, traditionalists believe it should be effected through a monastic transmission, supported by the laity. Without this, they believe they would probably wind up with a "watered-down" version of the Dharma. Monks give back to the community by running schools, giving spiritual advice, and presiding over holidays and festivals.

One of the key rituals of the Sangha is the fortnightly *patimokkha sikkhapada,* in which monks gather together and recite the 227 rules of monastic discipline (the Vinaya). At least four *bhikkus* must be present for this ceremony. This procedure is the norm for every Theravadin community across the world, since Theravada is not divided into sects or schools. However, finding four monks to witness the ceremony can be difficult in the United States, and monks often face a choice of carrying on the ceremony with fewer than four *bhikkhus* or gathering less frequently to find a time when more can convene. The Buddha did give his monks permission to change minor rules when circumstances demanded, but agreement has not been reached about whether the rules governing *patimokkha sikkhapada* are minor or not.

The Arhat

Theravada Buddhism holds that the ideal life is that of a monk, and that family life and possessions are hindrances to liberation. Only in monastic life can one become an arhat, or "worthy one." An *arhat* is one who has banished forever the Three Poisons (or defilements) of greed, hatred, and delusion. Only such a one is truly free. Laypeople unable to accept a monastic life must wait until another birth. By donating food and other resources to monasteries, laypeople gain merit that will help them to win a better birth next time around. Not all monks achieve the status of *arhat*, however. The term is reserved for those who are truly enlightened. The earliest texts describe the Buddha himself as an *arhat*, although later texts attribute wisdom and powers to the Buddha that go beyond that of the ordinary arhat.

While some Theravadins maintain that an arhat has attained permanent Nirvana during this life, most believe that entry into Nirvana can only be temporary while one is still living and breathing. Any kind of ordinary consciousness would obviate Nirvana. Thus, the Nirvana experience can only be a fleeting one while an arhat is still in this world. Those who have experienced such a state can say only that it is entirely "other," meaning different from ordinary experience. It is a state beyond suffering, and even beyond reasoning and description. It is generally described in negative formulation—unborn, unconditioned, uncreated, deathless, and so on.

Mahayana Buddhists often claim that to seek salvation by becoming an arhat is selfish, that one is obligated to defer Nirvana until the rest of the world is enlightened. Many Theravada Buddhists denounce this attitude as "soft," with no foundation in the teachings of the Buddha. They point out that the Buddha never said that his object was to save every living being. The path is available only to those people who are willing to accept the Eightfold Path. It is impossible to save other beings. Each and every person must make the effort to train, purify, and save himself or herself. The Buddha's final words were "Seek out your *own* salvation with diligence." This issue has been the main point of controversy between Theravada and Mahayana Buddhists down to this day.

Arhats *and Buddhas*

While it is generally said that the ideal of the Theravadin is the *arhat*, there is yet a higher goal—the *pratyeka Buddha,* one who "walks alone" and achieves entrance into Nirvana. This is a solitary path.

Theravadin Observances

In the Theravada countries of Southeast Asia, the Buddha's birthday is known as Vasak or Vesakha Puja, and, in the most efficient way, it serves to honor the Buddha's birth, Enlightenment, and Parinirvana all at once. The celebration occurs in the last full moon in May. People decorate their homes with paper lanterns and garlands; many communities also have displays featuring major events in the Buddha's life. Monks are offered special food and they lead the populace on a circumambulation (three times) of a shrine, stupa, or temple. In China, people will often wash a statue of the Buddha. This reflects an ancient tradition that says that the gods rained down scented water upon the infant Buddha when he was born. Chinese Buddhists will also often lead an image of the Buddha around in a procession, accompanied by cheering, incense burning, flower throwing, and, of course, the inevitable Chinese firecrackers. In Burma pipal (fig) trees are watered in honor of the Buddha.

Festivals include full-moon and quarter-moon days (*uposatha*), as well as three other days during the lunar cycle. Many Buddhists wear all white during *uposatha,* although it is not required by scripture, but seems to be merely a Sri Lankan custom that has somehow taken hold of everyone. In addition, there is a New Year festival in April (the end of the dry season) and several agricultural celebrations. During the New Year the elders and dead are honored, and past misdeeds are cleansed away.

Many Buddhists in Theravada countries all observe the beginning of the Rain Retreat (Vassa). During this period, monastics remain in their home temples to study and meditate. The laity present the monks (and nuns, where there are any) with special candles, which are burned throughout the retreat. They may also present other small gifts of food, toiletries, and money. At the end of the retreat (Pavarána Day), specially blessed water is sprinkled on the laity. The people, in return, often give new robes and other gifts to the monks. This is called the *kathina,* or robe-offering ceremony (see above). In Thailand, people celebrate the Loy Krathong festival on the full-moon night of the twelfth lunar month. People bring bowls made of leaves and filled with flowers, candles, and incense sticks, and float them in the water. Bad luck is supposed to float away with them. The traditional ceremony pays homage to the footprint of the Buddha on the beach of the Namada River in India. In Sri Lanka on the night of the full moon in August there is a special procession for a relic of the Buddha—his tooth. The tooth relic was brought to Sri Lanka in 371 C.E. from India. The tooth itself can never be seen, as it is kept deep inside many caskets.

Theravada Buddhists also honor the Buddha on the day of Asalha Puja, which occurs on the first full-moon day of the eighth lunar month (usually July). It commemorates the Buddha's first teaching (the turning of the wheel of the Dharma, or Dhammacakkappavattana Sutta) to the five ascetics at the Deer Park (Sarnath) near Benares.

Another important day in Theravada countries is Magha Puja Day (Fourfold Assembly or "Sangha Day"). This observance takes place on the full-moon day of the third lunar month, usually corresponding to March. It commemorates an important event in the Buddha's teaching life. After the first Rain Retreat at the Deer Park at Sarnath, the Buddha went to Rajagaha, where 1,250 arhats returned from their wanderings to pay respect to the Buddha. They assembled in the Veruvana Monastery with the two chief disciples of the Buddha, Sariputta and Moggalana.

Although Buddhists do not observe a Sabbath, there is a regular holy day, the *uposatha*, which occurs every other week, based upon the moon. Monks have special observances on these days, and occasionally the laity may also observe them, although it is not required. Laypeople generally observe this day by visiting a monastery and listening to the chanting and liturgy there. During this period, laypeople will observe an extra three precepts in addition to the five they already adhere to. In Sri Lanka, this is called Poya Day.

Rite of passage observances are also common in Theravada countries. One of the most important is the rite of initiation for a young boy. Here he becomes, for a short time, a novice monk. After a large family celebration, his head is shaved and he takes monastic vows. He spends the night in the monastery, and goes out begging with the monks the next day. In honor of his new spiritual maturity, even his parents bow to him. Usually, the boy leaves the monastery after a few days or weeks but he is now considered spiritually an adult, and may reenter the monastery at any time.

Theravada in the United States

Theravada Buddhism has a long, but narrow history in the United States. In America, New York, Boston, and San Francisco all saw their share of Buddhist converts. The words "American Buddhists" ceased to be strange, at least in cultured areas. Chicago, for example, was a branch home to the Maha Bodhi Society, an international Buddhist organization founded in India in 1891. This society was founded by Don David Hewavitarne (1864–1933), otherwise known as Angarika Dharmapala. Hewavitarne was the son of a wealthy furniture mogul in Colombo, Sri Lanka. He later came under the influence of Madame Helena Petrovna Blavatsky (1831–91) and Colonel Henry Steel Olcott (1832–1907), who had formally declared themselves to be Buddhists. However, they did not consider themselves to be Theravadins as such, although they took *pansil* in a Theravadin temple. They considered themselves to be "universal" Buddhists. Olcott, a one-time Presbyterian, wrote a *Buddhist Catechism* that went through forty editions before his death, while Blavatsky gained fame as founder of the Theosophy Society, which still exists, although in a rather attenuated form. Olcott and Blavatsky were probably the first American Buddhist converts (Blavatsky was a naturalized citizen) although the conversion did not occur on American soil, but, as mentioned in chapter 1, in Sri Lanka. Olcott's conversion did not occur without some disagreeable fallout. In his happiness at having discovered Buddhism, he wrote the *Buddhist Catechism* in 1871, even before formally becoming a Buddhist. This popular book, which is still in print, was viewed by many people as injecting Protestant elements into the Buddhist schools that he helped to form around the country.

Blavatsky and Olcott brought the teenage Hewavitarne to India. Dharmapala attended the 1893 World Parliament of Religions in Chicago, where he reportedly won many converts to Theravada Buddhism, captivating audiences with his flowing hair, mesmerizing glance, and powerful rhetoric. Although he had taken a vow of chastity and wore the robes of a monk, Dharmapala never confined himself to a monastery, but spread the word by active traveling and teaching. Much of his work actually took place in India, where he worked to restore Buddhism to the land of its birth.

Dharmapala is also responsible for the conversion to Buddhism of C. T. Strauss, a Swiss-American businessman, who lived in New York. This is said to be the first formal, public conversion to Buddhism on American soil. (Others had done so unofficially or privately.) The event occurred in 1893, after Dharmapala delivered a lecture at the World Paliament of Religions. Strauss remained loyal to his new faith for the rest of his life, writing *The Buddha and His Doctrine,* a nonmystical, clear-headed, rationalistic defense of Buddhism, in 1922.

Today, most Theravada Buddhists are immigrants from Southeast Asian countries like Sri Lanka, Thailand, and Cambodia; there are perhaps 775,000 in the United States. However, Theravada is rapidly gaining ground with Euro-Americans in the Insight (Vipassana) Meditation movement.

Contemporary Theravada Temples

The first Theravada temple in the United States was the Buddhist Vihara Temple, built in 1966 in Washington, D.C. It served mostly the diplomatic community. Today, Theravada temples or monasteries exist in most states. In Thailand and Cambodia, a temple is called a *wat,* but in Sri Lanka it is known as a *vihara*. In the United States, the designation of the monastery is dependent on the nationality of the founder.

During the 1970s, refugees from Vietnam, Cambodia, and Laos settled in the United States, establishing many tight-knit Buddhist communities. Venerable Taungpulu Sayadaw and Dr. Rina Sircar, from Burma, founded the Taungpulu Kaba-Aye Monastery in northern California, and Ajaan Chah founded the Wat Pah Nanachat, a forest monastery in Thailand for training Western monks.

Important American Theravada and related Vipassana centers today include Ruth Denison's Dhamma Dena in Joshua Tree, California, and Henepola Gunaratana's Bhavana Society in West Virginia, which is the first Theravada forest monastery in the United States. Other important centers include Jack Kornfield's Spirit Rock Meditation Center, Larry Rosenberg's Cambridge Insight Meditation, and the Vipassana Metta Foundation on Maui.

Several ecumenical organizations in Theravada, such as the Buddhist Sangha Council of Southern California (BSCSC), the American Buddhist Congress (ABC), and the Buddhist Council of the Midwest (BCM), attempt to promote understanding between all branches of Buddhism. The BSCSC is made up of ordained monks, nuns, and ministers from all the major Buddhist traditions (Theravada, Mahayana, and Vajrayana) and from all Buddhist ethnic origins (American, Burmese, Cambodian, Chinese, European, Japanese, Korean, Laotian, Sri Lankan, Thai, Tibetan, and Vietnamese). The council has as its primary goals greater communication, understanding, and cooperation among Buddhist groups in southern California. The ABC is a nonsectarian council of organizations and Sangha representing all traditions and ethnicities.

One Theravadin group, the NAMO TASSO, made a concerted attempt in 1991 to develop a more "culturally American" and "neo-monastic" profile. (The words "namo tasso" are the opening words of the Pali chant *Buddha vandana,* and mean "Hail to the Buddha.") Its original mission was to "evolve a neo-monasticism employing insights from renewing contemplative traditions, psychology, etc., while maintaining the basic integrity and commitment of Buddhist monasticism as a tool for Enlightenment." As constituted, the organization failed, and although it apparently still exists, it seems to have abandoned its effort to support Theravadin monasticism. Like most other Theravadin organizations in the United States, its emphasis is now on Vipassana meditation.

Another important Theravada group is the Bhavana Society, established by Sri Lankan-born Henepola Gunaratana in 1982. The Bhavana Society is a residential retreat open to laypersons as well as monastics located in West Virginia. The society, while conceding in some respects to American cultural norms, also maintains Vinaya regulations.

Gunaratana is a notable exponent of the Sri Lankan tradition, which works to develop *sati,* or mindfulness, a concept he thinks is hard to define not because it is so complicated, but because it is so simple. According to him, the characteristics of mindfulness include "mirror thought" (being precisely and only aware of what is presently occurring), nonjudgmental observation, impartial watchfulness, nonconceptual awareness, nonegoistic alertness, goal-less awareness, and (perhaps somewhat paradoxically) participatory observation, meaning that the meditator is the observer and the observed at the same time. Gunaratana remarks that while *sati* is objective, is it not unfeeling or cold.

Gunaratana finds it easier to describe mindfulness in terms of its actions, which include recalling us to what we are really supposed to be doing, seeing things as they really are, adding nothing and subtracting nothing from what is there ("bare attention"), and seeing into the true nature of all phenomena. When fully developed, mindfulness sees deeply into the three marks of existence (suffering, or *dukkha*; impermanence, or *anicca*; and the doctrine of no-soul, *anatta*) immediately and directly, so that they require no fuller explanation.

The Thai forest tradition, which originally developed in the northeast of that country, but has flourished in the West, emphasizes using meditation to understand the basic laws of karma. This is not completely "other" than the Sri Lanka tradition, just a different focus.

Acculturation

One of the most divisive issues in the Theravada monastic community, as it attempts to establish itself in a cold climate, is the matter of clothing. The Buddha permitted monks to wear three articles of clothing, an undergarment, a loose top piece, and a double-layered cloak. These thin cotton robes traditionally, however, are not substantial enough to stand up to the fierce winters of many American localities, and many *bhikkhus* don thermal underwear. They wear socks, too—with sandals. (Some have even donned sneakers.)

However, this is currently a matter of debate. Some monks feel that it might be better to eschew monastic garb altogether, as it creates a rift between Theravadins and the American community at large, who regard them as strange and outlandish. They believe the robes, far from commanding respect the way they do in the Theravadin cultures, serve instead to widen the gap between them and others. (Sometimes the monks have been mistaken for Hare Krishna Hindus, which they feel does not help their image.) So far monks have rejected the abandonment of their traditional robes, although, as mentioned, they often choose additional items of clothing for comfort during the cold weather.

Another acculturation problem is related to relationships between the sexes (which for Theravada monks never becomes "sexual relations.") In Theravada countries monks never touch members of the opposite sex. However, in the United States there is some discussion about permitting them to shake hands when greeting women, and otherwise adhering to American cultural norms in this regard.

Some acculturation problems have been more serious than a controversy over greeting styles. A tragedy that took place in 1991 at the Thai Theravadin temple near Phoenix, Arizona, Wat Promkunaram, highlights the acculturation issue. Two local teenagers, in search of gold and other valuables, massacred nine temple residents, including a seventy-five-year-old temple nun and her grandson. Unfortunately, the massacre was not only a tragedy in itself, but cultural differences between the native Thais and the American investigators created serious tensions. The monks did not understand why the killing scene, which was also the shrine room of the temple, had to be cordoned off, and the handling of the bodies of the murder victims was also deeply distressing. Instead of allowing the monks to handle the deceased according to their own customs, the bodies were shipped off, autopsied, sent to a funeral home, and returned heavily made up and almost unrecognizable.

The killers, one of whom was a Thai native whose father frequented the temple, were later sentenced to 300 years in prison. The remaining monks, true to the Buddhist tradition of nonviolence and forgiveness, believe that they have been visited by the slain monks in dreams. They have built an outdoor memorial in their honor.

Vipassana Meditation

While Theravada Buddhism itself may not be popular among Americans, one of its main elements, Vipassana, or Insight Meditation, is one of the most rapidly growing movements in the United States. In fact, practitioners of this form of meditation are unlikely to identify themselves as Theravadin, or in some cases, even as Buddhists. Unlike traditional Theravada Buddhism, Vipassana tends to be organized around a particular teacher rather than around a community. And in contradistinction to nearly every other Buddhist tradition, a high percentage of Vipassana teachers, including several of the founders of the movement on American soil, are women. Vipassana has not abolished all links to the Theravada tradition, but since it is a lay movement, those links are tenuous. Jack Kornfield and Christopher Titmuss, both well-known figures in the Vipassana movement, were once monks, but have gone back to lay life. On the other hand, Vipassana meditation is an integral part of religious Theravadin practice. It cannot be said that practitioners of Vipassana form a separate school from traditional Vipassana, for they do not differ on doctrinal points. Even more interesting is the fact that many Buddhists from Zen and Tibetan traditions have sometimes adopted Vipassana practices. The vast majority of Vipassana practitioners are white and over forty years of age.

In conformity with traditional Theravada, Vipassana focuses on the spiritual practices of mindfulness (*sati*), lovingkindness (*metta*), morality (*sila*), and generosity (*dana*). In classical Theravadin Vipassana tradition, mindfulness, or the awareness of what is truly present, is considered the most important and often taught separately; however, in America, the emphasis has been on lovingkindness.

In both contexts, Vipassana has two components, the psychological and the spiritual. On the psychological level, it helps overcome negative mental states by removing impurities, *klesha,* or from the mind; on the spiritual level it helps develop mindfulness. In contemporary Western culture, the psychological elements have merged with and perhaps to some extent replaced the spiritual—for example, Jack Kornfield's Spirit Rock Center has a preponderance of psychologists among its teaching staff.

Vipassana is considered the most advanced kind of meditation by its practitioners. Literally, the word means "seeing in various ways." It bypasses *samatha,* or "calming meditation," that is traditionally practiced as a prelude to it. Its purpose is to develop insight into one's own mind and its mental processes, although the particular emphasis varies from tradition to tradition. In Burma and Sri Lanka, the focus is on at-taining awareness of the fleeting moment-to-moment existence of all phenomena.

The "insight" refers to an intuitive perception of the three marks of existence—impermanence (*anicca*), suffering (*dukkha),* and no-selfness (*anatta*). It is used to develop *satipatthana,* or right-mindfulness, and to purify the mind by eliminating conflicts and unproductive mind-states like hatred, anger, and lust. It is often used to help the practitioner develop an awareness of the fleeting nature of existence. In Buddhism a distinction is often made between the insight one gains after meditation ("bare" insight) and that which is gained without it ("dry" insight). The development of insight is an examination of mental phenomena (*namas*) and physical phenomena (*rupas*) through the direct experience of them. *Namas* and *rupas,* which appear briefly one at a time, should be noted with mindfulness, although each moment of study is extremely short, since mindfulness does not last and falls away just like the objects it examines. However, gradually a clearer understanding of these mental and physical realities can be accumulated. Insight Meditation is thus mostly concerned with purifying the mind and gaining insights into a more profound reality.

Another type of meditation is goodwill or loving meditation (*metta bhanava*). In the Theravadin tradition it is is a second form of meditation that balances Insight Meditation. Its purpose is to awaken the heart of compassion to the world of all beings. *Metta bhavana* is concerned with the development of wholesome qualities of mind, but can be developed only if one extends it to all beings without discriminating and without expecting anything in return. It should be free of selfishness or attachment. It is often accompanied by a kind of "forgiveness" meditation that is not done in Asia. This form of meditation is especially popular in America.

The focus on *metta* also brings American Theravada Buddhism close to the Mahayana tradition, with its emphasis on compassion. This meditation is usually a guided one, in which a leader helps the meditators through the various stages of the meditation. First, the students are asked to focus their compassionate attention on themselves by repeating a series of phrases such as "May I live in happiness, may I have joy," and so forth. Then the students are asked to focus on another person who has done them a kindness in the past. Third, students focus on someone they have no strong feelings about one way or another, and fourth on someone whom they dislike or are in conflict with. Last, students focus *metta* on all beings in the world. This practice goes back to the traditional methods of Theravada meditation, which often starts with *metta,* not insight, as its initial goal.

Buddhaghosa, the founder of Theravada Buddhism, used to say that among the forty conventional foci of meditation, only two were always beneficial—the development of *metta* and the recollection of death. To make his point about the latter clearer, Buddhaghosa recommended meditating upon a disintegrating corpse. A stickler for detail, he even listed the specific stages of a corpse suitable for meditation. These included a swollen corpse, a blue-green discolored corpse, a pus-filled corpse, a split-open corpse, a corpse mangled by dogs, a partly dismembered corpse, a completely dismembered corpse, a bloody corpse, a worm-infested corpse, and a skeleton. This meditation is very similar to the practice of medieval Christian monks, who often worked with a skull on their writing desk, to remind them of their impending physical dissolution. In this country, meditation upon corpses is inconvenient and probably illegal. American Theravadins concentrate on *metta.*

Meditators pick a quiet time, usually early morning or evening. It is believed that sitting twice for half an hour is better than sitting once for an hour, but the ideal is to sit for two hours daily. One is to choose a comfortable posture without leaning against anything; padded cushions and even chairs are acceptable. The eyes should be gently closed in order to focus on the breath. One should be aware of the breath but not try to control or change it. The three most important conditions for successful meditation are comfort, a straight back, and natural, easy breathing. Vipassana also makes use of walking meditation. Unlike walkers in the Zen tradition, they may walk at their own pace, usually for about forty-five minutes.

Today Vipassana is one of the most popular forms of Buddhism among North American converts. One reason for the popularity of Vipassana is that it dispenses not only with traditional Theravada rites, but also with textual and doctrinal study, a mainstay of traditional Buddhism. It centers on present existence and achieving goals in this life, not on the classical notion of Nirvana, or cessation of the cycle of birth, death, rebirth, and redeath. It is also extremely egalitarian. Clothing in Vipassana centers is casual, even for the teachers, and there are few if any religious images. People sit anywhere they like, not in the formal straight rows characteristic of Zen. Vipassana teachers bear no titles, and usually just go by their first names. It is strongly associated with lay practitioners, rather than monks, and it also seems to be less dependent on a particular national tradition than, for example, Zen, which still has strong Japanese associations. In fact, in America Vipassana has become so dissociated from its Theravadin roots that many Americans who practice it call themselves students of Vipassana rather than of Theravada.

The founder of the Vipassana movement was Mahasi Sayadaw (1904–82), a Burmese monk, whose teachings were imported to America by Jack Kornfield (b. 1945), Joseph Goldstein (b. 1944), Sharon Salzberg (b. 1952), and Ruth Denison. (Because so few Theravadin Buddhists have come to the United States, Vipassana meditation was mostly introduced by Westerners who traveled to Asia and learned it there.) Mahasi's approach was to dispense with the traditionally preliminary *samatha* (or tranquility) meditation and move straight into marathon sessions (3:00 A.M. to 11:00 P.M.) during a retreat that could last several months.

Mahasi's strong focus on meditation and personal experience was accompanied by a lesser emphasis on the monastic tradition and ritual. However, Mahasi's emphasis was still on a *samsara* marked by ignorance, greed, and hatred, a place to be left behind as soon as possible. Jack Kornfield, on the other hand, whose outlook is more Western, believes that liberation can be attained in this world. For Westerners, Nirvana is present in the immediate context, not in a separate sphere.

Goldstein and Kornfield learned the technique while in the Peace Corps, and both were invited to teach the subject at Naropa Institute (now University) in 1974, where they met Salzberg. Together, the three set up the Insight Meditation Center in Barre, Massachusetts. Currently there are over 150

Vipassana centers in North America. (This tradition is even stronger in Great Britain than in the United States, due to the fact that both Burma and Thailand, home to this tradition, were at one time part of the British empire.)

Kornfield, an Ivy League graduate, went through a hippie/drug/Haight Ashbury stage before returning to college and graduating with a major in Asian studies. He joined the Peace Corps, went to Thailand, and eventually became a monk in the Thai forest tradition, spending a year in silent meditation. When he returned to America, he found that his studies and meditation had not prepared him for the rigors of modern life and its complex relationships. He went back to school, eventually earning a Ph.D. in clinical psychology. In 1984 he left the Insight Meditation Center, feeling that Salzberg and Goldstein were focusing their Dharma talks too much on the traditional "defilements" of greed, hatred, and ignorance, and not enough on positive things. He established his own teaching center at Spirit Rock Meditation Center in Marin County, California. (It is only about fifteen miles north of the San Francisco Zen Center's Green Gulch Farm.) Kornfield, a prolific writer, is also important because he has insisted that abuses and misconduct by fellow Buddhist teachers be brought to light. The Spirit Rock Meditation Center was host to an all-Buddhist conference, ostensibly on the art of teaching; however, many of the women attendees revealed the sexual abuse they had suffered at the hands of their own teachers. Instead of covering up the scandal, this "elephant in the meditation hall," as Allen Ginsberg called it, was openly discussed. The outcome was the Insight Meditation Teacher's Code of Ethics, which addressed various issues of morality.

As mentioned, the most important center for Vipassana is the Insight Meditation Society (IMS) near Barre, Massachusetts. It was established as a nonprofit organization in 1975 on eighty wooded acres, on a site formerly occupied by a Catholic seminary and school. The IMS also runs the Barre Center for Buddhist Studies (BCBS), which was founded in 1989. The mission of the BCBS is to bring together scholars, teachers, students, and practitioners to study the doctrines of various Buddhist traditions both in their country of origin and in their new centers in the West.

Summary

Vipassana meditation is probably the only element of Theravadin Buddhism that has become part of the American Buddhist mainstream.

Chapter 4

Mahayana: The Second Turning of the Wheel

While Theravada Buddhism believes itself the most historically accurate Buddhist tradition, Mahayana (the Great Vehicle) considers itself the most spiritually developed. Mahayana is the branch of Buddhism found in China, Korea, Japan, and, perhaps to a lesser degree, Vietnam. Its distinct character is partly due to its absorption of Taoist, Confucian, and Shinto elements as it expanded.

The development of Mahayana is not associated with any specific person; rather, it is the culmination of a number of different historical trends and schools. It is thought to have emerged in northern India between 150 B.C.E. and 100 C.E., during a time when Buddhist universities were springing up; it is probable, however, that its roots go back much farther than this. Much new philosophical literature was being composed at this time.

Some of this new literature developed into the sutras of Mahayana Buddhism, most of which were probably written in Central Asia and China. While traditionalists complained that the new literature had no historical basis for claiming to be the word of the Buddha, its defenders asserted that they had received the teachings through deeply meditative states during which they were in contact with the Buddha.

Those Buddhists who accepted the new literature as canonical were those who became, in essence, Mahayanists, and they claimed that the new sutras represented a "second turning" of the Dharma wheel, a new revelation. For a long time they remained a minority group. They were first referred to as the Bodhisattva-yana, or the "vehicle of the Bodhisattva," as opposed to the Arahat-yana, or "vehicle of the disciple" of the earlier school. (Mahayanists later made up the word "Mahayana," to distinguish themselves from those they criticized as the "Hinayana" or "Lesser Vehicle." Theravadins, of course, reject the designation "Hinayana" completely, and most Mahayanists have given up using the term even among themselves, although it is still sometimes applied by Tibetan Buddhists.)

Very simply, Mahayana Buddhism grew out of the plain fact that not everyone can be monk or nun, and the idea that one could not achieve Enlightenment as a layperson was deeply unsettling. The Mahayana tradition recognizes the Enlightenment potential of everyone.

The Mahayana tradition formally includes both Tibetan Buddhism and Japanese Zen, but because these traditions have very large followings in the United States, and because they are significantly different in practice and belief from other branches of Mahayana and from each other, we will treat them separately.

Mahayana Teachings

The history of Mahayana—how and when and why it separated from the older traditions—remains obscure. The break was neither sudden nor complete, and the differences that separate the two traditions emerged only gradually. In the earliest days the division between Mahayana and other schools was fuzzy, and most lay Buddhists probably identified themselves only as "Buddhists" without regard to any particular school. In the end, however, certain clear distinctions emerge: the ideal of Theravada is the arhat, or perfect monk, while that of the Mahayana tradition is the bodhisattva, one committed to the Enlightenment of all beings. For Theravada Buddhism the premier virtue is wisdom; for Mahayana it is compassion. The center of Theravada Buddhism is the Sangha, or community of monks; for Mahayanists it is the community at large. For Theravadins, the Buddha is a man; for Mahayanists, he is limitless being. Theravada is fundamentally rational, Mahayana largely mystical.

There is also a difference between Mahayana and Theravada concepts of Nirvana. For Mahayana Buddhists, Nirvana is thought of not as a place or a state (as the Theravadins tend to conceive it) but as an opportunity to be liberated. It is an event to be realized in the here and now.

Canon of Sacred Texts

While the canon, or collection of sacred texts, was closed early in the Theravada tradition, meaning that no texts could be added, it remained open in Mahayana for many years, at least up to about 650 C.E. in India, allowing for the possibility of new revelation. Many of these texts are recorded in the Indian sacred language of Sanskrit. Most Mahayana sutras are longer than their Theravada counterparts, many of them running to hundreds of pages, in comparison to the early sutras which never run more than 100 pages each and frequently only go on for a page or so. In addition, the Mahayana texts are much more abstruse and difficult to penetrate, both because of their subject matter and the richly ornamented style in which they are composed.

Some of the major sutras of the mainstream Mahayana tradition include:

- The Prajnaparamita ("Perfection of Wisdom") Sutras: These sutras expound on the *shunyata* teachings of the Madhhyamika school, although all traditions in Mahayana honor them. They were composed between 100 B.C.E. and 100 C.E.
- The Heart Sutra: The very brief Heart Sutra (only one or two pages) condenses the great Prajnaparamita Sutras. It begins with a supplication to Avalokitesvara, the bodhisattva of compassion. It was probably written in China using Sanskrit sources.
- Yogachara Sutras: These are a group of loosely associated sutras, generally assigned to the Yogachara school.
- The Lankavatara Sutra: This text was one of the founding texts of very early Ch'an (Zen) teachings in China. It focuses on the study of mental phenomena and consciousness.
- The Mahaparinirvana Sutra: Literally, "the Great Passing into Nirvana," it fully expounds the concept of universal Buddha-nature. From the Mahayana perspective, it expounds the Buddha's final teachings. A related text is the Lion's Roar of Queen Shrimala. Both these sutras are cited as examples of "Buddha womb teaching."
- The Lotus Sutra: This is one of the oldest Mahayana sutras, and is especially esteemed by the Tendai and Nichiren schools. It discusses the concept of "skillful means."
- The Flower Ornament Sutra (Sanskrit, *Avatamsaka;* Chinese, Hua-yen): This long sutra has been described as the most "psychedelic" of all sutras. (Not surprisingly, it was a favorite of Jack Kerouac.) It describes the vision of Shakyamuni Buddha immediately after his Enlightenment. Many of its chapters are read as separate sutras.

- The Vimalakirti Sutra: This very popular sutra is not associated with any particular school, but is one of the most entertaining and readable of the sutras. It contains the famous scene of Shakyamuni revealing the true wonder of reality, by touching his toe to the ground. It is indicative of the Mahayana view of things that Vimalakirti, a rich man who adhered to the teachings of the Buddha and took the bodhisattva vows, was not a monk, but a layperson. This fact underscores the Mahayana view that one need not be a monk to attain Buddhahood, and that one can follow a holy life in the everyday world. The trick, of course, is that while one may live in the world, one must not become attached to it. The sutra says that Vimalakirti even frequented gambling halls and places of ill-repute, but only to save other beings, of course. Contemporary, socially active lay Buddhists note his activities with approval, and he indeed provides a model for a life dedicated to service in the world.

  However, Vimalakirti was not above a few tricks. By superhuman means, he produced on his own body outward signs of illness. When concerned friends, fellow townspeople, and even bodhisattvas came to inquire after his health, he took the opportunity to preach the Dharma to them, using his "sickness" to express the nonduality of all beings. To this end, he used his "thundering silence" to make his point. It was always very effective.

Besides the sutras, there is an additional group of texts called *shastras*, or treatises. These are systematic analyses of each Mahayana school based upon the relevant sutras.

The Cosmos

In the Mahayana worldview, there exist innumerable universes, each divided into one billion "world systems." The entire cosmos is thought to have a life span of 432 billion years. All universes are the product of karma, the law of cause and effect. Good actions create pleasure and bad ones pain. All are without beginning and without end. Six realms, called the Desire Realms, are present in this world. They are called "Desire Realms" because all beings in them, even the deities, are driven by desire or grasping. There are in fact twenty types of beings in the Desire Realms. The highest realm is inhabited by gods, who live in a paradise of gardens, music, and ambrosia. In Buddhist thought, gods are long-lived, but not immortal. They know they are going to die when their thrones become uncomfortable and they begin to sweat. Nearly all gods are reborn into a lower world, because they have made themselves drunk with pleasure and have not followed the Middle Way. There are also many hells in Mahayana thought, some hot and some cold. There are others called "trifling hell realms," arising from the karma created by an individual. These last for only a day or two. While many Theravadins share some of these ideas, the Mahayana tradition developed the idea of Buddha-lands, in the far "west" of the universe, where the Buddha of the Light, the Amitabha Buddha, presides. This Heaven is also available to human beings who ardently wish for a rebirth there and who have faith in the Amitabha Buddha. This idea of salvation by faith is not shared by Theravadins.

Shunyata *(Emptiness) and the Madhyamaka School*

Mahayana Buddhists also rejected the distinction between Nirvana and *samsara* in favor of a unified view of reality. According to Mahayana tradition, everything is *shunyata*, or emptiness. The word does not signify "nothing," but rather the fleeting, impermanent nature of all phenomena. This concept lies at the heart of the Mahayana tradition.

The doctrine was originally invented by second-century C.E. mystical sage Nagarjuna and further developed by his Madhyamaka school, which for this reason, is sometimes called the school of emptiness. For most Western people, it has little appeal—until it is understood. (To be fair, people of ancient Asia didn't care for the idea either. It was directly opposite to what the Hindu wise men taught, and seemed on the surface to be bleak and dismal. "If everything is empty, then nothing can happen," objected an opponent to the doctrine in chapter 24 of the Madhyamakaka-karika.) Yet to Nagarjuna, this was a true expression of the Buddha's Middle Way.

Others argued that the concept of *shunyata* meant that the Four Noble Truths, and hence all the Buddha's teachings, were also empty. Thus, Nagajuna and his cronies were trying to subvert them. The Madhyamaka philosophers responded that it was the notion of any part of reality as having a separate nature that subverted the Four Noble Truths. Nagarjuna became even more obscure, at least to Western minds, when he proposed his "four corner negation." First he set up the four logical possibilities of any two topics: x is y; x is not-y; x is both y and not-y; x is neither y nor not-y. He then went on to refute them all.

Emptiness, meaning lacking self-nature, is considered to be the central characteristic of all "Dharmas," or the basic unit of existence. According to the Prajnaparamita Sutras, the perfection of wisdom lies in realizing this emptiness. Madhyamikas (philosophers of the Madhyamaka school) concentrate on the problem of ignorance and delusion, and use the idea of emptiness to deny reality to the objects of delusion.

Emptiness is not "nothing," but the state from which all things (including nothing) arise. It is the fount of creativity, the freeing of the imagination. It is not the place where nothing can happen, but the dimension from which everything must happen.

Although it may seem to the uninitiated that emptiness is a negative way of looking at things, Mahayana philosophers maintained the contrary—*shunyata,* which is limitless, opens the way to universal wisdom and bliss.

Tathata *(Suchness) and the Yogachara School*

Another school of Buddhism, called Yogachara, was founded by Maitreyanatha, Asanga (the practitioner), and Vasubandhu (the theoretician) based on sutras that began to appear around the third century C.E., the most important of which are the Samdhinirmocana and the Perfection of Wisdom Sutras. Philosophers of this school were uncomfortable with the negative connotations of *shunyata,* although they agreed with its philosophical truth.

Yogachara preferred the term *tathata,* which can be translated as "thusness" or "suchness." In its form-aspect, emptiness is called *tathata,* or "thusness, " the so-called positive aspect of *shunyata.* (In fact, a whole separate line of thinkers, sometimes considered a separate school, especially by the Chinese, were the Tathagata-Garbha philosophers.)

The Yogachara school is also, especially in the United States, called the "consciousness only" school of Buddhism. Yogachara Buddhism is famous for its many cogent analyses of the nature of the mind, consciousness, memory, and phenomena.

Instead of concentrating on the problems of ignorance, as does the Madhyamaka school, the Yogachara school concentrates on analyzing the issue of independent origination, the interconnectedness or interbeing, of all things. They asked important questions about how karma gets transmitted through time. Like the Madhyamikas, the Yogachara school saw itself as preserving the Middle Way of the Buddha—going the center path between nihilism and substantiality, although the Yogacharans considered the Madhyamikas a bit too nihilistic themselves, while the Madhyamikas thought the Yogacharans erred on the substantialist side.

Interpenetration and the Hua-yen School

This Chinese school, developed by the so-called Five Patriarchs, is based on the Avatamsaka, or Flower Ornament Sutra (Hua-yen in Chinese). This school has elements drawn largely from Yogachara and Tathagata-Garbha thinkers. Making use of paradox, the Hua-yen school maintains that truth and falsehood encompass and interpenetrate each other, as do good and evil. The Hua-yen school became known as the Kegon school in Japan.

Nonduality

Mahayana doctrine insists on the utter nonduality of all phenomena; in a somewhat startling formulation of this thought comes the idea that even Nirvana and *samsara,* which are usually thought of as complete opposites, turn out to be one and the same thing.

The Mahayana Buddha

Although the Buddha is a great man in the Theravada tradition, in Mahayana, he can be much more. In some formulations he resembles a god, in others, a kind of universal principle. Some of the earliest and most interesting developments of the conceptions of the Buddha occur in the Lotus Sutra, which reached final form about 200 C.E. Here the Buddha announces that his Enlightenment occurred innumerable eons before this one, and that he has been teaching ever since in various guises, each of which is a manifestation of the heavenly Buddha.

In analyzing Buddhahood this way, Mahayana theorists of the Yogachara school developed the *trikaya,* or three-body, doctrine of the Buddha about 300 C.E.

- The transformation or appearance body (*nirmana-kaya*): This is the form in which the Buddha appears in the world. However, it is not a real body, but in some sense an illusion or fabrication. Mahayanists disagree about whether the Buddha has fleshly form or not. Some regard the transformation body as appearance only. When the transformation body dies, it returns to the heavenly Buddha.
- The bliss or enjoyment body (*sambhoga-kaya*): In this body Buddha appears to the bodhisattvas who have achieved the final stage of development. It exhibits the thirty-two major marks and eighty

minor marks that identify a Buddha. It is full of light, and each enjoyment body presides over a "Buddha Land."
- The dharma body (*dharma-kaya*): This is the body that is united with the eternal Dharma. This Buddha is identical with transcendent reality. It is beyond time and space, and has no qualifiable attributes.

A Buddha is a being who has awakened from the delusion that objective reality is different from subjective truth. In the Mahayana perspective, all sentient beings, human and animal (and sometimes even plants and rocks), are regarded as having Buddha seed and are capable of Awakening. In addition, the Buddha is regarded as having both an eternal and absolute nature, but also certain historical manifestations, as with Shakyamuni.

The Bodhisattva

The bodhisattva, or "awakened being," is a concept unique to Mahayana, but has several meanings. One way the word is understood is that of a human being who has become a "Buddha." There exist both earthly and heavenly bodhisattvas, but both groups strive for Enlightenment and also to help others. To this end, a person who is already well along the path to Enlightenment may take a "bodhisattva vow," to cultivate perfection.

Although neither the term nor the concept of bodhisattva was invented by Mahayana Buddhists, they opened the idea up, so that anyone, both layperson and monastic, could become a Buddha. It is also a name for certain celestial beings who are worshiped along with the Buddha.

The concept of the bodhisattva replaces the Theravadin ideal of the arhat. For Theravada Buddhists also there is only one Buddha—the historical person Siddhartha Gautama. For Mahayana Buddhists many Buddhas and bodhisattvas exist, and in many realms. Some are human, some divine. Some are saviors, some teachers. Some sources state that there are fifty-two stages to a bodhisattva's career.

Bodhisattvas are sometimes divided into three classes: beings who have achieved Enlightenment, beings who have vowed to attain Enlightenment, and already-enlightened beings who help others on their way to Enlightenment.

A bodhisattva is one who has attained the Six Perfections:

- Generosity (*dana*): This means there is no difference in status between the giver and the receiver. The bodhisattva willingly gives up possessions, family, life and limb in the service of others.

- Morality (*shila*): This is the natural outcome of the awakened mind. Eventually, conduct will become spontaneously pure, without effort. In the Mayahyana view, morality is not absolute, but depends upon the changing conditions of the world.
- Patience (*kshanti*): This word can also be translated as "tolerance." This can be achieved by meditations on lovingkindness and compassion.
- Energy, vigor, or effort (*virya*): This refers to the courage to keep on in the midst of difficult times. In this stage one practices mindful alertness.
- Meditation (*dhyana*): Meditation increases the effectiveness of the other *paramitas*. Although perfection of these meditative states permits the bodhisattva to enter a heavenly state, he refuses out of compassion and in obedience to his bodhisattva vows.
- Wisdom (*prajna*): This is the awareness gained through experience, not simple book learning. Through wisdom the bodhisattva understands dependent origination. It is sometimes called "wisdom-heart," or *bodhicitta*. At this point or at death, the bodhisattva could enter Nirvana, but the bodhisattva refuses out of compassion for all beings, just as he or she refused Heaven in the previous stage.

Although the Zen and Tibetan schools (which we examine in the following chapters) consider only the first six, most Mahayana traditions add an additional four perfections:

- Skillful means (*upaya*): This refers to knowing the best teaching strategy to help people out of their pain. One who masters this is called a *maha-sattva,* or a great being, or a heavenly savior.
- Vow or commitment (*pranidhana*): This includes the intention to liberate all beings. The bodhisattva has completely mastered the "transfer of merit" to help all beings.
- Powers (*bala*): These are psychic abilities, usually developed through meditation, used to gain insight into other beings' minds, to discover the best way to teach them.
- Knowledge (*jnana*): This is knowledge of the world as it appears to be. It should always be put in the service of wisdom. Here the bodhisattva is consecrated for perfect Buddhahood. Actually achieving Buddhahood is perceived as taking place in the Akanistha Heaven, the most rarefied of the pure-form Heavens.

Here are some of the most important bodhisattvas (and how to recognize them):

- Maitreya (literally, "loving or kind one"), the future Buddha, is the earliest mentioned of the bodhisattvas and featured in the Yogachara, Flower Ornament, Vimalakirti, and even some Pali sutras. This Bodhisattva is acknowledged by some Theravadin Buddhists, but is most honored in the Yogachara tradition. He symbolizes patience, meditation, and generosity. He often appears sitting in a chair rather than with legs crossed. This is the forerunner of the so-called Chinese laughing Buddha, who is also featured as Pu-Tai, a laughing Zen monk.
- Avalokitesvara (Kwan-yin in China) symbolizes compassion. Featured in the Heart and Lotus sutras, he represents generosity, skillful means, tolerance, and powers. He is most honored in Tendai and Pure Land. Often shown with many arms or heads, he wears a crown, and usually carries a lotus bud, symbolizing his compassion, and a wish-fulfilling jewel, for granting righteous wishes. The crown and royal robes he wears symbolize that he comes in close contact with the world. (Most of the other bodhisattvas are pictured as wearing monks' robes.) This bodhisattva becomes the compassionate female bodhisattva Kuan-yin in the Chinese tradition.
- Manjushri (literally, the "noble and gentle one" or "sweet glory") symbolizes wisdom, meditation, and right conduct. He is a "tenth stage" bodhisattva, meaning that he is seen as the greatest embodiment of wisdom, the wisdom that comes only after the highest meditation. He is most honored in Madhyamika tradition, but also in Zen and Ch'an. He is shown carrying a sword or a scroll (sometimes both). He often rides a lion.
- Samantabhadra (literally, universal worthy one) represents disciplined daily practice and symbolizes commitment, knowledge, meditation, and powers. He is featured in the Flower Ornament and Lotus sutras. He may carry a lotus or wish-fulfilling gem, and is depicted riding a six-tusked elephant.
- Vimalakirti (literally, undefiled name) is featured in the Vimalakirti Sutra. He represents powers, knowledge, wisdom, and skillful means. He is a layman. He is most honored in Zen and Chan Buddhism. He is often shown with an armrest, reflecting his invalid status.
- Bhaisajya-guru, heavenly bodhisattva, is the master of healing. He presides over the Pure Land in the eastern part of the universe. He is

able to cure illnesses and heal deformities, and give people insight into their own bad karma. Those who call upon him at death will avoid an unfortunate rebirth.

- Amitabha (Japanese, Amida; Chinese, O-mi-t'o Fo) is the heavenly Buddha of blissful light. He represents mercy and wisdom. He is especially important in Chinese Buddhism, and in Pure Land schools of both China and Japan. He rules the Western Paradise of Sukhavati, and is often shown wearing a jeweled crown. The sutras most associated with him are the Larger and Smaller Sukhavati-vyuha (Happy Land) and the Amitayur-dyhana (Meditation of Amitayus) sutras.

Each school of Mahayana may have its own favored bodhisattva. For example, the Madhyamaka school is associated with Manjushri, the bodhisattva of wisdom, while the Yogachara school favors Maitreya, the bodhisattva of the future.

Mahayana Virtue: Majoring in Compassion

The signal virtue of Mahayana is compassion, as opposed to, or rather, next to, the virtue of wisdom developed in Theravada traditions. Wisdom is not ignored, but must be used in the service of compassion. Enlightened or great compassion (*maha karuna*) is unlimited, and helps infinite numbers of beings to attain Enlightenment. It is not restricted to those who are "worthy" of it. True Buddhist compassion means feeling the sufferings of others as if they were one's own.

Skillful Means

Compassion by itself is not enough. It must be accompanied by wisdom. And in Mahayana, a certain kind of practical, even cunning, wisdom comes to the fore. One of the most notable doctrines of Mahayana Buddhism is that of *upaya,* or "skillful means." This doctrine, expounded in the Lotus Sutra and other texts, declares that the Dharma, while always one and the same, may be expressed differently to different people according to their situation and level of understanding.

Several metaphors and stories are used to explain this doctrine. The Lotus Sutra, for example, likens the Buddha's teaching to a gentle, nourishing rain that falls equally upon all beings, yet each being makes use of the rain to flourish in its own way. Thus the concepts of equality and individuality are perfectly merged. In another water image, developed in the Hua-Yen Sutra, the Dharma is compared to water, which is a uniform substance. Yet it takes on the shape of the container it is placed in. Even so, the Buddha's teachings conform to the spiritual capacity of each hearer.

The Laity

For Mahayana Buddhists, it is not necessary to enter the monastic life to reach liberation. The role of the laity is equal to, and in some cases greater than, that of the monks. This point is made clear in the Vimalakirti Sutra, one of the most beloved texts in the Mahayana tradition.

Mahayana Practice

Because Mahayana Buddhists conceive of the Buddha as something more than a man, they have a place for devotion and even prayer in their scheme of things. Many Mahayana traditions (including Zen, especially in Japan) use statues of the Buddha and offerings of incense, food, or candles. Partly this is an inheritance from indigenous religious traditions in India, China, and Japan. Partly it is symbolic. The Buddha, while venerated, is not worshiped, nor are Buddha statues idols. They are merely substantive emblems of the spiritual force of Buddhism, and no more (or less) real than the entire universe of forms and sense. They are an encouragement and initiation to look more deeply. Much the same can be said for chanting and other forms of devotional practice.

The Mahayana Vows

Like all Buddhists, Mahayanists take the vows of the Three Refuges, or Triple Gem: "I take refuge in the Buddha, I take refuge in the Dharma, I take refuge in the Sangha." (Some Mahayanists, especially in the Zen camp, interpret these words metaphorically, in which the Buddha represents "realization," the Dharma represents "truth," and the "Sangha" "harmony.")

Mahayana Buddhism celebrates the interdependence of all sentient beings. This concept has great importance in Western eco-Buddhism, as we will see. A Mahayana Buddhist takes Four Great Bodhisattva Vows, contained in the following chant:

I vow to liberate all beings, without number.
I vow to uproot endless blind passion.
I vow to penetrate the Dharma gates beyond measure.
I vow to attain the great way of the Buddha.

Chinese Buddhists are supposed to make forty-eight vows to alleviate the sufferings of others, in imitation of Kuan-yin, the Chinese name for Avalokitesvara.

Buddha-Nature

One key term in the Mahayana tradition is Buddha-nature or Buddha-mind, which is often used by Mahayanists in place of "liberation." All sentient beings possess the Buddha-nature; the challenge for human beings is to realize it.

Mahayana Celebrations

Ancestor Day is celebrated throughout the Mahayana tradition from the first to the fifteenth days of the eighth lunar month. It is believed that the gates of Hell are opened on the first day and the ghosts may visit the world for fifteen days. Mahayana Buddhists make food offerings during this time to relieve the ghosts' sufferings. On the fifteenth day, Ullambana or Ancestor Day itself, people visit cemeteries to make offerings to departed ancestors. (Many Theravadins from Cambodia, Laos, and Thailand also observe this festival.)

In Japan a similar holiday is called Obon; it celebrates the reunion of family ancestors with the living. It begins on the thirteenth of July and lasts for three days.

Kuan Yin's (Avalokitesvara) birthday is also celebrated by Mahayanists. In many parts of China and Tibet, Kuan Yin represents the perfection of compassion in the Mahayana world.

Theravada and Mahayana: Points of Agreement

While there are important differences between Mahayana and Theravada Buddhists, there is consensus on many important issues. In 1966 the World

Buddhist Sangha Council was convened by Theravadins in Sri Lanka, with the agenda of finding philosophical points of agreement. Both Mahahyan and Theravadi monks were in attendance. The Venerable Walpola Rahula drafted the following unanimously accepted statements.

1. The Buddha is our only Master.
2. We take refuge in the Buddha, the Dhamma, and the Sangha.
3. We do not believe that this world is created and ruled by a God.
4. Following the example of the Buddha, who is the embodiment of Great Compassion (*maha-karuna*) and Great Wisdom (*maha-prajna*), we consider that the purpose of life is to develop compassion for all living beings without discrimination and to work for their good, happiness, and peace; and to develop wisdom leading to the realization of Ultimate Truth.
5. We accept the Four Noble Truths, namely, *Dukkha,* the Arising of *Dukkha,* the Cessation of *Dukkha,* and the Path leading to the Cessation of *Dukkha*; and the universal law of cause and effect as taught in the *pratitya-samutpaada* (Conditioned Genesis or Dependent Origination).
6. We understand, according to the teaching of the Buddha, that all conditioned things (*samskara*) are impermanent (*anitya*) and *dukkha,* and that all conditioned and unconditioned things (*dharma*) are without self (*anatma*).
7. We accept the Thirty-seven Qualities conducive to Enlightenment (*bodhipaksa-dharma*) as different aspects of the Path taught by the Buddha leading to Enlightenment.
8. There are three ways of attaining *bodhi* or Enlightenment, according to the ability and capacity of each individual: namely, as a disciple (*sravaka*), as a Pratyeka-Buddha (solitary Buddha), and as a Samyak-sam-Buddha (perfectly and Fully Enlightened Buddha). We accept it as the highest, noblest, and most heroic to follow the career of a bodhisattva and to become a Samyak-sam-Buddha in order to save others.
9. We admit that in different countries there are differences with regard to the life of Buddhist monks, popular Buddhist beliefs and practices, rites and ceremonies, customs and habits. These external forms and expressions should not be confused with the essential teachings of the Buddha.

Major Contemporary Mahayana Sects

Current schools of Mahayana Buddhism include Tendai, Shingon, Pure Land, Nichiren, Zen (Ch'an), and Tibetan, among others. It should be noted that the differences among the schools are, at least to some degree, a matter of culture. For example, the varieties of Japanese Mahayana schools are strictly maintained, often with some degree of animosity between them, usually centering on the relative importance of meditation (Zen) and ritual chanting (Pure Land and Nichiren). Chinese Mahayanists, however, tend to mute the differences between schools, and it is not unusual to find a single temple honoring both Pure Land and Ch'an traditions. This is simply another aspect of the Chinese syncretistic spirit. It is actually rather difficult to find a Chinese Buddhist temple, even one primarily affiliated with Ch'an, that does not include chanting of some sort as part of the practice.

Pure Land Buddhism: The "Easy Path" to Enlightenment

Although most Americans associate Japanese Buddhism with Zen, the fact is that Zen has never been especially popular with most Japanese. The Pure Land school of Buddhism, on the other hand, while not especially well known in America, has historically been one of the most popular forms of Buddhism in its native country. In the United States, however, it's been a different story, especially with the European-descended convert "elite" class. Many of these people, both academics and practitioners, have regarded Pure Land Buddhism as too "ethnic" to take root here. This attitude ignores not only the importance of Pure Land Buddhism as a flowering of Dharma itself, but also the fact that Pure Land Buddhists, as Ryo Imamura wrote in personal correspondence to Charles S. Prebish, "welcomed countless white Americans into our temples, introduced them to the Dharma, and then often assisted them to initiate their own sanghas, when they felt uncomfortable practicing with us" (*Luminous Passage* 128).

As its name implies, Pure Land Buddhism focuses on the concept of the Pure Land or Western Paradise. Technically, there are four schools in Pure Land Buddhism, two of which exist in the United States: Jodo Shu, founded by Honen Shonin (1143–1212), who wrote a short explanation of his teachings, known as the Ichimai Kishonin, and sealed it with the imprint of his palms as testimony; and Jodo Shinshu, established by Honen Shonin's disciple, Shinran in thirteenth-century Japan. *Jodo* means "pure land," *shin* "true," and *shu* "school." So Jodo Shu means simply "pure land school," while Jodo Shinshu means "*true* pure land school."

Shinran abandoned his monastic vows and married, and in a revolutionary move, taught that all people were guaranteed liberation through the grace and mercy of Amida (Amitabha) Buddha. He shifted the effort from self-effort to help from the Buddha. (The same controversy emerged in Christianity in the "works versus grace" debate.) The movement was further popularized by the Eighth Successor, Rennyo (1415–99), who reaffirmed the rural, peasant foundation of the religion. Even though an elaborate leadership structure eventually evolved, Pure Land Buddhism still retained the loyalty of its base.

In Japan there are ten varieties of Jodo Shinshu alone, but only two of these came to America, Nishi Honganji ("The Western School of the Original Vow") and Higashi Honganji ("The Eastern School"). The Western School has by far the most adherents in the United States. It is this school that later became incorporated as the Buddhist Churches of America. Both branches are commonly known as simply as Shin Buddhism in the United States.

Central Features of Pure Land Belief

No one is really certain how the idea of the "Pure Land" developed. One theory contends its origins lie outside Buddhism and India, possibly stemming from Zoroastrian ideas or even the Garden of Eden. The other theory is that it originated in Buddhism and in India. There no Sanskrit word for Pure Land (Chinese, *ching-t'u*; Japanese, *jodo*), however, and the closest translation seems to be *vishuddha-ksetra* (buddha land). The Sanskrit term *sukhavati* is the most common direct translation for *jodo*. At any rate, the fully developed idea of "Pure Land" seems to have first come together after Buddhism entered China.

The foremost characteristic of Pure Land belief is the concept of the Pure Land, or Western Paradise. In folk imagination it is a paradise of gloriously gemmed trees, magical singing birds, and fragrant breezes. It is inhabited by both gods and humans, but has no ghosts or animals. On a more philosophical level, however, the Western Paradise stands for a transcendent state of being only a step away from Nirvana itself. Modern ideas combine the two notions, so that the Pure Land is indeed the Land of Truth, but it also contains real forms. (Other Pure Lands exist, but the Western Paradise is the most important.) Amida (Sanskrit, Amitabha) is

In the eleventh century, Buddhist monks began using gardens as a teaching tool, as well as an aid to meditation. Many Zen gardens represent reality on a smaller scale. They are designed to enhance mindfulness. Every plant, stone, and water drop is rich with meaning. Don Farber Photography.

the cosmic Buddha of light. He is venerated not only in Japan and East Asia, but also in Central Asia and Tibet.

One can enter the Pure Land (Ching-t'u in Chinese) only through the grace of the Amibha Buddha (Amida in Japanese, O-mi-t'o Fo in Chinese) or from another person who has stored up a superabundant amount of merit. Pure Land Buddhists believe that the grace of Amida Buddha and the faith (*shinjin*) of the believer are sufficient to achieve liberation. Faith is a gift that is bestowed by the Buddha, resulting from his compassion and wisdom. This concept is called *tariki,* which means "other power." Efforts deriving from the individual, *jiriki,* such as those practiced in Zen, are considered ineffectual. This notion makes Pure Land Buddhism quite different from more "orthodox" forms, which place responsibility for liberation squarely on the seeker. The state of openness to liberation is a spiritual transformation brought about in this life by the grace of Amida. Good works, therefore, do not lead to salvation. They are a manifestation of having been saved, a further example of the blessing of the Amida Buddha. Merit, which can be earned by good works, like vegetarianism, freeing animals, or even chanting for the benefit of others, is transferable in Pure Land Buddhism, and by transferring one's merit to another person, one is more likely to receive the merciful grace of Amithabha. Chinese Buddhists seem somewhat more likely than other Pure Landers to consider the possibility that the Pure Land can be made a reality on Earth. However, it is made clear that although the Pure Land is not the final goal, to be reborn in the Pure Land is to be given the opportunity to learn the Buddha's teachings directly, without distraction or distortion.

As Christians do with the analogous concept of Heaven, contemporary Pure Land Buddhists use (sometime interchangeably) three ways of talking about the Pure Land. For some, the Pure Land refers to a purified, ideal society that can be created here on Earth. For others, it refers to the realm of the mind and consciousness, a mind of Enlightenment. And for others, it retains its old, more literal meaning of a real place presided over by a bodhisattva in the world to come.

In Pure Land Buddhism, three sutras form the core of the teaching: the Sutra of Immeasurable Life or Pure Land (Sanskrit, *Larger Sukhavativyuha sutra*), the *Meditation Sutra* (Chinese, *Kuan wu-liang-shou ching*), and the Amida Sutra (Sanskrit, *Smaller Sukhavativyuha sutra*).

The Wang-sheng lun, a commentary on the Sutra of Immeasurable Life, says that one can be reborn in the Pure Land through five methods: (1) prostrating oneself before the Buddha; (2) calling on the Buddha's name and giving praise; (3) single-mindedly desiring to enter the Pure Land and concentrating on this goal; (4) visualizing the Pure Land, the Buddha, and bodhisattvas through the eyes of wisdom acquired by virtue of the above-mentioned concentration; (5) transferring to others the merit gained from the first four practices, so as to help them to enter the Pure Land along with oneself.

The larger of the Pure Land (or Happy Land) sutras tells us that millions of years ago the Bodhisattva Amida (originally a king who became a monk named Dharmakara) vowed to become a Buddha and to purify a land that would become his own realm when he achieved his goal. This land would contain all the excellences of all other Pure Lands, and its inhabitants would have all perfections, memories of previous lives, and the ability to see all other Buddha Lands. He also swore that unless forty-eight conditions about his land were met, he did not wish to attain Enlightenment. The most important condition or vow was the Eighteenth, in which Dharmakara promised the attainment of the Pure Land to those who called upon his name sincerely even if only ten times. Ten *kalpas* ago Dharmakara became the Amida Buddha, reigning over the Western Paradise, into which he can enable all sincere seekers and believers to be reborn. (Only those who slander the Dharma are forbidden entrance.)

Amida Buddha is said to be of a golden color of illimitable brilliance. He is seated on a lotus. Eighty-four thousand golden light rays emanate from his immense body. Each ray represents a materialized virtue. A halo, larger than millions of worlds, surrounds him. Because the Buddha is so large, unenlightened people cannot imagine him. Therefore, he may appear to them as being only eight or sixteen feet high, to make it easier for their minds to grasp.

Some Pure Land Buddhists consider the Pure Land to be a state of liberation, to which the bodhisattva can repair after death until such time as he is called back to the world of *samsara* to carry on his work of liberation. Once one has reached the Pure Land, one cannot regress.

Pure Land Practice

BCA worship services resemble in some ways a typical Protestant service, including the singing of hymns and reading from sacred scripture. The hallmark of Pure Land Buddhism is the chanting of the Nembutsu, a shorthand abbreviation of *Namo Amida Butso,* "the Name of Amida Buddha."

In everyday practice, the Nembutso chant or recitation is the most characteristic feature of Pure Land Buddhism. The practice originated in China, but in Japan it came to have a central importance, and not just in Pure Land. From the early Nara period (710–784) some form of Nembutsu was common; the Tendai sect also placed emphasis upon it during the Heian period (794–1185). However, with the rise of the Pure Land schools in the Kamakura period (1185–1333), Nembutso recitation took a central role. (In Tendai, the practitioner visualized the seated figure of Amida, while in Pure Land the mental emphasis is on the name.) Some controversy arose as to which was the most efficacious in obtaining merit: the number of repetitions or the sincerity of the chant.

When Pure Land Buddhism was introduced into Japan, Honen taught that the recitation of the Nembutso was a way to attain liberation. However, his disciple Shinran (1173–1263) altered the emphasis—the recitation of the Nembutso did not grant one liberation (only the grace of Amida can accomplish that) but instead is a chant of thanksgiving for already having obtained liberation. Today's Pure Land Buddhists all over the world understand the Nembutso as an expression of joyful gratitude and as a way of entrusting oneself to the Amida Buddha.

The Buddhist rosary, or *juzu*, consists of 108 beads. One explanation of the number of 108 is that it represents the number of earthly desires that ordinary people have. The beads form a circle with two strands, with three other strands ending in tassels. The strands are attached to the circle by a larger bead, called the father's bead, on one side and on the other side, a mother's bead. These beads represent the Buddha. Don Farber Photography.

Pure Land Buddhists practice their faith at home as well as in temples. They also carry *juzu*, a string of 108 major and four minor beads that works much like a rosary. Prayer beads are also used by other Buddhist schools.

Pure Land Celebrations and Observances

Pure Land Buddhists celebrate the Buddha's birthday (Hanamatsuri, or Flower Festival) on April 8, and the Buddha's Enlightenment (Jodo-E),

In Japan, April 8 is celebrated as the anniversary of the Buddha's birth. Since shrine visitors often bring a cherry blossom, the festival is also called Hana Matsuri or Flower Festival. Men, women, and children all wear kimonos. What you see here is a *hana mido*, or "flower temple," a miniature shrine. The tray is filled with sweet tea. © TRIP.

or Bodhi Day, December 8. They also celebrate Nirvana Day, February 15, when Sakyamuni Buddha died at eighty years of age. They also celebrate Shinran's birthday (Gotan-E) and the anniversary of his death, Ho-On-Ko, in January.

When a member of the Pure Land community dies, the name of Amida Buddha is chanted again and again. The body is washed and the head is shaved. On the funeral day, priests recite scripture and burn incense. Rituals to keep away hungry ghosts may be performed. The body may be cremated or buried, according to custom. A memorial tablet is taken back to the home and placed in a household shrine. After the funeral, memorial rites are held on the seventh day and annually thereafter.

At the year's end, there is a service called Joya E, when temple bells are rung 108 times to wipe out the 108 passions of human beings.

Pure Land in the United States

The very first Pure Landers probably came to the not-yet state (or even American possession) of Hawaii by accident; starting in 1839 shipwrecked

The long earlobes represent material wealth by the Buddha (originally they were lengthened by the wearing of many jewels) and the half-closed eyes meditation. Note the "third eye" in the center of the forehead. Photographer George Wittenberg. © TRIP.

Japanese sailors found their way to the islands. Many of them were members of the Jodo Shinshu sect. The first official emissaries of the sect, however, didn't come until March 1889, when the Rev. Soryu Kagahi showed up as a representative of the home temple Honpa Honganji, located in Kyoto. He then returned to Japan, with laypeople carrying on the services until more missionaries, notably Hoji Satomi and Yemyo Imamura, came in 1897, building a temple in Honolulu. The latter was an especially powerful leader of his congregation through difficult times that included racial oppression and hostilities during the sugar strikes. He worked to "Americanize" his people through starting Boy Scout troops, having services in English, and putting American-style pews in the temple. Not coincidentally, these measures made Buddhism seem less foreign to Americans. Imamura's religious justification was that Buddhism was not to be restricted to the customs of any one country, that it was a universal and adoptable religion.

Pure Land Buddhism won the praise of many early American observers. They felt that many of its tenets, which included a "Pure Land" similar to many Western notions of Paradise, was at least moving in the right direction. (By this they meant that Pure Land beliefs were close to what *they* thought was true.)

Japanese Buddhists also published a very early and influential English-language Buddhist magazine, *The Light of Dharma,* in San Francisco, running from 1901 to 1907. It was not a strictly Pure Land journal, however, for its many contributors included D. T. Suzuki, Shaku Soyen, and Dharmapala, as well as Western Buddhist scholars.

Japanese immigration to the United States is often divided into two periods. The first period, from 1885 to about 1907, was characterized by what is called the *dekasagi* immigration, in which people left their birth country to look for employment elsewhere and then returned with their accumulated wages. Early Japanese *dekasagi* immigration came to Hawaii first, between 1885 to 1894. Large-scale immigration to the mainland followed. In 1908, the second phase of immigration began, during which most immigrants, rather than being laborers, were farmers and small business people who intended to create a properous life for themselves.

At the time of the greatest influx of Japanese immigrants, in the late nineteenth century, Protestant churches (mostly Presbyterian and Methodist) committed themselves to converting the new Japanese immigrants. Most of these immigrants were Pure Land Buddhists. The Japanese were much more amenable to acculturation than the earlier Chinese had been, and many Japanese Buddhists feared that they would lose their Buddhism as they became more "American." And to a large extent, this did indeed happen. To counteract these missionary endeavors, and with help from Japanese emissaries of the Pure Land Sect, Buddhists in San Francisco established the Young Men's Buddhist Association (Bukkyo Seinen Kai) in 1898, a Buddhist version of the YMCA and forerunner of the Buddhist Church of San Francisco. Services were held on Sundays; they often began with sutra chanting, but included sermons, informal talks, or lectures. Study classes were conducted on Saturday nights; Monday nights were saved for non-Asians, who were becoming increasingly interested in Japanese Buddhism. Thus, from its inception, Pure Land Buddhism was geared to assimilating with Christian America. A Buddhist's Women's Association (Fujinkai) was also established.

Partly in response to the fear of assimilation, the first Buddhist temple was built in San Francisco in 1898, and a year later, on September 1, 1899 (after an exploratory mission a year earlier by two officials of Pure Land from Japan), the first two official and permanent Buddhist missionaries to the United States, Shuye Sonoda and Kakuryo Nishijima, arrived in San Francisco. They laid the groundwork for what was to become the Buddhist Mission of North America.

Most of the first temples were converted Christian churches, although other buildings were also used. Money to purchase, renovate, and maintain the temples was raised by membership dues, donations, and fundraisers. Each congregation also hired a resident priest and paid him a monthly salary plus honoraria. The first temples were administered by an all-male board of directors who annually chose officers and met monthly to conduct temple business.

Although their original goal was to minister to the Japanese expatriates (of whom there were about 10,000), Sonoda at least planned to spread the Buddhist doctrine among white Americans as well by occasionally offering services in English. One such ceremony, a celebration of the Buddha's birthday (Hanmatsuri), on April 8, 1900, attracted 150 white Americans, some of whom later tried to force the Japanese out of the country. One early American convert to Pure Land Buddhism was Robert Clifton (1903–63), born as Harold Amos Eugene Newman in 1903. He apparently became fascinated with Buddhism while studying at Columbia University, and in 1928 he moved to San Francisco to live with the Japanese community there. In 1933 he was ordained as a priest at the Honpa Hongwanji Temple, and was ordained again in Japan a year later. In 1951 he established the Western Buddhist Order (there is another organization of the same name, founded by Sangharakshita). Later still, in 1956, Clifton was ordained as a Theravadin monk in Thailand, whereupon he took the name Sumangalo, and still later studied Zen and then Tibetan Buddhism. He died in Malaysia before he could explore yet further traditions. He is an interesting, although not extremely influential figure.

It should be said that not all Pure Land Buddhists are Japanese. Chinese Americans, too, honor the Pure Land tradition, although Chinese are less likely to differentiate "their" brand of Buddhism from others, and often combine Pure Land elements with other traditions.

Acculturation

Pure Land temples played an important role in keeping the rapidly growing Japanese immigrant community cohesive. They were religious, social, and commercial centers all at once, especially in outlying areas. Interestingly, the temples also organized baseball leagues and Boy Scout troops modeled on the American plan. Thus the temples provided a critical support system for a people who faced increasing prejudice and hostility from Caucasian Americans. The Oriental Exclusion Act of 1924 barred new immigrants from obtaining citizenship, and there was continuing anti-Japanese agitation throughout the 1920s. Japanese were also limited in the amount of property they were allowed to possess. Despite this, by 1931, there were thirty-three active main temples, and by the start of World War II, there were a 100,000 Japanese Buddhists in the country (about half the total number of Japanese Americans altogether).

Until the Second World War, the head of the American branch of Pure Land was the *socho,* or local bishop, although the real power remained in Japan with the abbot of the sect. (The abbot was always a direct descendant of Shinran.)

The original name of the American Pure Land mission was the North American Buddhist Mission (NABM), or sometimes Buddhist Mission of North America (BMNA), which was in reality the former Young Men's Buddhist Association. In 1905 Koyu Uchida, the fourth director of the organization, changed the name to the Buddhist Church of San Francisco, possibly believing the word "church" had more positive associations for Americans than "temple." Uchida returned to Japan in 1923, and a year later the Japanese Immigration Exclusion Act was passed, which essentially halted the arrival of Japanese to this country. However, the 100,000 Buddhists already present were more than enough to sustain Pure Land Buddhism, and by 1931 there were thirty-three churches affiliated with the BMNA.

One of the most important persons in the development of American Pure Land Buddhism was Kenju Masuyama, formerly a professor of the Honganji Ryukoku University, who became the bishop of the church in 1930. He established a training center in Kyoto for new ministers, so that when they came to America they would be able to speak English, since a growing number of the nisei, or second-generation Japanese, no longer spoke Japanese. In fact, the tension developing between older and newer Japanese encouraged Kenju Masuyama to reorganize the church into sections designed to facilitate communication and training. Unfortunately, his efforts to "Americanize" the church were largely halted by the advent of World War II and its consequent disruption of the Japanese American community by putting most of them into internment camps.

In fact, it was in such an internment camp (the Topaz Relocation Center in Utah) in 1944 that the Pure Land Buddhist communities in this country had officially changed their name to Buddhist Churches of America

(BCA) and repudiated all ties to Japan. The official use of the word "church" was partly a result of the imprisonment of Japanese citizens in the internment camps. It was felt that "church" had a friendlier, less "intrusive" sound than "mission," just as "church" had earlier often replaced "temple." Despite their unfair treatment at the hands of the government, most Japanese American Buddhists still felt it was important to try to fit in. (In the internment camps it was required that religious services be conducted in English, and many Buddhists continued to do so even after their release and resettlement.) After the war, in August 1945, Bishop Ryotai Matsukage returned to San Francisco to reopen the headquarters of the BCA.

The BCA, centered in San Francisco, is the oldest formal Buddhist institution in the United States and one of the most stable. It has established over sixty temples throughout the country, including Chicago, Cleveland, Detroit, Minneapolis, Phoenix, and Washington, D.C. In contrast to Japan, where temples are largely inherited by the eldest son, American Pure Land Buddhists hire clergy to serve them, much the way Protestant Americans do. The priests are trained in this country, as opposed to Kyoto, often at the Institute for Buddhist Studies in Berkeley, California.

Today there are about 20,000 adult Pure Land Buddhists in the United States. The organization is headed by Hakubun Watanabe with its headquarters in San Francisco. Most Pure Land Buddhists are ethnic Japanese, and the sect has not had much impact on the larger stream of conversion to Buddhism. However, the organization does run two important centers: the American Buddhist Academy in New York and the Institute of Buddhist Studies (IBS) in Berkeley. The latter offers training for ordination and a master's degree in Shin Buddhist Studies, and publishes the influential Buddhist journal, *Pacific World.* Shin Buddhism stresses the Asian virtues of filial piety and respect for one's ancestors as an example of the grace bestowed by the Buddha. This carefully interweaves religious faith with cultural norms already in existence, strengthening its position in the community. These same values were carried to the United States by Japanese Shin immigrants.

To a great extent, the immigrant Shin Buddhist community has been insular and fairly closed to outsiders. Part of the reason is that the leaders still often come from Japan, with limited facility in English. A more important reason may be that the chief function of Shin Buddhism in America has been not to evangelize but to retain a sense of community among its worshipers. Leadership is also extremely hierarchical (in Japan Shin priests basically "own" their temples) and insists on Japanese cultural values, sometimes at the expense of strictly Buddhist ones. The general tenor of Shin Buddhism is also anti-intellectual, focusing on pious behavior exemplified by models of good behavior known as *myokonin.* These factors have made this brand of Buddhism unappealing to potential converts. Some attempts have recently been made to extricate the true Purely Land teachings from its cultural entanglements, but success has been limited.

In addition, it appears that Pure Land Buddhism may be on the decline in the United States, losing both members and ministers. Part of the decline may be traced to the fact that BCA, while it willingly accepts new members and even funds Pure Land promotion, does not aggressively proselytize, either within the Japanese American community or outside it. Young people usually stop attending services when they reach adolescence.

It is generally conceded that for Shin Buddhism to remain alive in the United States, it must become more multicultural and open to converts. Its current membership is almost entirely ethnic Japanese, many of whom have "inherited" the Pure Land tradition, and many scholars feel that its "otherworldly," "conformist," and "obedient" features make it unattractive to contemporary Americans, either Japanese or other. The clergy is aging, and many attempt to operate more than one temple. To recruit young people to the clergy, the BCA is attempting to increase both their salaries and benefits. In addition, a school has been established to educate English-speaking ministers. This has been extremely difficult, as the vast majority of highly educated Japanese Americans choose to enter technical and scientific fields rather than the humanities. The future of the BCA seems uncertain.

Tendai (Chinese, T'ien T'ai)

Tendai Buddhism is strongly rooted in the T'ien-t'ai Buddhist practice of China. In fact, T'ien-t'ai is named after a sacred mountain in southeast China. It was popularized by Chih-i (538–597), who wished to unify Buddhist doctrine already in China with freshly arriving texts from India. He recognized the relative validity of all Buddhist scripture and teaching, but also proclaimed T'ien-t'ai's reliance on the Lotus Sutra as the highest doctrine. He also affirmed the universal presence of Buddha-nature in all forms of existence, both animate and inanimate.

Tendai Buddhism was one of the first to give philosophical treatment to connect the Ten Thousand Universes in each moment of existence, an idea more subjectively developed by Nichiren, whom I discuss below. Although Tendai is widespread in Japan, it is little known in this country as yet, although it has importance as a precursor to the popular Nichiren and Soka Gakkai school.

Tendai was founded in Japan by Saicho (767–822), now known as Dengyo-Daishi, the "Grand Master of the Propagation of the Doctrine." This Japanese priest made a dangerous journey to China to study under the Sixth T'ien-t'ai Patriarch. When he returned to his temple on Mt. Hiei near Kyoto that he had founded in 788, he brought back T'ien T'ai, but also transformed it into an esoteric school with Tantric rituals and practices using mantras, mudras, mandalas, and meditations, and Pure Land practices. Tendai also includes specialized scholarship, arts, and nature worship. The great variety of teachings and practices gave rise to the term "Ekayana" (round teachings) school.

Bostonian William Sturgis Bigelow (1850–1926), a disaffected physician, studied both Shingon and Tendai Buddhism in Japan, as did Ernest Fenollosa (1851–1903), a poet and student of Japanese art. Bigelow came from the upper strata of Boston society, and counted among his friends Henry Cabot Lodge and Theodore Roosevelt. Bigelow felt isolated and lonely in his Boston Buddhism. His family rejected him, and he spent most of his time holed up in his Beacon Street home in the winter and his home on Tuckernuck Island in the summer. Besides being a committed Buddhist, he did much to promote understanding and appreciation of Oriental art in America. When he died, he asked that half his ashes be buried in Boston, the other half in Japan.

On November 5, 2000, a Jukai Kanjo ceremony took place at the Tendai Mission of Hawaii. At the time Jikai Clark Choffy of the Mitsugon-an, Joshin Jonathan Driscoll of Enmitsu-ji, and Monshin Paul Naamon of the New York Betsuin were officially recognized as Tendai priests authorized to teach Tendai Buddhism in the United States and Japan by the Tendai administration. Also, a district (*kyoku*) for the United States was established.

Nichiren and Soka Gakkai

Soka Gakkai is somewhat of an oddity in the Buddhist world. Often scorned by "traditional" Buddhists (both native and convert), it retains a vitality and growth curve that is the envy of those who are most suspicious of it. While considered a "new" Buddhism, its origins go back hundreds of years, to the monk Nichiren.

Nichiren (1222–82), the Founder

Nichiren Buddhism arose in Japan in the thirteenth century. It is one of the only Buddhist schools actually founded in Japan rather than in China, and its emphasis is not on meditation, but on practice, focusing on the Lotus Sutra.

Nichiren was born February 16, 1222, in Kominato, in what is now Chiba Prefecture, Japan. He was a fisherman's son who was born into turbulent times. Not only was there social unrest and civil war, but it even seemed as though Japan was getting more than its fair share of natural disasters. For example, a huge earthquake struck the then-capital, Kamakura, in 1257. Nichiren later wrote that horses and oxen had formed the habit of dying in the streets, and pestilence was everywhere. All these dire happenings contributed to the urgency of Nichiren's thought.

Nichiren's childhood poverty is in contradistinction to the early wealth of the Buddha, and gained many followers for him among the impoverished people. As a child he amazed everyone with his zest for spiritual knowledge, and it is said that when he was twelve years old he prayed to the bodhisattva Kokuzo that he would become the wisest person in Japan. He became a Tendai monk at age fifteen, entering the temple at Mt. Kiyosumi, and was ordained a year later. It is said that he completely assimilated the knowledge of the current schools of Buddhism, including not only Tendai, but also Shingon, Pure Land, Zen, and the six schools of the Nara period. He experienced doubts about all of them, and criticized Pure Land Buddhism for promising people happiness in the next life rather than in this one, although he shared its love for the Lotus Sutra, which he claimed to be the sole source of salvation for all. This twenty-eight-chapter sutra is divided into two parts. The first half describes the life and teachings of Shakyamuni, the historical Buddha. The second half describes the eternal Buddha. It is a rich and complex book, so complex, in fact, that Nichiren suspected it would be out of the reach of the average person. He decided that the heart of the book could be touched by devotedly reciting *Nam-myoho-renge-kyo*, or "All Hail to the Lotus Sutra!"

At last, on April 28, 1253, after a seven-day period of seclusion, Nichiren climbed a hill and stood to face the rising sun. He then recited the *Nam-myoho-renge-kyo* for the first time. At the time, he adopted the name

Nichiren, which means "Sun-lotus." (His birth name is said to be Zennuchimaro, or "splendid sun.")

Nichiren believed that everyone else was deluded about what Buddhism really was. For example, he called Zen monks "devils," and said they would all be thrown into hell. Eventually, he formed his own school apart from Tendai. He also considered himself to be the living embodiment of Boatsu Jogyo, a disciple of the Buddha who is mentioned in the Lotus Sutra. He reviled the other Buddhist sects in such strong "un-Buddhist" terms that his enemies have never forgotten it. For modern-day Nichiren and Soka Gakkai believers, however, Nichiren is himself an embodiment of the Buddha, or at least of the bodhisattva Eminent Conduct.

Because he challenged the entire Japanese religious and political establishment, Nichiren kept getting into trouble with the authorities. He was outlawed, sentenced to death, and exiled twice, but he somehow always prevailed in the end, a trait also found in many of his greatest followers. When he died he was given the title Daishonin, or "Great Sage."

Nichiren Belief

Nichiren believed that humans lived in the dark age of *mappo,* the terrible "third age" during which the Dharma was in decline. He was disgusted by the fact that most of the schools of Buddhism of his own day had been co-opted by the aristocrats, and he felt that his mission was to unite all people (not just the elite) in one tradition that would last throughout this dark period. Only when all people found the truth of the Lotus Sutra would the dark age of *mappo* pass away. In one of his writings, Nichiren unveiled the Three Great Secret Laws for the age of *mappo*:

- the object of true worship (the Dai-Gohonzon)
- the high sanctuary that must be built in this age
- the true invocation: *Nam-myoho-renge-kyo* (All Hail to the Wondrous Lotus Sutra)

While the Lotus Sutra, is holy for many other Mahayana sects, for Nichiren Buddhists it is the *only* valid one. This sole reliance on the Lotus creates somewhat of a problem for other Buddhists; it is a text that omits the story of the Buddha's Enlightenment, the Four Noble Truths, and the Eightfold Path, all of which are central Buddhist beliefs.

Yet for Nichiren, the Lotus Sutra replaces all other teachings. He focused attention on it rather than on the Pure Land or even the Amida

Buddha. Its value for Nichiren and his followers was twofold: first, it revealed that everyone was able to achieve Buddhahood; and second, it teaches that life is eternal.

Most of his philosophy is contained in his letters, or *Gosho*. He agreed with Shinran on the efficacy of chanting, although he favored a different chant, the *daimoku: Nam-myoho-renge-kyo*. This is the actual title of the sutra and, as noted above, it means, "All hail to the wondrous Lotus Sutra." (Nichiren came to believe that this was the proper chant on April 28, 1253.) These words are considered to be the heart of the text. Nichiren Buddhists use this chant as a means of obtaining Enlightenment; it is not a chant of thanksgiving like that in Pure Land Buddhism.

On October 12, 1279, Nichiren, who was a noted calligrapher, inscribed a mandala-like scroll, the Dai-Gohonzon, with both Chinese and Sanskrit characters that express the *Nam-myoho-renge-kyo*, which is written also in bold letters in the middle. On either side are written the names of mythical and historical figures. At the top is the name of Shakyamuni, the historical Buddha. In Nichiren's thinking, this Buddha represents subjective wisdom. The name of Taho, the mythical Buddha, who represents objective reality, is also present. Four more bodhisattvas, symbolizing the true self, eternity, purity, and joy (all qualities of Buddhahood), are also written. Lower down on the Gohonzon is inscribed the name of the demoness (Kishimojin in Japanese) who fed her own 500 children by killing human babies. (Her story is told in chapter 2.) In Nichiren, she represents "hunger," a legitimate drive that must be kept subservient to the nobler aspects of humanhood.

Gohonzon literally means *Go* (an honorific prefix), *hon* (foundation), and *zon* (esteem). It functions as a replacement for Nichiren; a personal relationship with Gonhonzon enabled his followers to attain Buddhahood. Today, the Gohonzon is believed to draw out the Buddhahood of each believer. It serves the same function as does a mandala in other Buddhist traditions, and, indeed, is regarded by its followers as a kind of mandala, a compendium of blessings.

Contemporary Nichiren Buddhists often place offerings—most typically candles, evergreens, and incense—before the altar where the Gohonzon is enshrined. Also, a cup of fresh water and perhaps fruit is generally placed in front of the Gohonzon in the morning. These offerings are all considered symbolic: water and food for life, candles for nonsubstantiability, incense to engage our senses and the truth of the Middle Way, evergreen to remind us of the eternity of life. Some people add personal articles as well.

Man kneeling before an altar in a Buddhist temple in Manhattan's Chinatown. Photographer Jeff Greenberg. © TRIP.

The Dai-Gohonzon scroll is dedicated to the happiness of all humankind. Nichiren's disciples would sit before it and practice *gongyo,* which means to recite the *daimoku* and also the part of the Lotus Sutra known as *Honen,* which declares all sentient beings have Buddha-nature. They also recite chapter 16 (*Juryo*), which maintains that Buddhahood arises from within. It is also common to ring a bell during *gongyo.*

Nichiren thought that conventional Buddhism was too centered in monasteries, not in the real world where he thought it belonged. For Nichiren, a Buddhist could be a Buddhist without a shaved head, monastic robes, or a vegetarian diet. He wasn't even particularly concerned with rules of behavior, for he felt that these were already part of societal norms.

All Nichiren Buddhists, of whatever school, are expected to work diligently for world peace. However, each school regards itself as the "true" Buddhism and looks upon other forms of Buddhism as inauthentic.

The first documented Nichiren visitor to the United States was Yoshigirai Kawai, who made an appearance at the 1893 World Parliament of Religions. He spoke about the saving power of *Nam-myoho-renge-kyo* and that it was not necessary for one to learn and study Buddhist texts in order to reach liberation. However, since his speech was entirely in Japanese, his American audience remained mostly in the dark about Nichiren.

Currently of the dozens of different Nichiren sects in existence, three took root in the United States: Nichiren Shu, Nichiren Shoshu, and Soka Gakkai.

Nichiren Shu and Nichiren Shoshu

In Nichiren Shu (also known as the Nichiren Buddhist Church of America), the Buddha is Sakyamuni; the Dharma is *Namu-myoho-renge-kyo,* which stands for the literal meaning of the Lotus Sutra; and the priest is Nichiren. Its adherents are mostly Asian Americans on the West Coast. It may be considered a kind of "umbrella" Nichiren school and consisted of about 4,000 temples at the beginning of World War II.

Nichiren Shoshu (The Orthodox or True Faith of Nichiren) was founded by Nikko Shonin (1246–1333). He left Nichiren's temple at Mt. Minobu in 1288 after arguing with the other disciples and in 1290 he established Taisekiji, the head Nishiren Sho Shu temple at Kitayama. Nichiren Shoshu possesses two documents, the *Minobu sojo* and the *Ikegami sojo,* which it believes proves conclusively that Nichiren selected Nikko alone to succeed him.

In Nichiren Shoshu the Buddha is Nichiren himself, the Dharma is the *Namu-myoho-renge-kyo* of the Three Great Hidden Laws, and the priest is Nikko. Shoshu has 724 temples throughout Japan and six temples (and numerous other meeting places) in the United States run by Japanese priests, who supervise dedicated laymen known as *hokkeko.* This word refers to the name that Nichiren himself bestowed on the lay believers on the occasion of the establishment of the Dai-Gohonzon. The head temple of Nichiren Shoshu is at Taisekiji, at the foot of Mt. Fuji, which has developed into a Great Dojo.

Today all the believers of Nichiren Shoshu throughout the world make pilgrimages to Taisekiji, the place to practice True Buddhism and a fountainhead for the movement for worldwide Kosen-Rufu.

The priesthood is important in Nichiren Shoshu, whose doctrine states that the priests correctly protect and transmit the True Law of Nichiren Daishonin, while the lay believers correctly practice this Buddhist Law expounded by Nichiren. Only when the laity and the priesthood unite, cooperating in mutual efforts toward the propagation of this faith, do believers think that they can achieve Kosen-Rufu, or world peace.

While the Lotus Sutra is the key text in Nichiren Buddhism, its adherents believe that it is a deeply symbolic text not easily understood. Only

Nichiren, from his enlightened position, could penetrate its full mysteries and find the heart of the mystery in the powerful *Nam-myoho-renge-kyo* chant. Nichiren called it the "king of sutras, flawless in both letter and principle." Other teachings he called "inferior," "provisional," and "transient." By definition, inferior, transient, and provisional teachings cannot lead one to Enlightenment or Buddhahood.

Enlightenment is found within oneself, and the *Nam-myoho-renge-kyo* chant is identified with life itself. Each element of the chant has a special meaning. *Nam* is derived from the Sanskrit meaning "devotion to" and thus, on one level, means "devotion to the Lotus Sutra," the key text of Nichiren Buddhism. It is a word of invocation, signifying the sacredness of the text to follow.

Myo represents the mystical Middle Way of life, the elusive flowing between existence and nonexistence. Nichiren Buddhism takes an expanded view of the Buddha's famous doctrine of the Middle Way. It doesn't simply mean compromise, but a way to overcome duality. For example, our life itself is the Middle Way (*chu*) between nonsubstantiality (*ku*) and the temporary existence we normally call life (*ke*). The ultimate truth about any aspect of life does not lie in its unceasing change (*ku*) or its static (although temporary) appearance (*ke*). The truth of an entity lies somehow between these two extremes, but all partake in some aspect of truth. In fact, the Japanese term for this concept is *santai,* the "three truths." The whole idea is to overcome our dualistic thinking. *Myoho* is also said to mean "life and death," with *myo* meaning death and *ho* meaning life.

Alternatively, *ho* refers to the manifestations of that mystic life, or to all phenomena. (Mystic doesn't mean "otherworldly" here. In fact, it means just the opposite. It refers to what is deeply this-worldly, or even everyday, which comes to the same thing, when one considers it deeply.) Together *myo* and *ho* translate as Mystic Law.

Renge is the lotus and represents the Mystic Law. The lotus produces its flowers and seeds at the same time, thus demonstrating the law of karma, in which the causes and effects of an action are embedded within each other. Thus it refers to the simultaneity of cause and effect.

Kyo is the Japanese word for sutra or teaching. Originally both *sutra* and *kyo* referred to a thread out of which cloth is made. Thus they are the underpinning of all laws.

For those who doubted that the whole of the Buddha's teaching could be encompassed in one chant, Nichiren responded that the whole of Japan, and all ideas associated with it, were encompassed by that one word alone:

Japan. In the same way, a person's name must in a few letters evoke that person's form, history, thoughts, dreams, and spirit.

In the thought of Nichiren, there exist ten states of life, taken from the ten worlds of earlier Buddhist cosmology. Each represents a way of responding to life, and each persona can experience all of them. They are as follows:

1. hell, a state of immense and unrelenting suffering
2. hunger, a state of insatiable desire and greed
3. animal life, a state ruled by instinct
4. anger, a state of conflict
5. tranquility, a state of rationality, characteristic of humans
6. joy, a state of bliss, sometimes referred to as a paradise
7. learning, a state of effort and growth
8. absorption, a state of self-realization
9. bodhisattva, a state of compassion for all beings
10. buddhahood, a state of Enlightenment

Only the last four states are considered "noble" because one must expend effort to experience them. The other six states, even that of joy, simply "happen" to a person without any effort on his or her part. Thus, while joy is positive, it carries no ethical merit. In contrast, the last four states are meritorious. However, it is also true that each state carries all the others within itself. This means that true Buddhahood is not some state divorced from all the others (even the lowest hell). All are connected, and all exist within everyday life. In Nichiren, the object is not to deny or avoid states of anger and suffering, but to transform them and to realize the Buddhahood that lies embedded in each of them. Even the most despicable of states can be used to gain knowledge or to experience the pain of the others. Each is not merely a step toward the Buddha, but a realization of Buddhahood in all its aspects.

In like manner, there is no ultimate separation between body and mind. They are equal and interdependent, a principle known as *shiki shin funi,* the "oneness of body and mind." "At each moment," Nichiren wrote, "life encompasses both body and spirit." For this reason, among others, Nichiren Buddhism does not focus solely on the spiritual aspect of life. It recognizes that the material and spiritual worlds are deeply interdependent. Chanting affects both the material body and the spirit, and helps them both. In fact, Nichiren contends that those religious traditions that place sole emphasis on the spirit turn their believers into unwitting hypocrites, because such an attitude is simply not tenable. We are physical creatures as well as spiritual ones, and religion should reflect both.

Nichiren Buddhists view all phenomena as distinct, yet linked. Reality is one, yet it can be analyzed into Ten Factors or modes. According to the Lotus Sutra, these are:

1. form (the physical appearance of things)
2. nature (the inner spirit or character of things)
3. entity (life itself). This aspect unites the first two aspects.
4. power (potential energy)
5. influence (power in the external world)
6. inherent cause (habit)
7. relation (external stimulus)
8. latent effect (hidden effect resulting from inherent cause and relation)
9. manifest effect (the manifestation of the latent effects)
10. consistency from beginning to end (all factors are harmonious)

The ten aspects are listed to show believers not only that life always changes, but how and in what way it changes. It should be noted that many of the changes and effects are internal and thus not readily or immediately visible. Yet taken in total, they comprise what Pat Allwright calls "the mechanics of life" (67). Further, each moment of existence contains "3,000 universes." This may seem like an arbitrary or poetical number, but it is actually derived by multiplying the Ten States (each of which contains all the others) mentioned earlier by the Ten Factors, and the Three Realms of Self, Other Beings, and Environment. This is a mind-expanding view of the universe, for it shows how each "frame" or moment of life interpenetrates deeply with each element of the cosmos. Some Buddhist philosopher-scientists have actually estimated that each frame has a duration of about one-seventy-fifth of a second. However, this way of viewing phenomena makes them a series of quanta rather than a continually flowing process, which is the more traditionally Buddhist way of viewing things.

For Nichiren Buddhists, one great glory of their faith is that it is instantaneous. It does not accept the assumption that one must work and practice and undertake strenuous effort to reach Buddahood. Like some Zen Buddhists, it claims that the practice (in this case chanting rather than meditation) is itself a manifestation of Buddhahood. Since cause and effect are simultaneous, it makes no sense, in the Nichiren doctrine, to claim that one takes steps toward Enlightenment. We are already there, and just need to realize and practice it.

Nichiren recognizes the connection between individual action and collective result. It is said that world peace cannot be achieved unless we individually learn to transform hatred into compassion and anger into productive energy.

Soka Gakkai and Soka Gakkai International

Soka Gakkai International USA (SGI-USA) is a global organization, and is currently the largest and most racially diverse Buddhist group in America. It states that its fundamental purpose is the happiness of all people; its pathways to that goal include overcoming one's fears and appreciating how one's life affects other people. Its goals are to contribute to peace, culture, and education based on the philosophy and ideals of the Buddhism of Nichiren. Its official core concepts include:

- the inherent dignity and equality of all human life
- the unity of life and its environment
- the interconnectedness of all beings that makes altruism the only viable path to happiness
- the limitless potential of each person to make a difference
- the fundamental right of each person to pursue self-development through a process of self-motivated reform or "human revolution"

Soka Gakkai believes that the best way to deal with the famous Three Poisons of greed, hatred, and ignorance is not to eradicate them but to transform them. They can be turned into the positive attributes of courage, compassion, and wisdom. This process is called *bonno soku bodai. Bonno* means "deluded impulses" referring to the Three Poisons; *soku* means roughly "equals"; and *bodai* means Buddhahood. This reinforces the concept that Buddhahood does not banish deluded impulses, but transforms them. Transformation; the process of change, is a key concept in Nichiren Buddhism. It is another way of saying that all people can attain Buddahood. In one way of looking at it, it is a process of great transformation; in another way, we are already there.

In the past, Soka Gakkai was scorned by "orthodox" Buddhists, especially Zen Buddhists, largely because silent meditation is not an essential part of Soka Gakkai practice. However, it is slowly winning greater acceptance among more traditional Buddhists for its continuing active work in making a real difference in people's lives and in the world at large.

Soka Gakkai was founded by Tsunesaburo Makiguchi (1871–1944) and Josei Toda (1900–1958). Makiguchi, who was brought up in a rural village, moved to Tokyo in 1901 and soon began a campaign for progressive reform in education, and in fact became a school principal. In 1928, Makiguchi joined Nichiren Shoshu, a denomination of Nichiren Buddhism. Some years later, his interest in combining a religious sensibility with secular success became the foundation for Soka Gakkai: the Value Creation Society (Soka Kyoiku Gakkai), which was formally established in 1930 as a lay educational movement. In the 1930s he published his *Soka Kyoikugaku Taikei (System of Value Creating Pedagogy)*. Makiguchi was certain that the pursuit of happiness, material wealth, and social responsibility were compatible goals if people were properly educated.

Makiguchi and Toda were imprisoned by the government in 1934 for "treason" and labeled "thought criminals." Their crime was really opposition to Shinto (the state religion) and their resistance to joining together with other Nichiren sects, most of which were intensely loyal to the government. Makiguchi died in prison of malnutrition and mistreatment on November 18, 1944, but Toda survived and was released in July 1945.

His survival might be credited to the fact that, according to his own account, he chanted the *daimoku* two million times. After his release, Toda "reinvented" Makiguchi's society by calling it simply Soka Gakkai, dropping the *kyoiku* ("education") part of the name. By combining it with Nichiren, he led the way to the development of a vital new religion, one that currently claims more than 750,000 families in Japan. While Makiguchi had also been involved with Nichiren, for him it had been on a personal rather than institutional level. Toda's successor, Daisaku Ikeda, internationalized Soka Gakkai and also took it back to its roots, emphasizing education.

Ikeda arrived in Hawaii on October 1, 1960, as part of a whirlwind tour that took him to San Francisco, Seattle, Chicago, Toronto, New York, Washington, São Paulo, and Los Angeles, all within less than a month; he returned to Japan on October 24. He was the first Soka Gakkai president to visit America. Since then Soka Gakkai has flourished. The entire tour was an example of *shakubuku*, or aggressive proselytizing, claiming a thousand converts a month. Rather frighteningly, *shakubuku* literally means "to break and subdue." As Ikeda raced across the country, he organized as he went, setting up a Soka Gakkai group at each stop. He appointed a leader for each group, and ordered each member to learn English, become a citizen, and obtain a driver's license. The original 500 members were Japanese; by 1960 there were more than 200,000 members, and, at its height thirty years later, the membership had grown to over 300,000, mostly non-Japanese and a large percentage of whom were young (between twenty-one and thirty years old). Soka Gakkai has also welcomed gay people into its membership.

It should be stated that the majority of these people have since become inactive; however, Soka Gakkai still retains over 100,000 current members, with about half of those regularly chanting and attending meetings. This may not seem like a vast number, but it is much larger than that claimed by the next largest Buddhist group, the Honganji Branch of Jodo Shinshu (Buddhist Churches of America).

Soka Gakkai opened its first headquarters as Nichiren Shoshu of America (NSA) in Los Angeles in 1963, and it retained that name for many years. The first director of NSA was Ikeda's Korean-born disciple Masyasu Sadanaga. Later, in 1972, as a sign of his Americanization he changed his name to George M. Williams. He had studied with Ikeda in Japan, had preceded him to the United States in 1957, and accompanied him on his tour. Williams was an energetic proselytizer and, as time went on, he encouraged various ethnic groups to hold meetings in their own languages if they desired (between 1963 and 1965 he had asked that all meetings be conducted in English) and soon services could be heard in Korean, Spanish, Japanese, and various Chinese dialects as well as in English. Likewise, various language and ethnic groups produced their own publications. Now separate meetings of the various language groups are held annually at the Florida Nature and Culture Center.

Some American men joined because they had married Japanese women while on tour of duty in Japan, and wished to convert. But Williams changed to a different tactic as the 1960s wore on. He instructed members of the group to go out into the streets, and invite any wandering hippies to come inside and attend meetings. Some of the meetings had an intellectual bent and introduced the new prospects to important aspects of Buddhist philosophy. Others were simply "chant-and-be-happy" meetings. African Americans were particularly interested in the new religion, and Williams soon acquired a number of both Caucasian and African American disciples. While Hispanics are still under-represented in Soka Gakkai, if one takes into consideration their numbers in the general population, they are present in higher percentages and raw numbers in this school than in any other branch of Buddhism. It is estimated that currently between 25 and 30 percent of Soka Gakkai members are black or Hispanic.

The rapidly growing organization held its first convention in Chicago in 1963, and in 1964 began publishing its own newspaper, *The World Tribune,* and a monthly magazine, the *Seikyo Times*. In 1968 it opened its American Joint Headquarters in Santa Monica, where it still makes its headquarters.

David W. Chappell, who has studied the demographics of Soka Gakkai extensively, estimates that currently the membership of SGI-USA has twice the percentage of black Americans found in the population as a whole ("Racial Diversity in the Soka Gakkai," *Engaged Buddhism in the West*). Chappell suggests three reasons for this: people, practice, and purpose. "People had joined because some individual Soka Gakkai had maintained contact with them, cared about them, and helped them believe in themselves, and through their support they found a practice that enabled them to improve their attitude and circumstances, that gave them a purpose that was larger than themselves, and that involved them in working with and helping others." Much of Soka Gakkai's openness to all people stems directly from the attitude of Ikeda himself, who has constantly stressed the unity of all peoples and who considers race and ethnicity "in large part fictitious." He has given speeches about the achievements of Sojourner Truth and honored civil rights activist Rosa Parks. (The latter, when asked to select one picture to represent her life, chose one of her shaking hands with Ikeda in 1993.) In addition, this is an optimistic, positive religion that encourages people to take responsibility for their own lives.

Soka Gakkai International was founded by Ikeda in 1975 as its honorary president. He was also president of the Nichren Shoshu at the time, but was ousted from that organization in 1979 by the priesthood, mostly for reasons of power and authority. Ikeda then went on to assume a full-time position in Soka Gakkai International, which he turned into an organization of real power.

Eventually, in November 1991, SGI-USA and NSA split into two separate groups, although structural changes had taken place in Soka Gakkai to facilitate that break more than a year before, in February 1990. (The high priest of Nichiren Shoshu excommunicated all members of Soka Gakkai. Some gave in and returned to the temple, but most stayed with Soka Gakkai. This meant that the adherents of Soka Gakkai had no priesthood, and so now consists entirely of laypeople.) Nichiren Shoshu Temple

(NST), as it calls itself, is a smaller group led by a priesthood, with a group of dedicated laypeople, or Hokkeko. In fact, the whole group is often called Hokkeko. The constellation of reasons for the split between the two groups is extremely complicated and beyond the scope of this book, but one of the central issues, besides the usual ones of money and power, had to do with which leader, Ikeda of the SGI or Nichiren Shoshu's High Priest Nikken Shonin, was the true spiritual heir to Nichiren Daishonin.

The rift between the two Nichiren groups has turned somewhat hostile. Soka Gakkai USA outlines its differences with Nichiren in four ways: views about equality, ideas about the Gohonzon, understanding of the heritage of the law, and, most important in their view, attitude and behavior. As to equality, Soka Gakkai sees its activities focusing on dialogue with all people, while Nichiren Shoshu is hierarchical in its beliefs. According to Soka Gakkai, the "heritage of the law" is available to all people, not just priests. Soka Gakkai also claims that Nichiren Shoshu priests were not only not doing enough to help establish peace throughout the world, but they were also "indulging themselves" too freely in worldly delights and not living up to the standards set by Nichiren. Soka Gakkai stopped including gratitude to the priesthood in their daily prayers, an omission that was highly upsetting to the priesthood. On its side, Nichiren Shoshu has charged that Soka Gakkai places far too much emphasis on Ikeda's work, honoring it even above that of Nichiren himself.

As for the Gohonzon, Soka Gakkai maintains that it is "a manifestation of [Nichiren's] life as an enlightened human being, and that it is no different from the enlightened potential within all ordinary people" (official Web site Soka Gakkai-USA). Nichiren Shoshu places more emphasis on the priests' interpretations of Nichiren's teachings.

As of this writing SGI-USA has seventy-one centers throughout the United States. SGI-USA is affiliated with the worldwide SGI organization that has more than 12 million members in more than 180 countries and territories, with its headquarters in Tokyo. President Ikeda has made a strong commitment to world peace (Kosen-Rufu), and SGI-USA has been granted status as a nongovernmental organization (NGO) of the United Nations.

Soka Gakkai's spread in the United States has been marked by two different kinds of missionary activity. In the first period, roughly corresponding to its first thirty years, Soka Gakkai was aggressively evangelistic (*shakubuku*), but beginning in the 1990s it entered a period of what it calls dialogue (*taiwa*).

One milestone in the Americanization of Soka Gakkai occurred on July 4, 1976, when during an intermission between two baseball games, Soka Gakkai (then still calling itself NSA) put on an elaborate patriotic show that illustrated the history of the country in song and dance. As a nod to its Japanese roots, however, the American participation in World War II was ignored, and like a good Buddhist, George Washington was depicted as saying his prayers in the "active lotus position," the same one Nichiren members use in their daily prayers.

Today there may be between 100,000 and 250,000 Soka Gakkai adherents in the United States, depending upon who provides the information and how "adherent" is defined. Most members of SGI-USA are American converts, including sizable numbers of Latinos and African Americans. (Tina Turner, Patrick Swayze, and Patrick Duffy of *Dallas* fame belong to this sect of Buddhism.)

Central Beliefs, Goals, and Practices

According to its charter, the stated principles of the Soka Gakkai, which are derived from the core concepts mentioned earlier, are to:

- promote an understanding of Nichiren Daishonin's Buddhism
- contribute to peace, culture, and education within society
- safeguard fundamental human rights and eliminate discrimination
- respect and protect freedom of religion and religious expression
- work together with other religions to resolve issues affecting humanity
- respect cultural diversity and promote cultural exchange
- encourage the protection of nature and the environment.

Certainly the most distinctive element in both traditional Nichiren and Soka Gakkai is the *daimoku,* which is chanted while facing the Gohonzen, the sacred scroll or holy tablet. The *daimoku* is so important to Nichiren and Soka Gakkai practitioners that they consider it to be the Dharma itself. Each practicing lay member owns and treasures a small paper Gohonzon, which is said to be a replica of Nichiren's original one. On it is written the *daimoku* in Japanese characters. The Gohonzon is kept in the domestic altar, and it is considered especially efficacious to recite the *daimoku* while facing it, a practice called *shodai.* Originally, before Soka Gakkkai and Nichiren Shoshu split, the high priest at Taisekiji (near Mt. Fuji) consecrated all new Gohonzons in a ceremony called *gojukai.* It was believed that the *gojukai* ceremony enabled the power of the original Gohonzon, inscribed by Nichiren himself, to flow through to the new Gohonzon. After the schism, members of Soka Gakkai were not allowed to receive the consecrated Gohonzons. The original Gohonzon, known as the Dai-Gohonzon, was housed in Taisekiji in a beautiful sanctuary largely built and funded by Soka Gakkai. After the rift between the two sects, however, the Nichiren Shoshu group tore down the sanctuary, a sad loss to architecture.

Nam-myoho-renge-kyo is chanted for fifteen or twenty minutes a day, either privately or in public, sometimes to the accompaniment of drums. The practitioner may also chant other passages from the Lotus Sutra, a text Nichiren Buddhists believe that Shakymuni himself composed during the last eight years of his life. The chanting of passages from this sutra is called *gongyo,* or assiduous practice. Some devout practitioners chant as much as two hours a day, for one hour each time. After the chanting, members talk individually about how their faith, the most important of the three elements central to Nichiren (the other two are study and practice), has made a difference in their lives.

In addition to chanting, SGI-USA members meet locally in informal neighborhood discussion groups. These gatherings, usually held in members' private homes, bring together a wide range of people to pray together, to study Buddhist precepts, and to discuss how they can be applied to daily life.

Unfortunately, Soka Gakkai got a bad reputation in some quarters for allegedly promoting the use of chanting merely to gain material things like money, automobiles, or even drugs. Part of the blame must be laid at the door of Soka Gakkai's second president, Josei Toda, who characterized the Gohonzon as a "happiness-producing machine." This has turned out to be a delicate issue. Indeed, some people were told that they could chant for whatever they wanted. It is true that especially during its earlier days, when it was NSA, Soka Gakkai recruited from all aspects of society and promised that chanting would result in the fulfillment of all desires. As a method of recruitment this worked, but only for the short term, especially when it could be seen that cars were not quick in coming.

The hope was that the chanting itself would serve to change and purify those desires. In the meantime, the all-accepting attitude of Soka Gakkai members proved extremely attractive to those people who would be not accepted by other religions unless and until they showed a sincere desire to change their lifestyle. Soka Gakkai took the people first and trusted that their acceptance and the power of the chants would do the changing. In a deeper way, it was understood that each person has Buddha-nature, even though the outer circumstances have not changed.

Chanting to achieve one's desires is an integral part of Soka Gakkai, but with certain restrictions. Members are not to chant to hurt others or even to "chant away their problems." They are expected to regard their difficulties as learning experiences they need to confront and deal with. They are encouraged to chant to change their own attitudes, and achieve generally recognized Buddhist values like equanimity, peace of mind, and world peace.

Such criticisms have more recently quieted down, while members of the organization become more attentive to the true goals of their practice, which is to produce peace of mind and proper focusing and realization, much the same way that meditation works. Despite this, some other Buddhists feel that Buddhism without meditation is not Buddhism at all. Such an attitude, of course, does not properly respect the tolerance and broad-mindedness with which Buddhism is identified. Nor does it give sufficient credit to the real changes Soka Gakkai and Nichiren Buddhism have made in the lives of countless people, including, through its promotion of world peace, people who have never heard of it.

Nichidatsu Fujii (1885–1985) and Nippozan Myohoji

Another offshoot of Nichiren is Nichidatsu Fujii, born in rural Japan, who claimed to be a direct disciple of both Shakyamuni and Nichiren. Like Nichiren, he favored the *Nam-myoho-renge-kyo* chant, but added a drumbeat to it for extra spiritual value. He called his school Nippozan Myohoji. He began his teaching when he was thirty-three years old (a year later than Nichiren himself, to demonstrate his respect for his teacher) and made his order international, going to outposts in Manchuria, China, Korea, and eventually India, in order to bring Buddhism back to the land of its birth. Here he met with and became a close associate of Mahatma Gandhi, who called him Guruji, or "spiritual master." Guruji was equally impressed by Gandhi and his nonviolent activism.

On his return to Japan after World War II, Guruji established a "peace pagoda." Today, there are about eighty of these peace pagodas around the world, including the United States. Guruji died in 1985 at the age of one hundred. He left no formal successor; there is a monk with special status but no real authority. Decisions are now made in consultation.

Their special text is the Rissho Ankoku Ron, a treatise by Nichiren himself. Monks and nuns take traditional vows of poverty, obedience, and celibacy, but true to the Nichiren heritage, they chant rather than meditate. Chanting, however, does not merely take place in front of an altar, but also during what can only be termed expeditions—walks lasting for months that cover up to twenty miles a day in all weather conditions. It is common for an individual monk or nun to walk for a year.

Nippozan Myohoji came to the United States during the 1970s as a largely monastic order. The person most responsible for bringing the school to America is Kao Shonin, who fell in love with the works of Thoreau, but was disturbed by the difference between Thoreau's peaceful message and the violence he saw perpetuated in American society. In 1978 he walked the twenty-mile distance between Boston and Walden every day for fifty consecutive days, during the bitter winter weather. He was joined by Clare Carter, who was ordained as a nun in 1981.Together these two are responsible for the construction of the New England Peace Pagoda. This pagoda, much of which was built by volunteer labor in only eighteen months, is located in the small town of Leverett, Massachusetts. This is also the religious center for the Nipponzan Myohoji Buddhist Order in North America.

Currently, there are only about ten monks and nuns in the United States, only two of whom are American and none of whom are very young. The lay community is larger; over 3,000 persons attended the dedication of the stunning white New England Peace Pagoda in 1985. An adjoining temple inspired by fifth-century Indian Buddhist architecture is being built. Yet another Sangha is being developed in Atlanta, Georgia, in what was formerly a crack house.

Nipponzan Myohoji temples in the United States are less elaborate than the ones in Japan, but are carefully decorated with altars and images of the Buddha and Nichiren, as well as flowers, food donations, and other ornaments, including tiny peace pagodas. Once a month, the nuns and monks fast, pray, and chant together for three days.

Nipponzan Myohoji considers itself to have a special tie with Native American peoples, who share their nonmaterialistic values, and work with Navajo and Hopi Indians for both land and human rights.

Other Japanese Sects

Besides Pure Land, Nichiren, and Zen (discussed in a later chapter), we should mention Shingon, the mystical and esoteric sect related to the Tibetan Vajrayana. In fact, it appeared as early as 1912 in Los Angeles. However, some of its more distinctive elements such as the chanting of mantras and the use of mudras, or sacred gestures, have been eliminated from the practice. Shingon is an esoteric school, arising during Japan's Heian period (794–1185), when Kukai, a monk, went to China to study (804–6). When he returned to Japan, he first became abbot of a Kyoto temple (809), and then in 819 founded a monastery on Mt. Koya, south of Kyoto. Kukai's work centered on the cosmic Buddha Vairocana, of whom the historical Buddha was only a manifestation, and who, according to Kukai, dictated sacred sutras to him. The most important of these sutras is the Sokushin-jobutsugi (The Doctrine of Becoming a Buddha with One's Body During One's Earthly Existence).

Kukai also united the concept of the Buddha Vairocana with the idea of the Dharmakaya, or Ultimate Reality. Shingon practice involves two sacred mandalas representing the two aspects of Vairocana, the Diamond World (*kongo-kai*) and Womb World (*taizo-kai*). Shingon was popular among the sophisticated Heian aristocracy of Japan, probably as much for its beautiful artwork as anything else. Eventually Shingon became a major Buddhist sect of the Heian period, with more support than Tendai Buddhism. While it has lost some of its popularity, it still remains an important sect with about 12 million adherents.

Chinese Buddhist Sects

Until recently, Japanese Buddhist traditions in America have been far more prominent than those from China. However, that is beginning to change, and it is estimated that there are currently about 150 Chinese Buddhist organizations in the United States, most in California and a lesser number in New York. This is a figure that can be misleading; many of these organizations are extremely ecumenical, not only featuring aspects of more than one of the five traditional Chinese schools, but also containing many elements of Taoism and Confucianism as well. This is standard Chinese practice, for the Chinese tend to combine various religious traditions. It is not unusual to find one person incorporating elements of Taoism, Buddhism, and Confucianism into his or her life. (Death rites, for example, may be Buddhist, while an exorcism may be Taoist.) In another context, the three words "Chinese," "American," and "Buddhist" have been assembled together in each of its six possible permutations, each one presenting a slightly different picture.

Most Chinese American Buddhists belong to one of these four organizations or an affiliate: The Dharma Realm Buddhist Association (for-

Buddhist temple near Central Park, New York. Photographer Malcolm Lee. © TRIP.

merly the Sino-American Buddhist Association), the Buddhist Association of the United States, the Institute of Chung-Hwa Buddhist Culture, or the Hsi Lai Temple. Although part of the general Mahayana tradition, most of the groups are eclectic, combining Ch'an, Pure Land, T'ien-t'ai, Tantra, and Vinaya. The same is largely true of Korean and Vietnamese Buddhism.

The Dharma Realm Buddhist Association

The Sino-American Buddhist Association was established on December 1, 1968, by Tripitaka Master Hsüan-Hua (1908–95), who came to the United States from Hong Kong in 1962. Its stated mission is to promote Buddhism in the West. In 1970 the Gold Mountain (Sagely) Monastery was founded in San Francisco, and the Buddhist Text Society was created, publishing a journal called the *Vajra Bodhi Sea*. The Buddhist Texts Society was expanded in 1974 to the International Institute for the Translation of Buddhist Texts. In 1971, Hsüan-Hua formally ordained several disciples. Some branch temples opened in Seattle (Bodhi Dhamma Center) and Los Angeles (Gold Wheel Temple).

In 1976, Hsüan-Hua founded and directed a large monastery in Talmage, California, called the City of Ten Thousand Buddhas. It covers over 488 acres and has more than 60 buildings. The Dharma Realm Buddhist University is located on this site. The organization was renamed as the

Dharma Realm Buddhist Association in 1984. Currently the organization has monasteries throughout the United States, two in Canada, and a temple in Malaysia. One of the interesting things about this organization is that in its earlier years, it appealed primarily to Americans of European descent, who subsequently advanced to leadership positions within the organization. Now it is again receiving support from its Chinese American constituency, resulting in the rather odd situation of European Americans giving Dharma instructions to Chinese Americans. It emphasizes a strict monastic tradition and adherence to the Vinaya. Buddhist study includes Ch'an, T'ien-t'ai, Pure Land, and Chen-yen, while chanting is Pure Land or Ch'an.

Hsi Lai Temple

The Hsi Lai Temple, in Hacienda Heights, California, established in 1978 but not completed until 1988, has been called the largest monastery in North America. (Its floor area is reported to be 102,432 square feet.) The parent organization is the International Buddhist Progress Society.

The words "Hsi Lai" are generally translated as "coming to the West." The temple is affiliated with the Lin-Chi (Rinzai) Fo Kuang Shan, which in its turn is the biggest Buddhist center in Taiwan, established in 1967. Fo Kuang Shan has centers in Hong Kong, Australia, Costa Rica, Malaysia, the Philippines, Russia, Switzerland, and other countries as well. It also has branch temples in several states. According to their Web site, "We at Hsi Lai are committed to serving as a bridge between East and West so that the Buddha's teachings of kindness, compassion, joyfulness, and equanimity might be integrated into our lives and of those around us to the benefit of all and that we might learn the ways to cultivate the wisdom to clearly understand the true nature of all things."

The temple enshrines the five great bodhisattvas: Samantabhadra, Ksitigarbha, Maitreya, Avalokitesvara, and Manjusri. It contains a Buddhist university, library, theme gardens, and press. It also acts as the headquarters of the Buddha's Light International Organization.

Undoubtedly, however, the temple is most famous to the American public for another reason. The Democratic National Committee took in $140,000 at an April 1996 fund-raiser featuring Vice President Gore at the site. The temple fund-raiser organizers were indicted on federal charges of laundering campaign contributions. The temple, also known as the International Buddhist Progress Society, was cited as an unindicted co-conspirator.

This is the Hsi Lai Temple, located in Hacienda Heights, California. It was inaugurated in November 1988 and is the largest Buddhist monastery in the United States. It encompasses 15 acres and has a floor area of 102,432 square feet. The temple combines Ming and Ching dynasty architectural styles. Photographer Tony Freeman. © TRIP.

The Buddhist Association of the United States

The Buddhist Association of the United States (BAUS) was established by C. T. Shen, a layperson and retired electrical engineer, in 1964. Having made a fortune in the shipping trade as well, he donated land in the Bronx to BAUS to found the Temple of Great Enlightenment in 1969. In 1970, he founded the Bodhi House on Long Island. In 1971 Shen also founded the Institute for the Advanced Study of World Religions at the Stony Brook Campus of the State University of New York. In 1980 he donated 125 acres in New York State to the Chuang Yen Monastery, which contains a thirty-seven-foot likeness of Vairocana Buddha, the largest Buddha statue in the United States. (Vairocana Buddha is one of the five transcendent Buddhas.) Shen has written rather extensively on the parallels between Buddhism and contemporary science.

Institute of Chung-Hwa Buddhist Culture

The Institute of Chung-Hwa Buddhist Culture is the headquarters of the Ch'an Meditation Center. It started as part of the BAUS Temple of

Great Enlightenment, but has since, due to expanding membership, founded its own center. Its founder, Sheng-Yen (b. 1930), studied Buddhist literature in Japan, and in 1975 received Dharma transmission from Ch'an Master Tung-chu in the Soto lineage. Three years later he received Dharma transmission in the Rinzai lineage, and became an abbot of the Nun Ch'an Monastery in 1978, coming also that year to the United States at the invitation of BAUS.

Vietnamese Buddhism

Vietnamese Buddhism presents its own perspective, although it is closely related to the Chinese model, at least the Chinese model after the Sung dynasty. It has connections with several Chinese schools, including T'ien-T'ai (especially in respect to doctrine), Hua-yen or Flower Garland school (metaphysics), and Chan, but draws its rules of discipline (Vinaya) largely from the Dharmaguptaka school, originally from South India. Temples in Vietnam are semi-independent and rely on traditional Mahayana texts like the Lotus Sutra and the Amitabha Sutra.

Two important teachers in the Vietnamese traditions are Thich Thein-An (1926–80) and Thich Nhat Hanh (b. 1926). The former came to the United States trained in the Rinzai branch of Zen, although he later adopted a broader approach. He ordained both monks and nuns. He is treated more fully in chapter 7.

The most important practice aspect of Vietnamese Buddhism is the gaining of merit or *punya* for rebirth in the Pure Land. This is a common thread in much Buddhist tradition. Buddhists can earn merit by supporting monks and nuns, paying for the construction or upkeep of temples, and making contributions for the printing of Buddhist books.

Meditation is not an important element in this tradition, and most Vietnamese Buddhists do not believe that meditational practices are effective for achieving liberation. Chanting sutras and calling upon the Amitabha Buddha are much more common practices.

Ceremonies are extremely important in the Vietnamese Buddhist tradition. Services are generally conducted three times a day, at dawn, mid-day, and dusk, and consist largely of invoking the name of the Buddha and of chanting sutras (the Heart Sutra, Lotus Sutra, and Amitabha Sutra are especially popular). Laypeople and monks often attend the temple together, but many persons also worship at home. At the new and full moons, a service of repentance, the *sam hoi,* takes place. Equally important are the so-called *via*-days of the Buddha or a bodhisattva. The major ones includes Tet, the Vietnamese New Year, which also celebrates the bodhisattva Maitreya, the Buddha's Enlightenment, the Buddha's birthday, the first full moon of the first month, and Ullambana (the Festival of the hungry ghosts, or Vu Lan), among others. These days are celebrated with chanting and praying. Animals are also often set free on these holidays.

Vietnamese Buddhism has remained almost purely ethnic in the United States. Converts are neither sought after nor drawn to this form of Buddhism. Its devotional chanting, strange festivals, and lack of a meditative tradition or well-articulated doctrine are not designed to draw attention from outsiders. Interestingly, one of the most famous Buddhists in the West, Thich Nhat Hanh, comes from the Vietnamese tradition of Buddhism; however, he no longer identifies himself specifically with that tradition and is far more honored among Westerners than among the religious "establishment" of his own school.

Korean Buddhism

Although several brands of Korean Son Buddhism exist in Korea, in the United States the predominant form has been Son, or Korean Zen. That school is treated in chapter 5.

Won

Won is a new, meditative form of Korean Buddhism, whose monks are allowed to marry. While primarily confined to Korea, it has established some centers in the United States, mostly in Philadelphia. Won Buddhism makes use of a meditation device consisting of a black circle on a white background, and for this reason is sometimes called the "circular" school.

Mahayana Buddhism and the Beat Generation

Zen Buddhism has always been associated in the United States with the Beat Generation and their cohorts: Jack Kerouac, Allen Ginsberg, Diane di Prima, and Harold Norse in the East and the "San Francisco Poets" Gary Snyder, Philip Whalen, Joanne Kyger, Albert Saijo, Lew Welch, Lenore Kandel, Will Petersen, and Bob Kaufman. Also influential were William Burroughs, Lawrence Ferlinghetti, Michael McClure, Kenneth Rexroth, and Anne Waldman. Feeling alienated from the mainstream Protestantism, Catholicism, and Judaism of their youth, they sought revived spirituality and a new consciousness from Buddhism. (Not all Beats were Buddhists, of course. Some, like William Burroughs, thought it

Vietnamese monk Thich Nhat Hanh, Zen Master, poet, peace and human rights activist. Don Farber Photography.

was interesting, but incompatible with a Western mind-set.) Others developed unusual combinations of Buddhism and Western religion. Jack Kerouac melded Catholic and Mahayana Buddhist practice, while Allen Ginsberg considered himself a Buddhist Jew. Still others, of course, rejected Buddhism or never considered it at all. East Coast Beats like Kerouac and Ginsberg came to Buddhism first and took it most seriously.

Jack Kerouac (1922–69)

Although Kerouac is often associated with Zen Buddhism, his interest in Buddhism was eclectic. He belonged to the general Mahayana tradition (in which he was largely self-taught). In fact, he often decried what he considered the more brutal elements of Zen—such as striking students who didn't get the right answer to a koan. He believed this kind of behavior on the part of the Roshi violated the compassionate spirit of Buddhism. He also referred to himself as a junior arhat, a term he borrowed from the Theravada tradition. Late in life, Kerouac began to see Buddhism as part of a larger Eastern spiritual tradition, and he abandoned Buddhism as his primary religious identification. At one point, he said that he left Buddhism because it preached against "entanglement with women."

In the 1950s Kerouac began reading important sutras, probably after first encountering Eastern philosophy in the works of Thoreau. (For a while Kerouac, like many others, including the New England Transcendentalists, confused Buddhism and Hinduism.) He found a copy of the Surangama Sutra, a large, unwieldy sutra known as Ryogonkyo in Japan, a text that celebrates spontaneity. It inspired him to write *San Francisco Blues.* Kerouac was aware of the dangers of his idiosyncratic understanding of Buddhism, and at one point confessed that he was "a poet using Buddhism for his own advantage instead of for spreading the law."

After reading the beautiful verse-biography of Buddha by Ashvaghosa, written about 100 B.C.E., Kerouac tried to attain Enlightenment, eventually envisioning "golden swarms of nothing . . . the thusness of creation." Kerouac's favorite Buddhist work was the Diamond Sutra, which he chanted daily. He called it the greatest of the sutras, and attempted to write his own version in "ordinary English."

In time Kerouac even wrote his own as yet unpublished biography of the Buddha ("Wake Up") and an original sutra at the urging of California Zen poet Gary Snyder (the Scripture of the Golden Eternity). He also wrote *Some of the Dharma,* based on his Buddhist readings. Novels reflecting Kerouac's interest in Buddhism include *The Dharma Bums, Visions of Gerard, Desolation Angels,* and *Tristessa,* a novel Kerouac thought illustrated the First Noble Truth. Of these works, *The Dharma Bums* received the most attention—positive from the Buddhist Churches of America, negative from most critics. Famously, his work was condemned as not writing but typing (a charge also levied against Gertrude Stein).

Kerouac spent a great deal of time meditating alone, which angered his family—they thought he was just being lazy. Partly from this experience Kerouac discovered that most Americans weren't ready for exposure to monastic, strongly meditative Buddhism. He complained to his friend Allen Ginsberg that all he had done was "attract attention." He thought a better American plan would be a meditation center without "rules." He said he was more interested in "pure essence."

Kerouac once wrote that he planned to achieve Nirvana by the year 2000. However, his alcoholism prevented him from achieving the strict spiritual discipline necessary for a true Zen experience. (In *The Dharma Bums,* Kerouac used the famous Zen cartoon "The Ten Bulls" to justify his drinking.) Kerouac was also afflicted with phlebitis, which prevented his sitting to meditate, although he continued to try, despite the pain it caused him. (On the other hand, he compared the euphoric effects of meditation to a "shot of heroine or morphine.")

Kerouac's enthusiasms might have put off orthodox practitioners. In a 1955 letter to Ginsberg, for instance, he explained that his understanding of everything as Mind had led him into a deep relationship with a piece of cellophane he found lying on the floor of a subway car. "The cellophane, when I looked at it, was like my little brother, I really loved it." His idea of a Buddhist diet might also have surprised more stringent practitioners. At one point he declared he would live on an "elementary" diet of salt pork, beans, figs, bread, peanuts, and coffee. What this odd assortment of foodstuffs would have done for his spiritual development (or digestive system) is unclear.

Allen Ginsberg (1926–97)

Allen Ginsberg, equally famous as a voice of the Beat Generation and a close friend of Jack Kerouac, became entranced with Buddhism when he first saw an exhibit of Chinese paintings at the New York Public Library. Other sources say that his exposure came from looking through a book of reproductions there. Ginsberg wrote his own defiant "Sunflower Sutra," the sunflower being a powerful symbol in his life, modeled after a poem by William Blake, whose mystic voice he heard speaking to him. For years, Ginsberg tried to repeat this experience, but without success.

His initial interest in Buddhism was brief, despite the urgings of his friends Snyder and Kerouac. Ginsberg came again to Buddhism later on his own, after a meeting with a Tibetan lama, Dudjom Rinpoche. Ginsberg also met Chogyam Trungpa Rinpoche in 1971. At the latter's request, Ginsberg established the Jack Kerouac School of Disembodied Poetics at the Naropa Institute in Boulder, Colorado, the only accredited Buddhist university in America. Later Ginsberg studied with Gelek Rinpoche in Ann Arbor.

Diane di Prima (b. 1934)

Diane di Prima was another Beat poet, and an associate of Kerouac, Ginsberg, and Gregory Corso. She studied with Shunryo Suzuki Roshi in

Gary Snyder and Allen Ginsberg. © Getty Images.

San Francisco at the Zen Center, and later with Chogyam Trungpa. Her poetry reflected her Buddhist interests, and she found interesting connections between Keats's concept of negative capability, the poetic imagination, and Buddhist philosophy.

Gary Snyder (b. 1930)

Poet/essayist/philosopher/ecologist Gary Snyder, the hero of Kerouac's *The Dharma Bums,* has personified a kind of active Buddhism for the past forty years. Snyder came to the San Francisco area in 1952 to study Asian languages at Berkeley. He left for Japan in 1956 to study Zen formally, and became a disciple of Rinzai Zen Master Oda Sesso Roshi. His first two books of poetry, *Riprap* and *Myths & Texts,* were published while he was in that country. Spending ten years in Japan in the 1960s as a lay Zen monk, he returned to California in 1969 to begin his life work of applying a Buddhist mind-set to important political and environmental issues. In his "Buddhism and the Coming Revolution" Snyder declared that "no one today can afford to be ignorant, or indulge himself in ignorance of the nature of contemporary governments, politics and social orders." In 1975 he was awarded the Pulitzer Prize for his book of poems, *Turtle Island.*

Chapter 5

American Zen

We are devoting a separate chapter to Zen Buddhism, although it is technically part of the Mahayana tradition. This is because Zen, while only one Buddhist sect among many in Japan (and not even the most popular of them), has in the United States achieved a degree of recognition unrivaled by any other Buddhist group until the recent emergence of Tibetan Buddhism (and that, too, will receive its own chapter). It should be noted that the American melting pot is not the recipient of solely Japanese-style "Zen," although that of, course, is the most famous. Chinese Ch'an, Korean Son, and Vietnamese Thien are also making their mark, sometimes in separate streams, sometimes blending in.

No Buddhist tradition has become so deeply ingrained in America as Zen. In fact, it is estimated that about 40 percent of all Buddhist groups in North America have a Zen orientation. The number is still growing, too, surpassed only by unaffliliated or non-denominational Buddhist groups.

At first the popularity of Zen may seem surprising. Zen's reliance upon meditation, "just-sitting" (*shikantaza*), and stillness may seem, at least on the face of it, as peculiarly un-American. But because of its fresh approach to spirituality and its perhaps serendipitous connections with the Beat poets, Zen has become in many ways the "normative" Buddhist tradition in America today, and is much more popular in the United States than in Japan, where this tradition, as we know it, first flourished. Actually, even Japanese Zen is an import from China, where the school is known as Ch'an. Alan Watts, at the beginning of his short study, *Beat Zen, Square Zen, and Zen,* remarked that "it is as difficult for Anglo-Saxons as for the Japanese to absorb anything quite so Chinese as Zen," implying that any importation is bound to involve distortion.

One reason that Zen is popular with Americans is owing to its no-doctrine, no-text, no-external authority, direct-experience approach to spirituality, an attitude that well suits pragmatic, free-spirited Americans.

Compared with other Buddhist traditions, Zen is self-controlled, elegant, unemotional, and, despite the offbeat quality of Zen riddles or koans, mostly deadly serious. Its strong discipline and rigid approach to Enlightenment make it a favorite for people looking for boundaries, goals, and a straight path. Whether or not this attitude is true to the real spirit of Zen is a point of controversy. Lin-chi, founder of the sect named after him (Rinzai in Japanese), said, "In Buddhism there is no place for using effort. Just be ordinary and nothing special. Eat your food, move your bowels, pass water, and when you're tired go and lie down." Somehow this simple advice transmogrified into week-long, sleepless meditation marathons, mind-breaking koans, and elaborate bowing and chanting practices.

The Asian Origins of Zen

If Buddhism began with a tree, then Zen Buddhism began with a flower. Legend tells us that the Buddha gave an entire sermon, merely by holding up a flower to his assembled monks on Vulture Peak. Only one monk, Kashyapa (later called Maha [the great] Kashyapa), understood what the Buddha meant, and smiled. This incident is often considered the true beginning of the great Zen tradition, a tradition that is outside the sutra (sacred books) and that does not rely upon words and letters. This principle is stated formally in this way:

> Not relying on words or letters
> An independent self-transmitting apart from doctrine
> Direct pointing to the mind,
> Awakening to one's original nature, thereby actualizing his Buddhahood

This does not mean that Zen automatically abhors all books and rejects all thinking. It reaches to a state beyond intellect, it is true, but that does not mean it abandons intellect or eschews logic. It simply rejects the scholastic notion that reality can be encompassed in books or understood solely through the intellect.

Zen also leaves open the possibility that Enlightenment can come suddenly and at any time, an important concept for impatient people. (The ancient Zen Master Hasigawa once said, "It might take three minutes; it might take thirty years," and then added, "I mean that!") That idea sits well with Americans, too—who are always in a hurry. Zen emphasizes that this knowledge comes directly from experience, rather than from learning handed down by teachers. This independence of thought is an American way of looking at things. In fact, if Zen weren't so completely Japanese, Americans might have invented it themselves.

Zen is part of a great Buddhist tradition called Mahayana, the Great Vehicle. However, Zen is very different from many other forms of Mahayana, and has developed a distinct tradition in the United States. Zen also owes much of its character to Taoism, an indigenous religion of China. Some elements, not as readily apparent in "classical" Buddhism, include the use of humor and paradox and a deep appreciation for nature. All forms of Buddhism and Taoism have a deeply developed concept of the impermanent nature of reality, which Taoism visualizes as a river.

Most startling about Zen is its irreverence. The Buddha himself started the trend, when he denied the relevance of the gods or the holiness of the Hindu scriptures, but Zen extended this disregard for holy things to its own founders. Many Zen stories illustrate this outlook, none more shocking perhaps than the saying of Ummon (Yun-Men in Chinese). Upon listening to an account of the miraculous babyhood of the Buddha, in which the infant took seven steps at birth and declared himself to be the Buddha, Ummon remarked, " I wish I had been there. I would have beaten him to death and given his flesh to the dogs to eat. At least that would have been some contribution of peace and harmony in the world." And in Rinai Zen, it is commonly said that the Buddha should be killed whenever he is met. The spirit of independent seeking is classical Buddhism, although its expression is certainly not.

The original "Zen" Buddhist was a monk named Bodhidharma, who, in the sixth century trekked up to China from his home in India, the birthplace of the Buddha. (Some sources claim that he came by sea to Canton in 470.) He is said to have upset Emperor Wu of Liang, who asked Bodhidharma how much merit he had accumulated through his pious deeds. The monk responded, "None whatever," and Bodhidharma was either (depending on the source) banished or left on his own.

In any case, he spent the next nine years staring at a wall in silence. He cut off his eyelids to ensure he wouldn't fall asleep too easily. He refused to accept any students until the day one prospective disciple cut off his arm to show just how serious he was. This rather extreme approach has given birth to a variety of anecdotes about eccentric Zen Masters, which in itself seems to have become part of the tradition, as has meditating facing a wall among Zen people.

Thus began the form of Buddhism we know as Ch'an (a Chinese corruption of the Sanskrit word *dhyana,* or "meditation"), which in turn became Son in Korea, Thien in Vietnam, and Zen in Japan and the United States. In China, it reached its height during the T'ang dynasty (c. 618–907). Ch'an and Zen have always been forms of Buddhism for the elite classes. More popular among the common people in both China and Japan has been Pure Land.

Because Zen in its fullest sense is a practice, not a philosophy (although it includes philosophy), almost all discussion of it (including this one) distorts it to some degree. To *really* understand Zen, it is necessary to practice Zen. When we only talk about it, it's like a finger pointing at the moon. The observer is likely to mistake the pointer for the object it is pointing at. Once the person sees the moon for himself or herself, however, we can safely take the finger away. But to practice Zen well, one must enter it wholly. It has been said that truly to enter into Zen is like plunging into an abyss. Only by this means can one be saved, but the reason is paradoxical. Only by throwing oneself into the abyss does one learn that the abyss does not exist.

In one important way, Zen reverts to the original intent of Buddhism, and that is its emphasis on personal experience. Although Zen Buddhism does have a written literature (the *goroku,* or sayings), nothing can make up for direct, personal knowledge. Written Zen literature is merely a way to wipe the mind clean. After the mind is cleansed, the literature can properly be regarded as trash, like a dirty napkin.

In fact, D. T. Suzuki, who is largely responsible for popularizing Zen in America, once proclaimed that Zen didn't teach anything, and was neither a philosophy nor a religion. It is a way to Enlightenment, nothing more and nothing less. It is a unique admixture of wild idiosyncrasy and rigid discipline—wild idiosyncrasy for the Zen Masters and rigid discipline for the students. In Japanese Zen monasteries, the student is expected to respond with an instant "Hai!" (Yes!) to each request from the Zen Master, whether he fully understands it or not.

Like other varieties of Buddhism, Zen presents a religious stumbling block to some Western seekers: the absence of God in Zen practice. Zen Buddhism does not deny the existence of God, but neither does it refer to God or make use of him in any way whatever. So while Zen is not officially "atheistic" it is certainly "nontheistic," in that it simply has nothing to do with God at all. In like manner, it does not posit the existence of an afterlife or Paradise, and conforms to the orthodox Buddhist view that there is no such thing as a self or a soul. (Thus, there is nothing to be saved.)

What, then, is Zen? The Sixth Patriarch, Hui-neng (638–713), said that the heart of Zen is "seeing into one's self-nature," and that this in turn is *satori,* or Enlightenment. This pronouncement replaced Bodhidharma's identification of Zen with "mind," a concept Hui-neng may have found too static in implication. (Hui-neng is credited with writing the famous Platform Sutra, a text that established meditation as a practice designed not to obtain a certain goal, but to achieve a calm mind.)

In brief, Zen is the doctrine of Suchness (or "Thusness"). One of the most famous statements of this doctrine was made by Ch'ing-yüan Weihsin, a Zen Master during the T'ang dynasty. He wrote:

> Thirty years ago, before I started to study Zen, I said, "Mountains are mountains and rivers are rivers." After I got my first insight into the meaning of Zen, with the help of a good teacher, I said, "Mountains are not mountains, nor are rivers rivers." But now, after having been Awakened, I say, "Mountains are truly mountains; rivers are truly rivers."

This is the whole course of Zen in a nutshell: the concept of Thusness. Enlightenment does not proceed by logical steps, but through intuitive leaps of ever increasing complexity and depth (if a leap can be said to have "depth"). Paradox abounds, and the result is a re-visioning and reconstruction of reality, as well as a radical transformation of consciousness. (In addition to the pure Zen value of the mountains and rivers saying, one could add a great deal of symbolic richness. In Chinese thought, mountains are Yang, the masculine, active, warm principle, while rivers are Yin, the feminine, passive, cool principle. The complexities of the interactions between Yin and Yang are the substrate of much Chinese thought.)

The mountains and rivers story illustrates a developing Zen understanding. In the first stage, one sees with ordinary eyes and understands with an ordinary mind. In the second stage, a Zen view has overtaken the vision, so that instead of seeing separate mountains and rivers, one sees their interconnectedness, their interdependence, so that they cease to be mountains and rivers, but become something deeper. In the third stage, one realizes the mountains are true mountains—not objectified by everyday physical vision nor occluded by the observer's intellect. The particular mountains and particular rivers do not lose their individuality, do not disappear into a vast, cloudy spiritual miasma, but are revealed as truly themselves in a pure, absolute, unobscured state. This state is identical with the mind/heart/ spirit of the one who has realized *satori,* a state of complete emptiness by which it achieves infinite capacity. The Chinese characters often translated as "emptiness" really mean "sky-like," a richer and more positive term.

The Two Schools of Zen

Traditional Zen Buddhism consists of two major schools: Soto and Rinzai (there are several smaller ones as well). The differences between the two main schools are fairly minor. One difference concerns the celibacy of monks. Celibacy is customary in Rinzai but not in Soto. The second difference concerns the use of koans, or special riddles, to help bring about Enlightenment. (Interestingly, the word "koan" originally referred to a "public document," which seems opposite to its current meaning). The use of koans is characteristic of Rinzai; their employment may bring on "sudden enlightenment." The Soto school of Zen relies upon meditation (*zazen*) alone. It also makes use of more ceremonies and rituals than does Rinzai Zen. In Japan, Rinzai is the more popular school; however, that trend is reversed in the United States, largely because the monks who brought Buddhism to this country were mostly Soto. So we will consider that sect first.

Soto Zen

Soto is the school of gradual enlightenment, as opposed to Rinzai, which emphasizes sudden enlightenment. In Japan, Soto was considered much less elitist than the aristocratic Rinzai. The main transmitter of the Soto tradition was Eihei Dogen (1200–53), a Japanese monk. Dogen believed that the Buddhism practiced in Japan was inauthentic, so about 1223 (or possibly earlier) he left his native land in search of the "true Dharma." Zen itself had been introduced into Japan by Dogen's older contemporary, Esai, whom Dogen had met and conversed with.

However, Esai's understanding of the Zen tradition did not satisfy Dogen. His main question was this: Since we all have Buddha-nature, why do we need to engage in meditation, koans, and other practices in order to attain it? The term "Buddha-nature" became extremely important in Zen. In fact, some Zen Masters, like Robert Aitken, explain that all the Buddha's

Robert Aitken and Jack Kornfield. Don Farber Photography.

precepts can be understood on three levels: the literal level, as taught by what he terms the Hinayana Buddhists and who are known by others as Theravadins: the compassionate level, as interpreted by other Mahayanists; and the essential ("Buddha-nature") level, as understood by fellow Zen teachers.

Dogen eventually came to understand Buddha-nature as something that exists fully developed in all beings, not as a "potential" that lies within us like a seed. Dogen did not limit his concept of Buddha-nature to living beings, either—he included all beings, living and nonliving, as *being* (not "having") Buddha-nature. The Buddha-nature neither transcends nor inheres in all beings. For Dogen, Zen was not the pathway to Enlightenment—it was an expression of Enlightenment. Nirvana is attained only by liberating oneself from both permanence and impermanence (*mujo*). In fact, to attain Nirvana, one must release oneself even from that idea. Nirvana (the state of ultimacy) and *samsara* (the world of fleeting existence) completely interpenetrate each other. There is ultimately no difference between them. When one conceives of Nirvana and *samsara* as occupying different spheres, one makes distinctions between them, assigning Buddha-nature to one and not the other. This is impossible. Since all beings are

Buddha-nature, there can be no distinction between beings or realms of beings. To express this concept, Dogen created the phrase, *mujo-bussho*: impermanence equals the Buddha-nature.

It was a radical way of being a Buddhist, but a perfectly logical one. In the more traditional understanding, living beings go through a birth-life-death process. Yet this same process can be detected in nonliving beings also, which appear and disappear over time. All beings, therefore, both living and nonliving, are caught up in the same cycle. And not only things in general. Each individual is constantly undergoing birth and death every moment, constantly living, dying, and being reborn. That is what change means.

Since all beings are Buddha-nature, Buddha-nature is without limit and boundary. This doesn't mean that all beings are subsumed in some vast, vague "Buddha substance," but rather that each being stands completely and is Buddha fully in itself. By *being* Buddha-nature, it can as easily be said that each being contains Buddhahood as vice versa.

Dogen's wanderings took him to China, where Ch'an Buddhism had existed for a millennium. At first, he met with no success in his spiritual quest, a failure he blamed largely upon his inability to find a suitable master. At last, however, he met with Ju-ching (1163–1228), an abbot of the Ts'ao-sung wing of Ch'an. Ju-ching had little patience with the strange riddles, incense burning, and sutra-recitations of other Ch'an sects: he recommended meditation alone as the path to Enlightenment. Dogen approved of this simple approach, and he became a willing disciple. (Dogen is thus considered the ancestor of Soto Zen, although he himself rejected any notion that he was a founder of a school. He simply believed he had found the Dharma.) Dogen's most famous written work is Shobogenzo, which was the first major Japanese Buddhist work actually written in Japanese. Earlier writers had preferred Chinese, just as church writers in medieval Europe preferred Latin to their native languages, and for much the same reason—it was considered more "scholarly," "classic," and likely to endure.

Under the tutelage of Ju-ching, Dogen achieved Enlightenment after about two years, and returned to Japan in 1227. Following the example of his Chinese master, Dogen recommended sitting meditation (*zazen*) as the way to awakening. In fact, in the whole history of Buddhism, only the great Sixth Patriarch, Hui-neng, attained Enlightenment without doing *zazen*. *Zazen* supporters claim he had done enough of it in previous lives to make up for the lack.

The word *zazen* comes from the Sanskrit word *dhyana,* which also means meditation. However, Zen meditation is somewhat different from that of other Buddhist schools.

For most schools of Buddhism, the goal of meditation is to attain a peaceful, quiet state of mind. It is used to collect and focus the mind. But for Zen Buddhists, meditation is more than this: it is the very key to Enlightenment. It is difficult to describe the proper frame of mind that Zen produces; it is described as alert but not focused on any particular object or thought. One term used for the experience is *shikantaza,* or "just-sitting." In fact, Dogen used an even more theologically loaded term when he discussed his sitting—he called it *shinjindatsuraku,* or casting off body and mind. Dogen maintained that while the Dharma was present in everyone, it could not be realized or attained without practice. But practice is not a "way to" realization or awakening; it *is* awakening. This is what he meant when he warned disciples not to "intend to become a buddha." However, as in everything Zen, there is a dissenting view (which in a nondualistic scheme turns out not be dissenting at all). It is expressed in a story about the Zen Master Baso (708–788) while he was still a student of Nengaku (677–744). It is said that Baso was doing *zazen* when Nengaku came up and started polishing a tile. "What are you doing?" asked Baso.

"I'm trying to make a mirror," said Nengaku.

"You can't make a mirror by polishing a tile," protested Baso.

"You can't turn into a Buddha by sitting *zazen,*" rejoined Nengaku. It might be remarked, however, that a highly polished tile can make a passable mirror. Likewise, sitting *zazen* may make a passable future Buddha. On the other hand, one might wonder about the quality of Baso's *zazen*; perhaps he was paying more attention to Nengaku than to his *zazen.*

Enlightenment is endless, Dogen believed, and practice is beginningless. Practice and enlightenment are one. According to Masao Abe, in his *Zen and Western Thought,* this identification of practice and enlightenment overcomes three pairs of dualities that stand in the way of liberation: subject/object, potentiality/actuality, and means/end. Likewise, Dogen identified being and time as one "event" and both are permeated with Buddha-nature. "All beings of the universe are joined together," he wrote, "and each one is Time." It was Dogen who first said, "Once firewood turns to ash, it cannot return to firewood." This statement is commonly cut off at this point, taken as the whole truth of what Dogen said and meant. But Dogen was specifically not drawing a picture of time having inexorable command over states of being. He went on to say, "However, you shouldn't understand from this that it was ashes afterward and firewood before. Firewood is beyond *before* and *after.*" In Zen thinking, each moment is what it is, just as each being is what it is, although both are continually changing. So each being is united with time in each moment. This might best be understood as thinking of time not as "flowing" but as "hopping." This keeps the idea of distinctness and motion that is also characteristic of contemporary particle physics theory.

The proper state of mind, Dogen taught, was that of *hishiryo,* a mental state balanced between thinking and not-thinking. It was not necessary, for example, to offer incense to an image of the Buddha. All that was necessary was *zazen.* There is nothing supernatural about all this, say Zen Buddhists, for the road to Enlightenment depends upon the effort and mind-set of the sitter alone. Grace and prayer do not come into the picture, for there is no one to pray to.

The answer to the question he had posed years before was simply this: that Buddha-nature was not after all ultimately different from the practices used to realize it. In other words, once one can meditate sincerely, all the non-Buddha covering of the mind and body falls away, and the seeker is left with the pure shining Buddha-nature inherent in all things. Becoming Buddha is another way of becoming truly oneself so to study Buddhism is to study oneself, and vice versa.

Soto Zen appeared in the United States about 1950, although the first major Soto temple was established the year before by Soyu Matsuoka in Chicago. The best-known Soto Zen Master in this country, however, was Shunryu Suzuki (1904–71). He is discussed more fully later in this chapter.

Rinzai Zen

Rinzai Zen formally began in China, where it was known as Lin-chi, after its founder, the rather frightening ninth-century monk Rinzai (again, Lin-chi in Chinese) Gigen. It is said that he used paradoxes and riddles (koans) to shake his disciples' minds free of their customary pathways and to leave them open to a new and visionary experience. He was also famous for shouting, presumably not in anger, but to startle his disciples into Awakening. Lin-chi said that the core of Zen was *jen,* the person (or sometimes *jen-tao,* the person-way, emphasizing the active nature of the idea). This person is one who is fully individualized, subjective, alive, and aware. Yet he is fluid, too, impossible to capture completely in phrase or look. This is truly the characteristic of all fully realized existence.

In Japan, Rinzai Zen is for the elite, and many of the samurai warriors were among the first Zen converts. In fact, medieval samurai used to train in Zen monasteries. The influence of each tradition is evident upon the other, and each relies upon intense concentration for mastery. Rinzai Zen is sometimes even called "Samurai Zen." It shows its militaristic side not only in the relationship between Master and disciple, but also in the confrontational way one arrives at Enlightenment—by trying to "break through" to *satori,* much as if one is laying siege to a fortified city.

Like Soto Zen, Rinzai places tremendous emphasis on meditation, but with a difference. In Rinzai, *zazen* is in service to the koan, or Zen riddle. Most Rinzai Zen practitioners begin their studies with silent meditation or breathing exercises and then work up to the koan, although there is no set rule about this. Rinzai Zen is sometimes characterized as less formal or ritualistic than Soto Zen, but it also involves more study, in the conventional sense of the term of using texts. Rinzai Zen gained wide prominence in the United States during the "Buddhist boom" of the early 1960s, although it has never equaled the popularity of the more quiescent Soto. The most intriguing element of Rinzai Zen is undoubtedly the koan.

The Koan

A koan is a riddle designed to break through the normal means of understanding and lead to *kensho,* a first experience of Enlightenment. Zen Master Philip Kapleau has called the koan an "expression of perfection." The study of koans is a spiritual practice unique to Rinzai Zen. Two great collections of koans, *The Blue Rock Record* and *The Gateless Barrier* (*Mumonkan* in Japanese), originally collected during the T'ang dynasty of ancient China, have been translated into English. To those not used to reading them, their harsh playfulness and lightning-quick mood changes may strike a jarring note, but once accustomed to the genre, one notes the appearance of distinctive patterns, themes, dilemmas, and even characters. Some become old friends.

Many of the koans are built around stories of the ancient Chinese Ch'an Masters, and some are taken from the life of the Buddha himself. In fact, as stated at the beginning of the chapter, the first koan is said to be the Buddha's silent "flower" sermon, in which the Awakened One merely held up a flower. One disciple, the great and wise Kashyapa, smiled. The others didn't know what to do. For this and possibly other reasons, Kashyapa was elected to succeed the Buddha as leader of the Sangha. The flower, of course, expresses utterly and completely both the fragile and transient nature of existence as well as the perfect beauty of the Dharma. It represents love, beauty, and the return of life. Yet at the same time, it is simply and purely a flower. This concept of an object being itself/being other than itself/being more richly itself is the very nature of Zen.

No koan has a logical, reasonable, or "right" answer. The koan is a means to go beyond itself, and certainly beyond logic. The answer to each one is something that must be experienced rather than solved. And each person must experience that answer for himself, not by looking it up in a book, repeating the answers of others, or trying to reason it through, but by intense meditation until, after reasoning himself into a box, the student arrives at an unexpected breakthrough—a transformation in consciousness and a new mode of perception. This is a painful and difficult process. Dealing with a koan has been described as having swallowed a red-hot metal ball, and being equally unable to spit it out or to keep it down. Yet this painful experience, this acute discomfort, is the first step to Enlightenment (*satori*).

This process is likely to take even longer in the West than in the East, because Westerners place such a premium on logic and reasoning. The East lacks this rational tradition and so is more open to other kinds of knowledge and awareness, including those based on meditation and intuition. It does seem to be the case that persons knowledgeable in Indian, Chinese, and Japanese symbolism and mythology may have an easier time with gaining at least a rudimentary knowledge of the koan.

Interestingly, some see modern particle physics as just beginning to catch up with Zen insight. In this science, subatomic particles can apparently simultaneously exist and not exist. In other words, they waver in a state (or series of states or motions) not captured by words like "exist" or "not exist."

The most famous koan in America is undoubtedly "What is the sound of one hand clapping?" This famous riddle was devised by the great, although somewhat fierce, Japanese Zen Master Hakuin (1686–1769), founder of Rinzai Zen. (Hakuin was also a poet, painter, sculptor, and calligrapher of note.)

The greatest koan of all, however, is a paradoxical story. Called Joshu's (or Chao-chou's) *mu*, it is the first koan in *The Gateless Barrier*, the first and most famous collection of koans. A monk asks his Zen Master Chao-chou (778–897): "Does a dog have Buddha-nature?" Chao-chou answers "Mu!" (pronounced like the "u" in "put") or, in some versions, "Wu!" These sounds have multiple associations—first to indicate the noise a dog would naturally make in answer to a question asked of it (especially the "wu" sound) or a sound generally interpreted as a negative in Chinese. In addition, Chinese linguistics comes into play. Chinese is a tonal language, and the same word can have different meanings when pronounced using varying tones. "Wu" means "No!" when pronounced in the second tone, but *satori* or "wakening" when pronounced in the fourth tone. The paradox is that according to all Buddhist teaching, a dog does have Buddha-nature. So why the negative answer—or the sound of a barking dog? This is the heart of the koan.

The apparent negativity of the *mu*-koan reflects the general perception that Zen is inherently negative. This is an easy mistake to make. After all, Zen writings and commentaries are full of words like *shunyata* (emptiness), no-thought, no-perception, no-mind, nothingness, and the like. This certainly sounds negative and nihilistic. But it isn't; it is just more Zen paradox. It goes beyond words to arrive at a state that is beyond their boundaries. The only way words can approach this state is through a negative construction. It doesn't mean that the state itself is negative. It means that only negatives can "free" the concept.

Zen is profoundly and absolutely affirmative. By absolutely affirmative, Zen teachers mean that it is not conditioned by the relativity of a negative. In Western thought, an affirmative implies that there is also a negative. But that is true only in a relative realm. In the absolute freedom of Zen, an affirmative does not necessarily imply the existence of a negative. Why should it? Does a cloud imply an anticloud, or a butterfly an antibutterfly? Of course not. Perfect freedom and affirmation exist in an absolute, not a relative way. The limits imposed by language and logic on truth make the absolute freedom of Zen a confusing concept only until one goes beyond all concepts and experiences this freedom for oneself. At that point one doesn't *know* the truth—one *becomes* truth.

Chao-chou gave us another famous *mondo,* or question and answer. (Since he lived to be 120 years old, he had plenty of time to come up with them.) In this case, a monk asked him, "What is the self?" Chao-chou responded, "Have you had breakfast?" "Yes," rejoined the monk. "Then wash your bowl," responded Chao-chou. Although one can be tempted to read this *mondo* as an abrupt brushing off of the inquisitive monk, the meaning is at once simpler and deeper. By telling this disciple to "wash his bowl" Chao-chou was emphasizing the Zen practice of concentrating on particulars rather than vague abstractions. In specific activity one can find meaning and Enlightenment.

Something not always understood by American Zen students is that koans often employ esoteric Chinese symbolism. For example, one famous koan concerns an ox (or a bull). "An ox walks past a window. First the horns go by, then the head goes by, then the neck goes by, then the body goes by. Why doesn't the tail go by?" Although there may be more than one answer to this koan, it might be important for the student to know that in Chinese thought, the tail symbolizes the ego and the concept of self. Knowing that fact might help the student answer the koan. Or it might not. Curiously, for a tradition that emphasizes thinking for oneself and perceiving truth directly, a great many books exist to help the student figure out the answer to various famous koans. It also seems to be true that no one ever quite gets a koan right without help from the Master. Cynical people might say that all this is designed to keep a Zen Master in disciples. (Once a student masters one koan, he is usually given another one, until he achieves complete Enlightenment.)

Some koans or teaching puzzles seem to have serious consequences. The ancient Chinese Ch'an master Teh-shan (780–865) used to literally come out swinging at his disciples. "If you speak I will give you thirty blows with my stick" he would announce. "And if you don't speak, I will also give you thirty blows with my stick!" Although this seems like a lose-lose proposition to us, to Zen students, it's a win-win. If one escaped from the koan by coming up with a suitable response, and consequently a higher level of understanding, one might avoid the beating. On the other hand, if one did not avoid the beating, Enlightenment was likely to strike (literally) during the process, an Awakening born from the failure of logic. Zen stories are full of instances of disciples reaching *satori* during a beating. A famous (and painless) example of this kind of solution is this noted problem: A man kept a goose in a glass bottle. The goose kept growing larger. The man did not want to break the bottle or hurt the goose. How does he get it out? "Look! It is out!" seems to have been a satisfactory response.

A very serious Zen story concerns the Zen Master Nansen (who also, by the way, answered the goose-in-a-bottle question satisfactorily). The story relates how Nansen came upon his monks arguing over which group of them had ownership of the monastery cat. Nansen picked up the cat and announced that he would slice it in half unless someone could say something to save it. None of the monks was able to come up with anything and here the resemblance to the biblical story of King Solomon ends. Nansen duly but regretfully sliced the cat in half. At this point, the monk Joshu entered the monastery and when asked how he would have saved the poor creature, simply put his sandals on the top of his head and walked out. Nansen is reported to have said, "Had Joshu been here, the cat would certainly have been spared."

This is a dark koan. Killing an animal is against the First Precept of Buddhism, do not kill. Why would Nansen have done such a thing? Only for the gravest of reasons: to help his monks reach *satori.* In his commentary on this story, D. T. Suzuki remarks that the sacrificed cat surely was destined for Buddhahood. The sandal-hatted Joshu is reported to have attained an age of 120 years; it was said of him that Zen sparkled on his lips whenever he spoke. (Some Zen Masters, like Philip Kapleau, assure us that Nansen didn't really kill the cat, and that the whole incident was mimed. Others aren't so sure.)

Serious attacks against people are also part of the Zen tradition, at least in legend. One noted Master, Chu-chih, was fond of responding to questions merely by lifting his index finger. One of his disciples decided to answer a question of Chu-chih in the same way. Chu-chih instantly reached out and sliced off the disciple's finger. As the disciple ran from the room, howling in pain, he looked back and saw Chu-chih smiling and with a raised finger. At that moment, as the disciple stared in horror at his own bleeding hand, he achieved *satori.*

Korean Son

Son is the dominant form of Korean Buddhism to reach the United States, although it should be said that many other Buddhist traditions also exist in Korea. As is the case with Japanese Zen, Koreans inherited the Son tradition from China, but unlike Japanese Zen, Korean Son never became institutionalized. In fact, its entry into that country was a rather rocky one. Imported Ch'an monks from China were considered unruly and combative by the Confucians in charge of the government. They were severely persecuted until 1895, before which time they were not even allowed to enter city gates. The Son monks were celibate, but during the difficult 1930s when Korea was under attack from Japan, the beleaguered order joined forces with the Kyo (Sutra) Buddhists into one group that was called the Chogye order. During the 1950s, a separatist group, the Tae'go, consisting only of married monks, was formed.

Korean Zen, or Son, in the United States is largely a product of the work of Seung Sahn (b. 1927), the Seventy-eighth Patriarch in his line of transmission in the Chogye order of Korean Buddhism and the first Korean Zen Master to live and teach in the West. He was born of Christian parents, but he became a monk in 1948. When he arrived in the United States in 1972, he got a job repairing washing machines, but soon, with the assistance of some students from Brown University, founded the Providence Zen Center, part of the Kwan Um School of Zen, a school which Seung Sahn says is a "lay order of bodhisattva monks and Dharma teachers who are married householders." Kwan Um is thus now considered an order independent of its parent Chogye order.

The Kwan Um school is an international organization of more than 100 centers, temples, and groups all around the world. (Seung Sahn prefers to use the word "temple.") Not all of them have survived, however, and the impression is that many of his students are transient. His books include *Ten Gates, The Compass of Zen, Dropping Ashes on the Buddha, Only Don't Know,* and *The Whole World is a Single Flower—365 Kongans for Everyday Life.*

Like other Zen sects, Kwan Um places a great deal of emphasis on meditation. Rather un-Zenlike, however, are the morning and evening chanting liturgies, which are more reminiscent of Korean folk practice than traditional Son. Seung Sahn places little emphasis on *zazen,* preferring what he calls "active Zen." He is an energetic proselytizer for a brand of Buddhism, which while not traditional, fits in well with American expectations and lifestyle.

Seung Sahn also revolutionized thinking about monkhood, when he established the rank of "bodhisattva monk" for persons who wish to be a monk but reject celibacy as a life-choice. Such persons generally still live in the monasteries and practice regular meditation and retreats. He allows even lay students to wear monk's robes, which has scandalized more traditional Son teachers. Seung Sahn made a breakthrough of sorts in Korean Zen when he appointed a woman, Barbara Rhodes (b. 1948) in 1977 as a Master Dharma Teacher, the first of his students to be so honored. (The title has since been changed to Ji Do Poep Sa Nim, equivalent to "Sensei" in Japanese Zen.) Rhodes, although raised as an Episcopalian, discovered Zen when reading D. T. Suzuki.

One of Seung Sahn's other students is Zen Master Tundra Wind (Jim Wilson). Wilson has now taken his own path. As a gay person, Wilson found conventional Buddhist teachings about sexuality conventional and stultifying. He changed the Third Precept ("No sexual misconduct") to

"Express the sacredness of sexuality." Purists may argue whether this is the same thing at all.

Another strand of Korean Zen is found in the person of Seo Kyung Bo (or Kyung Bo-seo) also of the Chogye order. He gave Dharma transmission to American Don Gilbert in 1973. Gilbert then took the name Ta Hui; he conducts services in a Korean temple in Carmel, California, where most of the practitioners are Korean.

Vietnamese Thien and Thich Nhat Hanh

The most famous proponent of Vietnamese Thien in America is Thich Nhat Hanh, but, although he traces his roots to the Zen tradition, his outlook and approach are so different from "orthodox" Zen that he will be treated separately in chapter 7.

There are a few Vietnamese Zen teachers in this country, but the most important is probably Thien-an, a Rinzai monk and Zen Master, who founded the International Buddhist Meditation Center in Los Angeles in 1970. Most of the other Vietnamese teachers are American and two of them, Karuna Prabhasa Dharma and Karuna Dharma, are women. Karuna Dharma, who was born in Wisconsin, took a course in Buddhism from Thich Thien-an at UCLA. She then became a student of Thien-an and took full ordination in 1976. She was given Dharma transmission in 1980 and became the spiritual head and director of the center.

Another woman teacher in the Vietnamese tradition is Roshi Gesshin Prabhasa Dharma (Gisela Midwer, b. 1931), a German-born practitioner who has lived in the United States since the 1960s. She began studying in the Rinzai Zen tradition (Vinitarucci lineage) in 1967 and was ordained as a teacher (Osho) in 1972 by Joshu Sasaki Roshi (no connection to Sokei-an Sasaki). Subsequently she became head priest of his Cimarron Center. However, eleven years later, in 1983, she left the Cimarron, because of alleged abuse by Joshu Sasaki. She also left Rinzai Zen, a harsh tradition she came to believe was not suitable for women and older people. She entered the Vietnamese school of the Most Venerable Thich Man Giac, Supreme Abbot of the United Vietnamese Buddhist Churches in America. In 1985 the Dharma Mind Seal Transmission of a Great Master was bestowed upon her by Thich Man Giac. She founded the International Zen Institute of America, which became a regional center of the World Fellowship of Buddhists, with three branches in Europe and two in the United States. She writes: "Zen training brings us back into the original unconditioned, free Mind—into the immediate direct experience of the non-dualism of Buddha and person, things and Mind."

Zen Monasteries

The Zen monastic system is more than 1,000 years old. It was developed by the Chinese Ch'an Master Pai-chang (720–814), whose name in Japan is Hyakujo. Hyakujo is famous for telling his monks, "A day without working is a day without eating." This pithy saying serves to explain his basic philosophy—that monks should not spend all their time sitting around and meditating, but should also do useful work, such as gardening, cleaning, and cooking. Every facet of the monks' life is strictly regulated, and the monks follow a set routine every day. In Japan, begging is also part of the monks' accepted occupations; they go forth, usually calling on regular patrons, for their allotments of rice and vegetables. American Zen Buddhists do not usually follow this practice, which is culturally alien to the United States.

Meditation is done in the *zendo*, or meditation hall, which is the heart of a Zen monastery. It is often a separate building from the rest of the monastery, and can be of whatever size is needed to accommodate the monks. Each monk is generally allotted a space of a *tatami* mat, traditionally six feet by three feet. Here he sleeps, sits, and meditates. Each also has a large quilt for bedding. His private possessions include his robes, some books, a set of wooden or lacquer bowls, and a razor. All can fit into a small lightweight box, which the monk can hang from his neck with a wide sash when he is traveling. The reason for the paucity of goods is obvious—the more things a person owns, the more closely he is tied to everyday existence. The whole point of monkhood is to achieve a different way of living.

In the tropical climate where the idea of monasticism was born, it was mandated for monks to eat only once a day before noon. In colder climates, however, including most of the United States, this rule is often relaxed somewhat. An evening meal, called a "medicinal" meal, is permitted, but it must be of the most frugal kind.

The monks eschew rich and elegant foods, confining themselves to simple rice, gruel, tea, and vegetables. Animal products are avoided.

Before eating, the monks recite the Heart of Perfect Wisdom Sutra, and take out about seven grains of rice from their bowls in remembrance of their departed ancestors. Meals are conducted in silence, with hand signals used to ask for more tea or rice. Wooden utensils are used. The first food is offered to the Buddhas and bodhisattvas, then the community is served. When the meal is finished, the monks wipe their bowls clean, stack them up, and carry them out in the same order in which they entered. This ritual eating practice is called *oryoki.* The name refers specifically to a set of nesting bowls given to each monk or nun upon ordination. The largest of these bowls is sometimes called the "Buddha bowl," referring to the one begging bowl that the Buddha allowed each of his monks to carry.

Many American monasteries alter or delete one part of the ceremony. In traditional Japanese monasteries, the monks wash out the bowls in plain or hot water (or the remains of their hot tea), and then drink the water. This is known as giving the water "rebirth." It is both thrifty and a nod to the understanding of the essential unity of all things. A verse is recited, offering this dinner remainder to the hungry ghosts. Although there is nothing unclean about this, since once is merely drinking hot water and the last particles of one's own dinner, the practice is repugnant to many Americans, and thus omitted in many monasteries.

Zen Ritual

While many people believe that Zen has no rituals, this is not really the case. The hallmark of Zen, *zazen,* or sitting meditation, is a ritual, as is the ritual bowing (*gassho*) that is performed before one's teacher or a statue of the Buddha. The offering of flowers and candles is also a ritual.

While in Eastern countries ritual is considered a way of honoring the Buddha, Western Buddhists turn ritual into a kind of meditation in its own right, something of benefit to the meditator rather than an offering to the Buddha.

Ordination (*Jukai*)

The process of becoming a serious student of Zen often involves the rite of *jukai,* or ordination. Ordination in the Zen tradition means simply that one has decided to enter the monastic community and vows to follow the Buddhist precepts. During *jukai* one generally takes the Three Refuges or Triple Gem, although this can vary from community to community. A student is usually given a Dharma name as well. Because of its serious nature, this ceremony is often considered of the greatest importance.

Zen Meditation

Meditation is the hallmark of both schools of Zen, but its method and goal are different from the kinds of meditation practiced in Christianity, Hinduism, or even in some other kinds of Buddhism, such as Theravada. The purpose of Zen meditation is not to concentrate the mind but to free it.

This is most obvious in Soto Zen, which avoids even the use of koan-study in order to achieve the free-floating condition that approximates, in the words of D. T. Suzuki, "a wafting cloud in the sky." While other kinds of Buddhism may concentrate meditative efforts upon a philosophical idea, Zen avoids doing so. The object is the clearing of the mind of all visualizations in order to realize that "form is emptiness, and emptiness is form," the key phrase of the Prajnaparamita Sutra. In Zen, even thinking about no-selfness leads paradoxically to the opposite idea and constitutes another chain to everyday life. Zen is a state beyond categories, which is one reason that talking about it, rather than practicing it, seems so futile.

For the most orthodox, *zazen* is performed sitting on a *zafu,* or black meditation cushion, in the full-lotus position, each foot resting upon the opposite thigh, knees on the floor. While this position is very comfortable for Asians, who are used to it, it can be agony for Americans, and is thus often modified in the United States to the half-lotus position, in which one foot is atop and the other beneath the opposite thigh. Another possibility is the "Burmese lotus" position, in which the practitioner crosses the legs, but rests both feet on the floor instead of the thighs. In the "Japanese" posture, a cushion is placed between the legs, while the knees and top of the feet are on the floor. Some people, however, can only meditate sitting comfortably in a chair or meditation bench. In any case, the back must be straight, or bent very slightly forward.

The eyes are open or half-open (some say two-thirds) and focused slightly downward, and in Soto Zen, the practitioners often face a blank wall. The hands are placed in an oval position, with the thumbs lightly touching, at the *hara,* about three inches below the navel. The *hara* was believed to be the seat of consciousness. This hand position is called the "cosmic mudra," or *hokkaijoin.* At first, practitioners practice counting breaths and banishing any wayward thoughts. When they become adept at that, they simply "follow" their breath without counting. Experienced and highly accomplished meditators are able to meditate in "full awareness" without following the breath at all. This is *shikantaza.*

Zen meditation may also be practiced in the form of *kinhin,* or walking meditation. It is often done outdoors, and usually lasts only about five minutes. Time for the walk is signaled by a gong or perhaps a bell. The meditators arise, bow to their cushions, and set off. One purpose of *kinhin* is to get the circulation started again after hours of seated meditation, and so is healthful as well as a mere change of pace. During the walk, the students, especially in Soto Zen, are expected to concentrate upon each movement and placement of the feet. One hand is placed in a fist and held at navel level; the other hand is wrapped around the first. Often the steps are to be timed with breathing, although it is often more convenient to time the steps with those of the person in front. Some Zen schools, notably that of Thich Nhat Hanh, use walking meditations in their own right, often in preference to sitting, and have established walking trails for that purpose.

Soto Zen practitioners walk slowly, as do Theravadins, but Rinzai Zen practitioners usually walk very quickly. (Part of this derives from their theory that one should hasten to achieve Enlightenment.) Both practices are observed in American Zen Centers of both Rinzai and Soto traditions.

Sesshin

The word *sesshin* means to collect the mind. It is a period of continual *zazen.* The practice is said to stem first from Shakyamuni himself, who reached Enlightenment after meditating steadily beneath the Bo tree, and secondly from Dogen, who also reached Enlightenment (dropping both body and mind) after a period of steady sitting meditation. Traditionally, *sesshin* sessions (the pun is impossible to avoid), each lasting a week, take place during both summer and winter "sojourns." During these periods, the monks rise earlier and sit later into the night. They listen to a sermon or lecture each day and study from Zen "textbooks," such as collections of sermons like *The Rinzairoku* or anthologies of koans like *The Hekiganshu.* During *sesshin* the monks have an interview with the Master. This interview, usually described as "tense," is called *samzen.* This is the more general term for this meeting. Another word, *dokusan,* is used by Rinzai Zen monks. In *dokusan,* the student offers a solution to the koan he has been given. He may also discuss problems he is having with Zen practice. However, the Zen Master never directly "teaches" the koan to the student; the student is supposed to figure it out on his own. (One famous Zen Master, Nakagawa Soen, who worked in both Japan and America and was known for his eccentricities, sometimes put a pumpkin on his sitting cushion in place of himself during *dokusan.* This sort of thing did not make koan-solving any easier.)

Some Zen Masters have said that a properly conducted *sesshin* involves sitting by oneself between one and three years. Not everyone, of course, is a suitable candidate for *sesshin.* However, American Buddhism is diverse, and there are a few places, most famously the Gold Mountain Monastery of San Francisco, which try to replicate Asian practices. In fact, the residents of this monastery are required to sleep in a sitting position, as well as adopt Chinese dress and diet.

Monastic Begging and Working

Another Japanese practice that has undergone modification is that of *takahatsu,* or religious begging. In Japan, aspirants go forth with a bowl to collect money and a bag to hold donated food. American culture, however, views begging as disgraceful or pathetic, rather than as a sign of spiritual development. Most American Zen institutions eliminate it or replace it with community service. For example, at the Zen Center in Rochester, New York, trainees were required to pick up trash on the street instead. While most Americans still did not see trash pickup as a religious discipline, they did appreciate the community service.

Monks also work to maintain their monastery. This physical work is called *samu,* and is undertaken in the spirit of an offering to the monastic community one lives in. It is part of all Zen training, and harkens back to a saying of the eighth-century Chinese monk, Pai-chang: "A day without work is a day without food." Dogen Zenji wrote a famous guide called "Instructions to the Cook," which is not only a cooking manual, but also, on a deeper level, a guide to liberation. A true Zen Buddhist might deny that there is a difference. Today most Zen monasteries prescribe alternate periods of work and meditation.

Zen Monastic Dress

Most monasteries in the stricter Japanese tradition favor black robes for residents and monks. (These persons also shave their heads or wear their hair very short.) Outsiders and visitors may wear street clothes. The priests, especially those who have received Dharma transmission, wear the most elaborate robes. Certain high-ranking persons may also wear the *kesa,* or bib. Who gets to wear the bib depends upon what school or monastery we are talking about. In some cases, it is awarded to those who have passed their first koan.

Zen Writings

As mentioned earlier, just because Zen considered itself to be transmission outside scripture does not mean that it has no writings. There are thousands of Zen works in existence—collections of koans, explanations of koans, and other writings on matters dear to the heart of Zen. Zen simply does not accept these writings as sacred in the sense that their reciting or reading can deliver one to *satori.*

Zen Chanting

Many American Zen communities practice chanting the Heart of Perfect Wisdom and other sutras, usually in English. Even though Zen officially considers itself independent of the authority of any sutra, the Heart of Perfect Wisdom Sutra (Prajnaparamita Hridaya Sutra) holds a special place in Zen affections. It supposedly contains the core precepts from the Buddha's teachings over many years. The sutra is addressed to Sariputta, one of the Buddha's greatest disciples. The main point of the sutra is the realization that the senses, the objects of the senses, the act of sensing, Nirvana, and even the Four Noble Truths of Buddhism are to some degree the products of a delusive mind. "Form is emptiness—and emptiness is form." It ends: "Gone, gone, gone far Beyond—gone fully Beyond! Awaken! Rejoice!"

Chanting is a basic Buddhist practice. It is done at least once a day, usually at dawn, in Zen centers throughout the world, including the United States. The chant may consist of words from a sutra, or teachings of past Zen Masters. In addition to human voices, much use is made of musical instruments. The most important of these include a bowl-shaped gong called the *keisu,* a standing drum with brass beads along the rim, and a wooden fish-shaped drum.

Unlike the chanting protocol in other Buddhist traditions, Zen chanting involves no swaying or rocking. The chanters sit perfectly upright with their hands in their laps, while each chants at his or her lowest natural pitch. Each chanter's pitch should at the same time blend into the dominant one. Just as the body does not sway during a Zen chant, the voice does not roam around the scale; the pitch should be steady. The source of the chant must come from the abdomen, like good singing, not from the throat, like most talking. In Zen centers, a chant book is often passed around to help the practitioners follow along, although considering the speed at which some of the chants are chanted, it becomes almost impossible for a novice to keep up.

Zen Buddhists may chant a sutra (the words of the Buddha or ancient Masters) or a *dharani,* an extended mantra. In the United States, a sutra is often chanted in English translation, while a mantra is chanted in its original language. That is because a mantra's power is believed to derive from its sound as well as from its inherent meaning. (Many of the mantras make no sense in any language—they are just a string of nonsense syllables.) A mantra is an audible, sacred formula designed to focus a meditation. It is believed to draw the chanter into a relationship with the unseen forces of the universe. The strength of the relationship depends partly on the mantra itself and partly on the efforts and character of the chanter. One who has pure motives and a high level of concentration will be more successful than one who does not.

American Zen also relies more heavily upon verbal dialogues or teachings between Master and students than is common in other parts of the world. Perhaps this is because Americans live in such a noisy world that they find silence unnerving. At any rate, it seems to be true that beginning American Zen students especially find the practice of dialogue a great help in developing their spiritual awareness. In addition, many Zen rites of passage, such as weddings, funerals, and ordinations, have been altered to fit more comfortably within American culture. None of these changes touch the heart of Zen—they merely make it more accessible.

Zen Bowing

Many Zen centers make extensive use of bowing. In Asia, bowing is a common form of greeting, and has little or none of the "abasement" characteristics that Westerners associate with it. However, even these associations have proved useful to Zen teachers, since they can use them in bowing practice to break down the shell of egoism that binds the spirit of many disciples.

Zen Work

The achievement of a Zen sensibility is not restricted to meditation, chanting, bowing, or working koans. It is an essential element of the Zen view of life that all aspects of work should be integrated into the life of a Zen monk or layperson. This understanding has been slow in coming to America, where the idea reigns that the religious life (prayer, meditation, chanting, and so forth) occupies a different sphere from the secular life (work, play, study). In Zen Buddhism, all are recognized as interdependent factors of existence.

Zen Reasoning, Antireasoning, and Beyond Reasoning

Logic was created to be of service to human intellect, and in its circumscribed role has provided that basis for scientific progress. But there is a limit beyond which logic is fairly useless. And beyond that limit lie many of the ultimate truths of human existence. This is a tremendously freeing revelation, since it means that happiness does not depend on learning syllogisms or figuring out quadratic equations. Happiness is something that surges up from the very wellspring of existence, without cause, boundaries, or "reason." It exists in and of itself, and is available to all who care to taste its riches. Like rushing water, happiness indeed is something to be experienced, not grasped.

Although it may seem otherwise, Zen teachers and practitioners have a reason for apparently nonsensical statements and illogical comments. That purpose is to present another viewpoint. The world we experience with our senses is not the whole world. It probably doesn't even approximate it. The same can be said of the process of reason or even the apparent truth of emotion. All of these give only vague indications at best—and tell downright lies at worst. They even contradict each other. How many people have acted against their reason or contrary to their feelings? How many have mistaken a stick for a snake or a leaf for bird? If the senses were necessary to know truth, persons who are blind, deaf, or paralyzed could not attain Enlightenment, and that is patently not the case. How many times have we discovered that words, or even thoughts, are inadequate to express experience? Truth must somehow be attained in a different way. "Empty-handed I go!" cries the Zen saying, "And behold the spade is in my hands!" Logical consistency is not the whole truth, or even an approximation of it. Can one "logically" explain a rock? No, a rock is what it is and no amount of explaining can reveal it. It is "this," and once its "thisness" is truly experienced, the rest of experience becomes true. All the universe becomes "this" at "this moment"—then no more. Abstractions and generalizations are broken by Zen the way a person can break a stick in half. This is not to say that sticks are trivial objects; in the grand scheme of the universe, there isn't all that much difference between a pebble and Mt. Everest. In addition, when the mind is prepared for Enlightenment, it may take only the lightest touch—the sound of a leaf touching the earth, the sheen on a beetle-wing, or an aromatic whiff of lavender—to ignite the experience into *satori*.

Is Zen a mystical religion? Perhaps, but not in the sense that is usually meant by mysticism. The aim of most mysticism is to raise the mystic up somehow—to have him unite to the power of God or heaven, or even in some way to become part of that ultimate divinity. Considering things in that light, Zen is a kind of antimysticism. It brings what is considered "divine," "holy," and "sacred" down to earth. Yet, paradoxically, this very practice brings out the "divinity" within us. This, according to its practitioners, is the power of Zen.

Satori

The goal of Zen is *satori*—the Japanese term for Enlightenment. But here is a paradox, expressed by Dogen, the founder of Japanese Zen. He said that to achieve a goal one must become a certain type of person—but once you have become that type of person, achieving the goal is no longer important.

But what is it—this Enlightenment, this Awakening? What does the light show us? Into what world do we awaken? What, in brief, *happens* to us? What do we know, what do we do? As one might expect, these are all the wrong questions. *Satori* is not an express package full of exciting surprises. *Satori* is not something given to one. It is something one enters into, something one becomes with one's whole being. It may help to use an example from the West.

Many Western people search for happiness. Different things make different people happy. For one person it might be a motorcycle, for another a healthy child, for someone else a lucrative or creative career. These things are prized because they bring "happiness." Once the goal is achieved, each person may claim to be happy, but each may in fact feel rather differently from the others—it's not something anyone can be sure about. Yet for each, "happiness" represents some sort of ultimate value. *Satori* is the same. It is an ultimate value. It goes beyond feeling, beyond sense, beyond intellect. It strikes at the heart of being, shatters it, and remakes it. What is the highest principle of Zen? According to Joshu: "The oak tree in the garden."

Women, Sex, and Zen

In Japan, an extremely patriarchal society, women are generally permitted to attend retreat (*sesshin*) only, not to be admitted to a monastery. There have been some exceptions, notably Peggy Kennett, but her life there was fraught with difficulty. During lectures women and men are expected to sit apart, and it is believed that women distract men from their work of trying to reach *satori*.

This out-of-date attitude has been discarded among Zen Buddhists in the United States. Most monasteries use shared facilities for study, meditation, work, and meals. Practitioners agree that proximity between the sexes produces tensions, but argue that equal (although somewhat different in kind) tensions exist in same-sex institutions. Some American Zen monasteries permit sexual relations between participants. However, such relationships between students and teachers are routinely prohibited as examples of power-abuse. Responsibility for maintaining the correct relationship between students and teacher lies directly with the teacher, who is supposed to be mature in his or her practice. This does not absolve the student of all blame, however, since Buddhism makes each person responsible for his or her own actions.

Zen Art

Perhaps the most pervasive influence Zen has wielded in America is through art, especially poetry. The acknowledged master of Japanese poetry was Basho (1644–94), the great Zen writer and teacher of writing. Here is his most famous poem:

An ancient pond
Frog plunges down in it
The sound of water.

Haiku is a delicate and particularly demanding form: in its classical Japanese form, it must be of three unrhymed lines of five, seven, and seven syllables, respectively. No similes, moralizing, or abstract language is permitted. The poem should stand on its own, letting the "meaning-making" come from others, if they are unable to accept the poem on its own pure terms. The subject is always nature, and the typical haiku contains both a "season" word indicating the time of year and an "aha!" moment corresponding to the Zen *satori,* or realization. That is a lot to ask of a seventeen-syllable poem! Many people compare the writing of Haiku to the practice of "just-sitting"—quietly allowing the meaning to break through in the poem, not struggling to put it there. In this respect a haiku is like a flower that opens naturally. The haiku is also immediate. The poem exists only while it is being written, Basho said. "After that it's just wastepaper." This idea pays equal homage to the Buddhist notion of impermanence, and the Zen concept of "Be here now."

In English, seventeen syllables don't "scan" as well as they do in Japanese, and most Haikuists interpret the seventeen syllables to mean "very short." Nowadays the subject is frequently something other than nature, and many haiku are humorous. All this being said, this form is very popular with both amateur and professional poets.

Two American poets powerfully influenced by Zen are Gary Snyder and Anne Waldman. Waldman has written nearly forty books, mostly poetry, and regards herself as a "language guardian" and considers poetry to be an example of *upaya,* or skillful means, to express the Dharma. She points to great Buddhist teachers of the past like Milarepa in the Tibetan tradition and Basho and Dogen in the Zen tradition who were also poets and writers. She points out that poetry is so essentially Buddhist in its exact appreciation of the "now" and its inexorable passing that it gives most poets, even non-Buddhist ones like William Blake, William Butler Yeats, Emily Dickinson, and Wallace Stevens, a strong Buddhist flavor to their writing. Gary Snyder, more fully discussed in chapter 7, an academically and experientially trained Zen Buddhist who studied Oriental languages at Berkeley, was a founding member of the Berkeley Buddhist Church (Jodo Shinshu-affiliated), and studied formally in Japan with Isshu Miura until the latter's death.

Zen Teachers

Although the Buddha's last words to his disciples were to "seek out your own salvation with diligence," finding a good teacher has become part of much Mahayana Buddhist experience, particularly in Zen. In his book, *Zen: Merging of East and West* Roshi Philip Kapleau has said, "You need a teacher to learn that there is nothing to learn." Zen, therefore, unlike Theravadan Buddhism, is organized around various teaching "lineages" rather than the monastic Sangha. Any teacher can give Dharma transmission to as many students as he or she thinks worthy; thus a number of legitimate lineages can be created.

One does not become a Zen teacher automatically after one is enlightened; a long period of maturing is necessary. This maturing period is known as "the long maturing of the sacred womb," a phrase derived from ancient Taoism. Since Zen Buddhism has no pope or central authority, anyone can call himself or herself a "Zen Master" without necessarily lying about it. However, obtaining Dharma transmission from a certified Zen line is something else entirely—and not easy to achieve.

The most common term for a Zen teacher from a recognized line is Roshi, which means "venerable teacher." This word is mostly used by the teacher's own disciples; it isn't really a title that is earned by completing a specific course of studies. The term is used somewhat differently in each Zen community. In most cases, only a Roshi is empowered to give Dharma transmission and thus create his own "lineage."

Normally, a Zen Master is one who has achieved a high level of spiritual insight, and who in fact may be considered to be fully enlightened. That is how Dogen defined the term back in 1235. Dogen also said that the true Zen Master follows what he knows to be the truth and has received Dharma transmission from his own teacher, making him or her the Master's spiritual heir. The disciple is recognized as being of equal or greater spiritual stature as the Master. This is a high standard, and as a matter of fact, in America many Roshis are accorded the title of Zen Master whether they have strictly earned it or not.

Roshis are not perfect humans beings in any case; they have flaws like everyone else. In the Zen tradition, however, it is said that the Roshi is fully aware of his failings, whereas ordinary people try to cover theirs up. It is true that some Roshis developed terrible reputations for drinking, but many Zen students found they could learn much even from such comparatively poor examples of Buddha-nature.

The tradition of unquestioning obedience and loyalty to one's Master is not easily accepted by most Westerners, especially in the United States, where people are taught to think for themselves. The almost sacred bond between Master and student is an Asian tradition that has no real parallel in America. This has created conflict and confusion in the minds of many American Zen students. The conflict doesn't weaken the appeal of Zen, however, which also places a good deal of emphasis on independent thinking. How much allegiance an American Zen Buddhist places in the Zen teacher is a personal choice.

Not every Roshi is right for every student. But when the student finds the one who *is* right, he or she is expected to commit to the Roshi entirely. The relationship between them is based on a powerful karma that defies ordinary bonds. Such a commitment means the student promises to make a mindful effort to follow the guidance of the Roshi, no matter how difficult—or even nonsensical—it may seem.

Another term for a Zen teacher is *sensei*. A *sensei* is an honorific term, but is not so advanced a title as *roshi*. A *sensei* may have received Dharma transmission from his Master, but he has not yet attained Enlightenment. A Zen Master may have more than one spiritual heir, and some Zen students have received ceremonial transmission from more than one teacher or lineage or even school.

Zen teachers are not always positive, reinforcing, or encouraging. They are tough, challenging, and at times, abusive. Their purpose is to help the student break through ordinary modes of thinking to achieve Enlightenment. This process is so difficult that it takes tough measures. As we mentioned earlier, the originator of Zen, Bodhidharma, is said to have cut away his own eyelids so that he could stay awake better during meditation.

But the real authority in Zen doesn't come from a teacher, but from within the practitioner. By "within" Zen doesn't mean the powers of reason, intuition, emotion, or memory alone—not even of all of them combined—but the "this-ness" of the practitioner at every moment. D. T. Suzuki remarked that the great truth of Zen was present in every person. (It seems odd even to quote Suzuki. If what he says is true, then it should not be necessary to refer to him as an authority on this matter.)

In addition to Zen Masters and Zen teachers, there are also Zen priests, persons authorized to conduct rituals and perform ceremonies. This is a hereditary position in most Zen lineages. However, one can be a monk, then a priest, or vice versa. In the Japanese tradition, priests (as opposed to monks) are not required to be celibate, and may marry and raise a family.

Dharma Transmission

One of the most important of all ceremonies in Zen Buddhism is *shiho,* or direct Dharma transmission. In this ceremony, a Master gives his robe to his disciple, thus symbolizing the passing of the lineage to a new generation. (These lineages can go back eighty or ninety generations of teachers, although it is now recognized that many of the records are corrupt or fictionalized.) It is said that more than the robe is received; the mind of the Buddha comes with it. In an important sense, during the *shiho* ceremony, Buddha meets Buddha, in the minds of the master and disciple. It is a solemn and important occasion, which signifies that the student has embodied the teachings of his Master. During the ceremony, it is said that the Dharma passes from the teacher's "heart/mind" directly to the student's "heart/mind." However, it may be more accurate to say that the Dharma transmission recognizes that the mind of the Master and the mind of the student are one. Nothing has to actually be transmitted at all, because they are identical. The word "transmission" in this understanding is a just a figure of speech.

A word with a similar meaning is *inka,* which means "seal of approval," and is used in the Rinzai tradition. In Rinzai, *inka* is given when the student has solved all the koans the Master has given him. In the Soto tradition, *inka* is given when the student has shown an acceptable level of insight, meaning that the Buddha-nature in him has been recognized. Receiving *inka* does not necessarily mean that the pupil has become enlightened.

Zen Comes to America

Although the first seeds of "American" Zen were sown in 1893 at the World Parliament of Religions by Zen Master Soyen Shaku (1859–1919), it had to wait half a century for its real flowering. In the Zen way of thinking, of course, Zen was always in America—the first missionaries merely recognized its existence and developed it.

Today Zen followers in America are mostly converts and of no particular ethnic group. Since there is no central administration, it's difficult to say how many Zen practitioners there are today in America—the U.S. Census Bureau no longer asks people about their religious preference.

Early Zen "Missionaries"

Soyen Shaku (1859–1919)

Soyen (or Soen) Shaku, a Japanese Rinzai Zen Master, was an important early promoter of Buddhism; in fact, for the entire first half of the twentieth century, practically all Zen Buddhism was directly from his lineage. Soyen Shaku received his training and later became a monk at the prestigious Engakuji Monastery. His own teacher, Imagita Kosen, from whom he received Dharma transmission when he was only twenty-four, was unusual in that he combined academic with monastic lessons, thus preparing his young disciple for a much larger role in the world than was customary for young Zen monks. In fact, Soyen Shaku studied English and Western philosophy at Keio University, which was established specifically for the study of Western culture. He also studied in India and Sri Lanka. One reason that he decided to come to America was to reverse the West-to-East missionary tide. Soyen Shaku felt that Buddhism had as much to teach the West as Christianity had to teach the East.

Although Soyen Shaku made an appearance at the 1893 World Parliament of Religions in Chicago, he made little initial impression, largely because of his difficulties with the English language. His real impact on America began when he returned to the United States in 1905 and began instructing Mr. and Mrs. Alexander Russell of San Francisco in the ways of Zen, especially koan study. This was a great coup for the Russell family; no other Zen Master was teaching foreigners at the time. He also traveled from city to city lecturing, and becoming gradually convinced that Americans were ready to be instructed in Zen. In 1906 he published *Sermons of a Buddhist Abbot.* This selection of translations of talks that he had given to his American students is the first translation of any Zen work in the United States.

Curiously, he came to this country over the objections of his fellow monks and abbot, who felt that "the land of white barbarians" was beneath the dignity of a Zen Master. But Soyen Shaku felt that the true future of Zen lay in America, that Zen had grown corrupt, bureaucratic, and old in Japan. Upon embarking, he wrote in his journal:

> When the time comes
> A person rises to the occasion.
> Overcoming difficulties
> He sports as he masters his emotions.
> Resting his head on a staff of olive tree
> He gazes out on the vast sea.
> Monk's robe falling from his shoulders,
> Striding a great whale,
> His thoughts dwell constantly
> On this plan of one hundred years.
> How is he to announce himself, he wonders,
> This Buddhist disciple of non-self,
> As the blue mountains
> Of his destination draw near?

As a delegate to the 1893 World Parliament of Religions in Chicago, Soyen Shaku made many important Zen converts in the United States. His most important contact, however, was Paul Carus of Open Court Publishing, a great promoter of religious inquiry, who had emigrated to this country from Germany during the 1880s.

Sokei-an Sasaki (1882–1945)

Soyen Shaku's brother-in-Dharma (which means they shared the same teacher) was Sokei-an Sasaki, who first came to the United States in 1906. (His original name was Shigetsu Sasaki, and he had been trained as a dragon carver.) He returned to Japan in 1919 for more Zen training, was declared a Roshi in 1928, and finally went to New York, where he founded the Buddhist Society of America in 1931. The society became the Zen Institute of America in 1945, and was later renamed the First Zen Institute. Sokei-an married Ruth Fuller Everett in 1941, who was (not coincidentally) Alan Watt's mother-in-law. She is regarded as one of the first great American Buddhist women. Sokei-an, despite the fierce reputation of Rinzai Zen, was a gentle teacher, reporting in his later years that even five minutes of meditation was too much for most of his students. Sokei-an was interned during World War II. His health was irreparably damaged and he died in in 1945.

Dwight Goddard (1861–1939)

A former American Protestant missionary, Dwight Goddard, after converting to Zen Buddhism, used his missionary skills in attempting to found an American Buddhist monastic movement in the United States. He self-published the Buddhist Bible (American edition) 1934, a collection of both Theravada and Mahayana traditions. (This collection served as one introduction to Buddhism for Jack Kerouac and the Beat poets.) Two years later, Goddard established the Followers of Buddha, which he proposed as a celibate monastic movement with two monasteries, one in California and one in Vermont. Neither materialized.

D. T. Suzuki (1869–1966)

Diasetzu Teitaro Suzuki came to the United States in 1897 to work with Paul Carus as a translator at the Open Court Publishing Company in LaSalle, Illinois. Their association continued until 1909. Carus had originally asked Soyen Shaku, but the latter's poor English made him decline. He suggested instead his student Suzuki, whose English was excellent. Suzuki also helped Soyen Shaku spread the teachings of Zen, mostly by translating as Soyen taught. (Suzuki's Dharma name, Diasetzu, means "Great Stupidity," which means not "stupid" in the usual sense but having the ability to empty the mind in order to receive Enlightenment.)

Suzuki returned to Japan to study Buddhism further. In 1911 he married Beatrice Lane, an American Theosophist and graduate of Radcliffe. Suzuki came back to the United States in 1936, first to Hawaii and California, staying until the outbreak of the Second World War. Under the auspices of the Rockefeller Foundation, he returned to New York in 1950, when he was over eighty years old, and he taught Buddhism at Columbia University until 1957, when he retired.

Altogether, Suzuki wrote more than 100 works in both English and Japanese; he also founded the English-language *Eastern Buddhist* in 1927, which he and Lane edited together. He was also president of the Cambridge Buddhist Association. His lectures and books propelled him into popularity during the middle part of the twentieth century. His specialty seems to have been his ability to use language to explain the futility of language, a paradox that delighted and inspired his American audiences.

Although he was an essentially modest and shy man, Suzuki's influence spread beyond America, and many of the most brilliant minds of the

D. T. Suzuki. Courtesy of the Library of Congress

century were deeply influenced by him: John Cage, Erich Fromm, Allen Ginsberg, Karen Horney, Aldous Huxley, Carl Jung, Jack Kerouac, Thomas Merton, Gary Snyder, Arnold Toynbee, and Alan Watts, whom he met in England in 1936 when he was lecturing there. He was featured in the *New Yorker* and even, rather oddly, in *Vogue*.

Although Suzuki experienced *satori* while meditating on the famous *mu*-koan, technically he never received Dharma transmission, a Master's seal of approval authorizing him to transmit Dharma and to select a student to succeed him. He was neither a Zen priest nor a Zen Master. He thus technically represents a break with, rather than a continuation of, Soyen Shaku's lineage.

Nyogen Senzaki (1876–1958)

Nyogen Senzaki was born not in Japan but in Siberia, where it is said that a Japanese Shongon monk found him at the side of his mother's frozen body. The experience may have been responsible for his contracting a case of tuberculosis; luckily he was cured in the monastery. Because he was of mixed parentage, his prospects in racist Japan were grim. To save him from opprobrium, the monks decided to raise him themselves in the monastery. He began his religious life studying the esoteric Shingon system of his foster father, but also came under the influence of Soto Zen and studied Western, especially German, philosophy. (He was particularly fascinated by Immanuel Kant.)

One of Soyen Shaku's students, and brother-in-Dharma to D. T. Suzuki, Senzaki came to California in 1905, disillusioned (like his teacher Soyen Shaku) with the fossilized, materialistic state of Japanese Zen. He even compared Buddhist temples to chain stores. He also derided the Japanese military spirit, a spirit apparently supported by many Japanese Zen monasteries. Like Soyen Shaku, he stayed with the Russell family, and was especially impressed by Mrs. Russell, whom he considered a great friend of Buddhism.

He studied American culture for twenty years, forbidden by his Master to teach, or even, it is said, "utter the letter 'B' of Buddhism." It was a lonely time for him, for Senzaki had little command of English and spent his time doing hard, menial jobs. (He tried to make a living in the hotel business, but failed.) In 1925, the twenty years over, he set up what he called his "floating *zendo,*" so named because it had no settled abode. He laughingly called himself a "mushroom monk," rootless, and without flowers, branches, or seeds. (Interestingly, the name "Nyogen" means "no such person.") He was the first Zen teacher to set up permanent residence in the United States. Senzaki cautioned his students about taking Zen concepts too literally or seriously. Zen was experience, not intellectual conceptions, and Senzaki did very little formal teaching. He established *zendos* in both San Francisco and Los Angeles, remaining at the latter until he died. It was a peculiar sort of *zendo*—no statues of the Buddha, and meditations took place in chairs rather than on the customary cushions.

Senzaki was interned during World War II, along with many others, at the Heart Mountain relocation camp in Wyoming. While there, he started a *zendo* he called "The Meditation Hall of the Eastbound Teaching." He was struck by the way the Zen teaching seemed continually to move east—from China to Japan to California—and thence to Wyoming.

Like D. T. Suzuki, Nyogen Senzaki never received formal Dharma transmission from his Master, so he is not represented on the official Zen lineage charts. It is not clear what, if anything, Soyen Shaku had against Senzaki, but Robert Aitken, one of his pupils, suggests it may have been

Senzaki's outspoken denunciation of many aspects of Japanese Zen (which Soyen Shaku privately shared). Senzaki wore no robes, assumed no title, and attracted no glitzy crowd of American disciples. He even let his hair grow, to protect the Dharma, as he said "from ridicule," and he furnished his apartment in Western rather than Japanese style. But his spirit has had a lasting impact, for he showed that living Zen was as important as teaching it. He died on May 7, 1958. At his death a full-scale, seven-day *sesshin* was held in his honor—the first one in the United States.

Haku'un Yasutani (1885–1973)

Haku'un Yasutani entered a Rinzai temple when he was five years old; at eleven he transferred to a Soto temple and became a monk. He continued to study and write treatises on the Shobogenzo by Dogen, and at thirty he married and started a family. Marriage, or his profession as an elementary school teacher, however, did not interfere with Yasutani's interest in Buddhism, and in 1927 he attained *kensho*. His teacher, Dai'un Sogaku Harada, gave Yasutani Dharma transmission (*inka-shomei*) in 1943, when he was fifty-eight years old. Dai'un Harada (1871–1961), of the famously cold Hosshinji Monastery, was extremely influential in American Buddhism, though he never set foot in the United States. (Philip Kapleau, however, did study in Japan with him.) He was extraordinarily unusual in having received Dharma transmission from both the Soto and Rinzai schools. He shocked his Japanese Zen compatriots by giving lectures, rather than teaching nonverbally, in the traditional Soto method. He was also quite free with the encouragement stick. (Sometimes this Harada is confused with Shodo Harada. They are not the same. Shodo Harada was a Rinzai teacher.)

Although he never became a permanent resident, Yasutani made several teaching visits to the United States between 1962 and 1969, He taught a militaristic style of Zen reminiscent of the samurai tradition, which included long periods of silence and whacking poor sitters with the encouragement stick. Because of the close connection between them, Yasutani's school is often called the Harada-Yasutani school of Zen.

Yasutani continued to teach for the next thirty years, and his lineage includes such famous American Zen teachers as Philip Kapleau and Robert Aitken. Eventually, however, Yasutani broke from both Rinzai and Soto schools and founded his own Zen school, alongside the much larger Soto and Rinzai traditions, the Sanbo Kyodan ("Three Treasures Association" or "Order of the Three Treasures"). Sometimes, however, it is merely called the Harada-Ysutani-Yamada lineage, rather than a separate school.

Yasutani placed a balanced emphasis on koan and *zazen*. His students lived in their own homes, and kept their own jobs. He also incorporated the use of retreats to replace traditional monastic training, an innovation that made his school accessible to laypersons.

Yasutani is largely known to Zen students today through Philip Kapleau's *Three Pillars of Zen*, in which his lectures are featured. These lectures were themselves largely derived from Yasutani's own teacher. By the time of his death, he had left Dharma transmission to Koun Yamada in Japan and to Eido Tai Shimano and also to Philip Kapleau and Robert Aitken in America.

Eido Tai Shimano (b. 1932)

Eido Tai Shimano began his Zen career as a monk in the Rinzai Ryutakuji Monastery in Japan. He was encouraged to come to America in 1957, first to Hawaii and then to New York, where he revived the Zen Studies Society founded by D. T. Suzuki. He worked as a translator for Yasutani Roshi, but was given Dharma transmission by Nakagawa Soen. Eido Tai Shimano also founded the International Dai Bosatu Monastery in New York. He was one of the first to observe that the great turning point in America came about 1960, when Zen ceased to be primarily an intellectual pursuit and became a living practice.

Philip Kapleau (b. 1912)

Philip Kapleau, whose mother was Jewish and whose father was nominally Russian Orthodox, founded an Atheist's Club when he was thirteen years old. (This aspect of his religious sensibility never changed.) He became a court reporter and went to night school to become a lawyer, although ill health made him give up this dream. Although he was turned down for active service for the same reason during World War II, he did go to Nuremberg as a court reporter for the Department of Defense; in 1946 he went to Japan for the War Crimes Trials in Tokyo. This is when he first became interested in Zen, and he went to visit D. T. Suzuki, although he admitted the Master's ideas were too advanced for him at the time.

He was the first American student of Yasutani. He returned to the United States, and attended lectures at Columbia, but went back to Japan in 1953, where at age forty-one, he began formal Zen practice. He worked at it there for twelve years. He spent six months at Ryukuji Monastery with Nakagawa Soen, then studied for three more years with Harada at Hossinji, which was famous for its bitter weather and severe schedule. The harsh monastic life there caused Kapleau serious health problems, and he ended up as Yasutani's student (Harada's main Dharma heir) with his own living quarters. He was ordained as a monk by Yasutani in 1961. Kapleau received permission to teach from Yasutani (but was not given Dharma transmission) and returned to America in 1965.

In 1965 he wrote *The Three Pillars of Zen,* based upon the notes he took, with the special permission of his teacher, on the *dokusans* between him and Yasutani. (Kapleau's training as a court reporter must have come in handy for this endeavor.) This is the first book to describe Zen training, as opposed merely to Zen principles. It has since been translated into a dozen languages and has sold over a million copies.

In 1966 Kapleau founded the Rochester Zen Institute in Rochester, New York, which now has affiliates throughout the United States and Canada. The Zen center, which is most closely tied to the Rinzai tradition, uses English for services and adapts Western clothing. Kapleau's decision to translate the Heart Sutra into English caused a break between him and Yasutani in 1967. Yasutani has insisted that it only be chanted in Japanese. Because of the break between them, Kapleau never received full, formal Dharma transmission. This means that on the books, at least, the Rochester Zen Center is not part of any recognized Zen lineage, a serious matter in Zen circles. However, Kapleau's students remain deeply loyal to him, and point out that his purity of conduct and his degree of Enlightenment set him above many Zen teachers who have received Dharma transmission. Kapleau, now retired, left his own line of students, including Albert Low (b. 1928) and Michael Danan Henry (b. 1939), who now work with Robert Aitken.

Toni Packer (b. 1927)

Originally a student of Kapleau, half-Jewish, German-born Toni Packer broke with him in 1981. Although she was Kapleau's star pupil (he reportedly asked her to take over the Rochester Zen Center when he retired), she felt increasing doubts about Zen and its inaccessibility. She established her own independent center, The Springwater Center for Meditative Inquiry and Retreats, which is not only non-Zen, but even non-Buddhist. However, her meditative retreats, with their one-pointed attention to the "here and now," are definitely influenced by Buddhism. The split between Packer and Kapleau was not entirely amiable, although Kapleau retained his great regard for her. Still, as a result of her leaving, the Rochester Zen Center suffered, partly because Packer took many members with her. Others left because they were disillusioned with both sides. Today Packer maintains a strict nondenominational stance, and no longer identifies herself as a Buddhist, believing that such labels serve only to divide spiritual seekers. (This is a position with which the Buddha himself might have agreed.)

Nakagawa Soen (1907–84)

Nakagawa Soen first came into contact with Senzaki when the latter read his poems in a magazine. He spent a lot of time on top of a mountain scavenging berries and prostrating himself to the sun. In his spare time he wrote haiku. Soen Nakagawa arrived in the United States on April 8, 1947. Auspiciously, April 8 is the day Japanese Buddhists celebrate the birthday of the Buddha. He would have come to America sooner than he did, aided by contributions from Senzaki and his students, but was prevented by the outbreak of World War II. He spent the war in a temple at the base of Mt. Fuji. On the 21st of each month, Dai Bosatsu Day, he bowed across the ocean and mountains to Senzaki in his internment camp in Wyoming. Senzaki was doing exactly the same thing.

Soen Nakagawa was known for his eccentricities. Although he never formally took up residence in the United States, he did visit regularly. His students love to recount tales of his oddness, many of which revolve around the Japanese tea ceremony. He reportedly, on different occasions, performed the ceremony with instant coffee rather than tea, floating on the Dead Sea, and using imaginary bowls and tea. He also took his students on a nighttime walk outside Jerusalem, chanting loudly and reciting the famous *mu*-koan. Supposedly all the neighborhood dogs began to bark back at the MU! syllable, thus answering the koan for themselves. He would also don women's clothes from time to time. When Nakagawa Soen died at the Ryukuji Monastery in Japan, half his bones were buried there. The other half are buried in America.

Joshu Sasaki (b. 1907)

Joshu Sasaki came to the United States in 1962. Before that he had been a Rinzai monk and abbot at the Shoju-an Temple in Japan. His first *zendo* was his garage, but later he and his followers (incorporated as the Rinzai Zen Dojo) established the Cimarron Zen Center in Los Angeles in 1966 and Mt. Baldy Zen Center in 1971. He also established the Bodhi Manda Zen Center in New Mexico, which holds a major summer seminar for both scholars and practicing Buddhists. Today, Zen meditation centers in this tradition are spread throughout the United States, Canada, and Puerto Rico. In Joshu Sasaki's opinion, traditional Rinzai koans are not suited to the American temperament, and he replaced them with other exercises.

Maurine Stuart (1922–90)

Nakagawa Soen transmitted Dharma to five people. Four were male and Japanese. One, Maurine Stuart, was female and North American. Born in Saskatchewan, Canada, she was a concert pianist and head of the Cambridge Buddhist Association (CBA), an organization founded by Elsie Mitchell and others in 1957. (Interestingly, both women's introduction to Buddhism came from The *Story of Oriental Philosophy* by L. Adams Peck, a penname for Elizabeth Barrington. This well-written and accessible book, published in 1928, covered Hinduism, Confucianism, and Taoism, but it was the final chapter on Zen that caught Stuart's attention. She never afterward traveled without this volume.) She married an American by the name of Freedgood, and for many years used this name.

Stuart first studied under Yasutani Roshi, but encountered Soen Roshi in 1968, when he was a guest lecturer at the Zen Studies Society of which she was a member. It was, figuratively speaking, love at first sight. He gave her the Buddhist name Myoon, or "Subtle Sound," and informally and privately transmitted the Dharma to her. (Confusingly for some, Stuart was also ordained formally by Eido Roshi in 1977, and was given the Buddhist name Chico, or "Wisdom Light." Later the relationship between them soured, and Eido got into trouble amid allegations of sexual misconduct and financial mismanagement.)

Stuart was famous for visiting people in their own homes to teach Zen, and she conducted a class in *zazen* at the exclusive Exeter Academy in New Hampshire. She also led frequent all-women *sesshins,* which were hugely successful. Stuart maintained that there was not much difference between teaching Zen and teaching the piano. She said that just as the piano is an instrument for the music, the practitioner is the vehicle for Zen. However, she also believed that formal practice including *zazen, sesshin,* and *dokusan* was essential. Rather unusually for a Zen Master, Stuart never visited Japan, much less studied there. Two years after she died, her lineage was recognized by Robert Aitken and his Diamond Sangha, of the Rinzai Zen school.

Robert Aitken (b. 1917)

Robert Aitken was born in Philadelphia, but his family moved to Hawaii when he was five years old. He was introduced to Zen while spending three years in a POW camp in Japan during the Second World War. (He had been captured as a civilian the day after Pearl Harbor during his stint as a construction worker in Guam.) His experience as a POW was not the horrible ordeal that it was for many American prisoners. Although his diet was poor, there was no barbed wire and he was not forced to work. In fact, one camp, the former British Seaman's Mission, had a large, if somewhat outdated library, from which Aitken could nurture his passion for literature.

One day, a guard showed up waving a newly published book, R. H. Blyth's *Zen in English Literature and Oriental Classics.* Aitken read it straight through ten times. By happenstance, Reginald Blyth, born a British subject, was interned with Aitken in 1944 when all the prisoner camps around Kobe were combined. Blyth, a friend of D. T. Suzuki, became a tutor to Aitken, introducing him to essays by Suzuki and teaching him Japanese.

When the war was over, Aitken returned to Honolulu, ill and psychically damaged, although he continued to be interested in intellectual issues. He married in 1947, and moved to California, where he embarked on a course in Japanese studies at Berkeley. In the same year he met the Zen teacher Nyogen Senzaki (discussed earlier), who gave Aitken the Zen name Chotan, which means "Deep Pool." He also gave Aitken some practice in working on koans, but Senzaki's gentle style was not rigorous enough to meet Aitken's needs.

In 1950, Aitken, having completed his master's degree, received a $1,000 fellowship to study Zen in Japan. He went without his wife and son, and began his studies at the Engaku Temple in Kamakura, where Senzaki and D. T. Suzuki had both trained. At his first *sesshin,* he was introduced to the Japanese Zen practice of bowing before and after services. He found it unnerving, having previously been an intellectual rather than a traditionally practicing student of Zen. He soon changed monasteries, studying at Ryutakuji, where he became acquainted with Nakagawa Soen, a friend of Senzaki's and accomplished writer of haiku. The bowing practices still bothered him, however, and he got sick on a diet consisting largely of rice gruel and pickled radishes. (Later on, Aitken became a rather fervent admirer of bowing.) After contracting dysentery, he returned to Hawaii to deal with a failing marriage and subsequent divorce. He moved back to Los Angeles, got a job teaching English at Krishnamurti's Happy Valley School, and met his second wife, Anne Hopkins, whom he married in 1957. Anne eventually became a Zen Buddhist.

The two traveled to Japan on their honeymoon, and on their return to the United States, opened a Buddhist bookstore in Honolulu, where they had moved so that Aitken could be near his son. With his wife, Aitken founded the Diamond Sangha in Honolulu in 1959. (Aitken later opened a Zen center in Maui.) Although the original Sangha consisted only of the Aitkens and one other couple sitting *zazen,* it grew rapidly. Their center was part of the Harada-Yasutani school of Zen, the Order of the Three Treasures (Sanbo Kyodan). This order was established by Haku'un Yasutani in Kamakura, Japan, in 1954. (As mentioned above, Harada was Yasutani's own teacher. He was a Soto Zen Master who placed much more emphasis on *kensho,* a first experience of enlightenment, than is usual in this school, and which connects him more closely with the Rinzai school.) This school is an independent sect of Zen, having officially broken with the Soto tradition from which it emerged.

The Aitkens also began the *Diamond Sangha Newsletter.* The name comes from the great Diamond Sutra—and also from Diamond Head on Wakiki Beach. From 1962 to 1969 Aitken worked for the University of Hawaii; he also became active in the anti–Vietnam War effort. In 1969 Aitken retired from the University of Hawaii and moved to Maui to begin the Maui Zendo. The *zendo* became famous locally, and much to the Aitkens' consternation, the local police and other officials sent troublemakers, drug addicts, and mentally disturbed people to the *zendo* for the Aitkens to take care of.

While routine in the Maui Zendo was strict, the Aitkens made many adaptations to American sensibilities. They provided English translations of the sutras and started an experimental kitchen to test recipes. (Aitken's own unhappy experience with the traditional Zen monastery diet of gruel and pickled radishes may have given him the idea.) In addition, the Maui Zendo has dropped the traditional *jukai* ceremony, celebrated when a student passes the famous *mu*-koan. The Aitkens thought it prompted too much competition.

Aitken received Dharma transmission from the Japanese Master Yamada Koun in 1974, the only Westerner so honored by this Roshi.

However, Aitken never took monastic vows, continuing to live as a married person until the death of his wife Anne. His Sangha thus represents a lay stream of Zen, which includes both Soto and Rinzai aspects. It uses English in its rituals, is not authoritarian, and gives full equality to women. Aitken's specialty is Buddhist ethics. (Rather unsurprisingly, Aitken's dedication to peace and total nonviolence caused him to be investigated by the FBI during the 1950s.)

In 1986, after several difficult years, the Maui Zendo was sold, and the Diamond Sangha purchased property in Palolo Valley to begin anew. Aitken has given full transmission as independent Masters to Nelson Foster of the Honolulu Diamond Sangha and Ring of Bone Zendo in Nevada City, California; Patrick Hawk of the Zen Desert Sangha in Tucson, Arizona, and Mountain Cloud Zen Center in Santa Fe, New Mexico; Joseph Bobrow of Harbor Sangha in San Francisco, California; and Jack Duffy of the Three Treasures Sangha in Seattle, Washington. Other Sanghas were established around the world, including Argentina, New Zealand, and Australia. However, in 1999 John Tarrant of the Pacific Zen Institute in Santa Rosa, California, removed himself and his California Sangha from the Diamond Sangha and founded the well-known Pacific Zen Institute.

One of the more notable things about Aitken's career is the large number of Roshis under whom he studied, each for varying lengths of time. His experience with a broad range of Zen styles and traditions has stood him in good stead over the years.

According to Helen Tworkov, longtime editor of *Tricycle,* Aitken is the "unofficial American dean of Zen." He was also a founder of the Buddhist Peace Fellowship (BPF) in 1978, an affiliate of the Fellowship of Reconciliation. Aitken "updates" Buddhist principles to make them relevant in today's world. He once observed that the Buddha did not live in a time when the world was threatened by imminent extinction. He is a radical pacifist, and has demonstrated against everything militaristic, from the draft to Trident submarines, and he steadfastly withholds that part of his income tax that he believes goes into the military budget. However, Aitken does keep his peace activities and his Zen activities as somewhat separate enterprises. Zen students are invited but never coerced into participating in actions undertaken by the BPF. Even during the drug-infested 1970s, Aitken kept himself true to his Buddhist vows about nonuse of intoxicants and insisted his students do the same.

For Aitken, peace activities and *zazen* are closely connected. *Zazen* serves to quiet, collect, and strengthen the mind. Without his daily sitting practice, Aitken believes he would have burned out long ago. He assiduously insists on that aspect of practice for his students.

Aitken aroused some controversy among both Buddhists and Christians when he gave Dharma transmission to one of his students, Father Patrick Hawk, who was a Catholic priest. Among Buddhists, he was roundly criticized by Philip Kapleau, among others, who believes that the teachings of the two traditions, especially in regard to the no-self doctrine, are incompatible. Followers of Aitken merely point out that Kapleau never formally received Dharma transmission himself and suggest obliquely that some sour grapes may be involved. Among Zen Roshis, Bernard Glassman, Seung Sahn, and Jiyu Kennett have also given ordination or Dharma transmission to Christian clergy. This is a practice begun by Yamada Roshi. Yamada's teacher, Yasutani, did not approve of the practice.

Shunryu Suzuki (1904–71)

Shunryu Suzuki ("Crooked Cucumber") is sometimes confused with D. T. Suzuki, but there is no relation between them. For one thing, Shunryu Suzuki was of the Soto school, while D. T. Suzuki was Rinzai. Shunryu studied at Eiheji ("Temple of Eternal Peace"), one of the "great root monasteries" of the Soto Zen tradition. Dogen founded this beautiful temple and monastery in the thirteenth century; in fact, he is buried there. Here Shunryu learned not only how to meditate, but how to sweep, walk, clean, and fold his clothes. This emphasizes more than anything how much of Zen is not just religious practice, but a way of life. (For example, there is no Catholic or Protestant or Jewish way of sweeping, walking, or folding clothes—but there is a Soto Zen way.) Shunryu Suzuki was an opponent of Japan's entry into the Second World War, a stand that alienated him from the Zen establishment.

In obedience to a long-felt dream, Shunryu Suzuki came to the United States in 1959. He originally came to America with a three-year appointment to Sokoji, a Soto Zen temple on Bush Street in San Francisco's "Japantown," originally built as a synagogue. The temple had been founded in 1934 by Hosen Isobe, a Soto missionary. Suzuki's mandate was to serve the Japanese immigrant community, but he soon found that he had more success among Americans, especially when it came to *zazen,* or sitting meditation. Americans seemed willing to show up at 5:40 A.M. to begin sitting, although less willing to actually become monks. This seemed to puzzle Suzuki, who once commented, "You Americans are not quite monks and not quite laypeople." This indeed, is part of the American Buddhist dilemma.

One of his motives was to bring the best of Japanese culture to America. Discouraged by the masses of junk targeted for export to America, Suzuki felt it was important to let Americans have a chance to experience something truly Japanese—not the cheaply painted cups and umbrellas that passed for Japanese craft. Suzuki often spoke of Zen as the art of seeing "things-as-it-is." (He used this apparently ungrammatical phrase deliberately.) He taught that as soon as we begin to intellectualize about something, we are no longer seeing that thing in its pure state. Instead, we see a distortion created by our own minds.

One of the great concepts that Suzuki brought to the West was that of "beginner's mind." He came upon the idea by accident, when, as a young man in Japan, he was engaged as translator to a formidable Englishwoman, Miss Nona Ransom. Miss Ransom, a Quaker, had no knowledge of Buddhism and no particular desire to learn until she observed Suzuki's attentions to a small Buddha image she kept in her residence (as an artwork, not an object of veneration). When she asked him why he paid such profound respect to an idol, Suzuki took the opportunity to explain the idea that the statue was a mere reminder of the Buddha-nature that exists everywhere. Miss Ransom became increasingly impressed with Buddhism and eventually started sitting *zazen* herself. Thus Suzuki became aware that a "beginner's mind" could grasp the essential components of Buddhism perhaps more easily than those who had had years of exposure to the outward forms of the tradition. He thought that the essence of Zen was "just-sitting" and objected when his students thought they should "get" something from it. He felt meditation was its own reward. He was also a great proponent of ceremonial bowing, which he thought was good practice for self-centered Americans.

Suzuki was fascinated with the openness of the American mind to Zen precepts, and the famous edition of his talks, *Zen Mind, Beginner's Mind,* is a perennial best-seller. He is also the author of *Branching Streams Flow in the Darkness: Zen Talks on the Sandokai.*

Shunryu Suzuki founded the San Francisco Zen Center (SFZC) in 1962, an institution that became a crucible of ideas and movements during the 1960s counterculture revolution. It is so famous that it is usually known simply as the "Zen Center." In 1966, the San Francisco Zen Center acquired an old country resort in Tassajara Hot Springs (now Zen

Mind Temple), a former residential hotel at 300 Page Street (now Beginner's Mind Temple), and Green Gulch Farm (now Green Dragon Temple) in Marin County in 1972. In 1969, the Zen Center, with its largely American membership, left Sokoji for good, keeping it as a parish for its original Japanese community.

Other teachers associated with SFZC (although some have moved to found other Zen institutes) have included Zentatsu Richard Baker, Dainin Katagiri, Tenshin Reb Anderson, Sojun Mel Weitsman, Zoketsu Norman Fischer, Zenkei Blanche Hartman, and Jiko Linda Cutts. (Note that the American Roshi all have adopted Japanese names in addition to their American birth names.) Danin Katagiri (1928–90) came from Japan in 1964 and was a great help to Shunryu Suzuki. He founded his own *zendo* in Minneapolis after Suzuki's 1971 death from liver cancer.

One of the most interesting members of the Zen Center was surely Tommy Issan Dorsey (1933–90), a former drag queen and drug user, who became an honored Soto Zen Roshi ministering to gays. Some considered him to be a bodhisattva, and he was known more for his caring ministry than for any particular teaching. For many years he was abbot of the Hartford Street Zen Center.

Jakusho Kwong (b. 1935)

Jakusho ("Bill") Kwong is a Chinese American, born in Santa Rosa, near Sonoma Mountain, California, the present home of his Zen center, called Genjoji, "the Way of Everyday Life." His parents were illegal immigrants from Canton, and Kwong grew up under a severe, exacting physician father who insisted that he get a Chinese as well as an American education. Kwong rebelled, however, and was eventually released from the torture of his father's teaching. He worked hard for commercial flower growers, and later regarded the endless, backbreaking toil as a kind of training for Zen. When he became old enough, Kwong enrolled in the commercial art course at San Jose State College, where he met his future wife Laura, another Chinese American. They were married in 1957.

Jakusho Kwong's Zen training has taken place entirely in the United States, and he came to Zen through art, which appealed to him through its stark and simple beauty. He visited Sokoji Temple in San Francisco, presided over by Shunryu Suzuki, but at first found it, with its high wooden pews, too much like a church, and not enough like a Zen temple for his liking. However, he returned again and again, and in 1960 was given the *rakusu,* or monk's bib, at the *jukai* ceremony. (In 1970 Laura also went through the *jukai* ceremony.)

Kwong was eventually made *tenzo,* or monastery cook, a job offered only to senior monks. In the fall of 1970 Suzuki appointed Kwong as head monk at the Tassajara Center, and died the following year. Kwong has stated that Suzuki made him his Dharma heir, although no handwritten document exists. For some Zen followers of Suzuki, this clearly meant that their teacher had not intended Kwong to be his Dharma heir. However, the issue is disputed, and Suzuki may simply have died before he was able to formally transmit the Dharma. Kwong was, however, able to carry on his priestly duties at the Mill Valley Zendo where he had been officiating, but he was not permitted to teach. (Roshi Richard Baker was established as Suzuki's Dharma heir, and was ordained in the Mountain Seat Ceremony two weeks before Suzuki died. At the time Baker was one of only seven Americans who had received recognized Dharma transmission.)

These events combined to produce a schism between the San Francisco Zen Center and Kwong. In 1973, Kwong moved to Sonoma, and relinquished all ties with the San Francisco Zen Center. Several years later, he received Dharma transmission from Suzuki's son, Hoichi in Japan, although there remained some ambiguity about Hoichi's ability to confer it.

In the tradition of classic Soto Zen, *zazen* lies at the heart of Kwong's practice, and it is considered an expression of Enlightenment, not simply the path to Enlightenment. However, Kwong realizes that *zazen* is not suitable to all persons, and he also offers walking meditations, chanting, and ritual bowing as additional kinds of meditation. Kwong had little patience with Beat poet Jack Kerouac's brand of Buddhism, which he regarded as rootless and undisciplined. (Jack Kerouac is discussed in chapter 4.)

Kwong's Sonoma Zen Center is rural, austere, and rigorous. Full-time residents may work, but the meditation hours are demanding. Few people in the United States are able to make the traditional sacrifice of a career in order to become a monk. Most people do only temporary residencies at Sonoma. Kwong emphasizes the crucial role the Sangha plays in Buddhism, as it helps develop compassion. Solitary practitioners still have what he calls "rough edges." He acknowledges, however, that the Sangha is the most difficult of the three traditional refuges for American Buddhists to accept. This is one reason why he offers a month-long retreat in July for group practice.

Kongo Langlois (b. 1935)

Kongo Langlois began his spiritual search in the Hindu tradition, but switched to Zen Buddhism in 1960 when he met Soyu Matuoka, who founded the Zen Buddhist Temple of Chicago in 1949. He was ordained a Soto priest in 1967, and in 1970 received Dharma transmission and was appointed abbot of the temple, after Matsuoka left for California. In 1976, he was given the title of Roshi, and in 1987 was given *inka* in the Rinzai school by Asahina Sogen. Despite his high accomplishment, Langlois seems to stand aside from the main currents of Zen Buddhism in the United States, and as a result is somewhat unknown outside his immediate circle.

Richard Baker (b. 1936)

Richard Baker was born in Biddeford, Maine, of scholarly parents and an influential family. (His father taught at Harvard and his mother was a poet.) Baker attended Harvard, majoring in European history and architecture, but considered himself, and was considered by others, an "outsider." He left Harvard for a year and joined the merchant marine but later returned to Far Eastern studies at Harvard. In 1960 Baker took a bus to San Francisco. He got a job in a book distribution center, and went looking for a Zen Master. He met Shunryu Suzuki. Baker would say later that he was not studying Zen Buddhism—he was studying Suzuki. One reason the two "clicked" was that Suzuki felt he had no time to "prepare" anyone, but felt that Baker, with his rich background of New England Transcendentalism, came already prepared. In 1966, just before the opening of the Tassajara Monastery, he made Baker a priest and gave him the Buddhist name of Zentatsu Myoyu.

Baker returned to school at the University of California at Berkeley, studying, among other things, Asian history. He also organized the first LSD conference in 1966, although Baker himself was not a serious LSD user. Like many others, he felt the use of drugs to attain Enlightenment an interesting theory. Later he came to view LSD and other psychedelic drugs as obstacles to wisdom and counseled against their use.

In 1968 Baker and his family went to Japan to study (and to gain Zen prestige and authority, which was at the time awarded only to those who had studied in Japan). The family stayed at first in poet and Zen scholar Gary Snyder's home. Baker did not return permanently to the United States until 1971.

As mentioned earlier, Baker was ordained as Suzuki's Dharma heir and served as abbot of the Zen Center from 1971 to 1983. Dharma transmission, by the way, is just as much about temporal power as it is about spiritual enlightenment. Two weeks after Baker was installed as abbot, Suzuki died. He was the second Western abbot of Buddhist monastery (Peggy Jiyu Kennett being the first), but Baker had a keener talent for publicity and became much better known.

Under his leadership, the Zen Center grew at an almost frenetic pace, going from an annual budget of $6,000 to $4 million in fifteen years. He was instrumental in the Zen Center's purchase of Tassajara Zen Mountain Center (he first encountered the spot on a camping trip), which become the first truly American Zen monastery, and the 115-acre Green Gulch Farm, the last against the wishes of most senior members of the center. Altogether, the center's properties were worth about $20 million. Green Gulch proved to be a success, however, particularly with California Governor Jerry Brown, who liked to hold private parties there. Baker also helped set up the profitable vegetarian Greens Restaurant at Fort Mason and the Tassajara Bakery in San Francisco, as well as the Alaya Stitchery and the Green Gulch Greengrocery. More conventionally, Green Gulch included the Shunryu Suzuki Study Center, which offered classes and conducted lecture/seminars. In *his* mind, Baker is responsible for creating the entire Zen Center, although he gives Suzuki credit for creating the teaching. In his own teaching, Baker emphasized the yogic aspect of Zen, as well as its relevance to contemporary social issues, especially the antinuclear movement.

Baker's charismatic, energetic personality made many things possible, but also created difficulties for him and the Zen Center. Baker did not choose an abstemious lifestyle as abbot of the Zen Center. He possessed an enormous number of robes (a large collection for each location), as well as a large number of books (the same ones for each location), plus a white BMW that cost $21,000 in 1980. His daughter received $10,000 to go to college. He grew aloof from most of the students, traveled a great deal, and was seldom available to help disciples with their practice. Most dangerously, he fell in love with a married woman he claimed was a friend, but whom others regarded as his student.

Baker came under pressure from the community to resign as abbot in December 1983 amid allegations of sexual misconduct and abuse of power, both physical and psychological. His finances were also questioned. This was the first time that the community of a Zen center took matters into its own hands over the wishes of its abbot. While Zen has the

Green Gulch Farm overview. San Francisco Zen Center.

reputation of being antiauthoritarian, in actual practice, Zen abbots often retain a viselike control over their institutions.

Baker supposedly walked 120 miles to Tassajara, but reports differ about how far he actually walked (some say he hitched a ride) and the reason for the walk in the first place. Some claimed that the walk was penance for his actions, although Baker himself denied it. (He did write a letter of apology, however.) He left the center and was replaced by Reb Anderson.

Presently Baker is the spiritual head of Dharma Sangha with locations in Colorado and Germany. He still teaches and lectures, although his writing output has been small. The uproar caused by the whole affair was considerable and had long-lasting effects. Many students sided with Baker and left. The remaining members were left in turmoil. In July 1987 Baker gave Dharma transmission to Philip Whalen, one of the Beat poets. Today Whalen is abbot of the Hartford Street Zen Center in San Francisco, which ministers primarily to gay men.

Although the Zen Center had only two abbots in its first twenty-one years, between 1983 and 2000, it installed several, including Dainin Katagiri

(1984–85), Tenshin Reb Anderson (1986–95), Sojun Mel Weitsman (1988–97), and Zoketsu Norman Fisher (installed 1995).

Like Richard Baker, Reb Anderson had been a student of Shunryu Suzuki; however, he received Dharma transmission from Baker, Suzuki's successor. Anderson himself got into trouble when he chased a man he thought had mugged him into a house and pulled a gun on him. He said he had gotten the gun from a suicide victim he had happened across in Golden Gate Park four years before. (No one seems to have noticed the body, although Anderson claimed he had meditated by it for three days, an old Buddhist practice. It is not a Buddhist practice, however, to chase would-be assailants down the street with a gun.) The police, understandably puzzled by the whole episode, charged Anderson with displaying a weapon in public. The entire episode is so bizarre that further comment seems superfluous. Anderson was placed on six months' administrative leave, and to forestall the development of any more problems with a single wayward abbot, SFZC installed two abbots at the same time, first Anderson and Weitzman (who was also abbot of the Berkeley Zen Center) and then Norman Fischer and Blanche Hartman. Currently the co-abbess is Jiko Linda Cutts, who was installed in 2000.

Hakuyu Taizan Maezumi (1931–95)

Like Shunryu Suzuki, Hakuyu Maezumi was a Soto Zen Buddhist and son of a priest. (He was ordained in the Soto lineage at the age of eleven and received Dharma transmission from Hakujun Kuroda.) However, he also received Dharma transmission from Rinzai Masters, studying koans with lay Rinzai Master Koryu Osaka in Tokyo, from whom he received *inka*. Because of his unusual and ecumenical training, Maezumi never adhered to the Soto tradition alone.

Maezumi arrived in Los Angeles in 1956 to work at the Soto Zenshuji temple, which was the headquarters of the American Soto school, but which at the time catered only to Japanese Americans. In 1969 Maezumi founded the Zen Center of Los Angeles (ZCLA), attracting many American followers. This center continues to be extremely influential, having as many as fifty affiliates. During this time he also became a disciple of Haku'un Yasutani, and in 1970 he received Dharma transmission from him as well (in Japan). Thus Maezumi had Dharma transmission from three teachers in three different lineages (all of which were imported to the United States), a highly unusual accomplishment.

In 1976, Maezumi founded the Kuroda Institute for the Study of Human Values, which advances Buddhist scholarship. Maezumi also established the White Plum Sangha, a student association dedicated to spreading Dharma throughout the country. Important figures associated with the White Plum Sangha include Charlotte Joko Beck, Jan Chozen Bays, and John Daido Loori. Altogether Maezumi had twelve Western Dharma heirs; besides those previously listed are Bernard Glassman, Dennis Genpo Merzel, Gerry Shishin Wick, John Tesshin Anderson, Nicolee Jiyo Miller-McMahon, and William Nyogen Yeo.

Maezumi, true to his "double training" emphasized both *shikantasza* ("just-sitting") and koan study, in much the same way Dai'un Harada had done. Altogether, Maezumi founded six temples across the United States and Europe, which are formally allied with the Soto Zen headquarters in Japan.

Maezumi was not an abstemious monk, and his indulgence in both women and alcohol caused a crisis in the ZCLA. There were also questions about money. Eventually Maezumi entered an alcohol treatment program, but a great deal of damage had already been done to his school. Maezumi died rather suddenly in Tokyo, at age sixty-four. Before his death, Maezumi gave Dharma transmission (*inka*) to Bernard Tetsugen Glassman, who succeeded Maezumi, Dennis Merzel, Charlotte Joko Beck, Jan Chozen Bays, and John Loori, among others. His third Dharma heir, Charlotte Joko Beck, began practicing with Maezumi in 1965. In 1983, she left ZCLA and began her own center in San Diego. A year later she gave up her robes, and she claims no special title.

Maezumi's fourth Dharma heir, Sensei Jan Chozen Bays, began practicing with Maezumi at the ZCLA in 1973. She was a married woman with three young children, but Maezumi made sufficient alterations in his teaching methods to allow her to practice as fully as possible. Bays was one of the people with whom Maezumi had sex, although she says it was a very minor part of their relationship. This opinion was not shared by either her husband or Maezumi's American wife, and neither marriage survived the scandal. Currently she teaches semi-independently at the Zen Community of Oregon in Portland.

Bernard Tetsugen Glassman (b. 1939)

One of Maezumi's first, and subsequently chief, students was Bernard Glassman (universally known as "Bernie," despite his Zen name of Tetsugen,

Bernard Glassman. Don Farber Photography.

"One Who Penetrates All Subtleties"), who was born of Jewish immigrant parents in Brooklyn, New York. Glassman began studying with Maezumi in 1968, and completed his koan study in 1976. To do so, he had moved himself and his family, consisting of his wife Helen and two children, into Maezumi's Zen Center of Los Angeles in 1971. At the time he was working on his Ph.D. in applied mathematics and helping McDonnell-Douglas develop a proposed interplanetary shuttle system. In 1976 he decided to devote himself full-time to Buddhist practice and administering the ZCLA.

Glassman eventually experienced two *dai kenshos,* and received Dharma transmission at two Soto temples in Japan: Eihei-ji and Sojiji. He is the first American Zen Master to have completed koan study and also to have been ordained as Zen priest. He received *inka* in 1995, shortly before Maezumi's death. Glassman's first *kensho* occurred in 1970, very early in his training while studying the *mu*-koan under the direction of Osaka Koryu Roshi. Glassman's second *kensho* occurred a year later, when he was still working at McDonnell-Douglas. He was studying the *mu*-koan with Maezumi, and had a breakthrough in a carpool. The other members of the carpool thought he was having an attack of some sort. (The earlier *kensho* seemed to have a much more peaceful effect, in which Glassman felt his oneness with all beings, including a tree. This *kenso,* too, however, involved a lot of hugging and crying.) In 1979, at the request of Maezumi, he opened the Zen Community of New York (ZCNY), as both spiritual head (abbot) and general director.

Glassman sees incorporation of Buddhism and social activism as a top priority. He has worked to establish clinics, bakeries, and other services (which are also profitable) for the poor. He founded the Zen Community of New York and the Zen Peacemaker Order (along with his wife Roshi Sandra Jishu Holmes). The three major principles of the Zen Peacemaker Order are "not-knowing"; "just-sitting," or *shikantataza*; and the "way of enlightenment," or *butsudo*. In fact, he often equates "just-sitting" with "bearing witness."

Glassman retains some of the most conservative elements of Zen customs, such as having personal attendants, yet he is also willing to drive the bread vans and place meditation cushions in circles. He favors work practice over traditional *zazen* and koan study, stating that the latter do not provide him sufficient interaction with his students. He considers work a fully Zen form of training, not just to make a living. Nor does he find any disconnect between Zen practice and the business or corporate structure of America. He says that his Zen bakery may look like any other bakery on the outside, but that "inside" it is different.

Because of his positive attitude toward the world of business and his unusual combination of ancient Japanese ways with contemporary America, Glassman naturally invites criticism from both "liberal" and "conservative" Zen camps. Glassman is an autocratic leader, holding fast to the importance of his lineage. While he believes that the Sangha is indeed a true community, he also considers the true Sangha to be an *enlightened and committed* group, not just a random collection of people who wander in for a weekend retreat.

One of Glassman's most interesting exploits was the ZCNY's purchase of Greyston, a twenty-six-room mansion built in 1868 by James Renwick Jr. The mansion made an odd sort of *zendo*; in fact, some people began to call it the "Zen Hilton." Glassman was formally installed as abbot at Greyston on June 6, 1982, in an elaborate, very traditional ceremony, known as *shinsanshiki,* which included the formal "stepping down the mountain" of Maezumi Roshi in order to make room for his Dharma heir. (The Greyston was sold in 1988 and the community moved north to Yonkers.)

Glassman is famous for founding, along with his late wife Anne, the Zen Peacemaker Order (ZPO), whose primary tenets include "not-knowing," "bearing witness," and "healing." (The complete list is offered in chapter 7). "Not-knowing" refers to a state of open-mindedness, doubt, and avoidance of fixed opinions. It has even been called "Zen agnosticisim." "Bearing witness" is strongly connected with the concept of "engaged Buddhism" and is associated with Glassman's famous "plunges" into the darkest and most poverty-stricken corners of the American landscape. The third concept of "healing" refers to the healing of the entire world, but always beginning at home. (This is one reason why he chose Yonkers for his community headquarters.)

Glassman's latest enterprise has been his establishment of the Order of Dis-Order in 1999. (The acronym is OD.) Glassman took up the study of clowning under a mentor, Mr. YooWho, alias Moshe Cohen, the American Coordinator of Clowns Without Borders. He remarks that he finds putting on a red nose liberating, and often visualizes those with whom he is speaking as also having a red nose. He says it gives one an entirely different perspective—in fact, the motto of the OD is "Not Being Here Now." He also called the group the OD Peacemakers. Currently Glassman is working on developing an order of minstrels.

One of Glassman's most important achievements in American Zen Buddhism is the dialogue he has managed to undertake with members of other faiths, including Judaism, Islam, and, most particularly, Catholicism.

John Daido Loori

John Daido Loori is currently resident abbot of the Zen Mountain Monastery in Mt. Tremper, New York, a residential retreat center, Zen monastery, and training center for both lay and monastic men and women. It has its own publication company, Dharma Communications (DC), a nonprofit educational corporation. DC publishes the quarterly *Mountain Record Journal,* and operates the DC press, DC Video, DC Audio, DC Interactive Multimedia, Dharma Telecommunications, and even a monastery store. In addition, the monastery runs a prison program and a Zen environmental studies center. It is also the heart of an umbrella organization called the Mountains and Rivers Order (MRO), a name that stems from Ch'ing-yüan Wei-hsin's writings.

Loori began as food chemist and amateur photographer, and the latter occupation led him to study Zen art and meditation. He was ordained in 1977, and bought the land on which the Zen Mountain Center now stands. Like his teacher Maezumi, Loori is proficient in both *shikantasza* ("just-sitting") and koan study. He has received transmission in both the Rinzai as well as Soto lines of Zen Buddhism.

He is a prolific author, having written *Mountain Record of Zen Talks, Eight Gates of Gates, Still Point, Two Arrows Meeting in Mid-Air,* and *The Heart of Being: Moral and Ethical Teachings of Zen Buddhism.* He has developed a training program at the monastery based on what he calls the "Eight Gates" of Buddhism: *zazen,* personal relationship with a teacher, study, liturgy, precepts, art practice, body practice, and work practice.

Peggy Kennett (1925–96)

Curiously, the first true American Zen Master was an Englishwoman. Born into a conservative Christian family, Peggy Theresa Nancy Kennett was first drawn to Buddhism when a classmate brought in a statue of the Buddha to her schoolroom. Not believing that she had a future as an English Buddhist, however, Kennett sought to fulfill her spirituality by participating actively in the Church of England, hoping eventually to be ordained, an impossibility for women in the Anglican Church during the 1940s. Kennett also took degrees in music from the University of Durham and served in the Royal Navy.

Kennett lost the minor ecclesiastical post she had held ("just for being a woman," she said later), and devoted herself full-time to learning about Buddhism, first as a Theravadin, then, inspired by D. T. Suzuki, who visited the country, as a practitioner of Zen. She also met Chisan Kho, the abbot of the Sojiji Monastery, when he came to England. He invited her to Japan and she agreed. Like Dogen before her, Kennett began to travel in search of Dharma. She was thirty-six years old.

Kennett was ordained as a Rinzai priest in 1960 in a Chinese temple in Malaysia. She then went on to Japan, where she studied with Chisan Koho Zenji, abbot of the Soto Sojiji Temple. Her Buddhist name was T'su Yu, "Compassionate Friend." (In Japanese, the name was pronounced "Jiyu.")

Kennett became the first Westerner and first woman to achieve the distinction of receiving ordination in both Rinzai and Soto traditions, an extremely rare and difficult feat for anyone even now. In fact, she was the first woman to study at the Sojiji Temple since the fourteenth century. The fact that she was the only foreigner and the only woman in the temple did not disturb her unduly: she regarded the entire situation as her koan—a seemingly impossible riddle to be solved. Despite prejudice and hardship, Kennett persisted in her practice; after only six months in the monastery she attained her first *kensho*. In 1963, she received Dharma transmission and became a Roshi, a Zen Master entitled to teach others.

In obedience to her vision, after the death of Chisan Koho Zenji, Kennett traveled to the United States in 1969 with two of her Western disciples, and established the Zen Mission Society. A year later, she founded the Shasta Abbey (first called "The Reformed Soto Zen Church") in northern California, a seminary for Zen monks. It was in fact an outgrowth of the Zen Mission Society in Japan, which in 1978 changed its name to the Order of Buddhist Contemplatives. She used a method derived from both the Rinzai and Soto traditions.

Kennett introduced a number of changes into her Zen Buddhist seminary, for which many traditionalists chastised her. Her monks use knives and forks rather than chopsticks, and she preferred carpets to the traditional mats. In addition, she designed nontraditional robes for her students. (Her father had been a tailor.) The new robes were brown rather than traditional black, because in Kennett's mind, white skin and black robes made an unhealthy-looking contrast.

More important, her language seems to be more sympathetic to the Western concept of a personal god than is acceptable in classical Zen, and she passed on Dharma transmission to a much higher number of her monks than is usual—over 100 of them. (Her new Roshis, however, have been more wary about handing over Dharma transmission.) Also, in contradiction to the Soto tradition (but not Rinzai), Kennett maintained that only celibate monks had a real chance at Enlightenment; people mired in relationships were too distracted by them. This belief also goes back to Theravada Buddhism, but Kennett received this message directly during her third *kensho,* or enlightening vision. This in itself was unusual. Most Zen Masters have had one or at most two *kenshos*. Kennett had four. (She had illustrations of them drawn up on the wall of the ceremony hall at Mt. Shasta.) She saw golden Buddhas, balls of light, ribbons of light, and Shakaymuni Buddha himself. She also saw herself as a sad, lovely woman of the previous century. Kennett was criticized for these visons, even by her own disciples. They are not common or expected in Zen meditation, and are often regarded as *makyo,* or illusions of the senses. Kennett continued to have them.

Kennett died in 1996, and despite her spiritual achievements, always claimed matter-of-factly: "There is nothing special about me; I am neither holy nor unholy, enlightened nor unenlightened. I was born Peg Kennett and I will die Peg Kennett." Jiyu Kennett is one of the few women Roshis in the Soto tradition.

The Very Special Case of the Beat Poets

While the Beat poets own the honor of introducing the idea of Buddhism to the American public at large, they stand outside the main tradition of Zen Buddhism as it has grown roots in this country. (The exception is the poet Gary Snyder, who is a serious Zen Buddhist by any standard.) In fact, the Beat poet brand of Buddhism is sometimes referred to as "lunatic Zen." It took its inspiration from Zen, but was not part of any recognized school, nor did it found its own school. Of course, it would not have been in the spirit of Beat to do such a thing anyway. The Beats were mostly attracted to Zen by its spirit of rebellion, spontaneity, and unorthodoxy, rather than for its deeper insights. The Buddhism of the Beat Generation, again with the exception of Snyder, belongs more to the world of literature than to religion. The primary example is Jack Kerouac's *The Dharma Bums,* based largely on the experiences of Snyder.

Alan Watts (1915–73)

Born into a Fundamentalist English family, Alan Watts was one of the most famous Western Buddhists of the 1960s. He never went to a university, but read voraciously and studied Buddhism with Christmas Humphreys and other prominent British Buddhists. The Indian philosopher Krishnamurti, who came out of the Hindu tradition, also influenced him.

Watts came to New York in 1938 with his wife and mother-in-law, Ruth Fuller Everett (1883–1967). All worked with Sokei-an Sasaki, and Ruth Fuller Everett married the latter in 1944. Ruth Fuller Everett Sasaki, who became a Rinzai priest in Japan, is an interesting figure in her own right, a Western woman who insisted upon a completely Japanese style of Zen. (Her Dharma name was Eryu, or "Dragon Wisdom.")

In the 1940s Watts became an Episcopal minster, and published his immensely popular *The Way of Zen* in 1957. (Watts also wrote about the Taoist tradition.) The main Buddhist idea that Watts grabbed hold of and expounded upon was the concept of *anatta,* or "un-soulness." He felt that the idea of an individual ego was the main problem with Western philosophy.

Although Watts is sometimes associated with the Beat poets, and he was friends with some of them, he never approved of their appearance or lifestyle, especially their use of marijuana. However, he did share their rebellious attitude, particularly in regard to sex.

One of Watts's most influential works was an essay entitled "Beat Zen, Square Zen, and Zen," in which he opposed both the "Beat" Zen of

Kerouac and company and the "Square" Zen of those who slavishly imitated Japanese Zen, both of which he felt distorted true Zen. Of the Beats, Watts averred:

> Beat Zen is a complex phenomenon. It ranges from a use of Zen for justifying sheer caprice in art, literature, and life to a very forceful social criticism and "digging of the universe" such as one may find in the poetry of Ginsberg, Whalen, and Snyder, and, rather unevenly, in Kerouac who is always a shade too self conscious, too subjective, and too strident to have the flavor of Zen.

Like the Beats themselves, Watts was a tremendous populizer of Zen, but also like them, he misunderstood some of its most essential aspects, possibly due to lack of formal training in the practice.

The 1960s and Buddhism

The hippies of the 1960s were the natural heirs to the Beats. The hippie movement was always larger and more grassroots than the Beat movement, but shared many of its basic assumptions about society and culture. However, the 1960s generation was less elitist and less intellectual than their predecessors, and gravitated less to the severe, rather ascetic style of Zen than to more freewheeling forms of religious expression. Many, in fact, protested that the liberal use of LSD produced an experience similar to *satori* without the effort involved, perhaps missing the essential Zen point that the effort involved is part of the experience. Understandably, perhaps, when these psychedelics turned to Buddhism, it was often to the more colorful Tibetan versions. Hinduism, on the whole, was more popular.

Acculturation

Zen doesn't have to be Japanese to be authentic, especially when we consider that the original "Zen" Masters were Chinese and called their practice "Ch'an." American Zen has chosen to follow the heart of Zen teaching, often by modifying or even eliminating some prominent Japanese features. For example, as mentioned earlier, American Zen practitioners often do not sit in the full-lotus position, which is extremely difficult for most Westerners.

For another example, let's take the practice of *sesshin* (extended sitting), a hallmark of Zen. The purpose of *sesshin* is to stop the normal functioning of the psychological mind. In *sesshin,* Japanese Rinzai Buddhists sit in silence (and mostly without sleep, although they are allowed to doze off between 1:00 and 3:00 A.M. while sitting on their cushions) for seven (or eight or even ten) days and nights. It is not for nothing that this ordeal is often called a "monk-killer." In America this process is usually considerably modified, with most groups sitting about fourteen hours a day, not counting meals. During *sesshin* they concentrate upon a koan. (Soto Zen Buddhists have *sesshin* also—without the koan.) A special *sesshin,* Rohatsu, is observed in the winter to memorialize the Buddha's Enlightenment, which in Japan is celebrated in December.

In Japan, during *sesshin,* students are often shouted at, shoved, and beaten with sticks (euphemistically called *kyosaku,* or "encouragement sticks," and used in both the Rinzai and Soto traditions). Most American Zen institutes eliminate the humiliating aspects of this process, believing that it is not essential to Enlightenment, and may even have the opposite effect. In the United States, only one or two people have the authority to use the encouragement stick; in Japan, all the monks take turns, a kind of reversal of what we might expect. However, in nearly every Zen center in the United States, only students willing to be struck with the encouragement stick have it applied to them. These students indicate their permission by making a bow at the right moment. Ancient Japanese Zen Masters were considerably more violent, twisting noses, or even on occasion, if stories are to be believed, cutting the fingers off disciples. The reverse, of course, wasn't permitted; any student striking a teacher accumulated a lot of bad karma, although there is a Zen story about a student hitting his teacher, presumably in delight, *after* he had attained Enlightenment.

Some of the more "foreign" terms of the koan are given English or American equivalents, although American Masters don't usually go so far as their Japanese predecessors did. (When Zen first came to Japan, the early Zen Masters had no hesitation about translating Chinese names into Japanese ones, in order to reduce their foreignness.) However, other important elements of *sesshin,* such as the Roshi's commentary, which is given daily during *sesshin,* are retained.

Dokusan, the formal meeting between Zen master and student, is a highly ritualized affair in Japan. However, in the United States it is much more informal. Students may not only discuss the koan they have been given, but also general difficulties associated with practice.

American Zen students do not invest their koan study with the same kind of literary approach characteristic in Japan, in which monks engage in written explanations, which are written in Japanese and graded by the Roshi. More advanced assignments are to be completed in Chinese. These practices are not followed in the United States.

Training Methods

One major difference that exists between Zen monasteries of Japan and those of the United States is their divergent teaching methods. G. Victor Sogen Hori, in his essay "Japanese Zen in America," has vividly pointed out that in Japan, teachers use the same methods to teach proper work habits and correct chanting as they use to teach koans. What this means is that when a student makes a mistake, he is simply admonished (sometimes in a very loud voice) that he is wrong. He is never told exactly what is wrong or how to fix it. So if a novice cook prepares a meal incorrectly, the monks refuse to eat it, and the cook has to eat the leftovers himself and figure out what went wrong. The purpose of such hard teaching is to help the student himself figure out what is wrong, instead of feeding him the right answers. The harsh treatment also encourages the student to learn as fast as possible. Most Zen teaching centers in America have abandoned these training methods, which while possibly effective in Japan, simply don't work in America. Only in koan training, in which the teacher is a Roshi and not a mere monk, are Japanese methods used. And even here, as mentioned earlier, the harshness of the training has been considerably modified to meet American sensibilities.

In general, the sharp Asian distinction between "monk" and "layperson," as well as what Americans regard as the slavish attitude of students toward teachers present in many Asian traditions, are muted in most American Buddhist communities. On a related issue, Americans do not take easily to the strict hierarchical structure of Japanese Zen, especially in the matters of absolute obedience of disciple to Master. In Japan (and in Theravada countries, too), the monastery records the date the novice entered the monastery. This date determines his seniority. Every senior monk has authority to correct his juniors, and the correction can be harsh. This is simply not the usual American custom or culture, the way it is in Japan.

However, this does not mean that American Zen is necessarily more democratic than its Japanese counterpart. Zen is an authoritarian tradition in any guise, and in America, the authority is often given to the "staff" as opposed to a single, all-powerful abbot. Novice monks generally do not have any particular part in decision making for the group as a whole, or much input into the progress of their own training. Because American Zen monasteries do not usually impose the "every senior monk can correct every junior monk" rule, it sometimes happens that a student develops what can be an unhealthy dependence upon his own Roshi, without the refreshing correction of other monks. In addition, such rigid formalities as the Japanese tea ceremony, have never appealed to the vast majority of American Zen Buddhists as anything more than a curiosity.

Helen Tworkov has pointed out an interesting conflation of American Puritan and Zen values. The notoriously Spartan, sparkling clean Zen meditation halls appeal to many Americans brought up with at least the remnants of a Puritan sensibility. Zen offers the same atmosphere, although for a different reason—it appeals to the Japanese aesthetic of purity and simplicity. Accidental or not, there is here a meeting of minds.

Another problem of acculturation has to do with organization and leadership. In Japan, Soto Zen is a vastly bureaucratized behemoth, with each temple and monastery answering to a higher authority. Technically, this authority is operative in the United States as well, but such authority is attenuated and largely ignored. In consequence, most American Zen institutes are largely on their own. In addition, the Asian style of government by autocracy doesn't always jibe well with American democratic values, although it can work when the leader is seen as charismatic. In Asia it doesn't make any difference. The abbot is the abbot, no matter how profound (or not) his insights and abilities appear.

Ceremonies and Formalities

As might be expected, a major point of difference between Japanese and American Zen is the attention paid to rites and ceremonies. Japanese culture (not just Japanese Zen culture) prizes elaborate ceremony, while free-and-easy Americans often prefer to do without it. The difference has become a bone of contention. For example, it is the custom in Japan for a Soto monk to have his hair cut upon entering the monastery. A photo is taken of this event (of course, this is a certainly a fairly recent innovation) and housed at the Soto headquarters. Similarly, the Japanese authorities refused to accept the Dharma heir status of many famous American Zen students until they went through the proper rites—in Japan. The fact that they had done so already in the United States meant nothing.

American Zen Holidays

Many American Zen Buddhists celebrate the traditional holidays of Japanese Zen. These include celebrations typical of any religion (weddings, funerals, and ordinations) but also seasonal observances such as the Buddha's birthday, death day, Founder's Day; New Year's Day; and in a nod to America, Thanksgiving, which is given a Buddhist flavor.

In addition, there is a monthly confession/repentance ceremony (usually public) that goes back to the original Buddhism of the Sangha. The central lines of the repentance verse read: "All evil actions committed by me since time immemorial, stemming from greed, anger, and ignorance, arising from body, speech, and mind, I now repent having committed." These lines are repeated three times.

There is another monthly ceremony dedicated to the aid of impoverished people throughout the world. Some temples and meditation centers also celebrate the renewal of the Ten Precepts either monthly or every other week. The ceremony may include chanting and bowing to the Buddhas or bodhisattvas.

Chapter 6

Tibetan Buddhism: The Diamond Vehicle

What started as an unmitigated disaster for the country of Tibet turned into a spiritual gift for the Western world. The disaster was the Chinese invasion of Tibet in 1959. Before the invasion, it is estimated that about 20 percent of the Tibetan population were lamas (Buddhist monks). An untold number of them, and of lay Tibetans as well, were tortured and murdered, and over 6,000 monasteries were destroyed. The Dalai Lama and thousands of others, including the most important of the lamas, were forced into exile.

However, this exile resulted in the dissemination of Tibetan Buddhism into all parts of the world. As the Tibetan people, both laypersons and monks, were forced from their homeland, they brought with them their priceless texts and treasured rites. What had hitherto been an unknown and mysterious practice from a remote and mysterious land flowered into one of the most respected and widely known branches of the great Buddhist tradition. (A recent Web search revealed 206 Tibetan Buddhist monasteries and meditation centers in the United States alone. Today, Tibetan Buddhism really exists only outside the devastated land of its birth.)

Philosophically Tibetan Buddhism, or Vajrayana, is part of the great Mahayana tradition, although it has peculiarities that require it to be treated separately. The term "Vajrayana" comes from the name for the scepter of the ancient Ayran god Indra. Indra carries a powerful thunderbolt (*vajra*); however, the word also means "diamond" or "indestructible." The practitioner of Vajrayana is thus heir to both the power of the thunderbolt and the indestructibility of the diamond.

The main difference between Vajrayana and the tradition from which it sprang is in the means it uses, not its goal. Vajrayana claims that it provides its practitioners a more skillful, faster way of getting from suffering to Buddhahood. Tibetan Buddhism is practiced not only in Tibet, but also in neighboring Himalayan countries, and so for that reason alone, many prefer the word "Vajrayana," which has a philosophical rather than a geographical reference.

Technically, Tibetan Buddhism is divided into orthodox Tibetan, Tantric, and Vajrayana sects, but these differences are comparatively minor, and the terms are used indiscriminately in the United States.

In recent years, Tibetan Buddhism has been kept in the public consciousness by Hollywood. Such films as *Kundun, Seven Years in Tibet,* and *Red Corner* are only the latest expression of Tinsel City's longtime fascination with the wild splendors of Asia. (Frank Capra's *Lost Horizons,* from James Hilton's novel of the same name, came out in 1937.) In fact, Richard Gere earned the wrath of the motion picture industry when, during the 1993 Academy Awards ceremony he denounced China's oppression of Tibet and asked the audience to direct their thought waves to Deng Xiaoping to free Tibet. He was then banned by the academy. Gere, thus a kind of exile himself, spends a lot of time in Dharamsala, the current home of the exiled Dalai Lama.

Hollywood's current interest in Tibet and in the Dalai Lama has had an enormous impact on American understanding of this exotic form of Buddhism. Curiously, the Dalai Lama was not even permitted a visa to get into this country as recently as 1979—the U.S. government was at the time extremely anxious not to offend China. Things changed, however, after the massacre at Tiananmen Square in Beijing, and public sentiment for Tibet became overwhelming. When the Dalai Lama was awarded the Noble Prize in 1989, his standing as an international leader became impossible to ignore.

Tibetan Buddhism is the last Buddhist tradition to gain entrance in the United States, with the first Tibetan lamas arriving during the late 1950s. It owed its start to the great Indian scholar Shantirakshita and also to the missionary Padmasambhava. (Padmasambhava is discussed more fully below.)

Today, about one-third of the Buddhist centers in North America adhere to the Tibetan tradition, and altogether there are more than 400 groups claiming allegiance to the exotic and mysterious Vajrayana, the Diamond Vehicle. Currently there are about 10,000 Tibetan exiles and immigrants in the United States; a large number of Americans have converted to Tibetan Buddhism.

The Dalai Lama in France. Photographer Andrea Alborno. © TRIP.

The History of Tibetan Buddhism

Tibetan Buddhism began as a development of the Mahayana tradition. Buddhism came to Tibet in the seventh century C.E., both from India and from the Buddhist kingdoms in China. Before Buddhism arrived, the mass of people conformed to the indigenous religion of Bon. Very little is know about this religion, but it seems to have shared most of the features of Mongolian Shamanism, including nature worship, as well as psychic and ritual sexual practices.

King Trisong Detsen (755–797) protected and nourished the new religion. There exist today four recognized schools of Tibetan Buddhism: Kagyu, Gelugpa, Nyingma, and Sakya. Each school has its own internal lineage, which refers to the lama-student connection that has persisted, often over centuries. Each of the traditions can also be found today in the United States.

Tibetan Buddhist Beliefs

Many Tibetan Buddhists believe that the correct way for beginners to learn Tibetan Buddhism is to begin with Theravada Buddhism, proceed to Mahayana, and thence to Vajrayana. However, some students choose to approach Tibetan Buddhism more directly.

In many respects, Tibetan Buddhism seems much closer to the Western concept of a religion than does Zen (see chapter 5) or Vipassana (see chapter 3). With its colorful gods, abstruse texts, elaborate worship practices, and mysterious chanting, it seems a curious mixture of traditional Buddhist philosophy, ancient polytheistic faith, and mystic insight. What makes Tibetan Buddhism most compelling to many is its attitude of secrecy. The highest teachings are made known to students only after many years of practice, and can be revealed only by a guru. While the sacred Tantric texts reveal the secrets, they are "coded" so that the reader is in the dark about their true meaning.

Tibetan Buddhists have a number of deities, a word not often encountered in other branches of Buddhism. Chief among them is Tara, a savior-bodhisattva. She is one form of the bodhisattva Avalokitesvara, said to arise from his tears when he saw the horrors of hell and the sufferings of its inhabitants. Tara comes in various colors, but the most common are the Green Tara and the White Tara.

Sacred Texts or Canon

The sacred texts of Tibetan Buddhism are known as Tantras. They explain complicated meditative practices that were originally designed for those who have already completed Mayahana training. They were composed later than the sutras of traditional Mahayana Buddhism (not appearing "in public" until the sixth century or so) and have sometimes been associated with weird rituals and dark magical practices. One reason for this is that in Tantric Buddhism, many "forbidden" behaviors relating to food, drink, and sexuality are permitted (sometimes only symbolically) in order to achieve a spiritual purpose. For example, the Hevajra Tantra asserts that the world is entrapped by lust, and only lust can unbind it.

Tantra also exists in the Hindu tradition, and Tibetan Buddhism makes use of mantras largely borrowed from Hinduism. In fact, Tibetan Buddhism is sometimes called Mantrayana because of the use it makes of mantras. The most famous of all mantras is Om Mani Padme Hum ("Hail to the Jewel in the Lotus"), which honors Avalokitesvara.

Unlike the open tradition of the rest of Buddhism, Tantrism is secretive, and its practitioners believe that the highest secrets can only be passed on from lama to disciple. The texts themselves are written in a highly symbolic language called "twilight speech" so that their meaning is obscured from the casual or inappropriate student.

The Tibetan canon consists of the *Kang-yur* and *Teng-yur,* the written words of the Buddha as well as commentaries by learned Indian Masters. These two collections occupy 104 and 273 large volumes, respectively.

Tibetan Practice

While Tibetan ritual is complex and exotic, it is extremely friendly, and most outsiders and novices are made to feel more at home than is often the case in Zen or Vipassana centers. The center of Tibetan practice is that the student envisions himself as a Buddha and the world as a sacred mandala.

Veneration of Lamas and Gurus

In the Tibetan tradition, a lama is a monk authorized to teach. The honorific "Rinpoche," or "precious," is accorded to such a one as a title of respect. Above the ordinary level of lama, however, are two higher ranks, that of *khenpo* (in the Nyingma and Kagyu traditions) or *geshe* (Gelugpa and Sakya traditions) and that of *tulku.* To achieve the rank of *geshe* or *khenpo,* the aspirant must spend fifteen or twenty years in rigorous academic study. The *geshe lharampa,* although still ranked as a *geshe,* has completed several more years of work. Even higher is the *tulku,* one who is recognized as the reincarnation of a deceased lama; this is not a recognition one can reasonably expect to "earn." The concept of *tulku* is mostly confined to the Nyingma and Kagyu traditions. *Tulku*-naming was common in Tibet, and the practice has recently spread to the United States.

Few Westerners have been accorded the rank of *khenpo,* which requires an enormous amount of study and high oral and reading fluency in Tibetan. It also requires finding a lama who is willing to undertake the task of teaching a Westerner. Students take special vows of obedience (*samayas*) to their "root guru," and each lama traditionally has his own way of teaching.

Two of the most prominent Western *geshes* are Georges Dreyfuss (Geshe Sangye Samdup), who is Swiss and currently a professor of Indo-Tibetan Studies at Williams College, and Michael Roach, who teaches at the Asian Classics Institute in New York City. Spotting a *tulku* among Westerners is more frequent than in earlier times, but it is still not a common occurrence.

A high lama is considered a reincarnation of a Buddha (not just of another lama, as is a *tulku*), and respect for him approaches worship. He delivers lectures from a gilded throne, even in the United States. Visiting Tibetan lamas are often driven about in limousines and accompanied by a worshipful entourage. One is expected to pay the same worship to a lama or guru as one would to a god or living Buddha, no matter what faults or defects of character he may display. (These faults seem to be more easily on display in the commercial environment of the United States or even of India than was the case in the rural, isolated Tibet of years past.)

Shamatha (Samatha)

Shamatha is also known as tranquility meditation, and is most common in the Gelugpa school. Its purpose is to calm the mind so that a combination of insight and intuition can lead one to a vision of true reality, or emptiness (*shunyata*).

Correct *shamatha* uses the nine stages of the mind. These are:

1. directing the mind toward the object of meditation
2. stabilizing the mind
3. continually renewing attention
4. confining attention to the object
5. taming the mind
6. calming the mind
7. refining the mind
8. collecting the mind
9. *samadhi:* the highest state of meditation in which both subject and object disappear

It also uses the six powers:

1. hearing the teaching
2. reflecting on the teaching
3. concentrating on the teaching

4. clearly comprehending the teaching
5. concentrated energy on the teaching
6. natural confidence

Finally, it makes use of the four mental activities:

1. connecting the mind to the object
2. reestablishing attention
3. uninterrupted attentions
4. dwelling effortlessly

It can easily be seen that these methods are all interconnected and that "natural confidence" and "dwelling effortlessly" appear to come after a great deal of "unnatural effort." The meditation posture and breath control of *shamatha* is similar to that of Zen, although the specific goal is not Enlightenment but tranquility.

Tonglen

Tonglen is the Tibetan practice of "sending and receiving" (*ong* means "sending out" or "letting go," and "len" means "receiving" or "accepting"). It is a way of connecting with suffering. In this meditation, the practitioner concentrates on neutralizing the evils of the world in purifying breaths, which are then sent out through exhalation into the world. Thus, when he breathes in, he takes on the sufferings of the world; when he breathes out, he breathes out joy and happiness.

Ngondro

Ngondro is Tibetan for body, speech, and mind. It refers to practices designed to clear away negativity from each of these aspects. Mudras, or sacred gestures, dissolve impurities from the body. Mantras, or sacred sounds, do the same for speech, and *samadhi,* or deep meditation, performs the same function for the mind. Each of these likewise corresponds to one of the three sacred bodies (*trikaya*) of the Buddha: *nirmanakaya* (the transformation or emanation body, which is the visible historical form of the Buddha), *sambhogakaya* (the "enjoyment body," through which the Buddha exists as a transcendent, eternal, celestial being or an archetypal deity sometimes called the Tathagata Buddha), and the *dharmakaya* (the "truth" or "reality" body, referring to the essential Absolute Reality of Buddhas, sometimes called "emptiness," or *shunyata,* because it is "empty" of all finite characteristics).

Although the specific practices of *ngondro* may vary from one lineage to another, all generally involve full-body prostrations before an altar or image of the Buddha. This is done to purify the heart.

Typically, *ngondro* starts with 100,000 full prostrations before a shrine, repeating a prayer the entire time. Normally this takes a couple of years to complete. In a full prostration, the practitioner begins standing and ends face down on the floor with arms outstretched in front. Then he rises to begin again. Whatever its spiritual benefits, it is excellent exercise.

The initiate then visualizes Vajrasattva ("the diamond being"), a purifying Buddha. Vajrasattva is generally conceived of as being white (a unification of all five colors), holding a thunderbolt (*dorje*) in his right hand and a bell in his left. The thunderbolt symbolizes the indestructibleness of Vajrasattva, and the bell symbolizes his compassion. The practitioner recites the 100-syllable mantra associated with him 100,000 times.

The third step is a ritual mandala offering of colored rice, jewels, and coins. This offering is to be made 100,000 times. The word "mandala" is actually a Sanskrit word meaning circle, polygon, community, or connection. Mandalas, which can be made of paper, fabric, or sand, are inside an enclosed sacred space, usually consisting of concentric circles. The sand mandala is especially interesting. It is made from colored sand over a period of several days; shortly after its completion, the mandala is destroyed. This emphasizes the Buddhist view of the transitory nature of things. Fire is also considered a purifier.

The outer form of the mandala is a geometric design called a yantra. (Sometimes yantras, which are much simpler than mandalas, are used instead of them.) A deity is depicted in the center. Every detail carries a special meaning. Each mandala is unique and each serves a different purpose. Some mandalas are so-called cosmic mandalas, which purport to transmit ancient knowledge about the development of the universe. The cosmic mandala is usually enclosed by a fiery circle, which stands for transformation. More personal mandalas include the "medicine Buddha," which is used for individual healing rites. For Tibetans, the mandala represents an imaginary palace with four gates, each gate facing a different direction. It is upon this palace that one meditates.

The disciple is also supposed to repeat a short prayer to his guru one million times. Obviously this sort of thing can't be done in a day, or even a year, although it supposedly can be done in about two years if one is on a retreat the entire time and does little else. After *ngondro,* one is allowed to go forward to *abhisheka*, or empowerment.

Abhisheka

This Sanskrit word is variously translated as "anointing or sprinkling," "initiation," "empowerment," "consecration," or "transmission of power." It can take up to a year to learn the basics, wherein the disciple learns to envision himself as a god.

In this ritual, a lama initiates a student into a particular meditation practice and authorizes him to practice it himself. The initiation rite has four stages: (1) vase initiation (*kalabhisheka*), (2) secret initiation (*guhyabhisheka*), (3) wisdom initiation (*prajnabhisheka),* and (4) fourth initiation (*chaturabhiseka*).

The initiation is accompanied by the corresponding *sadhana* ("means of accomplishing or achieving"), a special liturgical text that describes the proper technique for visualization-meditation. This careful utilization of sights, sounds, and mental states is especially evident in the form of the Vajrayana ritual of meditation. Vajrayana rituals have a visual component (usually envisioning a deity), an auditory component (recitation of the mantra); and a mental component (the identification of the meditator with the object of meditation; this produces the realization of nonduality and emptiness).

In the Vajrayana initiation, the disciple receives the keys by which he may experience and re-create the sacred universe, which is another term for Enlightenment. One key is a vision of the tutelary deity; the second is a verbal formula, or mantra, associated with that tutelary deity. Fanciers of Tibetan Buddhism tout the fact that Vajrayana meditation and ritual is more effective than Zen or Vipassana because it uses the very "distractions" that other forms of meditation try to get rid of. This is one reason that they claim it is a faster road to Enlightenment than more "traditional" Buddhism.

Sadhana

Sadhana, a word used in Hinduism also, is technically any spritual practice. But for Tibetans, *sadhana* takes on special meaning. In this tradition, *sadhana* can usually be divided into three stages. In the first, the initiate takes refuge and dedicates accumulated merit for the Enlightenment of all beings. In the second or "developing" stage, the initiate visualizes and then "dissolves" or "carries over" a deity. In the visualization, the initiate visualizes not only the deity, but also his abode, his posture, his clothing, and his ornaments. In the final stage, the initiate offers prayers and asks for blessings. The visualization is accompanied by chanting. Very few Americans are considered advanced enough to be adepts at *sadhana*. In fact, most visualizations are considered to be fraught with danger, although they confer high spiritual blessings as well. The entire ceremony was formerly extremely secret, but during the nineteenth century it began to be open, even to the laity.

Mahamudra

In Tibetan Buddhism, *mahamudra* represents a perfected level of meditative realization: it is the inseparable union of wisdom and compassion, of emptiness and skillful means. It is a system of teaching employed by all but the Nyingma school.

Diet

The harsh climate of Tibet does not provide enough crops for a nutritionally complete vegetarian diet. Culturally Tibetans have always relied upon the yak for food and sustenance. Native Tibetan Buddhists, therefore, have traditionally included some meat as part of their diet; in fact, the Dalai Lama became ill after experimenting with a totally vegetarian diet in India. American Tibetan Buddhists, however, have ample sources of vegetarian foods, so they do not need to resort to a meat-enhanced diet.

Prayer Flags

Prayer flags are characteristic of Tibetan Buddhism. These flags are inscribed with auspicious symbols, mantras, prayers, and invocations. They may also bear traditional Buddhist symbols. They are said to bring happiness, prosperity, and long life.

They are generally put up at the beginning of the Buddhist year and left to fly in the wind and deteriorate naturally. The wind is supposed to loosen the prayers from the fabric and send them flying off into the ether, where, presumably, they will be heard by the gods.

Death Rites

Tibetan Buddhists have cultivated the art of dying for millennia. Indeed, death has its own literature, *The Tibetan Book of the Dead*, which is packed with instructions about how the recently deceased person may avoid rebirth and enter Nirvana.

Tibetan Buddhism is unique in its development of the concept of Bardo, an intermediate state (not place) between death and rebirth. In contemporary thinking, the term is applied to any transitional state. While much of this advice seems irrelevant to modern-day Americans, the idea of using a transitional period in life to regroup and redirect one's spirit is both highly relevant and powerful. Bardo can also refer to the place between two states of feeling or thinking. It is described as a gap or emptiness in which true realization of Enlightenment is allowed to penetrate. When one is actually *in* one kind of state, it is impossible to be open to another. Only the emptiness of the in-between state allows one to experience growth and development into another. It is, as Pema Chodron, an American Buddhist nun in the Tibetan Kagyu tradition, writes, "the perfect training ground." It is the place where, by letting go, one can experience the present moment in all its fullness—and emptiness.

At the moment of dying, one glimpses a glorious luminous something/nothing, that is, Enlightenment. If the disembodied former-person, who is "survived" by this consciousness, can attend to this luminosity and keep faithful to it, all will go well. Unfortunately, that doesn't happen very often. Fear, springing from unresolved karma, springs up and deludes the consciousness. The leftover consciousness may wander around Bardo for up to forty-nine days, at the end of which time, if it hasn't achieved Enlightenment, it will enter into a new birth, usually brought about by the sight of a pair of human beings having sexual intercourse. If the "consciousness/spirit" is attracted to the woman, it will be reborn male; if to the male, it will be reborn female. It is said that the consciousness/spirit becomes angry when it cannot participate in the sexual activity, and that anger is what ensures that it will be born anew. Thus the fatal three—ignorance (of Enlightenment, even when it is right before one), desire (specifically, in this case, sexual desire), and anger (arising from an unfulfilled desire)—produce the conditions that bind us again and again to the wheel of life.

Women in Tibetan Buddhism

Currently there are many nuns in Western Tibetan Buddhism, although this school of Buddhism does not grant full ordination to *bhikshunis*. Jetsunma Ahkon, who is considered below, was recognized as a *tulku*. And Pema Chodron (Deirdre Blomfield-Brown), an American disciple of

Chogyam Trungpa, is the resident director of Gampo Abbey in Nova Scotia. A Native American, Dhyani Ywahoo is recognized as a teacher in both the Nyingma and Kagyu schools. She is also a teacher in her native Cherokee tradition.

Schools of Tibetan Buddhism

There exist today four recognized schools of Tibetan Buddhism: Kagyu, Gelugpa, Nyingma, and Sakya. Each has its own internal lineage, which refers to the lama-student connection, often persisting over centuries. Each of the traditions can be found today in the United States.

The Nyingma School

Nyingma is the oldest of the Tibetan schools; literally the word means "school of the ancients." Its founder was Padmasambhava and the monks Vilamalmitra and Varochaina in the eighth century. Legend tells us that Padmasambhava arrived in Tibet when he was over 1,000 years old, and used his great magical powers to conquer the native demons. He then traveled throughout Tibet, spreading the good news of Buddhism to one and all. However, Nyingma Buddhism, despite its destruction of the ancient demons, remains much closer to the native religion of Tibet (Bon) than any other variety of Buddhism. While some Nyingma monasteries were established, most lamas were isolated teachers, healers, diviners, rainmakers, and workers of magic and miracles. Since the fifteenth century there has been an independent school of Nyingma teachings; these are not included in the official Tibetan canon, the Kangyur-Tengyur.

The main teachings of the Nyingma tradition are known as Dzogchen, a Tibetan word meaning "great perfection." It is also called *ati-yoga,* or "extraordinary yoga." It reportedly reveals the most definitive and most secret teachings of the Buddha. Lonchenpa and his commentary on it are authoritative in this tradition. According to its adherents, Tibetan Buddhism represents "the last extant wisdom culture to survive intact from ancient times" (Lama Surya Das). Because Tibet was so remote and isolated, Tibetan Buddhists believe that they alone were able to preserve completely in an undistorted form the teachings of the Buddha. (Theravadins and Mahayanists believe the same thing, of course, but for different reasons.) It does seem true that certain Buddhist sutras and commentaries written in Sanskrit were lost in India during the Muslim invasions of northern India, but were later discovered intact in Tibetan monastery libraries. Unusual among Buddhists, the Nyingma order has married lamas, which has made this order appealing to Americans.

Probably the last great Tibetan teacher of this school was His Holiness Dudjom Rinpoche (1904–87). Although he had no formal education, he became one of the greatest and most famous scholars in Tibet. He collected and published the Nyingma Kama, the original oral transmission of the Nyingma lineage. He restored many old texts and revealed profound teachings of his own. Dudjom Rinpoche was recognized as the first official representative of the Nyingma community during the Tibetan diaspora.

The United States is now home to Lama Tharchin Rinpoche, one of Dudjom Rinpoche's main disciples. He was raised in Dudjom Rinpoche's monastery and completed the traditional three-year retreat under his guidance. He came to the United States for health reasons, where he met with Dudjom Rinpoche in San Francisco. In this last meeting before Dudjom Rinpoche's death, Dudjom Rinpoche exhorted Lama Tharchin Rinpoche to "turn the wheel of Dharma in the West" and preserve the Vajrayana lineage for future generations. He was one of the very last *lharampa geshes* to receive this extraordinarily high degree in Tibet.

Nyingma was first brought to Berkeley, California, in 1969 by Tarthang Tulku, who founded the Tibetan Nyingma Meditation Center. He emphasized the importance of full-body prostrations, having his students begin with practicing 100,000 of them. He also began a publishing house, Dharma Publishing, which publishes his own teachings and also other translations from Tibetan and Sanskrit. The Nyingma Institute in Berkeley now offers a complete course of meditation and teaching; it consists mostly of "native" Americans, along with some ethnic Tibetans. In 1975 Tarthang Tulku began a "temple city" in Sonoma County, California, called Odiyan, which includes a nature preserve.

In 1988, the Vajrayana Foundation was established as a nonprofit organization, and in 1991, Tharchin Rinpoche founded Pema Osel Ling Retreat Center in California and the Orgyen Dechen Cho Dzong in Hawaii in 1994. Over twenty-five students are in or have completed the three-year retreat in America under Lama Tharchin Rinpoche; the College of Buddhist Studies and Tibetan Arts Institute have been established, and plans are underway to build a traditional gompa and stupa. The Vajrayana Foundation hosts numerous lamas and artists in addition to resident lamas Orgyen Thinley Rinpoche and Tulku Thubten Rinpoche.

Venerable Lama Tharchin Rinpoche is a Dzogchen master of Vajrayana Buddhism. He is also a master artist. Don Farber Photography.

One unique branch of the Nyingma tradition is Aro Gar. The Aro Gar lineage, also called the Mother Essence lineage, emanates from a succession of enlightened women. The Aro Gar was the place in the Himalayas where Khyungchen Aro Lingma (1886–1923), the source of this lineage, lived in a community of practitioners that formed around her and her son Aro Yeshé (1915–51), the latter of whom received pure vision transmission directly from Yeshé Tsogyel, the female Tantric Buddha. Aro Gar is a nonprofit organization, serving the United States and the Americas. It works closely with Sang-ngak-chö-dzong and its sister organizations in Europe, dedicated to bringing the "white tradition" of the Nyingma school to the West. The Aro Gar is a nonliturgical, nonmonastic tradition that specializes in the teaching and practice of Dzogchen. The Aro school has found some favor in the West because of the emphasis it places on the importance of everyday working life as sexual equality and the spiritual dimension of romantic relationships. In the United States the Nyingma school has focused more intently on meditative, devotional, and Tantric practices than academic textual study.

Another Nyingma organization is the Chagdud Gonpa, founded by Chagdud Tulku Trincpoche, a meditation master, Tibetan physician, and artist. Chagdud Rinpoche fled his native land in 1959, and came to the United States in 1979, where he created the Chagdud Gonpa Foundation in 1983. Its stated purpose is to provide instruction in the traditions of Vajrayana Buddhism, especially the arts, philosophy, and meditation practices. The foundation's North American headquarters are in Rigdzin Ling, located in the Trinity Alps region of northern California, fifty miles west of Redding. It administers over twenty Chagdud Gonpa centers in both North and South America.

Teachers of the Nyingma School

Tarthang Tulku (b. 1935), an incarnate lama of the royal family of Sogpa, escaped from Tibet to India in 1959, where he spent time as a professor of Buddhist philosophy. He was sent West by the leaders of his order. Tarthang Tulku Rinpoche arrived in the United States in 1968, and established the Tibetan Nyingma Meditation Center (Padma Ling) in 1969 in Berkeley, California. The next year he founded Dharma Publishing. In 1973 he founded the Nyingma Institute.

Another important teacher in the Nyingma tradition is Sogyal Rinpoche. Born in the Kham region of eastern Tibet, Sogyal Rinpoche was recognized as the incarnation of Lerab Lingpa Tertön Sogyal, a teacher to the thirteenth Dalai Lama, by Jamyang Khyentse Chökyi Lodrö, one of the most outstanding masters of the twentieth century. In 1971, Rinpoche went to England, where he studied comparative religion at Cambridge University. In 1981 he established the Rigpa Fellowship, which has a major center in Santa Cruz, California. "Rigpa" is a Tibetan word meaning "the innermost nature of the mind." The Rigpa Fellowship is now an international network with centers and groups in eleven countries around the world. Sogyal Rinpoche is the author of the popular and well-received *Tibetan Book of Living and Dying*. Over 1.6 million copies of this classic have been printed, in twenty-seven languages and fifty-four countries.

Lama Surya Das (b. 1950), who was born Jeffrey Miller, began his long voyage into Buddhism in 1970, after the student killings at Kent State. A friend of his was one of the dead, and in an eerie coincidence the name of another killed student was the same as his own. Soon after, Miller packed his bags and headed east, finally arriving in Kathmandu when he was twenty years old. The name Surya Das was given to him by a Hindu, not a Buddhist, teacher. He attached himself to a Tibetan lama named Yeshe, and began to learn the language of Tibet and of Tibetan Buddhism. Miller is associated with the Nyingma tradition, but is also eclectic in his approach to Buddhism, which extends beyond the Tibetan school. In fact, Surya Das helped develop the Western Buddhist Teachers Network, which includes Tibetan, Theravada, and Zen teachers from Europe and America.

In 1980, Surya Das joined the first Nyingma retreat center for Westerners, in Dordogne, France, where he completed two traditional three-and-a-half-year retreats under the guidance of Dudjom Rinpoche and Dilgo Khyentse Rinpoche, with Tulku Pema Wangyal and Nyoshul Khenpo Rinpoche. In 1984, he became a lama in the Non-Sectarian Practice Lineage of Tibetan Buddhism. Currently Surya Das has his own "Ask the Lama" column on the Web.

In 1991 Surya Das founded the Dzogchen Foundation to help Western students gain access to Tibetan teachings; in fact, Dzogchen, a formless meditation technique, is considered to be the most "accessible" Tibetan Buddhism for Western students, although it also is thought to be the highest teachings in the Nyingma tradition. Surya Das teaches this

Lama Surya Das, born Jeffrey Miller, is one of the most important and well-known Western Buddhist mediation teachers and scholars. Courtesy of Mark Ryan.

technique to anyone interested, whether they have had the long years of training traditionally required or not. (In his opinion, educated, sophisticated Americans are already prepared in a way that rural, illiterate native Tibetans were not, and who needed the preparation training.) According to its adherents, Dzogchen is the ultimate practice of Tibetan Buddhism. Only the Nyingma lineage practices it in full, although all four sects of Tibetan Buddhism practice it to some degree.

An extremely controversial *tulku* is Hollywood actor Steven Seagal, who was officially recognized as such in 1997 by Penor Rinpoche, supreme head of the important Palyul Nyingma order. Critics claim that not all Seagal's behavior has suggested his legitimate status as a *tulku*. Seagal, who has been a practicing Buddhist for twenty years, claims that his past lives are unimportant.

Jetsunma Ahkön Lhamo (b. 1949), an American woman in her forties with three children, was also recognized as a *tulku* by His Holiness Penor Rinpoche. (She was born Alyce or Alice Zeoli in Brooklyn. She was also known as Catharine Burroughs—Burroughs was the name of her third husband, and she decided she didn't feel like an Alyce anymore when she met him.) According to her own account, from the age of nineteen on she had a series of dreams that instructed her in meditation, although she was unfamiliar with the practice. In 1981, when she was married, the family moved to Washington, D.C., where she gave readings and consultations.

In 1985, she met His Holiness Drugwang Pema Norbu (Penor) Rinpoche, an important Nyingma lama, in fact, the eleventh throne holder of the Palyul lineage and the same man who would later recognize Steven Seagal. Although he did not immediately declare her to be a *tulku*, he took charge of her life. She bought some land near Poolesville, Maryland, and soon Penor Rinpoche and some other Nyingma lamas performed certain divinations, the results of which convinced them she was indeed a *tulku*, in this case a reincarnation of a seventeenth-century *yogini* (female *yogin*), named Ahkon Norbu. She was a character known for her wildness and her healing ability. The original Ahkon was associated with the Palyul Monastery in Tibet. Her meditations were said to have kept the monastery strong. When she died and was cremated, rainbows appeared, a fairly common occurrence with Tibetan holy people. (The same thing happened with Chogyam Trungpa.) Her skull reportedly flew into the air and was found several kilometers away. Part of this skull is now in Poolesville, sealed inside the stupa and attached to a polished cedar log, which has been intensively prayed and meditated over by a Tibetan lama specializing in stupas. The relic had been lost when the Chinese bombed the monastery, but it mysteriously resurfaced later. The skull can always be recognized because it has AH inscribed on it. Another important relic inside the stupa is a finger bone of Migyur Dorje. Penor Rinpoche brought the finger bone (in fact, he brought a whole hand) out of Tibet when he and 2,000 monks fled the place in 1950. He gave the finger to Jetsunma.

Jetsunma is the first Western woman to be recognized and officially enthroned in 1988 as a *tulku* and holder of the Palyul lineage. Jetsunma's being recognized as an adult caused a bit of a stir, as this is something that never happens in Tibet. The enthronement attracted national media attention. Despite this apparent breakthrough for women, Westerners still await the announcement of a reincarnated lama in the form of a young girl; so far the only children to be recognized as reincarnated lamas of any tradition have been boys. Most of them also live in Tibet, India, or Nepal.

In 1994 Penor Rinpoche and Gyatrul Rinpoche declared Jetsunma as an incarnation of White Tara. She presently is in change of the Tibetan temple in Poolesville, Maryland, Kunzang Palyul Chöling (KPC)—a shortened version of its full Tibetan name, Kunzang Odsal Palyul Changchub Chöling, meaning "Fully Awakened Glorious Dharma Continent of Absolute Clear Light." She has a large following, although both her sexual ethics and her financial handling of the center have been questioned. She has been accused of cohabiting with young male students, as well as with spending a great deal of the center's money on herself, especially on clothing. Her center is known for its many stupas, of varying sizes and quality, and projected 100-foot statue of the Buddha. Like many other American practitioners, Jetsunma has great respect for lay practitioners (she herself has never taken monastic vows). The Nyingma tradition to which she belongs is also less monastically inclined than the other Tibetan schools.

*The Kagyu School (*Kaygupa*)*

Although Kagyu was the last main Tibetan order to be brought to the United States, arriving only in 1970, it ultimately traces its origins back to Marpa, a saintly, if somewhat crusty, lama. Although Marpa gets official credit for beginning the Kagya school, it probably wouldn't have lasted without the energetic help of Milarepa, Marpa's disciple.

Milarepa (c. 1052–1135) was a one-time sorcerer who became one of the greatest Tibetan adepts, a Fully Enlightened One, and a national hero.

His psychic feats included *tumo,* the ability to turn up the body heat to such a pitch that one can live in complete comfort in the most bitter of Tibetan winters.

Unfortunately, Milarepa got off to a rather bad start for a Fully Enlightened One. He studied under Lama Yungtun-Trogyal ("The Wrathful and Victorious Teacher of Evil") and quickly perfected himself in the Black Arts. He began his own career in grand style at his cousin's wedding by filling the room with vermin and then conjuring up a scorpion the size of a yak. The scorpion pulled down a pillar of the building, killing thirty-five people, but sparing his aunt and uncle whom Milarepa wanted to live so that they could suffer more. To be fair, he only did it to please his mother, who disliked that branch of the family.

Still, Milarepa regretted being such an obedient son, and he decided to reform himself by studying with a more moral lama, Marpa. Marpa realized Milarepa needed a lot of work and took to beating him on a regular basis. He also had him build and rebuild a tall tower for him several times over.

At last, the surly saint was satisfied with Milarepa's carpentry and initiated his disciple in the mysteries of the "Short Path to Enlightenment." It was also about this time Milarepa dreamed his house was destroyed, and his mother too. He hastened home, found it was all true, and gathered up his mom's bones in a little brown bag, which he used as a pillow for the rest of his life.

Milarepa took up life as a hermit, living at first on nettle broth, which turned his skin green. Eventually, however, it is said he was transformed into pure intellectual light. At that point he forwent the nettle soup and dined upon ambrosia.

At the age of eighty-four, Milarepa died after knowingly ingesting some poisonous curds. (Curds are quite a comedown from ambrosia, but about on a par with nettle soup.) He was ready to die, he said, and entered Nirvana with a song. (All accounts agree that Milarepa was a superlative crooner, breaking into song at the oddest times.)

A more direct founder of the Kagya school was Naropa (1016–1100), although he himself never went to Tibet, but remained a professor at the Indian Buddhist University of Nalanda. His teachings reached Tibet through his disciples.

The Kagyu school eventually split into subsects, the most important of which is the Karma Kagyu. The head of this denomination is called Karmapa, and his lineage is identified through reincarnation. The line of the Karmapas is said to be self-announced, because each incarnation leaves a letter predicting his next rebirth. When a lama dies, he leaves a letter instructing his disciples how to find his reincarnation. A search party then goes forth to discover the child, who is given special schooling. All great Kagyu teachers regard His Holiness Karmapa as the embodiment and source of all of the blessings of the lineage. The current head of the sect is Ogyen Trinley Dorje, who was born to nomadic parents in 1985 in the Lhathok region of Tibet. He currently resides in India. The Kagyu school in the United States emphasizes devotional, meditative, and Tantric practice over academic work.

Teachers of the Kagyu School

In the Kagyu school, the first well-known missionary lama was Kalu Rinpoche. He did not live permanently in the United States, but made many trips there between 1971 and 1989, the year of his death, establishing a permanent retreat center near Woodstock, New York. He is well known for starting his disciples with a simple visualization practice in which they identified themselves with the bodhisattva or compassion. (This is considered a safe visualization, even for beginners, without some of the attendant dangers of more advanced practice.) Kalu also expected his disciples to do three-year retreats, during which time they were encouraged to sleep upright in a "meditation box."

His disciples included Lodru, who became the head of the Californian Kagyu group Kagyu Droden Kunchab (KDK). Other Kagyu communities include the Karma Triyana Dharmachakra (KTD) and Shambhala International. The latter was founded by Chogyam Trungpa (1939–87), who was trained in both the Kagyu and Nyingma schools. Chogyam Trungpa was part of the *rimed* ("unbiased") movement, which advocated greater ties between different Tibetan schools.

Chogyam Trungpa is often recognized as the first Kagyu teacher with a mission primarily to the United States. Born in a village in eastern Tibet, he was recognized as an incarnation of the eleventh Trungpa Tulku, and thus an emanation of the Buddha, when he was thirteen months of age and established as abbot of the Surmang Monasteries. He was forced to flee Tibet during the Chinese invasion in 1959. Eventually he moved to England and was educated at Oxford, where he had received a Spaulding Fellowship to study comparative religion. He was well-known for his excellent skills in colloquial English.

In 1969 he was involved in a serious automobile accident in which his car ironically ran into a joke-shop. He later said the accident freed him

Chogyam Trungpa Rinpoche was a pioneer in bringing the Tibetan Buddhist teachings to the West. Don Farber Photography.

from materialistic desires and brought him again in touch with wisdom. He officially renounced his monastic vows (he had in effect renounced them long before) and married a sixteen-year-old English girl, Diana Phybus, the next year; he also started drinking, possibly as a result of the accident that left his left side paralyzed and prevented him from wearing his religious dress, which had a bad effect upon him. In 1966 he wrote *Born in Tibet,* an autobiographical account of his youth, when he escaped (barely) from Tibet during the Chinese invasion.

He came to America in 1970, settling in Boulder, Colorado, where he established the Vajradhatu organization, a network of many other groups, in 1971. Trungpa acquired such notable followers as William Burroughs, Allen Ginsberg, and John Cage. The Buddhism he taught is sometimes called "crazy wisdom," perhaps in honor of its affinities to the Beat writers. (In fact, Ginsberg was a teacher at Trungpa's Naropa University until his death in 1997.) Trungpa's teachings were in many ways unorthodox, but he acquired the widest following of any Tibetan lama in the United States. (He is famous for inventing a square meditation pillow he called a *gomden,* which apparently many Western students found more comfortable than the traditional round one.)

Trungpa eventually moved the center of his operations, which is called Shambhala International, to Halifax, Nova Scotia, largely on account of its remoteness. There is also a group retreat center in Barnet, Vermont. In addition, Shambhala runs the Naropa Institute in Boulder, Colorado (Naropa was an abbot of Nalanda University), which fosters what it terms "contemplative education."

Trungpa specialized in the kind of meditation called *tonglen,* or meditation of compassion, characterized by ritualized in-and-out breathing. He also instituted month-long retreats known as *dathuns.* Only after many years did he initiate some students into the Tantric practices of his native Tibet. He encouraged his students to learn about other Buddhist traditions, including Theravada, Mahayana, and Zen.

Shambhala International recognizes three pathways or gates to Awakening: Vajradhatu, Shambhala, and Nalanda. Vajradhatu is a mixture of traditional Tibetan, Zen, and Theravada Buddhism (reflecting Trungpa's *rimed* heritage). It encompasses systematic meditation (both *shamatha* and *vipassana*) training and academic study.

Shambhala, sometimes called the "Sacred Path of the Warrior," is an innovative method particular to this school, although some believe that it derives from ancient Tibetan practice. This secularized program begins with the "Heart of Warriorship" workshop. Altogether there are five levels: the Art of Being Human (experiencing the world as "sacred"), Birth of the Warrior (recognizing habits and fears), Warrior in the World (developing confidence), Awakened Heart (opening the heart and intuition), and Open Sky (learning to trust oneself).

Nalanda, which takes its name from a medieval Indian Buddhist University, is the path of wisdom through appreciation of art and culture, attempting to integrate them into everyday life. Subjects include traditional arts, health, education, and business. The arts taught include the Japanese imperial court music and dance (*gagaku* and *bugaku*), *chado* (the tea ceremony), calligraphy, archery, *ikebana* (Japanese flower arranging), equestrian arts, music, poetics, and "Mudra Space Awareness." There are more than 100 Shambhala centers around the world; all are united under the control of Shambhala International in Halifax. In the United States

Shambhala runs one residential contemplative community in Vermont and two in Colorado.

Despite his popularity, Trungpa had his share of detractors, most of whom complained about his smoking, heavy drinking, and sexual activities with his own students. When he died (probably of cirrhosis of the liver), his body was packed in salt. This simple preservation enabled his students to meditate with the corpse for about two months. Then the late Chogyam Trungpa was wrapped in gauze, soaked in butter, and burned. At the funeral, several rainbows appeared in the sky, which were observed even by the most skeptical.

After his death, a period of dissension among his disciples ensued. Trungpa appointed an American, Osel Tendzin (Thomas Rich), as his successor or Vajra Regent, in 1976. The "Regent" means that Tendzin was appointed to look after Trungpa's students until Trungpa, the *tulku* and Master, was incarnated once more. Tendzin met Trungpa in 1971 in Boulder and became his disciple. Tendzin shared his Master's taste for promiscuous sex. He contracted AIDS and engaged in unprotected sex with both male and female students. Apparently he passed it on to at least one other person, who died from the disease. Tendzin was quietly forced into retreat in Ojai, California, where he died of AIDS in 1991.

In 1995, leadership of Shambhala passed to Trungpa's eldest son, known as Sakyong, or "Protector of the Earth." (His full name is Sakyong Mipham Jampal Trinley Dradil.) Recently Sakyong has been acknowledged as the reincarnation of a previous Kagya teacher.

One of Trungpa Rinpoche's lasting legacies is the Great Stupa, located near Fort Collins, Colorado. In the early 1970s Chogyam Trungpa founded the 552-acre Rocky Mountain Shambhala Center (RMSC). It contains the Great Stupa, a $2.7 million monument that combines classic Buddhist iconography with modern technology. The 108-foot-high structure was designed to last 1,000 years, and contains a 20-foot-high gold Buddha. The Buddha itself houses part of Trungpa Rinpoche's skull and spine, left over from the cremation. Unlike most stupas, which are completely sealed, this one houses meditation rooms. The stupa was consecrated August 18, 2001.

Another important teacher of this tradition is Kalu Rinpoche (1905–89). Kalu was born in far eastern Tibet, and began his monastic career at age thirteen. At twenty-five, he began a twelve-year wilderness retreat in the mountains, living an ascetic, wandering life. He was also a teacher of the present Dalai Lama. In 1957, he was appointed the abbot of

Jangchub Choling Monastery in Bhutan and became the personal chaplain of the royal family. In 1965, Kalu established his own lineage monastery of Samdrup Targye Ling at Sonada, near Darjeeling, in India. From 1971 Kalu traveled extensively, establishing Dharma centers and retreat facilities in Europe, the United States, Canada, and Southwest Asia.

Pema Chodrun is a disciple of Trungpa; the abbey that she opened at his request in 1983, Ganpo Abbey, is the first Tibetan monastery, rather than lay-operated center, in the West. She did the fund-raising herself. Chodrun took her *bhikkshuni* precepts in 1981 at a mass ordination in Hong Kong. The spiritual director of the abbey is Thrangu Rinpoche, who believes that the abbey will eventually become a center for Buddhists of all persuasions. He also recognizes that American (including Canadian) culture will permanently change the face of Buddhism. The abbey has already begun the process by having men and women practice together. Women taking full *bhikkushini* vows will be able to ordain other women.

The Sakya School

The Sakya school had its heyday several centuries ago, and while still very much a living tradition of Tibetan Buddhism, it is not now as well-known as the other three schools of Tibetan Buddhism. Its teachings, however, are closely related to those of the Kagyu school.

The leadership of the Sakya school is hereditary, and its history is legendary. The name Sakya itself derives from the Tibetan *sa-skya,* which means "white earth." The holy family who became the hereditary leaders of this lineage are known by three names: "Lha Rig," "Khön," and "Sakya." According to official doctrine, the Sakya lineage began with a race of celestial beings who descended from the Clear Light Heavens in the Realm of Form to take up residence in the snow mountains of Tibet for the benefit of sentient beings. These were known as "Lha Rig," or "The Celestial Race."

The historical founder is considered to be Khon Konchog Gyalpo (1034–1102), who built the first temple-hermitage, the Gorum Zimci Karpo, in 1073 on the white patch of earth, marking the beginning of the Sakya lineage. The present head of the school is the forty-first Throne Holder of Sakya, His Holiness Sakya Trizin Ngawang Kunga (b. 1945) of the Drolma Podrang. There are many *tulkus, khenpos*, and *lharampa-geshes* of this tradition, both in Tibet and scattered throughout the world.

One of the key teachings of this school is the concept of the "triple vision," referring to the three views of the world: that of an ordinary person, that of a devout practitioner with insight into reality, and the fully integrated view of an awakened Master or Buddha.

The most important canonical work of the Sakya tradition is Lamdre (Lam-'bras), "The Path and Its Result." This work maintains that one cannot attain Nirvana by abandoning *samsara* (the cycle of birth and rebirth), because the mind is the root of both *samsara* and Nirvana. When the mind is obscured, it takes the form of *samsara* and when freed of obscurations it is Nirvana. Thus, one needs to work, through meditation, to realize his or her nonduality. Today, in America, the Sakya school (along with the Gelugpa school) has flourished primarily as an academic nexus for the study of Tibetan Buddhism.

Teachers of the Sakya School in America

In 1961, Deshung Rinpoche, previously abbot of the Tharla Monastery, came to the University of Washington in Seattle. Although he eventually began to teach the Dharma to Western students (at the request of Kalu Rinpoche), his main academic focus was on working with scholars in Tibetan language training and translation. Equally important, however, was his establishment of a resettlement community in Seattle for displaced Tibetans.

Lama Thartse Kunga, who came to the United States with the Gelugpa lama Geshe Wangyal (about whom, more below), founded one of the earliest Sakya centers in America, the nondenominational Ewam Choden Tibetan Buddhist Center, in 1971. This monastery hosts lamas from all four Tibetan traditions. Other important institutions in the Sakya school include the Sakya Center for Buddhist Studies and Meditation in Cambridge, Massachusetts (founded 1980), and the Sakya Phuntsok Ling Center for Tibetan Buddhist Studies and Meditation in Silver Spring, Maryland (founded 1986).

The Sakyas celebrate the following holy days from the Buddha's life:

- Miracles of the Buddha: from the first to the fifteenth of the first month.
- Milestones in the Buddha's life: (a) the birth of Shakyamuni Buddha, seventh day of the fourth lunar month; (b) entering the womb; (c) attaining complete Enlightenment at dawn; and (d) passing into

Parinirvana at dusk, all on the fifteenth day of the fourth lunar month.

- The first turning of the Wheel of Dharma on the fourth day of the sixth lunar month.
- The Descent from the Divine Realms: Shakyamuni agreed to descend on the fifteenth day of the ninth lunar month and actually descended on the twenty-second of the ninth month.

In addition, there are regular monthly holy days: the eighth, fourteenth, fifteenth, twenty-third, twenty-ninth, and new moon. The full moon and solar and lunar eclipses are also considered auspicious.

The Gelugpa School

The Kagyu school remained dominant in Tibet until the fifteenth century, when it was surpassed by the reform movement eventually known as Gelugpa, the order to which the Dalai Lama belongs. The founder of this school was Tsongkhapa (1357–1419); Tsongkhapa's nephew was hailed as a reincarnation of Avalokitesvara. When he went to Mongolia to make converts, he was hailed as the Dalai ("Ocean") Lama. This seems odd, as Mongolia is not known for its seacoast. At any rate, the word "Dalai" refers to the fact that the Dalai Lama is an "ocean of wisdom."

The current (fourteenth) Dalai Lama is Tenzin Gyatso. He is both the political and spiritual head of Tibet, at least nominally, and he is an assured statesman for the cause of Tibetan freedom and independence. He won the Nobel Peace Prize in 1989. On his several visits to the United States, he addressed both religious and political concerns. His work has given life and impetus to the many organizations devoted to Tibetan autonomy, including the U.S. Tibet Committee, the Tibet House, the International Campaign for Tibet, the Free Tibet Campaign, and Students for a Free Tibet. Other groups dedicated to the cause include the Milarepa Fund and Concerts for a Free Tibet, both instituted by convert Adam Rauch of the Beastie Boys band. The Dalai Lama's own monastery in Ithaca, New York, the Namgyal Institute of Buddhist Studies, is a branch of the Dalai Lama's charter monastery in Dharamsala, India. It provides traditional Tibetan studies for Westerners under the oversight of a board of directors consisting of three Tibetans, one Western *geshe,* and three other Westerners.

Hollywood has also produced two major motion pictures featuring Tibet: *Seven Years in Tibet,* directed by Jean-Jacques Annaud; and *Kun-*

dun written by Melissa Matthiessen, herself a Tibetan Buddhist and then wife of Tibetan Buddhist Harrison Ford, and directed by Martin Scocese.

One of the most interesting aspects of the Gelugpa school is its concept of the doctrine of *anatta,* or no-selfness. It carefully distinguishes between a "transactional" self, a provisional being that lives and works in the world, and some ultimate essential Self whose existence is denied. This commonsense view of "no-self" has a great deal to recommend it, for it answers the question, if there is no "self" then who is writing this book or buying potatoes or feeding the basset hound? No, the answer is plain, it is the provisional self, the result of the temporary interplay of the five *skandhas,* literally "heaps," referring to the aggregates of senses and perceptions that we mistakenly refer to as "self." It is only when we dig a little deeper and try to find the nature of this "self" that we run into trouble. For while the "self" rises and decays, it never abides. There is no essence to it at all.

Like the Sakya school, the Gelugpa school in the United States has largely been academically oriented.

Teachers of the Gelugpa School

The first important lama of the Gelugpa school (or indeed of any school) of Tibetan Buddhism to enter the United States was Ngawang Wangyal (1901–83). Although born in the Mongolian province of Astrakhan, Wangyal studied at the Drepung Monastery in Lhasa, Tibet, and received his *geshe* degree in 1938. He came to the United States (New Jersey) as part of the general Tibetan exile, taught courses at Columbia University, and truly established Vajrayana Buddhism in America. He also founded the Lamaist Buddhist Monastery of America (renamed the Tibetan Buddhist Learning Center in 1986). This became one of the foremost institutions for promoting Tibetan Buddhism in the West. Wangyal ordained Robert Thurman, the first ordained American Tibetan monk. (Originally part of the Gelugpa school, Thurman now advocates his own special kind of American Buddhism. He currently holds the Jey Tsong Khapa Chair of Indo-Tibetan Buddhist Studies at Columbia.) He also ordained Jeffrey Hopkins, who is now a professor of Indo-Tibetan Studies at the University of Virginia.

In America, one of the most important of the Gelugpa school institutions is Drepung Loseling Institute. Located in Atlanta, Georgia, with assistance from Emory University and under the patronage of the Dalai Lama, Drepung Loseling Institute follows the legacy of Drepung Loseling Monastery of Tibet. Its mission statement lists its two major purposes:

1. To contribute to North American culture by providing knowledge of the Tibetan Buddhist arts and sciences, in terms of both theoretical and practical training, to academic students/researchers and the general public within the context of the authentic Tibetan framework
2. To help preserve the endangered Tibetan culture, which today leads a fragile existence in the exiled refugee communities in India and Nepal

Independent Schools

Not all Tibetan groups are aligned with one of the main four branches of Tibetan Buddhism.

Kadampa School

Literally meaning "oral instruction," the Kadampa school was founded by Atisha (982–1054). While Buddhism was degenerating throughout most of the rest of Tibet, the Kadampa school saw its main job as preserving intact the writings before they were distorted or destroyed. They also developed a powerful system of mind-training practices that are still in use in Tibet today. The Kadampa school has been almost totally subsumed in the Gelugpa school, but there are efforts toward reviving it. Currently the Kadampa Meditation Center in New York State is the first Kadampa temple in North America. It was founded in 2000 by Geshe Kelsang Gyatso, who brought this school of Buddhism to the West in the 1970s and is assiduously working to expand it. Kadampas would like to found a temple in every large city in the world.

Chökling Tersar Foundation

Chökling Tersar (literally, "new treasures of Chökgyur Lingpa") owes its name to the great Tibetan Buddhist Master of the nineteenth century, Chökgyur Lingpa (1829–70), who reportedly held seven lines of transmission. His teachings are widely practiced by both the Kagya and Nyingma schools of Tibetan Buddhism. His writings are supposedly scriptures that were concealed by the eighth-century founder of Tibetan Buddhism, Padmasambhava, with the express wish that they should be uncovered at specific times in the future. (Padmasambhava/Chökling Tersar was not brief. The writings take up forty volumes and 30,000 pages.) Chökling Tersar believes that this literature should be studied and practiced as an addition to the traditional canonical scriptures of Tibetan Buddhism. They contain not only advice on how to live, but also important prophecies. According to its charter:

> The independent American branch of the Chokling Tersar tradition is concerned with preserving, translating and disseminating these teachings, in the most authentic and principled way possible. The Chökling Tersar Foundation aims at doing so by first inviting learned and authentic holders of the Chökling Tersar lineage to lecture and provide appropriate spiritual counsel corresponding to the current public demand in the USA. These teachers will be invited from the various monasteries and learning centers belonging to the Chökling Tersar tradition in Nepal, India and Tibet.

Acculturaton of Tibetan Buddhism to America

Despite coming from an authoritarian, nondemocratic tradition, Tibetan Buddhism, for the most part, adapted quickly to American customs. It has been the general practice for Tibetan monks to set up a center, and then leave its upkeep and administration to senior American students. Most Tibetan monasteries are now firmly under American control, even though they may retain the nominal leadership of a Tibetan lama. Religiously, however, the essential elements have remained unchanged. The Dharma passes through the *geshe* and *tulku.*

Whether because of the inherent power and mystique of Tibetan Buddhism, or because of the tragedy of its birthplace, Americans are drawn to this rich and occult tradition. Tibetan lamas and their teaching continue to be in great demand.

Chapter 7

Contemporary American Buddhism: The Third Turning of the Wheel

One of the most amazing things about Buddhism is its ability to assimilate—to transform itself, like a living being, in order to accommodate itself to many cultures and diverse peoples. For many, it still savors of the rare, foreign, and exotic (which is, of course, a part of the attraction). Yet its roots are constantly deepening as it adjusts to the American climate. And while Buddhism is still a minority religion in America, its reach is growing beyond the culturally elite, educated, spiritually sensitive, and culturally powerful people who first embraced it.

What we are calling here contemporary American Buddhism is a subset of the general phenomenon known as Western Buddhism. Neither of these terms is as clear as one might wish. In the first place, many of the leaders of "Western" Buddhism, such as Thich Nhat Hanh, are not Western. Second, "Western Buddhism" in itself is not a sect or a school; neither is contemporary American Buddhism. Both these terms simply refer to Buddhism as it has developed in Western culture. In some cases, not much development has taken place at all; an entire group may have simply "relocated" without changing anything except its address. In other cases, it is almost impossible to recognize a connection between the "American" group and its roots. We use the term "contemporary American Buddhism," therefore, to denote a host of trends, organizational patterns, doctrines, and central concerns—some of which may be identical to Eastern Buddhism, and some of which are strikingly different. To make things even more complex, "Western" Buddhism is now going East again, and many traditional Buddhist cultures have turned with growing enthusiasm to some of the innovations of the West.

Americans are, above all, pragmatic people, and the practicality of Buddhism enchants and challenges them. And since this ancient tradition offers them many ways of being Buddhists, Americans are likely to sample them all, and to take what they find "works best." Buddhism itself began as a practical philosophy. The Buddha pointed out that if one were struck by an arrow, one's first job is to remove the arrow, not discover who shot it or from what motives. Buddhism is itself a superbly practical practice. This is the critical juncture at which Buddhism and America meet and prosper.

Some Buddhists, of course, both native Asian and convert American, object to what many of them call the co-optation of Buddhism by American culture. While many of these people make valid points, the truth is that such cultural change is inexorable. Buddhism has always changed as it has moved from culture to culture, and one of its more curious aspects has been the almost complete lack of ecumenical communication between schools when they all met in this country, until very recently. There are few doctrinal or practicing points of similarity between Theravada, Pure Land, and Soka Gakkai Buddhism, but each confidently identifies itself as Buddhist. The traditions can meet and even blend fruitfully in this country. While some inevitably object, it will happen nonetheless. Differences between the schools may always exist, but all will become "Westernized" as they encounter a world that even the Buddha could not have imagined. But he would have remained untroubled, for he above all others recognized impermanence and change as the very order of existence. He knew the Dharma would flow with it. As Lama Surya Das pointed out simply, "It's new times, new places."

A growing number of American Buddhists, currently about 13 percent, do not affiliate with any particular tradition. This is certainly a reflection of Americans' tendency not only to choose their own religious beliefs, but also to freely combine and amalgamate them. In religion, as in nearly everything else, Americans are individualistic and eclectic. In general, nonaffiliated Buddhist groups tend to be extremely democratic; many, but not all, have a formal leader. They may form out of devolution to a special chant, sutra, meditative practice, or style of worship. Some attract special constituencies like women or gays. Some are organized around a particular issue like nuclear disarmament, human rights, or environmental work.

The Heartland Sangha, of Evanston, Illinois, founded in 1989, may be a typical example. It is affiliated with the American Buddhist Association. This group of American Buddhists, led by Gyomay Kubose, practice a "nondualistic, pan-sectarian Buddhism drawn from the original teachings of Gautama Buddha, Jodo Shinshu, Zen Buddhism, and engaged Buddhism."

Their center includes members from several Buddhist traditions. Their simple mission statement includes:

- To live the teachings by their fellowship and support each other
- To explore the meaning of "Oneness" and develop insight into the teachings of the Buddha
- To work to make the community a better place
- To develop their spiritual Buddhist practice

Engaged Buddhism

Western Buddhism does not stand upon some celestial mountain, isolated from the rest of the planet. Not only would such a posture be impossible (even the most remote of monks is affected by air and water quality), it is not part of the Buddhist philosophy. While engaged Buddhism is certainly not the only form of Buddhism practiced in the West, and is not uniquely a Western phenomenon, it has become strongly entrenched in the Western Buddhism tradition. Engaged Buddhism is one path Buddhists use to attempt to solve the interconnected crises in which the contemporary world stands embroiled: nuclear perils, ethnic discord, environmental degradation and global warming, poverty, and psychopathic terrorism and criminality.

Thich Nhat Hanh

We owe the term "engaged Buddhism" to the exiled Vietnamese monk Thich Nhat Hanh. Of course, "engaged Buddhism" is only one choice for this new Buddhism. Dr. B. R. Ambedkar has suggested "Neo-Buddhism," a rather uninspired choice, while Bernard Glassman only half jokingly offers a "Supreme Meal." Kenneth Kraft has a more traditional suggestion: *Lokayana,* or "Earth Vehicle." But it is Thich Nhat Hanh's "engaged Buddhism" that seems to have stuck. Although never acknowledged as a great Ch'an Master in his native Vietnam, he has become one of the most influential of all Buddhist teachers of any school in the West.

Thich Nhat Hanh was born in 1926 in a Vietnamese village. His birth name was Nguyen Xuan Bao. When he was sixteen years old, he entered Tu Hieu Monastery, of the the Lieu Quan school of Vietnamese Zen

(Thien) in Hue. Here he was given his Buddhist name, which means "one action," a particularly portentous although apparently serendipitous choice, as he was actually named for an eleventh-century Master. He was fully ordained in 1949. However, his request to modernize the ancient curriculum was rejected, and as a result he and five other monks left the monastery to practice Buddhism their own way.

He opened the first Buddhist high school in Vietnam and helped to establish An Quang Buddhist Institute, a center for both Buddhist studies and political activism in Saigon (now Ho Chi Minh City) in 1950. He was also appointed editor-in-chief of *Vietnamese Buddhism,* the first organ to carry his expanded views of Buddhism.

According to Thich Nhat Hanh's thought, each being is distinct, separate, and yet part of a whole that includes society and the natural world. All of these are constantly changing. When he established his Order of Interbeing, he perfectly captured the Buddhist way of experiencing the world. Thich Nhat Hanh also coined the term "engaged Buddhism" to express the same idea in a more active form. Charles S. Prebish points out that this engaged Buddhism actually consists of three intertwined strands: Nhan Gian ("Buddhism for Everyone"), Nhap The ("Going into the World"), and Da'n Than ("Getting Involved").

The Order of Interbeing and the Unified Buddhist Church

In 1966 Thich Nhat Hanh founded Tiep Hien Order (Order of Interbeing) in Vietnam; this is the beginning of "engaged Buddhism," a Buddhism based on both Theravada and Mahayana traditions. According to its charter, its mission was to "actualize Buddhism by studying, experimenting with, and applying Buddhism in modern life." In February of that year he ordained six laypersons, three men and three women. From its inception and into the present, the order includes all four membership categories of the original Buddhist community: monks, nuns, laymen, and laywomen. Ordinees in the Order of Interbeing agree to abide by the Fourteen Mindfulness Precepts that Thich Nhat Hanh believes come from the Buddha's original teachings. These precepts are carefully framed so that they include openings for societal, as well as individual, action. (Interestingly, Thich Nhat Hanh has said that he believes that Maitreya, the Buddha-to-Come, will not arrive in an individual form, but as a community, or Sangha.) In their own words, the precepts are are follows:

1. *The First Mindfulness Training: Openness*

Aware of the suffering created by fanaticism and intolerance, we are determined not to be idolatrous about or bound to any doctrine, theory, or ideology, even Buddhist ones. Buddhist teachings are guiding means to help us learn to look deeply and to develop our understanding and compassion. They are not doctrines to fight, kill, or die for.

2. *The Second Mindfulness Training: Nonattachment from Views*

Aware of the suffering created by attachment to views and wrong perceptions, we are determined to avoid being narrow-minded and bound to present views. We shall learn and practice nonattachment from views in order to be open to others' insights and experiences. We are aware that the knowledge we presently possess is not changeless, absolute truth. Truth is found in life, and we will observe life within and around us in every moment, ready to learn throughout our lives.

3. *The Third Mindfulness Training: Freedom of Thought*

Aware of the suffering brought about when we impose our views on others, we are committed not to force others, even our children, by any means whatsoever—such as authority, threat, money, propaganda, or indoctrination—to adopt our views. We will respect the right of others to be different and to choose what to believe and how to decide. We will, however, help others renounce fanaticism and narrowness through practicing deeply and engaging in compassionate dialogue.

4. *The Fourth Mindfulness Training: Awareness of Suffering*

Aware that looking deeply at the nature of suffering can help us develop compassion and find ways out of suffering, we are determined not to avoid or close our eyes before suffering. We are committed to finding ways, including personal contact, images, and sounds, to be with those who suffer, so we can understand their situation deeply and help them transform their suffering into compassion, peace, and joy.

5. *The Fifth Mindfulness Training: Simple, Healthy Living*

Aware that true happiness is rooted in peace, solidity, freedom, and compassion, and not in wealth or fame, we are determined not to take as the aim of our life fame, profit, wealth, or sensual pleasure, nor to accumulate wealth while millions are hungry and dying. We are committed to living simply and sharing our time, energy, and material resources with those in need. We will practice mindful consuming, not using alcohol, drugs, or any other products that bring toxins into our own and the collective body and consciousness.

6. The Sixth Mindfulness Training: Dealing with Anger

Aware that anger blocks communication and creates suffering, we are determined to take care of the energy of anger when it arises and to recognize and transform the seeds of anger that lie deep in our consciousness. When anger comes up, we are determined not to do or say anything, but to practice mindful breathing or mindful walking and acknowledge, embrace, and look deeply into our anger. We will learn to look with the eyes of compassion at ourselves and at those we think are the cause of our anger.

7. The Seventh Mindfulness Training: Dwelling Happily in the Present Moment

Aware that life is available only in the present moment and that it is possible to live happily in the here and now, we are committed to training ourselves to live deeply each moment of daily life. We will try not to lose ourselves in dispersion or be carried away by regrets about the past, worries about the future, or craving, anger, or jealousy in the present. We will practice mindful breathing to come back to what is happening in the present moment. We are determined to learn the art of mindful living by touching the wondrous, refreshing, and healing elements that are inside and around us, and by nourishing seeds of joy, peace, love, and understanding in ourselves, thus facilitating the work of transformation and healing in our consciousness.

8. The Eighth Mindfulness Training: Community and Communication

Aware that lack of communication always brings separation and suffering, we are committed to training ourselves in the practice of compassionate listening and loving speech. We will learn to listen deeply without judging or reacting and refrain from uttering words that can create discord or cause the community to break. We will make every effort to keep communications open and to reconcile and resolve all conflicts, however small.

9. The Ninth Mindfulness Training: Truthful and Loving Speech

Aware that words can create suffering or happiness, we are committed to learning to speak truthfully and constructively, using only words that inspire hope and confidence. We are determined not to say untruthful things for the sake of personal interest or to impress people, nor to utter words that might cause division or hatred. We will not spread news that we do not know to be certain nor criticize or condemn things of which we are not sure. We will do our best to speak out about situations of injustice, even when doing so may threaten our safety.

10. The Tenth Mindfulness Training: Protecting the Sangha

Aware that the essence and aim of a Sangha is the practice of understanding and compassion, we are determined not to use the Buddhist community for personal gain or profit or transform our community into a political instrument. A spiritual community should, however, take a clear stand against oppression and injustice and should strive to change the situation without engaging in partisan conflicts.

11. The Eleventh Mindfulness Training: Right Livelihood

Aware that great violence and injustice have been done to our environment and society, we are committed not to live with a vocation that is harmful to humans and nature. We will do our best to select a livelihood that helps realize our ideal of understanding and compassion. Aware of global economic, political, and social realities, we will behave responsibly as consumers and as citizens, not supporting companies that deprive others of their chance to live.

12. The Twelfth Mindfulness Training: Reverence for Life

Aware that much suffering is caused by war and conflict, we are determined to cultivate nonviolence, understanding, and compassion in our daily lives, to promote peace education, mindful meditation, and reconciliation within families, communities, nations, and in the world. We are determined not to kill and not to let others kill. We will diligently practice deep looking with our Sangha to discover better ways to protect life and prevent war.

13. The Thirteenth Mindfulness Training: Generosity

Aware of the suffering caused by exploitation, social injustice, stealing, and oppression, we are committed to cultivating loving kindness and learning ways to work for the well-being of people, animals, plants, and minerals. We will practice generosity by sharing our time, energy, and material resources with those who are in need. We are determined not to steal and not to possess anything that should belong to others. We will respect the property of others, but will try to prevent others from profiting from human suffering or the suffering of other beings.

14. The Fourteenth Mindfulness Training: Right Conduct

(For lay members): Aware that sexual relations motivated by craving cannot dissipate the feeling of loneliness but will create more suffering, frustration, and isolation, we are determined not to engage in sexual relations without mutual understanding, love, and a long-term commitment. In sexual relations, we must be aware of future suffering that may be caused. We know that to preserve the happiness of ourselves and others, we must respect the rights and commitments of ourselves and others. We will do everything in our power to protect children from sexual abuse and to protect couples and families from being broken by sexual misconduct. We will treat our bodies with respect and preserve our vital energies (sexual, breath, spirit) for the realization of our bodhisattva ideal. We will be fully aware of the responsibility of bringing new lives into the world, and will meditate on the world into which we are bringing new beings.

Trainees also agree to practice sixty days of complete mindfulness (full concentration on the present moment) each year. Monks and nuns are forbidden to engage in sexual relationships.

Thich Nhat Hanh's work is now based in Plum Village, his monastic training and retreat center near Bordeaux in France, which he established in 1982. Plum Village contains five "hamlets" and is home to about 100 persons in addition to a transient population who come for retreats.

He also founded the Unified Buddhist Church (Eglise Bouddhique Unifieé) in France in 1969, largely as a response to the Vietnam War. The Unified Buddhist Church Inc. (UBC), a nonprofit corporation, was founded in 1998 to officially represent Thich Nhat Hanh and his Sangha in the United States. It is a sister organization of the Unified Buddhist Church founded in France. The UBC in America is represented by Sr. Annabel, abbess of the Green Mountain Dharma Center, which is near Woodstock, Vermont. The Green Mountain Dharma Center acts as the headquarters of the Unified Buddhist Church in the United States.

Thich Nhat Hanh came to the United States in 1961 to study religion at Princeton. During the early 1960s he taught Buddhism at Columbia, but he returned to his own country in 1964, where he established the Van Hanh Buddhist University in Saigon. It was during this time that he wrote *Engaged Buddhism.* As a peace activist, he was branded as a communist traitor by the South Vietnamese government. He narrowly escaped an assassination attempt, and returned to the United States in 1966. He spoke widely to American audiences, both to the public at large and to government officials, including members of Congress. He also inspired such human rights activists as Martin Luther King Jr., who nominated him for the Nobel Peace Prize in 1967. (However, his peaceful approach was considered *too* peaceful by some antiwar activists, who were as angry and violent as the people they opposed.) His compassion for all people was clearly revealed in the turmoil that followed the beating of Rodney King in 1992. He said, "When I first saw that video on French TV I felt that I was the one being beaten, and I suffered a lot . . . But as I looked more deeply, I saw that the policemen beating Rodney King were no different from myself. They were doing it because our society is filled with hatred and violence . . . We are all the policemen and the victim."

Thich Nhat Hanh's main assistant through the years has been Cao Ngoc Phuong; her Buddhist name is Chan Khong, which means "True Emptiness." She met Thich Nhat Hanh in 1959 when she was a university teacher in Vietnam, and was one of the original people ordained into the Order of Interbeing.

While Thich Nhat Hanh is not a permanent resident of the United States, his work has had a particular resonance among Buddhists of all schools. Individual communities of engaged Buddhism exist in Maine, North Carolina, Montana, and Pennsylvania. Today Thich Nhat Hanh continues to offer retreats throughout the world, including many in the United States, some specifically for veterans of conflicts such as the Persian Gulf War. Some critics of Thich Nhat Hanh have charged that he fails to address underlying causes of conflict (which they see as rooted in class and power structure rather than in individual frailties) or that he fails to give attention to traditional monastic practice. However, the vast majority of Buddhists of all schools find Thich Nhat Hanh a powerful voice for both Buddhism and social change.

Roots of Engaged Buddhism

Engaged Buddhism, by which we mean Buddhism formally committed to social change, environmental activism, and economic justice, is a rather new, or at least newly recognized, phenomenon. A few Buddhists find it so different from traditional Buddhism that they classify it as a fourth vehicle (*yana*) of Buddhism, along with Theravada, Mahayana, and

Vajrayana. It focuses more on the world than on the inner mind, and it is powerfully active rather than quietist. Robert Thurman even stated in a fall 1992 interview with *Tricycle,* "Meditation is not the main point of Buddhism. The main point is a new vision of relationships, a vision of compassion that led to the Buddha's strong commitment to social transformation. That's why the Buddha really could have dreamed America."

However, the seeds of engaged Buddhism lie within the older Buddhist traditions. Its emphasis might be new, but engaged Buddhism is a natural development and outgrowth of all schools of Buddhist thought and practice. It can also be argued, as Robert Aitken does in his *The Mind of Clover,* that Christianity and Western ideas in general had a powerful influence on Buddhist activism.

The signature Buddhist attributes are compassion and wisdom, which together form mindfulness (*sati*), and Western Buddhists are wisely and compassionately engaged in this world. Mindfulness not only includes awareness and direct perception of the fleeting nowness of phenomena, but also includes elements of memory and hope, of being able to look long into both the rich history and the uncertain future of the Earth. When the Buddhist scriptures speak of millions upon millions of *kalpas* (long ages), it is not just a figure of speech—they really mean it.

Buddhism is uniquely suited to a socially active role. It regards all beings as valuable and worthy of enlightenment. Buddhism embodies what Jewish philosopher Martin Buber called the "I-Thou" relationship, which placed beings in true and equal relationship, rather than the objectified "I-It" mode that is so unfortunately common. Immanuel Kant, another philosopher, made the same point when he said we should treat others as ends rather than as means. Thus the ancient Buddhist philosophy flows naturally into the most contemporary of Western thinking.

Buddhism recognizes the destructive power of greed, hatred, and delusion, and though these features were first identified as harming the individual person, they are equally destructive to the world around us. Buddhism understands that just as human beings as individuals are not separate from other human beings, the human species is not separated from other species. Plants, humans, and other animals live together in a delicate symbiosis. And all of us depend in turn upon the fragile network of water, air, and earth that sustains us. This is what Buddhism means when it talks about the interdependent origination, a balance between unfettered individualism and mindless collectivism. Bernard Glassman, a Zen Roshi long committed to the idea of service, said that the depth of a person's realization is made visible by that person's service to others. Since we are all one, an enlightened person could not help caring for other people. For Glassman, this is just common sense, not some altruistic "social action."

Understanding without acting is hollow, and Buddhism, with its doctrine of *maha karuna,* or great compassion, has become one of the most socially and environmentally activist of the world's religions. Because Buddhism is impartial, its compassion is not limited to fellow Buddhists, or, for that matter, fellow human beings. Animals, plants, air, earth, and water—each is worthy of respect. It is this respect for the original nature of all beings, and ultimately the identification of all beings that gives Buddhism its special role in saving our planet. Anne Waldman, Buddhist poet and activist, has affirmed this role for Buddhism. The bodhisattva vow, she believes, is Buddhist Activism 101 (*Tricycle,* Spring 2002). The bodhisattva vow binds the practitioners to alleviate suffering throughout the world of sentient beings; therefore, activism is a "must" for caring Buddhists all over the world.

This does not means that all Western Buddhists are in agreement about the role of Buddhism as a force for change. There are differences in emphasis and approach. For some, social activism seems to pull Buddhists back too fiercely into a world of grasping and struggle. Others believe that solving the world's problems is best undertaken through individual improvement rather than broad social action. Like mindful people of all religious traditions, Buddhists feel both called to act in the world and the need to rise above it. This means responding to crises promptly and with compassion, but always remembering that all things on Earth, including the Earth itself and all its inhabitants, are transitory beings.

The disconnect between private practice, which has always been so essential to Buddhism, and public policy has proved painful indeed. Some Buddhists find themselves split between a "citizen-self" and a "spiritual-self." This became particularly evident after September 11, 2001, in the wake of the terrorist attack on the World Trade Center and Pentagon. Like other Americans, Buddhists found solace in their beliefs, but at the same time were conflicted about how to apply their compassionate and peaceful philosophy to the demands and feelings of the moment. In destroying complacency, in shaking confidence, and in wounding hearts, the terrorist attack brought home the painful reality of the First Noble Truth—that all life, even in the privileged "god-realm" (as Chogyam Trungpa Rinpoche called America) involves suffering. It also presented Buddhists with an awesome challenge: how to respond both as Buddhists and as Americans.

Yet the citizen-self and spiritual-self turn out to be two aspects of one person. All of us live in both a public world and private world. And since

Buddhism stresses the interconnectedness of all beings, justice is never a matter that can be left in someone else's hands. We all share this planet, and everyone is part of some society and culture.

Although anger is often considered a beneficial emotion in American culture, Buddhism generally regards anger as clouding the mind, as making good decisions less likely, as the Venerable Thubten Chodren writes in *Working with Anger.* It also makes Americans look bad in the eyes of others. Responding to attack with rage and anger is, in Buddhist thinking, not only useless, but senseless. No such thing as "righteous anger" even exists in most Buddhist thinking, although some Buddhists like Joanna Macy counsel people not to fear anger, and believe it has its place. At one point, Macy calls anger "good energy" and notes that Tibetan Buddhism is full of wrathful images of the gods and even of the Buddha. In one depiction he has fangs. Anger against hatred, greed, and ignorance is warranted in her view, although she also notes that if given proper "room" inside the psyche, anger can transform into something more positive.

Since we are all one, we should attempt to heal our wounds (as both aggressor and victim) rather than attack what is really part of our own being. This does not mean that aggressors should be allowed to continue their aggression. As the Vietnamese monk Thich Nhat Hanh wrote in *Tricycle: The Buddhist Review* about the terrorists responsible for attacks: "We must lock them up with compassion." Compassion can be passionate and even fierce. But it cannot be colored by anger and still remain compassion.

Teachings on Contemporary Controversies and Issues

Since Buddhism is a religion that encourages people to think for themselves, it provides no easy answers to difficult questions, only guidance. One of the greatest areas of conflict is the division between absolute and relative positions, a division that can apply to almost every ethical dilemma. For example, the First Precept states, "Do not kill." It is an absolute prohibition. But the doctrines of emptiness and nonduality held by Mahayanists teach that everything is one, and that there is finally no killer and nothing to be killed, a view that could be ungenerously interpreted as "Well, since there is no killer and nothing to be killed, it doesn't really matter what you do."

Buddhists have managed to navigate successfully between this Scylla and Charybdis (or in more contemporary terms, between a rock and hard place) by invoking the virtue of compassion. Compassion is based on understanding the feelings of individuals and the knowledge that such individuation is an artifact of ceaseless change, and whose existence, while real, is nonetheless being reborn and dying every instant. This broad, but sensitive view is simply a manifestation of the Middle Way, which leads us to making good decisions based on both wisdom of how things really are and compassion as to how they can be.

War and Peace

Buddhists are strong, sometimes radical, pacifists who condemn war as an outgrowth of the three poisons (hatred, greed, and ignorance or delusion) that serves the cause of nationalism, a kind of super-ego. Thus nations as a whole are subject to the same "three poisons" as individuals are. Anger against enemies must transform itself into compassion, greed into giving, and delusion into wisdom. Of course, this transformation is not instantaneous, and to this end Buddhists cultivate the foundational virtue of patience.

Scriptural foundation for such a strong, nonviolent stance is firm. The Buddha said:

> "They insulted me, hit me, beat me, robbed me."
> For those who brood on this, hostility is not quieted.
> "They insulted me, hit me, beat, robbed me."
> For those who do not brood on this, hostility is quieted.
> Hostility is quieted by nonhostility. This is an enduring truth.

However, since Buddhism is never absolutist in its claims, it expects each Buddhist to reflect deeply on the options available to him or her, and make the best decision possible in light of Buddhist precepts.

Some Buddhist teachers, like Thich Nhat Hanh, Daisaku Ikeda, and Robert Aitken, teach that killing is never permitted, while others point to a Buddhist sutra that tells of a bodhisattva who killed a pirate in order that the 500 merchants on the ship would be saved. Even so, the bodhisattva had to be reborn in hell for a moment in consequence of his action. Even in the rare instances where killing or other retaliation seems to be permitted, it is emphasized that the doer must be acting from compassion only, such as to save the lives of innocents. It may not be done from motives of expediency or revenge. Despite their generally peaceful history, there are a few instances in which Buddhists have engaged in war. The Buddhist

"White Lotus Society" freed China from Mongol rule in 1368, and Japanese Zen Masters often supported their empire's imperialistic designs. Still, these instances are very rare; Buddhism is usually successful in uniting its nonviolent theory with peaceful practice. However, some renowned Buddhist teachers such as the Tibetan Chagdud Tulku Rinpoche wrote in the *Buddhist Peace Fellowship Newsletter* (winter 1991) in connection with the Persian Gulf War, "As we aspire to peace we cannot deny the possibility that each of us may be confronted with the need for wrathful intervention in order to prevent greater harm."

Buddhists who hold a position of absolute nonviolence maintain that once we eliminate violence as a possible option, it encourages us to think more creatively about peaceful ways to attain just goals. This can be done by first analyzing and then eliminating the causes of war—hatred, greed, and ignorance, each of which is responsible for the conditions that lead to violence. Hatred is often based on perceptions of racial, religious, ethnic, or ideological differences; greed is based on the desire for the wealth or property of others, and ignorance is based on the deluded notion that other people are essentially different or even other than ourselves. These false concepts produce terrible suffering, and happiness, which is the goal of everyone, cannot be achieved by inflicting suffering on other people. In Buddhist thought, nonviolence need not be passive, but rather an active way to work in the world. The depth of the Buddhist opposition to war was first demonstrated in Vietnam on June 11, 1963, when Thich Quang Duc, an elderly monk burned himself alive to protest the Vietnam War. A student of Thich Nhat Hanh, Nhat Chi Mai, followed suit on May 16, 1967.

Another Buddhist peace activist is Paula Green (b. 1939), who founded the Karuna Center for Peacebuilding, where she offers training programs in nonviolent social change. Her work has led her and her husband Jim all over the world to lead workshops. She will go only at the invitation of the host countries.

Concern for world peace is not limited to widely known Buddhist groups such as Zen. In 1973, two American monks from the Hsuan-Hua's City of Ten Thousand Buddhas undertook an 1,100-mile pilgrimage across the country in an effort to promote peace.

Soka Gakkai International-USA and the Peace Movement

Daisaku Ikeda of Soka Gakkai International-USA has received the United Nations Peace Award for his work toward global nonviolence. Peace, he maintains, is not merely an absence of war, and the goal of humanity should be to create a culture of peace. Barriers to peace include isolationism, the illusion of "efficiency," greed, poverty, environmental responsibility, and nuclear negativity. In his book *For the Sake of Peace,* he discusses seven "paths to global harmony":

- The path of self-mastery, in which inner reform and the "internal republic" replace the reliance upon external and abstract reform. It also includes replacing the "lesser self" with the "greater self," which is interwoven with the forces of the universe.
- The path of dialogue and tolerance, which dispenses with prejudice and stereotyping. Dialogue is an intrinsic part of the Buddhist tradition, and Ikeda quotes the Lotus Sutra, which proclaims that bodhisattvas "are clever at difficult questions and answers." The bodhisattvas themselves are masters of dialogue, and possess certain characteristics that set them apart. First, they are strict with themselves. Second, they are compassionate toward others. And third, they are unrelenting against evil. Ikeda uses the analogy of a lotus, which rises from the mud to flower in the pure air. But it never forgets its roots.
- The path of community, in which Ikeda advocates rethinking the idea of competition, and which addresses the need for a world community.
- The path of culture, which talks about the role of art in building peace.
- The path of nations, which considers the role of the UN.
- The path of global awareness, which considers sustainable development and related issues.
- The path of disarmament, which addresses the most immediate and savage danger to world peace.

Soka Gakkai focuses on public education, including such efforts as petition drives, seminars, pro-peace publications, and exhibitions. The SGI's Women's Peace Committee has published a twenty-volume work, *In Hope of Peace,* that chronicles the experiences of women who lived through World War II. It has also sponsored peace forums and published thousands of essays by people who have experienced war firsthand.

SGI has assembled an internationally traveled exhibit on the dangers of nuclear arms. It was first presented at the UN in 1982 and has since traveled to over sixteen countries. It has been viewed by well over a million people worldwide.

On a local level, the SGI-USA's Youth Peace Committee has held conferences focused on the issue of violence in the community, in which law enforcement officials, social workers, and citizens work together to find answers.

A group known as Nipponzan Myohoji, which like Soka Gakkai is an offshoot of Nichiren Buddhism, has also been active in the peace movement, largely through "walking for peace" movements and the building of white "peace pagodas" around the world. The head monk of Nipponzan Myohoji in America and founder of the New England Peace Pagoda, Kato Shonin, is also a board member of the famous Buddhist Peace Fellowship, which is discussed below.

The Buddhist Peace Fellowship and the Peace Movement

The Buddhist Peace Fellowship (BPF) was founded in 1978 by Robert and Anne Aitken, Gary Snyder, Nelson Foster, and Joanna Macy. It began because its founders were concerned that the Buddhism they were practicing had distanced itself from the social problems of the day, and had become aloof and even elitist. Many Buddhist teachers, especially those from the Zen tradition, even discouraged social outreach programs, feeling that they interfered with an individual's ability to reach Enlightenment. The group felt that such teachings flouted the Buddha's own compassionate stance.

This unusual group is not associated with any particular Buddhist school or teacher; Joanna Macy (b. 1929), for example, grew up as a committed Presbyterian/Congregationalist, and she retains strong feelings for Christianity, although she no longer calls herself a Christian. Although born in Los Angeles, Macy grew up in New York City, where she attended a French lycée, and studied religion at Wellesley College. Eventually she received a Ph.D. in Buddhist Studies from Syracuse University, but also studied general systems theory. Macy was able to combine fruitfully these two fields in her subsequent work. In fact, her doctoral dissertation concerned analogies between Buddhism and general systems theory. With her husband Fran she lived all over the world, raised three children, and even, for a time, worked for the CIA. Her interest in nuclear disarmament began in the 1970s, thanks to a nudge from her college-age children.

The BPF is a nonprofit organization affiliated with the Fellowship of Reconciliation and international peace consortium. It is also part of the International Network of Engaged Buddhism. BPF is a completely nondenominational group, working not only with Buddhists of all schools but also with Christian and Jewish groups. The BPF is a largely homegrown movement, with most of its founders being Euro-Americans from the Zen and West Coast Vipassana traditions. However, it also includes a substantial membership from the ethnic Japanese Jodo Shinshu community.

One major contribution the BPF has made to the engaged Buddhist movement is to establish a doctrinally sound Buddhist basis for its action. It has carefully combed through sacred texts from all Buddhist traditions, including Theravada, Zen, Tibetan, and Pure Land, finding canonical support for its various positions on peace and other reforms.

Two important members of the BPF, Therese Fitzgerald and her husband Arnold Kotler, eventually split from the BPF and founded their own organization, The Community of Mindful Living. This organization and the BPF have resumed friendly relations, however.

BPF currently has about 4,000 members. Its mission statement includes the following:

- Recognize the interdependence of all beings
- Meet suffering directly and with compassion
- Appreciate the importance of not clinging to views and outcomes
- Work with Buddhists from all traditions
- Connect individual and social transformation
- Practice nonviolence
- Use participatory decision-making techniques
- Protect and extend human rights
- Support gender and racial equality, and challenge all forms of unjust discrimination
- Work for economic justice and the end of poverty
- Work for a sustainable environment

The BPF focuses on democracy and human rights around the globe, particularly focusing on Bangladesh, Burma, Vietnam, and Tibet. In general, it has emphasized the structural basis for war and violence. Although it recognizes that individual action is important, it has also stated that it is "naïve and counterproductive" to think that single persons can successfully oppose large corporations. (Members of the Fellowship call that the "cowboy theory of history" and comment that it doesn't work.)

The BPF also has a prison project and runs the Buddhist Alliance for Social Engagement (BASE), a manifestation of the bodhisattva vow to save all sentient beings. The guiding light behind the BASE movement has been

Diane Winston, who trained in Vipassana with Joseph Goldstein and U Pandita Sayadaw. She felt a disconcerting split between those Buddhists who engaged in social action and those who routinely meditate, and found that few committed Buddhists of her acquaintance did both. Her efforts to combine both activities were largely responsible for giving BASE its current structure and outlook. BASE is a good deal more domestic in its outlook than is the BPF in general, and its emphasis may reflect a developing trend in BPF itself.

BASE provides a community-based structure for participants to spend six months in full- or part-time service, combined with Buddhist practice. It has five main components:

- Service/social action (*seva*): In the social action segment, participants are required to work twenty to thirty hours a week in community service such as hospices, prisons, or soup kitchens. Some participants are paid for their work; others are volunteers.
- Wisdom training (*pannya*): In the training or wisdom portion, students work with a teacher to learn how to apply Buddhist precepts to social issues and collective action.
- Dharma practice (*samadhi*): The third element is Dharma practice or twice-weekly meditation. There are also monthly retreats of one to five days. The purpose of meditative practice is not only to help reach Enlightenment, but to gather strength for the hard work of the organization.
- Community (*sangha*): Community refers to the community of participants; BASE hopes to develop an entire network of caring Buddhist associations.
- Commitment (*adhitthana*): Commitment means that each participant is expected to truly commit time to what he or she signed up for, usually six months.

The BPF has also been active in the disarmament movement and the Anti-Land Mines Campaign.Today the BPF has sixteen chapters across the United States. Its newsletter eventually became the quarterly journal *The Turning Wheel,* edited by Susan Moon.

One weakness of the BPF stems from what most Americans consider its greatest asset—its democratic and nonhierarchical structure. For cultural reasons, many Japanese, Chinese, and Tibetan people find the informality and democratic nature of BPF daunting or even inappropriate, and the organization has had to work hard to draw them in. Some critics complain also that BPF is not a truly national organization, with most of its functions taking place on the West Coast.

Zen Peacemaker Order

In 1996, Bernard Glassman and his wife, Roshi Sandra Jishu Angyo Holmes (1941–98), co-founded the Zen Peacemaker Order, and later the Peacemaker Community, an international, interfaith group, working with all strands of the Buddhist (and other) traditions. It states its goals as a "commitment and spirit of broad-based inclusivity, service, interfaith communion and celebration, and to a lifelong peacemaking path that integrates work, training, and practice." The Peacemakers adhere to the following values:

The Three Treasures:

- oneness, the awakened nature of all beings
- diversity, the ocean of wisdom and compassion
- harmony, the interdependence of all creations

The Three Tenets, a life of engaged spirituality based on:

- unknowing, as the source of all manifestations and seeing all manifestations as the teachings of unknowing
- bearing witness, by encountering all creations with respect and dignity and allowing oneself to be touched by the joys and pain of the universe
- healing, by committing energy and love to the healing of self, the earth, humanity, and all creations

The Four Commitments, which were agreed upon by the representatives of 200 religions at the World Parliament of Religions held in Chicago in 1993:

- I commit myself to a culture of nonviolence and reverence for life.
- I commit myself to a culture of solidarity and a just economic order.
- I commit myself to a culture of tolerance and a life based on truthfulness.
- I commit myself to a culture of equal rights and partnership between men and women.

The Ten Practices:

1. Recognizing that I am not separate from all that is. This is the practice of Non-Killing.
2. Being satisfied with what I have. This is the practice of Non-Stealing.
3. Encountering all creations with respect and dignity. This is the practice of Chaste Conduct.
4. Listening and speaking from the heart. This is the practice of Non-Lying.
5. Cultivating a mind that sees clearly. This is the practice of Not Being Deluded.
6. Accepting unconditionally what each moment has to offer. This is the practice of Not Talking About Others' Errors and Faults.
7. Speaking what I perceive to be the truth without guilt or blame. This is the practice of Not Elevating Oneself and Blaming Others.
8. Using all of the ingredients of my life. This is the practice of Not Being Stingy.
9. Transforming suffering into wisdom. This is the practice of Not Being Angry.
10. Honoring my life as an instrument of peacemaking. This is the practice of Not Thinking Ill of the Three Treasures.

As is usual in Buddhist practice, the Ten Practices are stated negatively, so as to give the widest range of freedom of action. Zen Peacemakers also do daily *zazen*, observe a moment of silence at noon, and observe a monthly Day of Reflection. They also have an interesting form of practice called Plunges, in which one immerses oneself in a situation that is not one's usual habitat, such as a street retreat.

Human Rights and Racism

Contemporary Buddhists consider human rights to be of prime importance, and many Buddhist groups of all branches are actively involved in the political (as well as the spiritual) liberation of humanity. For example, Soka Gakkai works hard in the field of human rights education, especially with children's rights. Soka Gakkai in itself is the most the racially diverse of all Buddhist groups, and is dedicated to continuing that diversity. Nippozan

Myohoji works closely with Navajo and Hopi Indians in their struggle for land and human rights.

One Myohoji monk, Sasamori Shonin, organized the Quincentennial Peace Walk in 1992 from Panama City to Washington, D.C., to chronicle 500 years of repression of indigenous peoples in this hemisphere. Another Buddhist (of the Zen school) active in the struggle against racism is Sala Steibach, an African American nurse/midwife and feminist. She feels that it is important to begin using the "language of Buddhism" to address racism, just as Rita Gross has done for ecology and feminism.

Although, as mentioned, some kinds of Buddhism, notably Soka Gakkai, tend to be quite diverse, others schools, notably Zen, are less so. Ethnic Buddhists of all sorts, including Korean, Japanese, Chinese, and Thai, tend to have little interaction, not only with Euro-Americans, but also with each other. Fear of the unknown is not a specialty of Euro-American Buddhists, and as Kenneth Tanaka has remarked, there is "a human tendency to gravitate to those with shared background and interests for psychological and physical security." Buddhists, of course, are not exempt from the common weaknesses of the rest of humanity.

Homelessness, Sickness, and Poverty

Homelessness presents an interesting challenge for Western Buddhists. In India, where Buddhism was born, homelessness was not merely a condition of poverty faced by countless people; it was also actively encouraged for those who sought the religious life. Hindu holy men lived homeless lives; indeed, the final stage of a life dedicated to holiness was that of the wandering sage. The Buddha also left his own home to seek spiritual truth and never returned to a permanent home.

However, times and customs have changed, and even the Buddha sought shelter during the three months of the rainy season. So, both as a nod to new cultural norms and out of compassion, the idea of homelessness as an ideal has been abandoned. Even Buddhist monks reside nearly year-round in monasteries or some other permanent dwelling.

Notwithstanding the fact that Buddhism was born in a country where poverty was endemic and homelessness a fact of life for some and an ascetic ideal for others, modern Buddhism has taken an active role to alleviate suffering and poverty around the world. One Chinese Buddhist organization, the Buddhist Association of Wisdom and Compassion, has no temple and no Sangha, and considers the mission of Buddhism is to compassionately minister to the poor and downtrodden. It works to organize the distribution of money, furniture, medical care, and clothing to needy persons.

Soka Gakkai has raised millions of dollars to support the UN High Commission for Refugees, for example, and also has conducted many relief efforts to provide medical care and other services to the poor and disaster-stricken around the world, including Cambodia, Nepal, Peru, India, China, Yugoslavia, and Argentina.

The Buddhist Peace Fellowship has also worked hard to abolish world poverty and sickness. Robert Aitken believes that Western economies in and of themselves violate the Second Precept, "Do not steal," and in *The Mind of Clover* argues that it is the Buddhist's duty to fight for social change. With the help of a grant from the Kaiser Foundation, the BPF has sponsored mobile medical teams to treat displaced Burmese people along the Thai-Burmese border. They have also provided low-interest loans for "right livelihood" projects among the Tibetan exile community.

Killing and Mistreatment of Animals

Most contemporary engaged American Buddhists work hard to promote the welfare of animals. This practice has deep philosophical roots in classical Buddhism. The very essence of Buddhism is compassion. Animals share in the world of *samsara,* the ceaseless round of birth, suffering, death, rebirth, and redeath. Because animals, like human beings, are able to suffer, they deserve our compassion. In fact, in the Buddhist view, there is no essential difference between them and us; no insuperable barriers exist between the human and animal worlds. Any distinction we can make is tentative, and not always true. We might, for example, say that animals are not as intelligent as humans. As a general rule, this may be true. Certainly no animals can do calculus, but neither can most people. Besides, there is no reason why intelligence, just because it happens to be our "thing" should be a characteristic that marks us as superior to animals. Fish are better swimmers, birds can fly, polar bears can handle extremes of weather, even monarch butterflies can unerringly migrate thousands of miles without the help of a map. Even the family dog can predict a thunderstorm.

If we use morality as the distinguishing feature, we are in even more difficulty. Indeed animals don't seem to have a well-developed moral sense, and their actions are generally based on fear of punishment or hope of reward. However, the same can be said for most people. And while we can certainly point out individual examples of altruistic behavior, it is so uncharacteristic of our species that we call such people "heroes" and set them apart from the rest of the "herd." And there are animal "heroes" as well. Cats will save their kittens from a fire, dogs save their owners, and dolphins have been known to save perfect strangers from drowning, at no benefit to themselves.

And as for the idea that only human beings possess a "soul," Buddhists dismiss that idea right away in their central doctrine of *anatta,* which maintains that nothing has a soul, including humans.

Buddhists do not believe that animals were created simply for our use. The fact that we can thrive on the flesh of some animals means nothing since some animals can thrive quite well on ours. Buddhist doctrine teaches its adherents to love all living creatures, not just human beings.

Since Buddhism denies the concept of a "soul," even for human beings, nothing separates humans from animals except our capacity for greater insight (and thus the opportunity to be enlightened). But because of *samsara,* this opportunity will one day belong to each creature. Over and over, the Mahayana texts inform us that all beings have Buddha-nature and that no final Enlightenment is possible until all beings are enlightened. In addition, Buddhists approach others in an I-Thou way. Other beings are not "its," but "yous," not treated as means to an end, but as worthy ends in themselves. Animals do not exist merely for our benefit and comfort, and to impose suffering upon them is a violation of the most fundamental Buddhist precept: do not kill. The Hua-Yen (Flower Ornament) Sutra instructs us that by helping all sentient beings equally and without discrimination, we make all Buddhas happy.

In addition, ancient tradition preserved in the Jataka tales informs us that the Buddha had 123 rebirths as an animal, thus reinforcing the inherent connection between them and human beings. Some of his incarnations included that of a lion, a parrot, an ox, a hare, a monkey, and an elephant. And as Prince Mahasattva, the Buddha gave his life to save a starving tigress and her cubs. In fact, his big concern was that she was so hungry she might even eat the cubs herself. To save her from committing this grave sin, he gave his own body to the brood to eat. The animals' debt to the Buddha was repaid. It is said that after the Buddha's Enlightenment, a seven-headed cobra rose up, spread its hood, and protected the Buddha from a raging thunderstorm.

Milarepa, a Tibetan monk, who supposedly composed 100,000 songs, tells in one saga how he came upon a hunted deer, a hunting dog named Red Lightning Lady, and its owner, a certain Chirawa Gwunbo Dorje. The three, hunted and hunters, were locked together in pain and suffering caused by sins in previous lives. Milarepa, however, released them from their fear, greed, and anger by his compassion, prayers, and practice of the Dharma, thus setting them on the path of liberation.

Most Buddhists believe that it is worse to kill a person than an animal, on the grounds that human beings are uniquely able to achieve Enlightenment in their present form. Therefore, it is permitted to kill animals to save human lives, although it is not permitted to kill them merely to enhance our comfort (meat, shoes, belts, and so on).

The Maharatnakuta Sutra declares that one should "not discriminate among sentient beings." The Cullavagga, a Pali text, declares that all creatures, "those with two feet, four feet, no feet, or many feet," are deserving of the Buddhist's love and care. It makes specific reference to serpents, scorpions, centipedes, lizards, spiders, and mice, creatures that are usually on everybody's kill-list. The Metta Sutra declares, "With a boundless heart one should cherish all living beings."

A story from the life of the Buddha illustrates this principle. One day Devadatta, the Buddha's evil disciple (who was also his cousin), shot down a swan that was flying overhead minding its own business. The Buddha saw the cruel act, and patiently took out the arrow, cleaned the wound, and bound it up. The furious Devadatta demanded his swan back. When the Buddha refused to yield the animal to certain death, Devadatta took his cousin to the Council court for a legal opinion. The Buddha successfully argued that since he cared for the bird, it belonged to him rather than to the one who tried to kill it. From this the Buddhist Principle of Property was born: "A living being belongs to the one who loves it."

In the United States, in 1985 Brad Miller of the San Francisco Zen Center founded the Humane Farming Association, which instituted the famous and successful Boycott Veal campaign. Buddhists work not only to improve the lives of factory-farmed animals, but also to encourage people to eat less meat and dairy products in general. Less meat eating is not only humane to animals, but in the Buddhist view, healthier for human beings and for the planet as a whole, since meat-animals consume far more resources than they produce.

One organization that works on animal welfare issues is the Buddhists Concerned for Animals. This group protests factory farming, experimental animals, and animals imprisoned by the import/export trade, such as tropical birds. However, even more "mainstream" Buddhists honor this principle. For example, the Ding Gong Temple in Massachusetts observes an annual celebration featuring the release of shellfish, lobsters, and other denizens of the sea into Boston Harbor. The International Buddhist Association in El Cerrito, California, has freed thousands of fish, crabs, and turtles.

Vegetarianism

As a result of their concern for animals, most Buddhists (with the exception of the meat-loving Tibetans) are vegetarians. Laura Carter Holloway Langford produced the *Buddhist Diet Book* in 1886. Like many Buddhists she believed that a vegetarian diet was conducive to both spiritual and physical health. All killing is a violation of the First Precept, and Buddhism condemns the willful killing of animals (even mosquitoes). Chinese Buddhists have taken, as one their forty-eight vows in imitation of Kuan-yin, a vow to follow a vegetarian diet. The Dalai Lama has confessed that he has on occasion killed mosquitoes that were biting him, but he did so regretfully and felt remorse. Robert Aitken generally maintains a vegetarian diet, but will eat meat at a party if offered to him. "The cow," he reasons, "is dead. While the hostess is not" (quoted in Helen Tworkov's *Zen in America* 59).

The Vinaya, or ancient disciplinary code of the monasteries, explicitly forbids eating ten different kinds of meat, and even when one of the monks died from snakebite (a not uncommon occurrence), the Buddha advised compassion and friendliness toward the snake family. However, not all Buddhists are vegetarians. Tibetans are fond of beef (not many plants grow in Tibet), and Buddhists from Burma favor pork dishes in remembrance of the Buddha's last meal on earth.

Care for the Earth: Green Buddhism

Dogen, in the Mountain and Waters Sutra, declared "There is a world of sentient beings in a blade of grass."

Contemporary American Buddhists agree. They have taken a lead in the worldwide fight to save our planet from environmental depredation, and again, they can go back to a long Buddhist tradition for inspiration. When the Tempter, Mara, asked the Buddha by what authority he acted, the Buddha responded merely by reaching down and touching the Earth. And the Earth roared in response. The Earth and the Buddha are one.

All Buddhists are by nature and conviction environmentalists. Not only are all aspects of the environment connected in a complex web of interdependence, but Buddhism also teaches that we are truly brothers and sisters, since we all spring from the same source. Violence against the Earth is seen as a violation of the First Precept ("do not kill"), and taking its fruits to fatten an already swollen economy while poor people starve is seen as a violation of the Second Precept ("do not steal"). Both actions deny the essential unity of the Earth and its people.

Environmentally Active Buddhist Groups

Nichiren and Soka Gakkai Buddhism formulate environmentalism in the phrase *eho funi,* which means that life (*sho*) and the environment (*e*) are inextricable (*funi*). Nichiren wrote that life is like a body and the world around is like its shadow. When one bends, so does the other.

In like manner, the Buddhist Peace Fellowship works hard to educate members and other interested parties in how deeply a single, seemingly innocuous act can adversely affect the environment. The issue is always to show how the Buddhist concept of dependent origination gives us a clearer understanding of the relationship between ourselves and our environment. However, one connection between Buddhism and the environment is fortuitous; it just happens that the most recent rise in interest in Buddhism, and the most recent influx of Buddhist teachers into the United States, coincided with the rise of the environmental movement. The two turned out to be a perfect match. (The same set of circumstances is true for the women's and human rights movements as well.) The first Earth and Spirit Conference was held in Seattle in 1990, and it included Buddhist workshops. In the same year, the Dalai Lama came to Middlebury College in Vermont for a Spirit and Nature Conference.

Joanna Macy has suggested that Buddhism's response to the environmental crisis and similar issues has set in motion what she calls "the third turning of the wheel," and that an entirely new kind of Buddhism, separate from Theravada and Mahayana (including Zen and Tibetan), is being born. Others see Buddhism's response as completely in line with traditional teachings, and something that can be found in all schools. Whatever the case, it is clear that Buddhism's fundamental teaching of dependent origination, or *paticca samuppada,* is getting a whole new application.

In Buddhist thinking, violence against the environment is a kind of fratricide. An even deeper insight shows us that in the larger view, the environment truly is our very body. We breathe the air and drink the water and eat the fruitful offerings of the earth. In this way we incorporate the earth into our being. And when we die, our bodies return to the earth that produced them. In other words, there is a deep, flowing unity between ourselves, that which surrounds us, and that which we surround in the form of food and drink. This complex principle of unity and diversity is what Thich Nhat Hanh has called "interbeing," and he leads meditation retreats for environmental activists. (Because the Buddhist perspective places humans and nature within the same complex web, some Buddhists object to the term "environmentalism," which suggests a compartmentalization that does not in reality exist. They prefer the word "ecology" to express the sense of oneness between humans and nature.)

The Buddhist love for nature is very ancient. The Buddha's greatest disciple, Mahakashyapa, composed a song praising the glories of nature: blossoming vines, cliffs, clouds, brooks, and all the creatures of the wild—elephants, peacocks, deer, and monkeys. And Han-Shan, an eighth-century Chinese poet, scrawled his nature poetry on cliffs and trees. (For some reason, this was not considered graffiti.) And Basho, the greatest of the haiku writers, took nature as the very lifeblood of his poetry. For all these writers, nature was simply another unfolding of the Dharma. It resonated vibrantly with the Buddha's teaching.

To take refuge in nature was to take refuge in the Dharma itself. Sometimes the message of nature is that of joy, sometimes of suffering, sadness, or the passing of time. Like the Dharma itself, nature speaks to every human condition and bodies it forth. As Dogen, the first Master of Japanese Zen, advised, "You should study the blue mountains." He knew that the mountains contained the entire Dharma in their heights and depths. At one point he said, "Mountains are the ancestors of the Buddha." Although mountains are perhaps the powerful and commanding aspects of the landscape, he also noted "all mountains walk with their toes in the water." Again, the interconnectedness of all phenomena is not merely a natural fact, but the touchstone of Buddhist philosophy. This makes the Buddhist attitude toward nature one of friendship, not antagonism, as often tends to be the case in the West. As Daito (1282–1337), a Rinzai Zen Buddhist and poet, wrote, "If there is a sudden downpour, and I am caught without my umbrella, I'll just wear the rain for a raincoat."

In fact, one prominent American Buddhist environmentalist, John Seed, has said that he has given up meditating in favor of serving the rainforest through environmental activism, although he believes that his previous practice in meditation has allowed him to work "joyously" even without seeing the fruits of his actions.

The Japanese monk Myoe of Toganoo, a member of the mystical Shingon sect, wrote a letter to an island remarking that he felt the island was more than some "enlightened" and religious person, but was in fact an interesting and pleasant friend. In the same work, he debated within himself the idea of writing a letter to a big cherry tree he knew, but desisted, deciding that the neighbors would think he was crazy.

Buddhist concern for the environment is a natural outgrowth of *ahimsa*. The Indian monk Buddhaghosa talks about a wounded tree-spirit. And as we have already seen, a tree, the *Ficus religiosa*, or as it is known in Buddhism, the Bo tree, has a central place in Buddhism. Trees, which seem to many people to stand on the line between sentient and non-sentient beings, are particularly important to Buddhists. The Buddha himself achieved Enlightenment underneath the *pipul*, or Bodhi tree, and according to one legend spent seven days in the weeks after his Enlightenment staring unblinkingly at the tree of his Enlightenment. One of the Jataka tales even talks about one of the Buddha's incarnations as a kusha grass-spirit, and Buddhist monks were forbidden to cut down trees. According to Chi-t'sang of the Madhyamaka school, Buddhists specifically include plants and trees in the category of sentient beings, those that will be eventually enlightened according to the bodhisattva vow.

In Southeast Asia, where many forests are now threatened by logging, Buddhist monks all over the region are engaging in tree ordination, which consists of a series of rites and the wrapping of the tree in the saffron robes of a monk. This ritual serves to sanctify the tree and to protect it against logging. It also serves to raise the awareness of the local people about the importance of conservation. The idea is now being copied in California. All trees are Bodhi trees.

For those who doubt that trees and plants are sentient, cautious Buddhists ask how we can be absolutely sure that a particular being is *not* sentient. Chan-jan, a philosopher of the T'ien-t'ai school, theorized that we have no real way of knowing what is sentient and what is not. "Who can really maintain," he wrote, "that inanimate things lack Buddhahood?"

Western philosophers, of course, have generally scoffed at the notion of anything other than human beings as having spiritual value. Descartes went so far as to maintain that animals were incapable of feeling pain. (This remark is so obtuse as to make one wonder in what ways Descartes' reputation as a great philosopher is justified.) Descartes is also responsible for steering Western philosophy straight into the so-called mind-body problem, a problem found only in Western philosophy and directly stemming from his notion that the mind and the body are completely separate entities. The philosophical dead-end this approach led to is perhaps one reason why contemporary philosophers are discovering anew the age-old insights of Buddhism.

According to many Buddhists, all beings, sentient or not, share the quality of beingness and thus deserve respect. Eco-philosophers like the Norwegian Arne Naess have called the earth the Third Body of the Buddha. (In classical Buddhism, of course, the Third Body is the Bliss Body, the body that has achieved the final stage of development. Buddhist ecologists put an interesting twist on this perspective.) In addition, the Buddhist ideal of a simple life makes environmentalism practical. In traditional Buddhism, nature is considered the perfect venue for meditation, although some Zen Buddhists, especially of the Soto school, find it distracting. They meditate facing a blank wall instead.

What does nature mean to Buddhists? Buddhism does not see the environment as separate from humankind. We are all part of the same web, which, in a beautiful metaphor, is sometimes known as the Jeweled Net of Indra. The net is envisaged as studded with clear jewels, each reflecting the other. In such a way, too, the elements of the environment are bound together, and shine and reflect upon one another. We are each individual, yet each of us is tied to and reflects the others. Each of us is a jewel in the net.

And like everything else, nature is subject to suffering impermanence (*anicca*). Western philosophy (based on Plato) and Hindu philosophy (based on the Upanishads) agree that the "highest" reality is eternal and unchanging. Buddhist philosophers have always maintained this picture of reality was inaccurate. They point out (along with the pre-Socratic philosopher Heraclitus) that change itself is the only "changeless" characteristic of the universe. All things in the universe change, and to posit some higher order of being that does not change effectively removes that order of being from the universe as we know it. Enlightenment does not consist in moving "beyond" this universe, but in plunging ever more deeply into it. One cannot understand the cosmos by leaving it.

Buddhism is practical; its purpose is to show its adherents how to achieve release from suffering not by leaving the realm of suffering, which is impossible, but by finding a path that transforms our relationship to that realm. For this reason, among so many others, Buddhists are environmentalists. We cannot alter the way the universe works. We cannot halt the progress of the seasons. Yet our careless and brutal use of natural resources has degraded our environment to the extent that the changes that occur are detrimental. Legend tell us that Nero fiddled while Rome burned. Western science has "fiddled" with the environment to the point where it, too, is burning.

Thus nature, like everything else in the universe, is subject to suffering (*dukkha*). Fortunately, suffering has the power to awaken our compassion. When our compassion is aroused, we can reenvision our proper relationship to the Earth and can then take the steps to correct our behavior so that it respects the Earth and its ways, and sees itself a part of them, not as a separate and higher order of being.

Thus, the Western idea of separating ourselves and our ultimate values from the natural, existential values of the Earth, the entire process of Cartesian and Platonic duality, has resulted in our separating ourselves from that which is truest and deepest and of ultimate concern. Most simply, as Thich Nhat Hanh has written, "We should deal with nature the way we should deal with ourselves!"

Another way of looking at the environment is to see it as the logical enlargement of the Sangha, or Buddhist community. If we consider the word "community" to mean a group of related beings with similar goals and a common welfare, then indeed all beings can lay claim to community. For while Western people tend to see competition among beings as the core of life, a more complete vision would recognize cooperation and dependence as the true center. For example, the lion and the antelope may look like competitors, but the truth is that not only does the lion depend on the antelope (or similar creatures), but the antelope population also relies on the lion to keep the herd healthy and strong. This is *patiica samupadda*, dependent origination, in action. No being is utterly distinct; no being can exist in isolation on this Earth. Even a rock is embedded in the earth.

In the United States, groups such as Ecosattva, originating from Green Gulch Farm of the San Francisco Zen Center, works to preserve the forest. "I speak for the trees, for the trees have no tongues, " said the Lorax in Dr. Seuss's book of the same name. Buddhists, along with other environmentalists, are learning to speak for the trees. In this regard, Soka Gakkai has established an Amazon Ecological Research Center in Brazil, which has contributed to the protection of the Amazon Basin.

On the other hand, Buddhists, who are not romantics, do not shrink from recognizing that nature has a dark side. They don't romanticize or soften its savage power, and they recognize the damage it can do to human beings. For example, in 1998, the Texas Buddhist Association collected over $30,000 in donations to distribute to the victims of natural disasters, both locally and around the world, including the Yangtze River area flood, earthquakes in Her-bei Province, China, and in Afghanistan, a typhoon-flood in Taiwan, and hurricane damage in three southeastern states of the United States and in Mexico. This effort was led by the Jade Temple in Houston, which is a primarily Chinese Buddhist temple.

For Buddhists, care for the environment is not a matter of holiness but of common sense and practicality. For if we destroy our planet, there will be no place left to become enlightened. Nature is not the repository of the human or divine spirit. It is part of life, neither more nor less. We are bound to care for the Earth if for no other reason than that we have to live here.

This practical approach means that it is not necessary to regard nature with excessive awe or to think of it as sacred. But it is absolutely essential, and as such deserves respect. Respect for nature, and love for all the beings on this planet, have, from earliest times, been essential components of Buddhism. The Buddha himself was enlightened under a fig tree, and all traditions tell us that he was even born in a grove of beautiful Sal trees. According to the Sutta-Nipata, one of the earliest sutras, the Buddha says, "Know ye the grass and trees . . . Then know ye the worms, and moths and the different sorts of ants . . . Know ye also the four-footed animals small and great, the serpents, the fish which range on the water, the birds that are borne along on wings and move through the air." All beings, then, are worthy.

The Buddha was also well attuned to the relationship between human activities and environmental degradation. He forbade his monks to pollute rivers by throwing waste of any kind into them, and the early monastic code of disciple, the Vinaya Pitaka, describes how to build toilets so that they do not contaminate the area.

Buddhism considers three factors to be the ultimate destructive forces of the world: greed, hatred, and delusion. Each has adverse effects on the environment. Driven by greed, corporations cut down forests, buy up (or otherwise degrade) farmland, and pollute the air and water. Driven by hatred, we see the elements of the natural world (insects, fires, storms) as hostile and destructive, yet unwittingly exacerbate their negative effects by trying to micromanage the environment instead of allowing ourselves to grow with it. We are also deluded about the interconnectedness of all beings, and until we become enlightened, we will continue to inflict suffering on ourselves and others, not because we are evil, but because we are deluded.

Unhappily, Buddhist concern with the environment has caused what biologists Paul and Anne Ehrlich call a "brownlash" among some Christian conservatives, who aside from whatever beliefs they have in their theology about the environment, feel constrained to take the opposite view from Buddhists (or any non-Christian religion) on principle, no matter what the issue. Thus some Buddhists, like Christopher S. Queen, have stated they always act as a "small-b" buddhist for fear of stirring up this "brownlash."

Gary Snyder and the Environment

The American Buddhist poet and scholar Gary Snyder wrote, "We must become warrior-lovers in the service of the Great Goddess Gaia, Mother of the Buddha." Even in the 1950s, when environmentalism wasn't even a word to Americans, Snyder was drawing connections between Buddhism and the environment. He is a widely read author both in the American literary tradition and in environmental studies, making a profound impact in both areas.

In 1951 Sndyer read D. T. Suzuki's *Essays in Zen Buddhism*. Inspired, he studied both Chinese and Japanese at the University of California at Berkeley, then met Allen Ginsberg and Jack Kerouac. He mostly lived in Japan between 1956 and 1965, and studied Zen at Daitokuji in Kyoto.

Long before they became mainstream causes, Snyder advocated recycling, responsible stewardship of the land, and reduction of dependence on fossil fuel. He finds strength in the Buddhist doctrine of no-self, and advocates an outlook that goes beyond narrow individuality to embrace the whole of creation. As a committed Buddhist, Snyder believes that "family values" should develop and expand into "community values." For him this development must accompany the Awakening of the "wild mind." The wild mind is not chaotic or excessive, but self-organizing, self-disciplined, and self-maintained, with strength coming from the inside, not forced or coerced. For Snyder, Buddhism is an integral whole that includes devotional practices and myth as well as sitting meditation and philosophy. Currently, Snyder has helped establish the Yuba River Institute, which works in cooperation with the U.S. Bureau of Land Management to restore land.

Law and Order

The Buddha's attitude toward the underside of society was that all humanity is redeemable. If even a hell-being can one day attain Enlightenment, it is surely possible for a criminal to turn aside from evil ways and begin the path toward renewal. The Buddha's own life provides an example. On one occasion, the Buddha was chased by a fierce outlaw named Angulimala who liked to chop off his victims' hands and make a necklace from their fingers. (In fact, the name Angulimala means "necklace of fingers.") He spotted the Buddha and tried to run him down, yelling at him to stop. Rather amazingly, the Buddha did stop, and looked placidly at Angulimala. "I have stopped as you asked," he said mildly. "Isn't it time that you stopped, too?" Angulimala immediately understood the Buddha's point, that he should cease his career of terror. Awed by the simple courage and strength of the Buddha, he discarded his weapon and became a follower.

This doesn't mean that criminals should not be punished. The inexorable law of karma assures that evil actions produce a result painful to the doer, but ultimately rectifying to society. What it does mean is that punishment is not to be exacted by society as a vengeful act. The Buddhist Peace Fellowship in particular has been very active in prison work, including spreading the peaceful message of Buddhism among the inmate population.

Melody Ermachild Chavis (b. 1943) is an investigator and writer who works exclusively on death penalty cases. She also practices Zen Buddhism (and previously studied Tibetan Buddhism at the Nyingma Institute in Berkeley). She currently practices at the Berkeley Zen Center, where she is working with other feminists to make Zen less patriarchal.

The Economy

The term "economics" is a Western one, and the concept of economics as an academic field did not exist in ancient Buddhist cultures. This does not make it any less important from a Buddhist perspective, and recent Buddhist scholars have been at work applying traditional Buddhist thought to global network of finance.

The earliest scriptures set the tone for what is today the Buddhist attitude. The Sigalovada Sutta, for example, teaches that one should gather wealth in the same way that a bee collects pollen, gently, without hurting the flower or producer of the bounty. The Buddhist ideal of a simple life based on reducing desire (*tanha*) and cooperation is incompatible with a lifestyle based on conspicuous consumption and competition. In Buddhist culture, giving (*dana*) is more highly valued than gaining; thus a Buddhist society is not amenable to unbridled capitalism. Personal fulfillment is found in interconnection, not competition. In traditional Buddhist societies, surplus material, whether food, clothing, or money, is typically donated to the monastery for the maintenance of the monks and nuns.

By reducing one's wants, one can more easily follow the Second Precept: do not steal. Reducing wants is reducing temptation. By not wanting so many things, one more easily reaches peace of mind and contentment. Thus the ideal is not to gain more things, to continually pile up objects, filling attics, basements, closets, garages, and even hired storage sheds with possessions, most of which the owners have forgotten about. The ideal is not to *reduce* our insatiable, sorrow-causing desires. It is to *eliminate* them altogether. Modern capitalism feeds on greed, hatred, and delusion, and thus is bound to bring unhappiness. In addition, compassion, one of the chief virtues of Buddhism, acts as a brake on capitalism, as it teaches its practitioners to look upon others as fellow beings, not as competitors. This ideal is spoken of as *kalayana mitta,* or "good friends." Capitalism, on the contrary, breeds envy, followed by hatred and, ultimately, violence.

As a matter of fact, Buddhist economists believe that economics cannot be cordoned off, either from other academic disciplines or from the world it hopes to describe. They view economics not as an objective description of the way things are, but as a social and financial program to create the world the way it should be. Unbridled consumerism, perhaps an inevitable result of a capitalist society, is inherently inimical to Buddhist values. It is an economic system based upon greed, one of Buddhism's Three Poisons. From a Buddhist standpoint, it is also, as is now painfully obvious, destructive to the environment, hurtful to traditional economies, and soul-searing for its own participants. Contemporary Buddhists attempt to inject at least a little of the Middle Way mentality into the American economy, at present, it appears, without much success.

Of course, simple, self-supporting economies have been submerged in rampant consumerism, and the American economy is so complex that one cannot simply retire to the forest (what is left of it) and build a self-sustaining Buddhist community, even if one wanted to. Interaction with the "other world" is inevitable. However, Buddhists believe that in general the scale of the economy can be reduced. Small does not mean isolated. Small systems can interconnect and interweave, thus becoming large and small at the same time. This is the Buddhist ideal, which recognizes and appreciates every unit in the whole, but also sees the larger design.

Many Buddhists have embraced the philosophy of radical (and Buddhist) British economist E. F. Schumacher, as expressed in his *Small Is*

Beautiful: Economics as if People Mattered. As Schumacher wrote, "The Buddhist sees the essence of civilization not in a multiplication of wants but in the purification of human character." And character is formed through the work one does. If work is conducted in an environment of "dignity and freedom," it uplifts. (Such workers also, not coincidentally, produce more, although whether more is better is a subjective opinion.) If labor is performed under conditions of oppression or dehumanization, it degrades the human person.

Unfortunately, until recently economics has ignored the importance of ethics in its formulations. It has also largely ignored psychological factors such as hatred, greed, and ignorance (for Buddhists the three marks of existence) that are instrumental in the making of market decisions. Time is making it clear, moreover, that this isolated approach is no longer either desirable or feasible.

Buddhism takes issue even with treating economics as an objective science, first for reasons of impossibility and second from reasons of desirability. First, Buddhists believe that it is simply not possible for economics to be a science in the way that chemistry is a science. Economics is driven by human beings, and humans beings are largely driven by emotions, including anger, greed, and ignorance. Western science is finally coming to an understanding of internal and subjective values that are directly linked to the outside world. Second, it is not desirable to treat economics as if it were a science, since that would reduce what could be a beneficial force in the lives of millions to an academic discipline that lets the chips fall where they may. Only by injecting moral and ethical insights into the study of economics, Buddhists believe, can we hope to use it as part of a transformative process in society.

Buddhists believe that a real economy would be based on developing wisdom and compassion, not material goods, as our main assets. The ninth-century Buddhist wise man, Shantideva, clarified this doctrine when he maintained that all the happiness in the world comes from desiring the happiness of others, and all the suffering comes from attending to our own egos instead.

To build a functional and ethical economic system, Buddhist thinkers such as Thailand's Prayudh A. Payutto, Buddhist monk and nominee for the Nobel Peace Prize, asks us to look at the effects an economic system has on three levels: the individual consumer, society, and the environment. For example, the manufacture of a bottle of whiskey has implications that go far beyond the bottom line for the company that makes it. Its ill effects on the consumer may be obvious, but society itself pays for the drinking problems of each of its members. Additionally, the pollution produced by the distillery can have an adverse effect on the environment.

Nuclear Energy, Waste, and Disarmament

Although classical Buddhism has nothing to say (of course) about nuclear waste, contemporary Buddhists assume that the purposeful accumulation of large of amounts of deadly material goes against basic Buddhist principles. Joanna Macy, Buddhist scholar and writer, has suggested a creative Buddhist way for handling the problems of nuclear waste, until the day when safe alternative energy becomes widely available. Buddhism has a tradition of dealing comfortably with long spans of time called *kalpas,* periods lasting millions of years. For many people, a *kalpa* seems a flight of fancy, but perhaps it is not when it comes to the issue of nuclear waste: the half-life of plutonium is thousands of years.

When Macy attended a Boston conference in 1977 about environmental degradation, she had a dark and overwhelming vision of the possible destruction of the Earth. From her anguish was born her "despair and empowerment" work during the current nuclear crisis, which is designed to help activists work on critical issues without getting burned out. In 1979 she returned to Asia to work with the Sarvodaya movement, which teaches local villages the art of self-help.

Macy notes that much of the danger of nuclear energy has come about through inattention of workers and suggests that training in mindfulness as well as technology would go a long way toward preventing future Three Mile Islands. In fact, she developed the Nuclear Guardianship Project, a grassroots program for handling nuclear wastes, with this end in mind. Their mission statement reads:

> To curtail rampant radioactive contamination the Project calls for a halt to the production and transportation of nuclear wastes, and for citizen involvement in the responsible care of the wastes produced to date. It promotes the guardianship of the wastes at the points of generation in monitored, retrievable storage facilities. And it develops educational programs to begin the training in technical knowledge and moral vigilance required to establish and maintain the Guardian Sites. The Project

> recognizes that radioactive wastes represent our most enduring legacy to future life on earth.

Macy believes this better, more "mindful" training can make a big difference in protecting against what she calls "poison fire." She notes that even the strongest containers and deepest burial sites are not fail-proof. She even comments that one reason human beings have to remain on Earth is to keep the rest of the planet safe from the nuclear waste we have created. She also remarks that nuclear toxins are nothing compared to some of the evil and hatred that human beings have built up inside themselves.

Buddhists believe that their philosophy can play a big part in dealing with the problem of nuclear waste. The Buddha's last words were: "Seek your own salvation with diligence." For Buddhists this means that human beings must take responsibility for our past actions (all part of the law of karma). We are not to shrink from the dangerous and terrible task we have set for ourselves. Buddhism acknowledges the truth of Thich Nhat Hanh's observation that nuclear waste is the "most difficult kind of human garbage," but believes we must nonetheless make a mindful effort to deal with it. It is a perfect example of "collective karma."

Recycling

Recycling is a necessity, not a matter of political correctness, in traditional Buddhist cultures, but early Buddhism made a virtue of it nonetheless. Ananda, the Buddha's favorite disciple, once explained to an inquiring king that when new robes were received, the old ones became blankets. Old blankets became mattress covers and old mattress covers were turned into rugs. Old rugs were used as dust rags. Zen Buddhist literature is full of tales that denounce waste. One monk is scolded for throwing away a chopstick, another races wildly along a stream bank to retrieve a leaf of lettuce.

Politics

Buddhism denies the basic concept by which most countries, both dictatorships and democracies, are routinely run—the idea that people are inherently and unalterably selfish. While Buddhists acknowledge that this trait does crop up with alarming frequency, they believe it should be overcome and not pandered to. The way to do this is, of course, to turn to the Noble Eightfold Path, not the idea of "enlightened self-interest," and still less to violence and hatred, which is the way of most political systems around the world. The Buddhist objection to these means is more than ethical; it is logical as well. It is simply not possible to create an ideal society except by ideal means. This is merely karma, the law of cause and effect.

The Buddhist ideal polity would be small, to permit free access to leaders; culturally and socially diverse; and lacking in both extremes of wealth or poverty. This ideal, of course, goes back to the first Sangha, which welcomed rich and poor, men and women, educated and illiterate. But it was small enough to provide a rich interaction between its members. This is the kind of Jeffersonian government that Buddhists believe would produce the best person. Here Buddhists invert and rearrange John F. Kennedy's famous exhortation: "Ask not what your country can do for you; ask what you can do for your country." For Buddhists, it might be best phrased: "Create a country in which all people can be and do their best." Those who believe these values are unrealistic are on the wrong side of history. Important thinkers like Thomas Jefferson, Martin Luther King Jr., and Henry David Thoreau held them. People like Ralph Nader and Noam Chomsky still speak out in their favor.

Everyone, both liberal and conservative, recognizes that big government and massive state-run welfare programs create at least as many problems as they solve. They are inhuman and inhumane. Buddhism seeks solutions to social problems that are not "charity" or "welfare" but based upon the recognition of the interdependence of all life.

This is not an impossible dream, but it is a challenge to meet. While many religious people of all faiths find the very concept of politics polluting, more than ever Buddhists, following the lead of the Dalai Lama, are learning that "heart-politics," or political action springing from compassion and wisdom, may ultimately help lead all sentient beings toward Enlightenment. However, many Buddhists also agree that at least in present circumstances, it is not possible to be a full-time politician and a sincere Buddhist because of the intensely corrupting influences of the political scene. The Dalai Lama has managed it, but of course he is an exception.

Even lay Buddhists have run into their share of criticism from fellow Buddhists by participating actively in political affairs, as Robert Aikten found during the 1960s in his antiwar efforts. He ran counter to the counsel of Yasutani Roshi, who believed that all people are subject to their own karma, and that if drafted, people must serve. Aitken disagreed, and opened a draft-resistance counseling center.

Authority and Egalitarianism in the Buddhist Community

Equality is a modern idea, and in classical Buddhism, the teacher, who is considered to be enlightened, has all the authority, both moral and political. This notion goes deeply against the American grain. The two concepts are not intrinsically antithetical, however, since Buddhism acknowledges the interdependence and essential oneness of all beings. As long as this Buddhist concept is kept well in mind, Buddhist communities can run smoothly in the United States. Americans do expect a high moral standard from their leaders, however, especially from those who are supposed to be enlightened. If they behave in a manner that their students feel is incompatible with Enlightenment, the students are likely to rebel. This is unheard of in traditional Buddhist countries, most of which do not have a democratic culture. In these cultures, the leader's behavior is likely to be accepted, no matter how odd or even incompatible with Buddhist principles it may seem.

In America, the general rule seems to be that small communities tend to be informal and democratic, while larger ones, probably from necessity, are more structured and authoritarian. Many American Buddhist communities also have a different idea of what it means to be a teacher—and the criteria by which one attains that position—than do Buddhists in traditionally Buddhist countries. In addition, Buddhist monks in Asia, especially in Japan, usually have the opportunity to leave the monastery after they have mastered the necessary knowledge and received Dharma transmission and become teachers in their own temples. In America, on the other hand, there simply aren't scores of temples awaiting teachers. Thus American students have essentially nowhere to go and remain "stuck" in the monastery in which they were trained with no real chance for advancement.

Not all Buddhists are pleased with the incursion of democracy into their faith. Some Buddhists, like Sangye Khandro, maintain that the very essence of faith is to trust in sublime beings or in the person of the Master, in order to receive the blessing of wisdom. It means surrendering oneself entirely to the object of devotion. In Buddhism this object of devotion is the Buddha, represented by the spiritual teacher. The Buddha as the spiritual teacher has nothing to receive or gain when disciples offer themselves; instead, it is the disciples who benefit from having their pride and other passions cleansed. This view is a minority one, however, among American Buddhists.

The Media

Contemporary Buddhist thinkers such as Thich Nhat Hanh make the point that just as consumers and industry pollute the environment, the endemic violence of the media can pollute the mind.

In the Buddhist view, what we honor is what we get. If we honor big moneymakers, elite athletes, and fatuous entertainers above scientists, teachers, artists, gardeners, caregivers, and philosophers, we will have a society that reflects those values. The media, and the powers that control it, can manipulate minds to adhere to worthless goals and bad values. But Buddhism teaches that people can control their responses to stimuli, and by controlling their responses can change those stimuli. As long as people continue to buy advertised junk, pay exorbitant fees to entertain themselves at concerts or ball games, the longer and more deeply they will be enslaved by the stimuli they have been conditioned to crave. Only by shutting out the media and controlling it the way one can learn to control one's own senses can one be free of its noxious influence. Perhaps, with care, the media can become what it was intended to be, a means of communication *between* people rather than of control *over* them.

Drugs and Frivolous Entertainment

It may seem odd to group these two subjects together, but in the Buddhist view there exists a logical link between them, at least according to Thich Nhat Hanh. Both serve to distract the mind and to increase attachment to the world. Both, therefore, while not inherently evil, are things to be avoided by those who seek Enlightenment. Western culture, of course, officially and in principle objects to the use of drugs, but in practice promotes the use of many of the most dangerous ones, including alcohol and tobacco. To a Buddhist, there is no essential difference between alcohol, marijuana, LSD, and heroin—all work to cloud the mind and impair perception. Mindless movies, inane television, and silly books and Web sites work the same way—to distract attention rather than focus it.

As with the case of sexual misconduct, however, many Buddhist centers have been plagued with the problem of alcohol among its leaders. Maezumi and Chogyam Trungpa were both acknowledged alcoholics; indeed, it probably killed the latter, who died at age forty-seven of cirrhosis of the liver. Trungpa's successor, Osel Tendzin, also drank and engaged in immoral sexual behavior (he had AIDS and afterward knowingly had sexual relations with others), but because he lacked the charisma of his predecessor, he was ultimately not allowed to get away with it, although his behavior had been known to the board of directors for a long time before they took action.

Population Growth and Birth Control

Unlike many other religions, Buddhism has never regarded birth as an act of unqualified value or goodness. Traditional Buddhists regarded rebirth into the world of *samsara* as something to be avoided, not sought after. This stance has given today's Buddhists the moral authority to consider the current population explosion as a calamity for the Earth. Buddhists have always supported birth control, and the Buddhist conviction that we live in one, interconnected world is accompanied by the belief that it is not every individual's right to propagate as much as he or she chooses, especially when we consider that the planet's resources are distinctly limited. Since Buddhists regard all sentient beings as related, there is no particular pressure to preserve one's own genes or biological lineage over that of other people.

Human birth is regarded as precious only because the possibility of Enlightenment is limited to the human state (to which all beings will eventually come). This does not translate, however, into a competition among couples to produce as many able-to-be-enlightened beings as possible. Many Buddhists are especially horrified at the lengths to which some couples will go to have "their own" child rather than to adopt a needy orphan. This kind of behavior is regarded as full of unhealthy attachment and egoism.

Abortion

Most Buddhists regard abortion as a form of killing, and therefore a violation of the First Precept. However, it does not follow that all abortion is forbidden under Buddhist precepts. Buddhism generally holds to a middle, commonsense line between "no abortion is ever justified" and "all abortion is permissible." First of all, Buddhism stresses that abortion is always a serious decision, which requires utmost thought. It recognizes that the destruction of a potential life is a matter that can carry heavy karma. However, it also recognizes that some circumstances may leave a woman with no other choice. In these circumstances, it does not condemn such a decision. Buddhists generally support the right to choose, leaving the decision up to the individual, who must make it for herself or himself. Like thoughtful people everywhere, most Buddhists hope that the problem of abortion will lessen with increased attention to sexual responsibility.

Robert Aitken's attitude might be considered typical. While calling himself a feminist, he has performed ceremonies for aborted fetuses, and has even given fetuses Buddhist names. In Japanese, a fetus is sometimes poetically called a *mizuko,* or "water baby." Aitken has said that if consulted, he discusses options carefully with the woman, and if her decision is definite, he advises her to go through the procedure "with the consciousness of a mother who holds her dying child in her arms, lovingly nurturing it as it passes from life" (*Mind of Clover* 21).

Women and Buddhism

Buddhism has an advantage, at least theoretically, for women. Nothing in Buddhist doctrine makes them second-class citizens, and even Buddhist religious language is, as James William Coleman pointed out in his *The New Buddhism,* generally free of sexist language. "Since there is no all-powerful deity, Buddhism has no problem with the male 'god language' to which feminists have raised such strong objections." However, even the doctrinal openness of Buddhism to the concerns of women was no match for patriarchal Asian societies. In fact, problems started with the founder himself.

Although the historical Buddha established an order of nuns, he reportedly did so only reluctantly and under pressure from his wife, mother-in-law, and beloved disciple Ananda. The Buddha is reported to have commented that if that Sangha had been restricted to men, its reign would last for a thousand years; the admission of women cut that in half. This is not a promising remark for women's equality. In addition, women had to obey eight more precepts than monks did—and they were expected to be subservient to the men as well. And while women could obtain the rank of arhat, full Buddhahood was not possible for them until they were reborn as men; apparently a female Buddha was just too much to deal with.

While early Buddhism was fairly egalitarian, the Theravada tradition became more and more unfriendly to the idea of nuns. The literature become increasingly antagonistic toward them, and eventually the order of nuns was allowed to die out. For about a thousand years, there were no orders of nuns at all. However, despite what appeared at one time to be insurmountable obstacles, including the difficulties of a broken Dharma transmission, women are reestablishing their position in monastic Theravada traditions in Asia. This has been extremely difficult, since some Buddhists reared in patriarchal Asian environments refused to admit that women could reach Enlightenment. Like the Hindus, some of these Buddhists believed that women could best accumulate merit by serving males, in this case, monks.

Cultivating an order of nuns seems especially important since traditionally, most renowned Buddhist teachers have sprung from the monastic rather than lay line of Buddhists. In the Mahayana tradition, the way for women was in some sense easier, and even patriarchal countries like Japan and Korea offered monastic Zen training for women. Tibetan Buddhism honors women, at least verbally and in art. Images of powerful female deities abound, but this is also true in Hinduism, where women's lot is poor. However, Tantric scriptures do counsel their readers that one of the fourteen root downfalls is the denigration of women. Still, words are comparatively cheap, and it's a long way from "not denigrating" women to handing over positions of authority to them. This has not been done in traditional Tibetan cultures. Joanna Macy has written, "I was a woman before I was Buddhist or an activist, and a woman aware of oppression." She believes that Buddhist institutions have yet a great deal to learn from women.

In the Zen tradition, Robert Aitken is fiercely egalitarian, going so far as to call the Buddha "she" and urging the "feminizing of Buddhism," including translations. In this regard, Aitken seems to be following contemporary Western thought. In contemporary American Buddhism women are just as likely to be teachers and leaders as men are, and, in general, have equal authority. However, the most revered teachers are still from Asia, especially Tibet, and they are men. And of course, the Buddha himself, his images, and nearly all early influential teachers were males as well, so, like nearly every other worldwide religious tradition, Buddhism is still dominated by men, especially Tibetan Buddhism, whose leaders are still, almost by necessity, ethnic Tibetans. One interesting exception, of course, is Jetsunma (Alyce Zeoli), a recognized *tulku* who runs the Kunnzang Odsal Palyul Changchub Choling in Poolesville, Maryland. In the Zen tradition, important women teachers include Charlotte Joko Beck, Ruth Fuller Sasaki, Maurine Stuart, Jiju Kennett, Ruth Denison, Sharon Salzberg, and Joanna Macy.

Sexual Misconduct

Avoiding sexual misconduct is the Third Precept. It has traditionally been explained as meaning celibacy for monks (although traditions differ here) and no adultery for laypersons. The Buddha himself had nothing good to say about sex; he felt that it was one of the worst kinds of desires that kept people from achieving Enlightenment. In the world of the Sangha, women were a snare and temptation. His anxious monks inquired as to what to do if they should happen upon women. "Don't look at them," the Buddha advised severely.

"But what if I have to look at them?" persisted the monk.

"Then don't talk to them," the Buddha is reported to have said.

"And if we must speak to them?"

"Keep wide awake," counseled the Buddha, rather enigmatically. As mentioned earlier, he stated that it was better for a monk to insert his penis in the mouth of a venomous serpent than to have sexual intercourse. It is difficult to think of anyone with a greater dislike for, or at least distrust of, the sexual act. (When tempted, the Buddha advised his monks to meditate on the idea of a corpse. He actually provided several varieties to choose from, including pus-filled, dog-mangled, and rotten, and, to make the lesson even clearer, he sometimes brought his monks to burial grounds to view and smell and meditate upon the real thing.)

In the Sangha's Vinaya, or rules of discipline, all sexual activity is strictly forbidden, including masturbation and inappropriate touching of any person or animal. Even being alone with someone of the opposite sex was enough to get one kicked out of the Sangha.

The Mahayana tradition, in keeping with its celebration of Enlightenment in the midst of ordinary life, did not perceive sexual activity as a snare from hell the way the Theravada school did. Mahayanists felt that sexually active people were no further from Enlightenment than the celibate.

Because sexuality definitely places one in the here and now, perhaps they were even closer.

Official Zen doctrine (if there is such a thing) is essentially silent about the subject of sex. Perhaps the founders thought that not mentioning it might make it go away. Despite this, however, Zen monks developed a rather unsavory reputation for sexual exploits in Japan, Korea, and China.

Tibetan Buddhists reserve for sexuality a powerful role in Enlightenment. Recognizing sex as a potent force, Tibetans developed Tantra, in which sexual activity was a means to Enlightenment. In most cases, they simply visualized sexual activity, but actual practice is not unknown, although it is restricted to only the highest adepts.

Later Buddhists had a tolerant, commonsense attitude to sex. On a practical level, of course, it is easy to be celibate in a grim monastery in the lonely mountains of Tibet. It's a different story in contemporary American society. Thich Nhat Hanh has clarified the Third Precept for contemporary life by restricting sexual activity to people with a long-term commitment to each other—and to no one else. He also talks about protecting children from sexual abuse.

The current Dalai Lama stands by the Tibetan Lam Rim text concerning sexual ethics. This text specifically forbids sexual activity involving an inappropriate partner, organ, time, or place. Inappropriate partners include persons of the same sex. However, it also includes prostitutes paid for by "a third party," suggesting that prostitution paid for by the client falls within permissible sexual activity. And while prostitution is as common in the West as elsewhere, it is not considered ethical by any major religious tradition. Thus a similar case might be made for the allowance of homosexual behavior, which receives no more opprobrium than sexual activity with nursing or menstruating women, oral or anal sex, or even sex during the daytime, all of which were forbidden by the twelfth-century Buddhist teacher Gampopa (1070–1153). The same writer promised that those partaking of forbidden sexual acts would be reborn "in a place of much dust."

Unfortunately, many Buddhist residential centers have been rocked by sexual scandals. Richard Baker, Maezumi, Soen Sa Nim (a Korean Zen Master), Chogyam Trungpa, and others were involved in inappropriate sexual relationships with students. Sogyal Rinpoche, author of the bestselling *Tibetan Book of Living and Dying*, was sued for sexual damages in 1994. While in some cases, the community survived and even prospered despite the scandals, leaking word of the sexual improprieties has done nothing to enhance the reputation of Buddhism among outsiders. It is interesting to note, however, that some committed Buddhists, including the noted and Buddhist feminist Rita Gross, a student of Trungpa, profess to be much more concerned about the secrecy and hypocrisy surrounding the activities of some teachers. In this view, the actual misconduct itself is not disturbing. She makes the point that she personally never expected "too much" from a spiritual teacher in any case. She goes on to make a defense of sexual misconduct, mostly relying upon the position that women as self-determining adults should be able to make their own decisions. Specifically, in her essay "Western Buddhist Women," included in *The Faces of Buddhism in America,* she writes:

> I reject the frequent comparison of sexual encounters between spiritual teachers and their students to sexual contacts between bosses and secretaries or between professors and students. Secretaries and academic students rarely choose their bosses or professors in the way that Dharma students choose a spiritual mentor, and they usually cannot exercise the degree of discrimination that is required of a Dharma student vis-à-vis his or her guru. Most especially, I reject the comparison of the guru-student relationship to the therapist-client relationship.

She continues, "I want to suggest that those who adamantly condemn sexual relationships between spiritual teachers and their students are overly reliant on conventional morality, especially conventional sexual ethics, which are often erotophobic and repressive." To not a few observers, this defense appears so weak as to be laughable. As a matter of fact, during the early days of the Sangha, the only opinion for which a monk could be censured was maintaining that there was nothing wrong with sensual pleasure.

This problem seems to be one shared by many religious institutions with authoritarian structures, in which the religious leader is perceived as being somehow exempt from ethical codes that bind others. Osel Tendzin, the successor to Chogyam Trungpa, apparently believed that even though he himself had contracted AIDS, his great spiritual powers prevented him from passing it on to others. (Why these spiritual powers did not protect Tendzin himself remains a mystery.) In addition, spiritual teachers are often charismatic, and students feel that sexual intimacy somehow draws them into a circle of spiritual power. It is equally clear that an abundance of adoring young students places a great temptation in the path of any powerful leader. This, of course, does not make such behavior any less reprehensible. New, more democratic leadership, which does not revolve around any one teacher, seems to be helping to solve the problem.

In addition, many Buddhist organizations, such as the Buddhist Peace Fellowship and others with democratic leadership, have tackled the problem directly. The BPF has produced a set of ethical guidelines for Buddhist teachers, which is being distributed to Buddhist centers throughout the United States. It has also co-sponsored support groups and training for those who have suffered sexual abuse by teachers in the past.

Homosexuality

Classical Buddhist teachings make no special mention of homosexuality, and today, the topic is for the most part subsumed under sexuality in general, about which traditional Buddhism is notably conservative. The Third Precept in classical Buddhism prohibits sexual misconduct. While leaders such as the Dalai Lama have denounced persecution of gay people, the Buddha himself may not have been so indulgent, and one text tells us that he forbade the admittance of certain homosexuals—those who took the passive role during the sex act (*pandaka*)—into his order.

Modern American Buddhism is generally free of prejudice against homosexuality and treats it just like any other form of sexual expression. Robert Aitken is supposed to have remarked that those not in touch with their sexuality were not practicing Zen, and that *zazen* could not be done in a closet. Currently San Francisco is home to the Gay Buddhist Fellowship for men and the Dharma Sisters for gay women. The Gay Buddhist Fellowship regards its main mission as healing the internal homophobia with which many gay people are afflicted. Its mission statement proclaims: "We respect and care for each other in a compassionate way as an expression of the full realization of the Dharma. We cultivate a social environment that is accepting, open, inclusive, and caring." There is also the Hartford Street Zen Center in the Castro district of San Francisco, which ministers to gay people; the resident teacher is the famous writer and Zen Buddhist Philip Whalen (Zenshin Ryufu).

Even "mainstream" Buddhist monasteries like Spirit Rock have hosted retreats for gay people. And Soka Gakkai, often in the forefront of social change, since 1995, has offered same-sex "partnership ceremonies" for those members who request them. Among acknowledged American Zen Masters, Robert Aitken has been among the most vocal heterosexuals in his support of gay rights, and he has actively encouraged both gay and lesbian participation in Zen.

The Buddhist Monastic Tradition in the West

The order of monks and, to a lesser extent, nuns, is also present in American Buddhism, not as the only possible route to a deep religious experience, but as an acceptable one. Like Catholicism, Buddhism offers a variety of pathways to salvation.

Buddhist Therapy

Since Buddhism is more than a religion, it is not surprising to find it filling a therapeutic role in modern medicine. To cite only one example, psychologist Marsha Linehan's dialectical behavior therapy offers a Zen-based therapy, which combines Western assertiveness therapy with Eastern mindfulness training. Linehan, who considers herself a Catholic rather than a Buddhist, has learned how powerful Zen insights can be in working with self-destructive and even suicidal clients. She originally wanted to call her therapy Zen behavior therapy, but decided it would not be a good "career move." However, one might also ponder the negative associations of "dialectical," a term derived straight from Marxism.

William Alexander's *Cool Water: Alcoholism, Mindfulness, and Ordinary Recovery* shows how Buddhist teachings can be applied even to one of the most intractable of psychological problems, while Sogyal Rinpoche's *The Tibetan Book of Living and Dying* helps readers deal with the universal fear of death.

Death, Euthanasia, and Suicide

One famous Zen Master, Hakuin, is reported to have said, "Young man, if you are afraid to die, die now. That way you won't have to die twice."

While wanton killing and killing for pleasure are not permissible under the First Precept, "do not kill," Buddhism recognizes the right to choose one's own death, as long as one's motives are pure and unselfish, and as long as the desire does not stem from weakness.

Suicide is a kind of killing, and thus a violation of the First Precept. Since it is only in this life that one can achieve Enlightenment, it is a waste to kill oneself before doing so. Killing oneself does not result in escape from suffering, since one is reborn into another plane of existence with all suffering attached.

Buddhism does allow for the destruction of the self in the service of a higher good or to serve others. The primary example is the self-immolation of Vietnamese monks during the Vietnamese War. (Reportedly the heart of one monk did not burn and is now enshrined in a pagoda in Vietnam.) In that case, the monks were offering their pain and their bodies as a powerful message against the horror of war. It was not suicide per se, but a sacrifice whose natural outcome was the death of the sacrificer. This should be understood not as a sacrifice to some deity, but a sacrifice on behalf of human beings. While many people, including some Buddhists, criticized this action as violating the First Precept, others believed that it measurably shortened the war by waking up the hearts of the American people.

The burning monk's tremendous courage in the face of violent death has a long history in Buddhism. One Zen story relates how a general approached a seated Zen Master, shoved his sword against his chest, and announced, "Know this. I am a man who can run you through without batting an eyelash." The Master's response: "Know this. I am a man who can be run through without batting an eyelash." The general withdrew his sword and began to receive instruction.

Buddhism and Western Psychology

It may be helpful to begin by considering what the Buddhist concept of "mind" entails. It is not a substance identical to the brain or the "self." It is much more likely to be described as process or function than as a "thing." In much classical Buddhist literature the mind is compared to a river; in Zen, the word "mirror" crops up frequently. A river is flowing, never the same from moment to moment; a mirror reflects reality. The healthy mind, then, is clear and steady like a mirror, and, at the same time, clear and flowing like a river. It is a powerful balance of stillness and movement, yet not to be completely identified with either.

Buddhism shows its versatility in that it has spawned an entire movement in cognitive science, psychology, and psychotherapy. A brief sampling of essay titles from *The Psychology of Awakening*, edited by Gay

Watson, Stephen Batchelor, and Guy Claxton, may serve to illustrate the scope of the field: "The Foundations of a Buddhist Psychology of Awakening," by Geshe Thupten Jinpa; "Steps to a Science of Interbeing: Unfolding the Dharma Implicit in Modern Cognitive Science," by Francisco J. Varela; "Neurotheology: Buddhism, Cognitive Science and the Mystical Experience," by Guy Claxton; "Going to Pieces without Falling Apart: A Buddhist Perspective on Wholeness," by Mark Epstein; "Zen: The Challenge to Dependency," by John Crook; "Buddhist Psychotherapy or Buddhism as Psychotherapy?" by David Brazier; "Indra's Net at Work: The Mainstreaming of Dharma Practice in Society," by Jon Kabat-Zim; "The Structures of Suffering: Tibetan and Cognitive Analytic Approaches," by James Law; "Mindfulness of Breathing and Contemporary Breathwork Techniques," by Joy Manné; and "Four Noble Truths for Counseling: A Personal Reflection," by Eric Hall. It is also interesting to note that Spirit Rock, a Vipassana meditation center, has nine psychotherapists among its teaching staff of fourteen.

These and other writers explain how a thorough exploration of the Four Noble Truths leads from ignorance and suffering to knowledge and Awakening. As the patient works through the truths, he or she begins to accept his or her illness, search out its causes, identify a treatment plan, and then follow through. The Eightfold Path in itself works as a practical guide for many patients. Dharma-oriented therapists can use several concepts in Buddhist philosophy to work with their clients. One is the idea of *kleshas,* or "defilements of the mind." Therapists working with this concept attempt to help the patient rid his or her mind of the mental pollutants that have assailed it. Buddhism teaches that *kleshas* in turn cause unhealthy actions. Unpolluted, the mind is pure. This notion is in direct conflict with the Christian idea of "original sin." The Buddhist idea is that the luminous mind in itself has the capacity to heal itself; that pollutants do not come from within it. It is thus a positive and hopeful approach to dealing with mental stress.

Contemporaneously with helping the client cleanse the mind, the Buddhist therapist works to help the client develop awareness and the positive qualities within. In Buddhism these mental factors together are known as *caitta,* and include introspection, wisdom, concentration, and mindfulness. When these mind-qualities are awakened, the mind can cleanse itself of its polluting thoughts and habits.

Buddhist psychotherapy is thus intensely active and based on a medical model that the Buddha himself discussed, as described in the Cula Malunka Sutta, the sixty-third discourse in Majjhima Nikaya of the Pali canon. In an immortal analogy, the Buddha says, "Suppose a man were wounded by an arrow thickly smeared with poison, and his friends and companions brought a doctor to him. The wounded man would not refuse to have the arrow withdrawn before he knew who shot him or why. He would die before he had that knowledge, if indeed he ever got it. No, the arrow should first be withdrawn so that the healing can begin." Buddhist psychotherapy is likewise results-oriented. One major difference between Western and Buddhist psychotherapists is that in Buddhist psychotherapy, seated meditation and mindfulness practices are used.

However, Buddhism is not in itself psychotherapy; it is a religion, and its concerns are not limited to psychological adjustment. Some Buddhist thinkers and writers, such as Fred Pfeil, wonder aloud if the aims and underlying assumptions of Buddhism and Western psychology are so inimical to each other that a true Western practice of Buddhist psychotherapy is impossible. The main point of contention, of course, is the very concept of the "self." The goal of Western psychological therapy is largely to help the patient "find" and integrate the self, whereas Buddhism contends that no such entity as the "self" even exists, at least not in the form envisaged by Western psychologists.

Francisco J. Varela, who holds a Ph.D. in biological science from Harvard University, in his "Steps to a Science of Interbeing" suggests that cognitive science is beginning to show us a new, more Buddhist way of looking at the world and others. While the 1960s tended to view the self as an isolate in need of protection from others, the 1990s began to conceive of our relation to others as being that of interaction. Varela predicts that in the next ten years, cognitive scientists will have caught up to the Buddhist notion of "interbeing." The psychology of Awakening can at that point, he believes, become a real possibility: the place where mind and spirit meet.

However, it should always be remembered that no matter how many parallels may exist between Buddhism and psychotherapy, the ultimate purpose of each remains radically different. For Western psychotherapy, the final goal for a client is to become "adjusted" to society. For Buddhism, it is to become awake.

Buddhism and the World of Science

The publication of Fritjof Capra's best-selling *Tao of Physics* a couple of decades ago raised public awareness about possible connections between new science and ancient insight. Many people looked at the linguistic and thought parallels between Asian mystical literature and the newest discoveries in contemporary physics and came to the conclusion that either the ancients knew a lot more about how the universe works than they let on by the official cosmologies, or that the new findings in physics somehow proved that the mystical writings of ancient India were true and could be proved by science.

Such thinking, of course, misapprehends both the nature of science and the nature of mysticism (and certainly of Buddhist thinkers). While intriguing parallels certainly exist between the two, they are not identical. While Buddhism, in its original formulation, advocates something very much like the scientific method, most Buddhists maintain that the highway of science and the path of Dharma lead to different places. The end of science is knowledge. The end of Buddhism is liberation. Liberation is not to be found in any area of study. It cannot be replicated by others. It cannot be taught. It tells us nothing about the nature of quanta, microbes, or neurons.

However, once this is accepted, Buddhists, unlike followers of Christianity or Islam, have no objections to the findings of science in the field of evolution or anywhere else. The primitive cosmologies of ancient Buddhism are accepted as symbolic, rather than literal truths. As a tolerant, scientifically minded (if not scientific) religion, Buddhism remains open to science and welcomes scientific progress that does not hurt the environment, harm society, or dehumanize individuals.

Buddhism and Biotechnology

Because of its emphasis on *ahimsa* (no-injury), Buddhism is very alert to manifestations of suffering and bases most of its bioethical positions upon that realization. While practitioners of most other religions would agree with Buddhism's stance, Buddhism goes one step further than is acceptable to other religions. Ron Epstein, research professor at the Institute for World Religions, Berkeley, and lecturer in the Philosophy Department, San Francisco State University, has made an interesting point not likely to be considered by Christianity, Islam, or Judaism because of the different paradigms under which they operate:

> Because of the interrelation and ultimate non-duality of body, mind, and spirit . . . genetic engineering may adversely influence the potential of sentient beings to achieve transcendence and liberation. Because science deals only with the physical realm, no scientific experiment or methodology can

> possibly assess this kind of risk. Even if there is only a relatively small possibility of genetic engineering having a serious effect on the nature of the human spirit and its potential for transcendence, I think many of you will agree with me that it is a very serious cause for concern.

Eclectic and Independent Traditions

Not all Western Buddhists are "engaged" in environmental, political, or social causes. Many have developed their own traditions from a collection of Buddhist schools or teachings. One such example is Andrew Cohen (b. 1955), often called simply "Andrew." Cohen, who hails from New York City, founded the Moksha Foundation, which in 1988 became the International Fellowship for Realization of Impersonal Enlightenment, in Lenox, Massachusetts. Cohen, who studied Zen, Sufi (mystical form of Islam), yoga, Vipassana, and other traditions, maintains that no particular practice can create Enlightenment, for Enlightenment already exists within us, if we are willing to surrender everything we have to realize it. He calls his teaching "evolutionary Enlightenment."

Whither Western Buddhism?

Buddhism is very new to America. When we take a long view, even counting the "speeding up" of history due to instant communications, it should be recalled that in China, for instance, more than 500 years passed between the first introduction of Buddhism to that land and the arrival of Bodhidharma, the great missionary who founded Ch'an. It is the same in other Buddhist countries. If Buddhism has not become established in the United States, it may be because Americans have not yet found their Bodhidharma.

As Buddhism becomes more firmly implanted in American soil, it faces a number of challenges. Some have to do with the inevitable collision of an ancient tradition with the exigencies of contemporary America. Mendicancy, for example, is simply not acceptable to mainstream America. Monks must perforce handle money. Hierarchies tend to become more egalitarian and less gender-biased in society. Although monasteries continue to be a part of many Buddhist traditions, their methods of governance (male and autocratic) are slowly giving way to American democratic influences. Ways of practice are changing, with more and more emphasis on social engagement.

Although these changes are troubling to some Buddhists, most regard them as opportunities for the Dharma to grow. Buddhism has always accommodated itself to changing cultures and times. The original practice of the historical Buddha has little in common with that of Tibetan, Pure Land, or Zen Buddhism. There is a Buddhism for each culture, and for each person, and one Dharma for all.

Appendix

Note on Buddhist Names and Titles

The names and titles used in all brands of Buddhism can be extremely confusing to the beginner. There are alternate ways of positioning, and sometimes of spelling, Japanese names. Thus Nakagawa Soen's name is also given as Soen Nakagawa. This seems to be a matter of individual preference in anglicizing. Likewise, the word "Roshi" or "Master" is usually placed before the name in the United States, although Japanese practice would place it afterward.

Japanese Zen

Roshi: A Zen Master dedicated to teaching. He may also be an abbot, the director of the monastery, although the two positions are sometimes kept separate, with the abbot attending mostly to administration. Korean Zen does not use the term "Roshi." "Zen Master" is preferred.
Sensei: In Zen, a teacher, usually of a lower degree of authority than a Roshi. He may have received Dharma transmission from his teacher, but not Enlightenment.

Korean Zen (Kwan Um School)

Jo Do Poep Sa Nim: Equivalent to sensei. Formerly referred to as master dharma teacher.

Pure Land

Shonin: Title meaning "person of honor," used for a monk with superior attainments like Honen Shonin.

Nichiren

Daishonin: "Great Sage." Title given to Nichiren: Nichiren Daishonin.

Theravadin

Sayadaw: In Burma, the title for a Burmese monk, especially an abbot.

Tibetan

Lama: A religious master regarded by his students as an embodiment of Buddhist teachings. Now often a polite form of address for any monk.
Geshe: A learned monk, somewhat equivalent to a "doctor of divinity." Term is used in Gelugpa and Sakya traditions. Typically takes seventeen to twenty years of training. Few Westerners have received this degree.
Geshe lharampa: Geshe or khenpo with an "advanced degree." Typically takes an additional eight or nine years beyond *geshe.*
Khenpo: Similar to *geshe,* meaning a highly educated lama, *khenpo* is used in the Nyingma and Kagyu traditions.
Rinpoche: Honorific meaning "precious" given to especially qualified masters. Used after the name.
Tulku: Term and title for one who has been recognized as a reincarnation of a deceased lama. Used primarily in the Nyingma and Kagyu orders.

Who's Who in Buddhism

Note: Parentheses indicate a title, not a proper name.

Ahkon, Jetsumna (b. 1949)**:** Only Western woman recognized as a *tulku*. So identified by Penor Rinpoche of the Nyingma school.

Aitken, Robert (Roshi): Hawaiian-based Zen teacher of the Sanbo Kyodan lineage.

Amida (Japanese)**:** Amitabha, the heavenly Buddha of infinite light. Chief Buddha of the Pure Land sect.

Amitabha: The Buddha of infinite light. Represents compassion. Amida in Japanese; Amita or O-Mi-t'o Fo in Chinese.

Ananda (Sanskrit, *Ānanda*)**:** A cousin and disciple of the historical Buddha, noted for his phenomenal memory and devotion to the Buddha.

Asanga: Founder of the Yogachara school of Mahayana Buddhism.

Ashita: A seer who predicted the fame of the historical Buddha.

Ashoka (c. 268–239 B.C.E.)**:** Indian emperor, under whose tolerant reign Buddhism became widespread. His son and daughter became famous missionaries.

Asvaghos(h)a: Buddhist writer of the first century C.E. Composed a verse biography of the Buddha.

Avalokiteshvara (Sanskrit, *Avalokiteśvara*)**:** Literally, "one who looks down" or "one who perceives the self at rest." The celestial Bodhisattva of mercy and compassion, who takes pity on the world. Very important in the Tibetan tradition also, where he is known as Chenrezi. In the Chinese tradition this bodhisattva is female and called Kuan Yin. In Japanese she is called Kannon.

Baker, Richard (Roshi): Dharma heir to Shunryu Suzuki.

Beck, Charlotte Joko: Third Dharma heir of Maezumi.

Blomfield-Brown, Deirdre. See Chodron, Pema.

Bodhidharma (Sanskrit): Vastly learned Indian monk. Twenty-eighth Patriarch in line from the Buddha. Brought Buddhism to China.

Bodhisattva (Sanskrit; Pali, *Bodhisatta*): One who aspires to Enlightenment for the sake of liberating others, or one who experiences Enlightenment. Since he delays his own entry into Nirvana for the sake of others, compassion is his most notable characteristic. Bodhisattvas come in three varieties: enlightened beings, beings on the way to Enlightenment, and enlightened beings who help others on their way to Enlightenment. This figure is especially important in Mahayana Buddhism.

Brahma (Sanskrit, *Brahmā*): Vedic god who encouraged the Buddha to teach. Heaven.

Buddha (Sanskrit): "Awakened," from the word *budh,* or "ultimate mind." Enlightened or awakened one. Possibly related to the English "bud." In Mahayana Buddhism, the number of Buddhas is infinite.

Buddhaghosa: One of the founders of the Theravada school.

Carus, Paul (1852–1919): German-born American publisher who promoted Buddhism in his periodicals *Open Court* and *The Monist.* Collaborated with Soyen Shaku, D. T. Suzuki, and Angarika Dharmapala.

Chain-jan: A philosopher of the T'iten-T'ai school.

Chavis, Melody Ermachild: Zen feminist and activist against the death penalty. She practices at the Berkeley Zen Center.

Chodron, Pema (Deirdre Blomfield-Brown): Resident director of the Gampo Abbey in Nova Scotia. Kagyu school.

Cohen, Andrew (b. 1955): Founder of the Moksha Foundation. Eclectic.

Denison, Ruth: Pioneer of the Vipassana meditation movement.

Deshung (Rinpoche): Sakya school scholar and translator.

Devadatta: A disciple and possibly a cousin of Shakyamuni.

Dharma King: Another name for the Buddha.

Dharmapala, Angarika (1864–1933): Name used by D. H. Hewavitarne, Buddhist promoter. Joined Theosophical Society in 1884. Attended World Parliament of Religions in Chicago in 1893.

Dipamkara (Sanskrit, *Dīpamkara*): A previous Buddha.

Dogen (Japanese, *Dōgen*): Thirteenth-century founder of Soto Zen in Japan.

Gautama (Sanskrit): The clan name of the historical Buddha, Siddhartha.

Ginsberg, Allen: Beat writer.

Glassman, Bernard (Roshi): First Dharma heir of Maezumi.

Goldstein, Joseph (b. 1944): Pioneer of Vipassana meditation in the United States.

Green, Paula (b. 1939): Peace activist and feminist with links to Vipassana and Nippozen Myohoji Buddhist order of monks and nuns.

Gyatso, Tenzin Gyalwa (Dalai Lama, His Holiness the XIVth) (b. 1935): Exiled spiritual and temporal head of the Tibetan people.

Halifax, Joan: Zen teacher and hospice movement leader.

Harada, Sokagu (Roshi): Japanese Zen Master, trained in both Rinzai and Soto schools, and receiving Dharma transmission from both.

Hui-neng (Chinese) (637–713): The Sixth Patriarch of Zen Buddhism, counting from Bodhidharma. Author of the Platform Sutra.

Ikeda, Daisaku (b. 1928): Third president of Soka Gakkai.

Joshu Jushin (Japanese, Jōshū Jūshin form of Chao-chou Ts'ung-shen): Famous Chinese Ch'an Master and subject of many koans. His lips were said to shine with light.

Kalu (Rinpoche) (1905–89): Considered to be a "modern Milarepa."

Kanjizai (Japanese): Anther name for Avalokitesvara.

Kanzeon (Japanese): Another name for Avalokitesvara.

Kapleau, Philip: Zen teacher.

Kashyapa (Pali, *Kassapa*; or *Mahākāshyapa*, the "great" Kashyapa): Wise disciple and relative of the Buddha. He was selected to lead the disciples of the Buddha after his death. He also was reportedly the only disciple who understood the silent "flower sermon" of the Buddha, reportedly the first koan.

Katagiri, Dainin: Soto Zen teacher who works in the United States.

Kennett, Jiyu (1924–96)**:** British-born Soto Zen Master who worked in the United States.

Kerouac, Jack: Beat writer.

Kokuzo: A bodhisattva to whom Nichiren prayed for wisdom.

Kornfield, Jack (b. 1945)**:** Pioneer in bringing Vipassana meditation to the United States.

Kuan Yin: Chinese name for Avalokitesvara, the bodhisattva of compassion. Made forty-eight vows aimed at relieving suffering.

Kunda: Blacksmith who served the Buddha his last, fatal meal.

Kyungbo, Sunim: First Korean Zen Master to visit the United States.

Langlois, Kongo (b. 1935)**:** Appointed as teacher of both Soto and Rinzai Zen schools.

Loori, John: Dharma heir of Maezumi.

Macy, Joanna (b. 1929)**:** Buddhist scholar, activist, and eco-philosopher. Leading voice in peace, justice, and environmental movements. Resides in Berkeley, California, where she teaches at the California Institute of Integral Studies in San Francisco, the Graduate Theological Union in Berkeley, and the University of Creation Spirituality in Oakland.

Maezumi, Hakuyu (1931–95)**:** Founder of the Zen Center of Los Angeles.

Mahakashyapa (Sanskrit, *Mahākāśyapa*)**:** The "great" Kashyaypa, an honorific name for Kashpya, Buddha's great disciple and successor.

Mahasi, Sayadaw (1904–82)**:** Burmese monk and Vipassana meditation teacher.

Maitreya (Sanskrit)**:** Literally, "loving one." The bodhisattva of all encompassing love who will become the next Buddha. Also called Ajita.

Makiguchi, Tsunesaburo (1871–1944)**:** Founder of the Soka Gakkai movement. Died in prison.

Manjushri (Sanskrit, *Mañjushrī*): A bodhisattva who is featured in the Lotus Sutra and other sutras. The bodhisattva of wisdom and right conduct. Often depicted riding on a lion.

Mara: The Tempter.

Marpa: Early Tibetan Buddhist lama. An ancestor of the Kagyu school of Tibetan Buddhism.

Maya: Mother of the Buddha; sometimes "Mahamaya" in this usage.

Merzel, Dennis: Second Dharma heir of Maezumi.

Milarepa: Marpa's disciple. Ancestor of Kagyu school of Tibetan Buddhism.

Naess, Arne: Norwegian philosopher who coined the term "deep ecology."

Nagarjuna (*Nāgārjuna*) c. 150–250 C.E.): South Indian monk and mystic, a proponent of the doctrine of emptiness (*shunyata*) and founder of the Madhyamika ("Middle Way") school. He attempted to show the emptiness (*shunyata*) of the world through the relativity of opposites. His major work is the Mula Madhyamika-karika.

Nhat Han, Thich: Exiled Vietnamese monk and peace activist.

Nichiren (1222–82): Founder of Nichiren Buddhism.

Nirmanakaya (Sanskrit, *Nirmānakā*): Literally, "emanation body." Earthly form of the Buddha.

Padmasambhava: Founder of the Nyingma school of Tibetan Buddhism, and considered ancestor to most schools.

Rahula (*Rāhula*): Son of Siddhartha Gautama and Yasodhara.

Rich, Thomas: Osel Tendzin.

Saicho (767–822): Founder of the Japanese Tendai sect of Buddhism.

Sakyamuni or Shakyamuni: Literally, sage of the Shakya clan. Siddhartha Gautama, the historical founder of Buddhism. The first historically recorded Buddha.

Salzberg, Sharon (b. 1952): Pioneer of Vipassana meditation in the United States, with Joseph Goldberg and Jack Kornfield.

Samantabharda: The bodhisattva of practice and discipline.

Sasaki, Joshu: Early missionary of Zen Buddhism to United States.

Sasaki, Ruth Fuller (1883–1967)**:** Early missionary of Zen Buddhism to the United States. Favored a completely Japanese style of Zen.

Sasaki, Sokei-an (1882–1945)**:** Early Zen missionary to the United States.

Senzaki, Nyogen (1876–1958)**:** Early missionary of Rinzai Zen in the United States.

Seung San: North Korean Zen Master based in the United States.

Shaku, Soyen (1895–1919)**:** Rinzai Zen Master who spoke at the World Parliament of Religions in Chicago in 1893. Considered responsible for bringing Rinzai Zen to the West.

Shamano, Eido Tai: Zen Master active in the United States.

Shantideva: Ninth-century Buddhist sage who maintained that all the joy on Earth comes from wishing for the happiness of others, and that all the suffering comes from attending to one's own ego.

Shinran (1173–1263)**:** A founder of Shin Buddhism.

Shonin (1143–1211)**:** Honen Shonin, a founder of Jodo Shu, the Pure Land school in Japan.

Siddhartha Gautama: Personal name of the historical Buddha before his Enlightenment.

Snyder, Gary: Beat poet.

Soen Nakagawa (1907–1984)**:** Zen Master and poet.

Steinbach, Sala: African America Zen activist in the field of human rights and racism.

Stuart, Maurine: Canadian-born Zen teacher who specialized in making Zen more female-friendly.

Suddhodana: Father of the Buddha.

Suzuki, Daisetzu Teitaro (1870–1966)**:** Famous as the man who popularized Zen in the United States.

Suzuki, Shunryo (1904–71)**:** Soto Master and early teacher of Soto Zen and proponent of "just-sitting." Opened both the San Francisco Zen Center and Tassajara Mountain Monastery.

Taho: A Buddha appearing in the Lotus Sutra.

Tara (Sanskrit, *Tārā;* Tibetan, Dolma)**:** Savior goddess of Tibet. Form of Avalokitesvara.

Tarthang (Tulku): Founder of Nyingma school of Tibetan Buddhism in the United States.

Tathagata: The Buddha.

Tendzin, Osel: Disciple and Vajra Regent of Chogyam Trungpa.

Thurman, Robert: Jay Tsong Khapa Professor of Indo-Tibetan Studies at Columbia University. He is the first American to receive ordination in the Tibetan (Gelug) school of Buddhism. He received Upasaka ordination in 1964 and Vajracharya ordination in 1971, both from His Holiness the Dalai Lama. He has translated many classic texts from Tibetan to English and is a co-founder of Tibet House in New York City.

Toda, Josei (1900–1958)**:** Disciple of Makiguchi and second president of Soka Gakkai.

Trungpa, Chogyam (Rinpoche) (1939–87)**:** Tibetan Buddhist leader who established a center in Boulder, Colorado, in 1971, which has become the center of the Vajradhatu Organization.

Tsongkhapa (1357–1419)**:** Tibetan Buddhist thinker and founder of the Gelugpa order.

Vairocana: One of the five transcendent Buddhas. He is often depicted as making the mudra of supreme wisdom, and is sometimes considered Shakyamuni's cosmic counterpart. In Tibetan Buddhism, the Buddha of the center, Dhyani-Buddha.

Vimalkirti: Household bodhisattva featured in the sutra of the same name.

Wangyal, Ngawang (Geshe) (1901–83)**:** Mongolian-born, first teacher of Tibetan Buddhism to arrive in the United States.

Watts, Alan: British-born American writer; in the Beat circle, but not a Beat writer.

Williams, George M. (Masaysau Sadanaga)**:** Associate of Daisaku Ikeda and organizer of Soka Gakkai in the United States.

Yama: The Indian death-god and ruler of the various hells.

Yasodhara: Wife of the historical Buddha.

Yasutani, Hakuun Ryoko (1885–1973): Japanese Zen Master and missionary to the West. Student of Sogaku Harada. Visited the United States frequently between 1962 and 1969. Used both Soto and Rinzai methods.

Glossary

Pali and Sanskrit are cognate languages. Generally, Theravada Buddhists use Pali, while Mahayana Buddhists use Sanskrit.

Abbot: Chief priest of a temple or monastery.

Abhidharma (Sanskrit; Pali, *Abhidhamma*)**:** Literally, "higher teaching." Treatise commentary. A category of scriptures that analyzes the basic constituents of a person.

Abisheka (Sanskrit)**:** Literally, "anointing." Term used in Tibetan Buddhism for empowerment initiation.

Adi-buddha (Sanskrit)**:** A supreme Buddha.

Ahimsa: Nonviolence.

Anattā (Pali; Sanskrit, *anātman*)**:** No-self, the absence of a soul. One of the three marks of existence.

Ango (Japanese)**:** Literally, "dwelling in peace." Refers to a three-month mediation retreat that memorializes the three-month rainy season retreats of the Buddha and his disciples. Also refers to the one- to three-month training period in Zen.

Anicca (Pali; Sanskrit, *anitya*)**:** Impermanence, ceaseless change, one of the three marks of existence.

Arhat (Sanskrit; Pali, *arahat*; Chinese, *lohan*; Japanese, *rakan*)**:** Literally, "worthy one," one who has achieved a highest state of Enlightenment, extinguishing all defilements, one who is free of the ten fetters. The ideal of Theravada Buddhism and of early Buddhism, where the Buddha is described as an arhat. Not all monks achieve the status of arhat.

Arupaloka: Also called *arupadhatu*. The highest realm in the Buddhist cosmology. Sphere of Formlessness. A purely spiritual realm. One can be reborn in this realm through the practice of the four stages of formlessness.

Asura (Sanskrit; also *āsura*)**:** A demon or evil spirit. One of the six modes of existence. Sometimes considered a "higher" mode, sometimes a "lower" mode.

Avatamsaka (Chinese, *Hua-Yen*)**:** Literally, "flower ornament." Mahayana Buddhist scripture.

Avichi (Sanskrit, *Avīci*)**:** The hell of incessant suffering.

Avidyā (Sanskrit; Pali, *avijjā*): Ignorance through unawareness. Delusion. The first step in the cycle of dependent origination.

Avijjā: See Avidyā.

Bala: Powers. One of the Ten Perfections of a bodhisattva.

Bardo Thodol (Tibetan *Bardo Thödol*): Literally, liberation through hearing in the in-between state. *The Tibetan Book of the Dead,* a set of instructions for the dying and newly dead. Based on the teachings of Padmasambhava.

Bhadra Kalpa (Sanskrit): Literally, the "fortunate age." The present age.

Bhava (Sanskrit and Pali): Literally, "coming to be." The tenth link in the chain of causation.

Bhava-Chakra (Sanskrit, *bhava-cakra*): Wheel of life or chain of causation.

Bhāvanā (Sanskrit and Pali): Meditation, mind-development.

Bhikkhu (Pali; Sanskrit, *bhikkshu*): Monk in the Theravada tradition. A *bhikkhu* keeps the Ten Precepts and his daily life is governed by the 227 Rules.

Bhikkhuni (Pali; Sanskrit, *bhikshunī*): Nun in the Theravada tradition.

Bodhi (Sanskrit): Enlightenment or Buddhahood.

Bodhi tree (Bo tree): The tree of Awakening. Historically, the fig tree, or *pipul* tree, under which Buddha achieved Enlightenment. The scientific name is *Ficus religisosa,* and it is also sacred to Hindus. The current Bodhi tree at Bodhgaya is probably a descendant of the original. A cutting from the original now in Sri Lanka may be the oldest historical tree in the world.

Bodhicitta (Sanskrit): Literally, "mind of enlightenment" or "awakened heart." The aspiration to attain Enlightenment for the sake of all beings.

Brahma sound: Pure sound.

Bussho (Japanese, *busshō*): Buddha-nature.

Butsudo (Japanese): The way of Enlightenment.

Chado (Japanese, *chadō*): "Tea way." Way of referring to what is commonly called the "tea ceremony."

Chakravala: Iron mountains encircling the world.

Chakravartin (Sanskrit, *cakravartin*): Literally, "wheel-turner," an ideal monarch ruling according to Buddhist principles.

Ch'an (Chinese): Zen.

Chanoyu: Japanese tea ceremony.

Chöd (Tibetan): Body awareness technique used in Tibetan Buddhism. Practiced primarily in the Kagya school.

Dai-Gohonzon: Scroll inscribed by Nichiren containing Chinese characters for *Nam-myoho-renge-kyo,* "Hail to the Lotus Sutra!"

Daimoku (Japanese): Literally, "title." Central chant of Nichiren Buddhism: *Nam-myoho-renge-kyo,* "All hail to the Lotus Sutra."

Dakini (Sanskrit, *dākinī*): Manifestation of the feminine in Tibetan Buddhism. A semi-wrathful being. May appear as a person or a goddess.

Dana (Sanskrit and Pali, *dāna*): Generosity, charity, giving. One of the Six Perfections of a bodhisattva.

Dathun: Month-long meditation retreat in Chogyam Trungpa's school.

Dependent Co-arising (Sanskrit, *pratītya-samapāda*; Pali, *paticca samuppāda*): Another term for interdependent origination.

Desire Realm: The lowest of the three realms in Buddhist cosmology. Also called Kamaloka or Kamadhatu.

Deva (Sanskrit and Pali): Literally, "shining." A heavenly being or god.

Dhammapada (Pali): Literally, "path of virtue." Sayings of the Buddha.

Dharani (Sanskrit; *dhāranī*): A protective, magical formula.

Dharma (Sanskrit; Pali, *dhamma*): Literally, "carrying, or holding." The doctrine of the Buddha. His teaching, sometimes translated as "truth" or "religion." Also, the law of the universe, phenomena.

Dharma Ancestor: One from the past who achieved Enlightenment and taught the Dharma.

Dharma Chakra (Sanskrit, *Dharma-cakra*; Pali, *dhamma-chakka*): The Wheel of Dharma.

Dharma-kaya (*Dharma-kāya*): Literally, "dharma body" or "body of truth." The Buddha body of truth, referring to the transcendent qualities of the Buddha. The pure aspect of the universe.

Dharma seal: Emblem of the Buddhist law.

Dhatu (Sanskrit and Pali, *Dhātu*): Place, realm. Appears frequently in compounds words, such as *kamadhatu.*

Dhyana (Sanskrit, *Dhyāna*): Deep meditation. Also one of the Six Perfections of a bodhisattva.

Dhyanaparamita (Sanskrit, *Dhyānapāramitā*): The Perfection of Meditation.

Diamond Sutra (Sanskrit, *Vajrachchedikā Prajñāpāramita Sutra*): "The perfection of Wisdom that cuts like a diamond," thus known as "the diamond cutter" for short. Probably compiled during the fourth century. A Chinese translation of this work is dated 868 and is the oldest printed book in existence. This sutra is an important Zen text and incidentally, Jack Kerouac's favorite. Many koans are derived from it.

Ditthi (Pali): Views. Right views are the first step on the Noble Eightfold Path.

Dojo (Japanese, *dōjō*): Zen training center.

Dokusan (Japanese)**:** Literally, "going alone to a high [place or person]." Refers to the private interview between Master and student in Zen Buddhism in which koans or difficulties in practice or in understanding the Dharma are discussed. One of the most important elements of Zen training.

Dragon: One of the eight kinds of nonhuman beings who protect Buddhism. Appears frequently in the Lotus Sutra.

Dukkha (Pali; Sanskrit, *duhkha*)**:** Suffering, unsatisfactoriness. The basis for the Four Noble Truths, also one of the three marks of existence, along with impermanence (*anicca*) and no-self-ness (*anatta*).

Dzogchen (Tibetan, also *rdzogs-chen*)**:** The Great Perfection, or *ati-yoga* (extraordinary yoga) teaching, a system of training in the Nyingma school of Tibetan Buddhism. Its approach is more instantaneous than the Mahamudra system.

Eight Masteries: Eight meditation exercises for mastery of the senses.

Eightfold Path: Buddhist practice: right view, right thought, right speech, right action, right livelihood, right effort, right mindfulness, right meditation.

Engaged Buddhism: Application of Buddhist teachings to social and political problems.

Enlightenment: *Bodhi* or *satori.*

Fetters: Chains. The Ten Fetters are false conceptions and desires.

Form Realm: In Buddhist cosmology, the realm above the Desire Realm.

Four Noble Truths: Basis of Buddhist teaching. (1) Life is suffering. (2) Suffering is caused by desire. (3) There is a way out of suffering. (4) The way out of suffering is the Eightfold Noble Path.

Gandharva: A heavenly musician, one of the eight kinds of nonhuman beings who protect Buddhism.

Gassho (Japanese, *Gasshō*)**:** In Zen, a hand gesture in which palms are placed together in front of the chest, arms are parallel to the floor.

Gatha (Sanskrit, *gāthā*)**:** Hymn in American Pure Land Buddhism. Short sutra in praise of the Buddha.

Gaya: City in present-day Bihar.

Geshe: High-level lama.

Geta: Wooden clogs worn by Zen Buddhist monks.

Go-en (Japanese)**:** Karma.

Gohonzon (Japanese)**:** A sacred scroll in Nichiren and Soka Gakkai, upon which is inscribed the *daimoku.* It is the embodiment of the law of *Nam-myoho-renge-kyo.*

Gomden: Square meditation pillow invented by Chogyam Trungpa.

Gompa: Tibetan Buddhist monastery.

Gongyo (Japanese)**:** Literally, "assiduous practice." Nichiren practice of reciting the *daimoku* and other parts of the Lotus Sutra.

Gosho: The writings of Nichiren.

Great Vehicle: Mahayana.

Haiku (Japanese)**:** Zen-like poem of three lines and seventeen syllables, focused on nature and expressing a moment of Enlightenment.

Han (Japanese)*:* Wooden board that is struck as a call to Zen meditation.

Hara: Spot about three inches below the navel. Meditation and power center. Also known as *tanden.*

Hasan (Japanese)**:** Zen student who has experienced *kensho.*

Heart Sutra: A condensation of the Prajnaparamita Sutra.

Hīnayanā (Sanskrit)**:** Literally, "low vehicle." Pejorative name given by Mahayana Buddhists to a number of ancient schools. Now represented by Theravada Buddhism.

Hō'e (Japanese)**:** Literally, "Dharma clothing." Robe of a Japanese monk.

Hondō (Japanese)**:** In Zen, a hall for formal ceremonies and rituals. Usually a separate building.

Hosshō (Japanese)**:** Literally, "Dharma nature." True nature of the phenomenal world; it can be experienced during Enlightenment.

Hua Yen Sutra: Flower Ornament or Flower Garland Sutra. Late Chinese Mahayana sutra, derived from the Avatamsaka Sutra.

Iddhis (Pali)**:** Attribute or power. There are six supernatural powers developed by an arhat on the way to Buddhahood.

Indra's net: A metaphor found in the Avatamsaka Sutra illustrating the concept of dependent origination.

Inka (Japanese)**:** In Rinzai Zen, "seal of approval" given when the student completes his koan study. It is also generally required that one receive overpowering awareness of one's Buddha-nature, and to have integrated one's practice and knowledge into everyday life.

Interbeing: A condensed way of saying dependent origination.

Jaramarana (Sanskrit; Pali, *jarāmarna*)**:** Old age and dying. The twelfth link in the Wheel of Life or chain of causation.

Jataka: Literally, "birth story." A collection of 550 stories about the previous lives of the Buddha.

Jati (Pali, *jāti*)**:** Birth. The eleventh link in the chain of causation.

Jhana (Pali, *Jhāna*)**:** A state of concentration during meditation.

Jiriki or Joriki (Japanese, *jōriki*)**:** Literally, "one's own efforts." Considered an ineffectual means to salvation in Pure Land Buddhism, as opposed to *tariki.* Considered effectual in Zen.

Jodo (Japanese)**:** The Pure Land school.

Jūjūkai (Japanese; also *jūjūkinkai*)**:** The ten main precepts of Mahayana Buddhism.

Jukai: "Giving or receiving the precepts." The rite of ordination in Zen Buddhism, in which a student enters a Buddhist community and is given a Dharma name.

Juzu: Rosary-like beads used in Pure Land Buddhism.

Kalpa (Sanskrit; Pali, *kappa*)**:** An immense span of time—about 4 million years, part of the cosmic cycle. The length of a day and a night of Brahma. We currently live in the Bhadra Kalpa.

Kāmaloka: Also Kamadhatu, the Realm of Desire. The lowest of the three Buddhist realms. Its denizens include hell-beings, hungry ghosts, animals, demons, humans, and certain gods.

Kargu (Tibetan, *Kargü* or *Kagyu* or *Kagupa*)**:** Literally, "oral transmission." One of the four major lineages of Tibetan Buddhism. Founded by Naropa through Marpa and Milarepa.

Karma (Sanskrit; Pali *Kamma*)**:** Literally, "action" or "deed." The fundamental law of cause and effect or action and reaction through birth and rebirth.

Karunā (Sanskrit and Pali)**:** Compassion. Primary attribute of the Buddhas and bodhisattvas.

Kata: Ceremonial white scarf, customary gift in Tibetan Buddhism.

"Katsu!" (Japanese): A shout by a Zen Master that supposedly wipes out everything.

Kensho (Japanese, *kenshō*)**:** Literally, "seeing into" (*ken*) "one's own nature" (*sho*). In Zen, first breakthrough experience of *satori.* Although the words mean approximately the same thing, *satori* is often used to describe a deeper experience.

Kesa: "Bib" worn by certain Zen monks.

Khenpo: High-level lama in the Nyingma and Kagyu traditions.

Kinhin (Japanese): In Zen Buddhism, walking group meditation. Usually practiced between sittings, but occasionally by itself. Rinzai Zen practitioners walk very fast; Soto Zen practitioners walk in slow motion.

Klesha (Sanskrit, *klesa*; Pali, *kilesa*): Defilement of the mind, basis for unwholesome actions.

Koan (Japanese, *kōan*; Chinese, *kungan*)**:** In the Rinzai Zen tradition, a riddle or enigmatic brief story designed to lead one to *satori.* It cannot be solved by rational thinking.

Koromo (Japanese)**:** Blue or black robes worn by a priest in American Pure Land Buddhist tradition.

Kosen-rufu: Literally, "to declare and spread the Law [of Buddhism]."

Kshanti (Sanskrit, *kshānti*)**:** Patience. One of the Six Perfections of a bodhisattva.

Kuan-Yin (Chinese)**:** Avalokitesvara, often depicted with feminine features.

Kyosaku or Keisaku (Japanese)**:** Literally, "wake-up stick." The wooden "Awakening stick" used in some Zen schools. Usually two or three feet long, flattened at the end.

Lama (Tibetan, *blama*)**:** Literally, "none above." Tibetan teacher; identified as the present incarnation of a teacher of the past. Properly, a senior monk.

Lankavatara Sutra: Group of teachings concerning the study of consciousness.

Laughing Buddha: Chinese style of depicting the Buddha.

Loka (Pali)**:** World.

Lotus Sutra: (Sanskrit, *Saddharmapundarīka-sūtra;* Chinese, *Hokekeyo*)**:** Literally, "Sutra of the Lotus of the Good Dharma." A twenty-eight-chapter sutra especially sacred in Nichiren and Soka Gakkai Buddhism. It discusses the doctrine of skillful means.

Madhyamika (Sanskrit, *Mādyamika*)**:** Literally, "the Middle Way," a philosophical school associated with Nagarjuna in the third or second century B.C.E. Sometimes called the school of emptiness, it expounds the central ideas of Prajnaparamita literature.

Mahadeva: Buddhist council.

Mahamudra (Sanskrit, *Mahāmudrā*)**:** Literally, "great seal." System of teaching involving direct view and practice in the Kagyu, Gelug, and Sakya schools of Tibetan Buddhism. One of the highest teachings, representing a perfected level of meditative realization.

Mahaparinirvana Sutra: Mahayana sutra that purportedly expresses the Buddha's final teachings.

Mahayana (Sanskrit, *Mahāyāna*)**:** The Great Vehicle tradition, a radical reform movement, appearing about 400 years after the Buddha's death. It emphasizes the bodhisattva path and Enlightenment of all beings.

Mahoraga: A serpent-headed being, one of the eight kinds of nonhuman beings who protect Buddhism.

Maka Shikan: "Great concentration and insight." One of Tendai's major works.

Māna: Conceit, egotism. An important cause of suffering, or *dukkha*.

Mandala (Sanskrit)**:** Literally, "circle." Symbolic representation in two or three dimensions of the forces of the universe, used as a visualization aid in Vajrayana. Implies wholeness. Often depicted on Thankas. Found in Tibetan and Shingon schools of Buddhism.

Mandarava: Sweet scented red flower that blossoms in Paradise.

Mantra (Sanskrit; also *mantram*)**:** Sacred, magical, power-laden chanted syllables. They manifest certain forces of the Buddha. The most famous is *Om Mani Padme Hum*: "All hail to the Jewel in the lotus." A lotus is a symbolic flower in Buddhism, for while its roots remain in the mud, it blossoms in the air. It is thus a parable in itself.

Mantrayana: Another name for Tibetan Buddhism, or Vajrayana.

Mappo (Japanese)**:** Literally, the "decay of the Dharma." The present, degenerate age.

Matcha: Powdered green tea used in a tea ceremony.

Maya (Sanskrit, *Māyā*)**:** Literally, "deception." Refers to the changing world of phenomena.

Meru (Sanskrit; also Sumeru)**:** The world mountain, or *axis mundi*. It stands at the center of the world and is the dwelling or meeting place of the gods.

Metta (Pali, *mettā*; Sanskrit, *maitri*)**:** Lovingkindness, good-will, friendliness, the sincere wish for all beings to be happy.

Middle Way: Buddha's teaching to avoid extremes.

Mindfulness: Alertness.

Mondo (Japanese, *mondō*)**:** Zen stories in question-and-answer form, usually between teacher and student. Many later became famous koans.

Mudra (Sanskrit, *mudrā*)**:** Literally, "sign" or "seal." Ritual sacred gesture of the hand, used in the Vajrayana tradition. Used in conjunction with mantras.

Mujo (Japanese)**:** *Anicca,* or impermanence.

Mumonkan (Japanese)**:** The Gateless Barrier, famous book of forty-eight koans.

Nama: In Theravada, a mental reality.

Namarupa (Sanskrit and Pali, *Nāmarūpa*)**:** Literally, "name-form" or "mind and body." The fourth link in the chain of causation or wheel of independent arising. Also used as a paraphrase for the five *skandhas*.

Nam-myoho-renge-kyo (Japanese)**:** Literally, "Hail to the Lotus Sutra!" Mantra of Nichiren Buddhism, the ultimate Law.

Naraka (Sanskrit)**:** Literally, "hell." One of the three negative planes or modes of existence.

Nembutso (Japanese)**:** An abbreviated form of Namo Amida Butso or "Name of the Amida Buddha," an invocation of the Buddha's name by Pure Land Buddhists. Supposed to effect rebirth in the Pure Land.

Nen (Japanese)**:** Literally, "thought." One thought.

Nichiren (Japanese)**:** Literally, "lotus of the sun." Japanese school of Buddhism, based on the Lotus Sutra.

Nidana (Pali, *nidāna*): Link in the chain of causation.

Niraya (Pali): Hell Realm.

Nirmana-kaya (*Nirmāna-kāya)*: Transformation body of the Buddha. The earthly Buddha.

Nirvana (Sanskrit, *Nirvāna;* Pali, *Nibbāna*): Literally, "blown out." The cessation of suffering, liberation from birth and death, extinction of desire. In Theravada countries, escaping the cycle of birth and death.

Noble Eightfold Path: See Eightfold Path.

Nondro (Tibetan; also *ngöndro*): Body, speech, and mind.

Nundrel: Foundational practices in Tibetan Buddhism.

Nyingma school (Tibetan; also *rnying-ma-pa*): Literally, "school of the ancients." The oldest of the four main schools of Tibetan Buddhism. Brought to Tibet from India by Padmasambhava in the eighth century, and to the United States by Tarthang Tulku in 1969.

Ojuzu: Buddhist beads.

Ordination: Formal entrance into a period of study for the religious profession. In Buddhism, it does not mean that one has completed the process. A legal act that must be carried out in the presence of witnesses.

Oryoki (Japanese, *ōryōki*): Set of nesting bowls given to Zen monks and nuns upon ordination. The term may also refer to the practice of silent, ritualized eating that occurs in Zen monasteries.

Pali: Ancient language allied to Sanskrit. Theravada Buddhism is based on scripture written in this language.

Panca Sila (Pali, *pancha sīla*): The five great precepts of Buddhism, sometimes abbreviated *pancil.*

Paramita (Sanskrit, *pāramitā*): Literally, "that which has reached the other shore." Perfection. There are ten perfections or virtues in Buddhism.

Parinirvana (Sanskrit, *parinirvāna*): The apparent passing away of the Buddha's physical body. Ultimate Nirvana.

Patimokkha sikhapada (Pali, *pātimokkha sikkhāpada*): Fortnightly ritual in which Theravadin monks recite the 227 precepts of monastic discipline.

Patticca samuppada (Pali; Sanskrit, *prattiya samutapda*): Conditioned arising or the co-dependent origination of all phenomena; twelve links of causation.

Phassa (Pali): Contact or touch. The sixth link in the chain of causation.

Platform Sutra of the Sixth Patriarch: An important sutra in Zen Buddhism, relating the words and deeds of Hui-neng.

Prajna (Sanskrit, *prajñā*; Pali, *pañña*): Wisdom. One of the Six Perfections of a bodhisattva.

Prajnaparamita (Sanskrit, *prajñāpāramitā*): Literally, perfection of wisdom, the true understanding of reality. The Prajnaparamita sutras express the "great emptiness" doctrine of the Madhyamika branch.

Prayer Wheel: A revolving cylinder made of various materials. Used in Tibetan Buddhism to hold the attention of the practitioner.

Preta (Sanskrit; Pali, *peta*): Hungry ghost, a frustrated disembodied spirit, usually depicted with bloated belly and tiny mouth.

Priest: An official authorized to perform ceremonies and conduct rituals.

Puja (Sanskrit, *Pūjā*): Worship in the form of offerings of food, flowers, water, incense.

Punya (Sanskrit; Pali, *punna*): Karmic merit.

Pure Land (Jodo): In Pure Land Buddhism, a transcendent but not final state of rebirth. In folk imagination a paradise of singing birds, jeweled trees, and fragrant air. Also known as the Buddha field.

Rakshasa (Sanskrit, *rāksasa*): An evil demon.

Rakusu (Japanese): Biblike rectangular cloth given at the *jukai* ceremony, when the precepts are given. It represents the Buddha's garb.

Riddhi (Sanskrit, *rddhi*): Literally, "well-being." Supernormal powers.

Rimed (Tibetan, also spelled *rime,* or *rismed* and pronounced *ri-may*): Literally, "unbiased." Nineteenth-century movement to transcend differences between sects in Tibetan Buddhism.

Rinpoche (Tibetan): Honorific title in Tibetan Buddhism for spiritual Master.

Rinzai (Japanese): A school of Japanese Buddhism making extensive use of koans. In Chinese, "Lin-chi."

Rohatsu (Japanese, *rōhatsu*): Zen *sesshin* that commemorates the Buddha's Enlightenment, in December according to Japanese reckoning.

Roshi (Japanese, *rōshi*): Literally, "old man" or "venerable teacher." Senior Zen Master. In Japan, the title "Roshi" is reserved only for a handful of truly renowned Zen Masters. In America, however, it is accorded to anyone who has received Dharma transmission, when a Zen Master identifies a particular student as his spiritual heir. A Roshi may be a monk or a layperson.

Rupa (Sanskrit and Pali, *rūpa*): Matter or form. One of the five *skandhas* or aggregates, a physical reality.

Rupadhatu (Sanskrit, *rūpadhātu*): Also called Rupaloka, the middle of the three realms. The Realm of Forms. Realm of certain of the gods. No carnal appetites in this realm, but the capacity for pleasure continues.

Saddharmapundarika Sutra (Sanskrit, *saddharmapundarīka*): Lotus Sutra.

Sadhana (Sanskrit, *sādhana)*: Derived from *sadh,* to "arrive at the goal." In Tibetan Buddhism, a special liturgical text and associated visualization-meditation practices.

Saha: The present world, full of suffering.

Sake: Japanese rice wine.

Sakya: The clan to which Siddhartha Gautama, the Buddha, belonged. Hence his title "Sakyamuni," or sage of the Sakya clan.

Sal Tree: Tree under which the Buddha died.

Salayatana (Pali, *salāyatana*)**:** The six senses. The fifth link in the chain of causation.

Sam Hoi: Vietnamese service of repentance.

Samadhi (Sanskrit, *samādhi*): Literally, "to establish." State of the deepest meditation, total absorption. Characterized by tranquility and one-pointed concentration. Merging of subject and object into nonduality. One of the three "trainings," along with ethics and wisdom.

Samanera (Pali, *sāmanera*)**:** One who keeps the precepts, but who has not yet been ordained.

Samatha (shamatha): "Calming" meditation practiced in the Theravada tradition. Prelude to insight meditation or Vipassana in the Vipassana movement, but cultivated for itself in Tibetan practice.

Sambhoga kaya (*Sambhoga-kāya*)**:** Enjoyment or bliss body of the Buddha.

Sambo (Japanese, *sambō*): The Three Jewels or Three Gems (Buddha, Dharma, Sangha).

Samjñā (Sanskrit; Pali, *sammā*)**:** Perception. One of the Five Aggregates or *skandhas.*

Samsara (Sanskrit, *samsāra*): Literally, "wandering on." Used to denote the ceaseless cycle of birth, death, rebirth, and redeath.

Samu (Japanese)**:** In Zen, designated work service for the monastic community. It refers specifically to physical work.

Sangha (Pali; Sanskrit, *samgha*)**:** Literally, a "crowd." The Buddhist priesthood or monastic community. One of the three treasures, along with the Buddha and Dharma. In some traditions, the Sangha might be a priesthood. In America, the term might simply refer to an informal group of lay meditators. In the broadest sense, it includes all Buddhists.

Sankhara (Pali; Sanskrit, *samskāra*): Literally, impression or consequence. Mental impulses or mental formations. The second link in the wheel of dependent origination.

Sanron school (Japanese)**:** Literally, "three treasures." School of Chinese, Korean, and Japanese Buddhism.

Sanzen (Japanese)**:** Literally, "going to a master." Dokusan.

Sarvodaya Shramadana (Pali, Sanskrit)**:** The awakening of all beings. Village self-help movement begun in Sri Lanka.

Sati: Mindfulness, awareness. The two words are sometimes used as synonyms, but mindfulness carries the additional meaning of "remembrance" or "keeping in mind."

Satori (Japanese)**:** In the Zen tradition, Enlightenment or sudden Awakening, opening the eye of the mind. See Kensho.

Sattva: Literally, "a being." A being, especially a sentient being.

Sayadaw: Title for a Burmese monk.

Seiza: Literally, "sitting in silence." It refers to the Japanese posture of sitting on one's heels, and is an alternative to the lotus position for meditating.

Sensei: In Zen, a teacher, usually of a lower degree of authority than a Roshi. He may have received Dharma transmission from his teacher, but not Enlightenment.

Sesshin (Japanese)**:** Literally, "mind-gathering." One or more days (usually seven) of continual *zazen*. It is considered an essential part of Zen training in both Soto and Rinzai traditions.

Shamatha (Sanskrit, *samatha*)**:** Literally, "dwelling in tranquility." A form of meditation used in the Gelugpa school of Tibetan Buddhism. Its purpose is to calm the mind, which leads to the vision of true reality—emptiness (*shunyata*).

Shambhala (Sanskrit, *śambhala*)**:** A mythical kingdom of Tibetan Buddhism.

Shastra: A treatise.

Shiho (Japanese, *shihō*)**:** In Zen, especially Soto Zen, Dharma transmission.

Shikantaza (Japanese)**:** Literally, "sitting in awareness." In the Zen tradition, "just-sitting."

Shila or Sila (Sanskrit and Pali, *śila*)**:** Character, good deeds, morality, virtue. One of the Six Perfections of a bodhisattva.

Shin (also called Jodo Shinshu or Shin Shu)**:** Pure Land, a school of Japanese Buddhism that adheres to the teachings of Honen Shonin.

Shinjin (Japanese)**:** Faith, essential aspect of Pure Land Buddhism

Shoko: Offering of incense in American Pure Land Buddhist tradition.

Shramanerika (Sanskrit)**:** Novice nun.

Shravaka (Sanskrit, *śrāvaka*)**:** Literally, "listener." A disciple of the Buddha.

Shunyata (Sanskrit, *sūnyatā*)**:** Emptiness.

Siddhi (Sanskrit)**:** Literally, "achievement" or "complete ability." A power gained through yogic practices.

Socho: Bishop in American Pure Land Buddhism.

Sodo (Japanese)**:** In Zen, a formal hall for meditation and sleeping.

Soji-ji: Famous Soto monastery in Japan.

Soka Gakkai: Value Creaton Society, founded in 1930.

Soto (Japanese, *sōtō*)**:** With Rinzai, one of the most important Zen schools. Founded by the Chinese Ch'an master Tung-shan Liang-chieh and his student Ts'ao-shan Pen-chi in the ninth century. Brought to Japan by Dogen in the thirteenth century. It emphasizes *zazen* and gradual, as opposed to sudden, Enlightenment.

Sramana (Sanskrit)**:** Wandering mendicant.

Stupa (Sanskrit, *stūpa*)**:** A sacred mound, shrine, or monument containing a relic, real or symbolic, of the historical Buddha or another teacher of the Dharma. May be a focus of pilgrimage. About fifty stupas exist in the United States.

Sukha (Sanskrit)**:** Happiness, bliss, delight.

Sukhavati (Sanskrit, *sukhāvatī*)**:** Literally, "the land of bliss." The Pure Land presided over by Amitabha.

Sunyata: Empty of self.

Surangama Sutra: Probably compiled in China. The inspiration for Kerouac's *San Francisco Blues.*

Sutra (Sanskrit, *sūtra;* Pali, *sutta*)**:** Literally, "a thread." Buddhist scripture, especially the dialogues and sermons of the Buddha.

Tanden (Japanese)**:** Literally, "one" or "single." Meditation or power center of the body, located about three inches below the navel. Also called *hara.*

Tangka: A sacred scroll used for meditation in Tibetan Buddhism.

Tanha (Pali)**:** Literally, "thirst" or "grasping." The cause of suffering. The eighth link in the chain of causation.

Tantra (Sanskrit)**:** Literally, "continuum." In Buddhism, a text that contains esoteric teachings and magical ritual. Nonconformist path to realization.

Tariki (Japanese)**:** "Other power" or grace. In Pure Land Buddhism the way to achieve salvation or passage into the Pure Land.

Tathagata (Sanskrit and Pali, *tathāgata*)**:** Thus come and gone. The Buddha.

Tathagatagarbha (Sanskrit, *tathāgatagarbha*)**:** Literally, the "embryo" or "essence" of the Tathagata, or Buddha. Used to refer to Buddha-nature, which resides in all beings.

Tathata (Sanskrit, *tathatā*)**:** Literally, "suchness." Central doctrine of Mahayana, especially the Yogachara school. Frames the concept of *shunyata* in positive terms.

Teisho (Japanese, *teishō*): A Zen or Dharma talk.

Tenzo (Japanese): Monastery cook. A revered position, given to a senior monk.

Theravada (Pali): Teaching or Way of the Elders, the "southern" school of Buddhism. Predominant in South Asia. In America, closely related to the Vipassana and insight meditation schools.

Three Jewels or Three Treasures: The Triple Gem: the Buddha, the Dharma, and the Sangha.

Three marks of existence: Impermanence (*anicca*), suffering (*dukkha*), and no-self (*anatta*).

Three Poisons: Ignorance, greed, and anger/hatred. These lie in the center of the Wheel of Life.

Tibetan Book of the Dead (Tibetan, *Bardo Thödöl*): Text that gives instruction to the dying and newly dead about how to avoid rebirth.

Tipitaka (Pali): Literally, "three baskets." The Theravada canon, consisting of the Vinaya, Sutta, and Abhidhamma Pitakas.

Toban (Japanese): Assigned duties like cooking or cleaning.

Toku (Japanese): Power.

Trikaya Doctrine (Sanskrit, *trikāya*): Literally, "three-body." In Mahayana, three bodies: the "Appearance" or "Transformation" body, "the Dharma body," and the "Enjoyment" or "Bliss" body. In Zen the three Buddhas are three levels of reality.

Triple Gem: The vow taken by all Buddhists: "I take refuge in the Buddha, I take refuge in the Dharma, I take refuge in the Sangha."

Trisharana (Sanskrit, *trisarana;* Pali, *tisarana*): The Threefold Refuge or Triple Gem.

Tushita: Heaven in which the bodhisattvas live.

Udumbara (Sanskrit): A special flower that blooms only when the Buddha is among us.

Upadana (Pali, *upādāna*): Literally, "clinging." The "will to live." The ninth link in the chain of causation.

Upaya (Sanskrit, *upāya*): Skillful or expedient means by which Dharma teachings are made available to all.

Uposatha (Pali): Literally, "fasting." In Theravadin Buddhism, a day of fasting, ritual, and religious reflection. Occurs on the quarter moon.

Vajra (Sanskrit; Tibetan, *dorje*): Literally, "diamond," or "the indestructible." In Tibetan Buddhism, the thunderbolt symbol used in art and magic.

Vajrayana (Sanskrit, *vajrayāna*): Literally, the "Diamond Vehicle" or "The Way of the Thunderbolt." Tibetan and North Indian Buddhism, a late development of Mahayana. Traditionally considered a form of Mahayana that leads more quickly to Buddhahood than the traditional Bodhisattva path.

Vassa: Rainy period.

Vedana (Sanskrit and Pali, *vedanā*): Sensation. Can be pleasant, unpleasant, or neutral. One of the Five Aggregates or *skandhas*. Also the seventh link in the chain of causation.

Vesak: Holiday celebrating the Buddha's birth, Enlightenment, and Parinirvana. Named for the Indian month in which it occurs.

Vimalakirti Sutra: Popular Mahayana sutra that praises the abilities of laypeople by telling the story of the famous debate between Manjushri and Vimalakirti.

Vinaya (Pali): Literally, "taming." Special rules of discipline for monks and nuns.

Vinnana (Pali, *Viññāna*): Normal consciousness, one of the five *skandhas*. Also the subliminal consciousness, in which sense it is the third in the chain of dependent origination.

Vipaka (Pali, *Vipāka*): Literally, "ripening." The result of an action—one's "comeuppance."

Vipassana (Pali, *vipassana*): Literally, "seeing in various ways." Insight meditation in the Theravada tradition, designed to recognize the three marks of existence and to develop Right Mindfulness. Involved analysis of the nature of existence.

Virya (Sanskrit, *vīrya*): Energy, exertion, vigor. One of the Six Perfections of a bodhisattva.

World Honored One: The Buddha.

Yaksha (Pali, *yakka*): Disruptive supernatural being said to disturb the meditations of monks and nuns.

Yogachara: School of Mahayana Buddhism propounding the doctrine of "suchness" or "thusness." Founded by Asanga and others.

Zafu (Japanese): Round meditation cushion.

Zazen (Japanese): Sitting Zen meditation; does not involve visualization.

Zen (Japanese): Ch'an Buddhism.

Zendo (Japanese, *zendō*): Meditation hall for *zazen*.

Research Questions and Projects

1. How does the life or teachings of the Buddha compare to those of Jesus or Muhammad, who also founded world religions?

2. How does the Buddhism of convert American Buddhists compare with that of ethnic Buddhists?

3. Discuss the Buddhist influences in the works of Beat writers like Jack Kerouac, Allen Ginsberg, Diane di Prima, or Harold Norse. Or consider the Buddhist influences in the works of the San Francisco poets like Gary Snyder, Philip Whalen, Joanne Kyger, Albert Saijo, Lew Welch, Lenore Kendel, Will Petersen, or Bob Kaufman. Other writers who may exhibit Buddhist influences include Williams Burroughs, Lawrence Ferlinghetti, Michael McClure, Kenneth Rexroth, or Anne Waldman. For a shorter paper, you might wish to choose one particular work, such as *The Dharma Bums*.

4. Using Buddhism as an example, make an attempt to define religion. Explore the ways in which Buddhism fits a conventional definition of religion, and ways in which it deviates from it. Do you think some schools of Buddhism are more "religious" than others?

5. Examine the influence of a Japanese Buddhist emissary to this country. You may want to consider Shunryo Suzuki.

6. Examine the influence of a Tibetan Buddhist emissary to the United States. You may want to consider Chogyam Trungpa. Why was he such an influential figure?

7. Examine the influence of a Vietnamese Buddhist emissary to the United States. You may wish to consider Thich Nhat Hanh. How is the Buddhism that he advocates different from traditional Vietnamese Buddhism?

8. What are some major changes that have occurred in various Buddhist schools to acculturate to America? What things have not changed? You might divide your paper into (a) teachings and (b) practices.

9. Consider the Buddhist attitude toward the environment, the peace movement, or another contemporary issue. You might wish to compare this viewpoint with that of Christianity, Judaism, or Islam.

10. The proper place of sexuality in the life of Buddhist monks and laypersons is currently a matter of controversy. Research this debate.

11. Explain how the Buddhist attitude toward nature is a direct result of the Buddhist concept of nonduality.

12. Explore several types of Buddhist meditation, including the purpose and methods of each.

13. How do the ideals and goals of Buddhism compare with those of the European Enlightenment, particularly as expressed by the founders of the United States? What does "Enlightenment" mean in each case?

14. What aspects of Buddhism make this religion a likely choice for many Americans? What qualities does it have that discourage or repel others? What schools of Buddhism seem the best "fit" with American values and why?

15. How does the Buddhist monastic tradition compare with the Christian one? How have American Buddhist monks modified the ancient traditions of the Sangha to fit in with American life?

16. Select an issue of contemporary interest and discuss how Buddhist teachings may apply to it. How might these teachings coincide or differ from those of other religions? You may want to consider abortion, homosexuality, capital punishment, or pacifism.

17. What is the Buddhist worldview? How does that worldview validate the findings of modern science? With that of other religions? With mainstream Western philosophy? In what ways does Buddhism retain an "antiscientific" stance? How can these two aspects of Buddhism be reconciled?

18. What can the Four Noble Truths and the Eightfold Noble Path offer people living in contemporary society?

19. Compare and contrast the Buddhist concept of karma with its Hindu counterpart, or with the Islamic notion of fate, the Christian concept of predestination, or classical notions of determinations or free will. Which of these ideas seems to make the most sense today?

20. Compare the Buddhist concept of death, rebirth, and Nirvana with its counterparts in another religious tradition or in today's secular society.

21. Carefully develop the concept of interdependent origination and explain how it can be applied today. How does it fit in with contemporary environmentalism or social action?

22. According to Buddha, the Three Fires or Three Poisons are greed, hatred, and ignorance. Apply these concepts to contemporary society.

23. What are some of the major differences between Mahayana and Theravada Buddhism? Which do you believe is most adaptable to Americana and why? You may also wish to consider Zen Buddhism and Tibetan Buddhism in your analysis.

24. Consider the concept of *upaya,* or skillful means. How has it been applied over the ages and in contemporary American society?

25. Explore the various ways the Rinzai tradition makes use of the koan.

26. Opponents of Buddhism call it an escapist or even a selfish religion. Do you agree with that designation? Support your position with examples from the precepts and actual events.

27. Some people claim that Soka Gakkai is not true Buddhism, since it does not consider meditation necessary for Enlightenment, relying rather upon its chant: *Nam-myoho-renge-kyo.* Do you consider this objection a valid one? Why or why not? In either case, what do you consider the essential components of Buddhist belief?

28. Examine the various holidays celebrated in various Buddhist traditions. Which ones can be most easily observed in the United States? Explore how Buddhist holidays have acculturated to the American scene.

Resources

Buddhist Monasteries, Centers, Associations, and Institutions

This list is of necessity incomplete. It is reliably estimated that there are more than a thousand meditation sites alone throughout the United States, in addition to the numerous institutions, organizations, and monasteries.

American Buddhist Congress (ABC)
Theravada

The ABC was founded on November 12, 1987, to bring together Buddhists, individuals, and organizations of various Buddhist traditions and of diverse Buddhist denominations and ethnic backgrounds in America. It publishes the *Journal of the American Buddhist Congress.*
www.americanbuddhistcongress.org

Aro Gar
Tibetan Buddhism, Nyingma school
P.O. Box 330
Ramsey, NJ 07446
(201) 236-9373

Aro Gar is a nonprofit organization, serving the United States and the Americas. It works closely with Sang-ngak-chö-dzong and sister organizations in Europe, dedicated to bringing the white tradition of the Nyingma school to the West.

Aryaloka Buddhist Center
14 Heartwood Circle
Newmarket, NH 03857
(603) 659-5456
www.aryaloka.org/contact/contact_home.html

Affiliated with Friends of the Western Buddhist Order (FWBO), a worldwide network of meditation and retreat centers, communities, and ethical businesses.

Association for Asian Studies
1021 East Huron Street
Ann Arbor, MI 48104
(734) 665-2490

Boulder Shambhala Center
1345 Spruce Street
Boulder, CO 80302
(303) 444-0190

Buddhist Association of the United States (BAUS)

Runs the Chuang Yen Monastery in Carmel, New York. Holds Sunday morning meditation, a book discussion group, Yoga, and Tai Chi.

Buddhist Churches of America (Pure Land)
1710 Octavia Street
San Francisco, CA 94109
Bishop Hakubun Watanabe
Rev. Kodo Umezu
email: bcahq@pacbell.net
FAX: (415) 771-6293
Phone: (415) 776-5600

Buddhist Council of the Midwest (BCM)
Theravada

The Buddhist Council of the Midwest (BCM) is an organization for all Buddhist groups in Chicago and the Midwest area. It was officially incorporated as a nonprofit religious organization by the State of Illinois on October 21, 1987. The founding purposes as stated in the Articles of Incorporation are to foster the learning and practice of Buddhism; to represent the Midwest Buddhist community in matters affecting its membership; to pool resources and coordinate efforts by its membership to create an atmosphere of fellowship and cooperation.

Buddhist Peace Fellowship
P.O. Box 4650
Berkeley, CA 94704
(510) 525-7973

Buddhist Sangha Council of Southern California (BSCSC)
Theravada

Sponsors the Los Angeles Buddhist-Catholic Dialogue

Cambridge Buddhist Association
Nondenominational Buddhism
75 Sparks Street
Cambridge, MA 02138
(617) 491-8857
email: cambridgebuddhist@worldnet.att.net

The Cambridge Buddhist Association is a nondenominational organization founded by Shinichi Hisamatsu, D. T. Suzuki, Stewart Holmes, and John and Elsie Mitchell in 1957. The current resident director is the Ven. Dharman Stortz, a Zen monk with thirty years of experience in Buddhist meditation practices. The association conducts a regular schedule of *zazen* (Zen meditation), retreats, introductory periods for beginners, and Buddhist services at its temple and also maintains a large library. In addition, the CBA provides facilities for other Buddhist groups in the Boston area, which currently include the Community of Interbeing and the Sakya Institute. A quarterly schedule and newsletter are available on request.

Cambridge Zen Center
199 Auburn Street
Cambridge, MA 02139
(617) 576-3229
email: camzen@aol.com
www.cambrdigezen.org

Offers daily morning and evening practice, residential training, public talks, monthly retreats, introductory classes.

Chagdud Gonpa Foundation
P.O. Box 279
Junction City, CA 96048
(530) 623-2714
Chgdud Tulku Rinpoche

The foundation's purpose is to preserve Nyingma teachings and to provide instruction in the traditions of Vajrayana Buddhism, especially the arts, philosophy, and meditation practices. It sponsors many events and retreats throughout the year.

Chökling Tersar
Independent Tibetan tradition
Rangjung Yeshe Gomde, CA, USA
66000 Drive Through Tree Road, Leggett
(707) 925-0201
email: *choklingtersar@yahoo.com*
www.shedrub.org/main/CTF/

Community for Mindful Living
Thich Nhat Hahn
P.O. Box 7355
Berkeley, CA 94707
(510) 527-3741

Dharma Rain Zen Center
2539 SE Madison
Portland, OR 97214
(503) 239-4846
email: Staff@Dharma-Rain.org
Kyogen and Gyokuko Carlson, abbots

Offers Soto lay practice.

Diamond Sangha
Robert Aitken lineage
2119 Kaloa Way
Honolulu, HI 96822
(808) 946-0666

Drepung Loseling Institute
Tibetan Buddhism, Gelugpa school
2531 Briarcliff Road, Suite 101
Atlanta, GA 30329
(404) 982-0051
email: institute@drepung.org
www.drepung.org

Dzogchen Foundation
Lama Surya Das
P.O. Box 734
Cambridge, MA 02140
Nonsectarian practice lineage of Tibetan Buddhism.

Ewam Choden Tibetan Buddhist Center
Offers Tibetan language training, seminars, and meditation instruction. Founded 1971.

Gay Buddhist Fellowship
2215-R Market Street PMB 456
San Francisco, CA 94114
(415) 974-9878
www.gaybuddhist.org/followindex.html
The center focuses on the spiritual concerns of gay men.

Great Plains Zen Center
P.O. Box 3362
Barrington, IL 60011
(847) 381-8798
email: gpzc@greatplainszen.org
www.greatplainszen
Offers *zazen, sesshin,* workshops, personal interview with the teacher Sensei Myoyu Anderson.

Hartford Street Zen Center
57 Hartford Street
San Francisco, CA 94114
(415) 863-2507

Hermit's Gate
30 Spring Street
Livermore Falls, ME 04254
(207) 897-5850
hermitsgate.net

Guesthouse for spiritual practice.

Hidden Mountain Zen Center
Albuquerque, NM
(505) 248-0649
email: hiddenmt@aol.com
www.peacemakercommunity.org/hiddenmountain

His Lai Temple
Chinese (Lin Chi)
Hacienda Heights, CA

Insight Meditation Society
1230 Pleasant Street
Barre, MA 01005
(978) 355-4378

A retreat center offering a variety of programs for Vipassana meditators. Founded 1975, it sponsors retreats for both beginners and experienced meditators. Dharma talks, sitting meditation, walking meditations, work retreats, and long-term practice are all offered.

Institute of Buddhist Studies, Seminary and Graduate School
2400 Ridge Road
Berkeley, CA 94709
email: gtuadm@gtu.edu
www.gtu.edu

Offers graduate-level study leading to an MA (Buddhist Studies) degree, with a particular focus on Shin (Pure Land) Buddhism. Affiliated with Ryukoku University, Kyoto, Japan. The core, three-year program in Contemporary Shin Buddhist Studies offers in addition a systematic treatment of other Buddhist traditions, a precise study of the writings of Shinran, and preparation in classical and modern Japanese.

International Association of Buddhist Studies
Centered at the University of Lausanne
Lausanne, Switzerland
Translations

International Association of Shin Buddhist Studies
Publishes *The Pure Land: Journal of Pure Land Buddhism*

International Fellowship for Realization of Impersonal Enlightenment
P.O. Box 2360
Lenox, MA 01240
Phone: (413) 637-6000 or
(800) 376-3210
fax: (413) 637-6015
email: ief@andrewcohen.org
www.andrewcohen.org/home/default.asp

Kadampa Meditation Center
47 Sweeney Road
P.O. Box 447
Glen Spey, NY 12737
Phone: (845) 856-9000
Toll free: 1-877-KADAMPA (1-877-523-2672)
Fax: (845) 856-2110
email: nfo@kadampacenter.org

Offers ongoing meditation and study programs_for all levels of experience. Has a wildlife sanctuary.

Kunzang Palyul Choling
Nyingma School of Tibetan Buddhism
18400 River Road
Poolesville, MD 20837
(301) 428-8116
www.tara.org/index.html

Offers twenty-four-hour peace prayer vigil, many stupas, and a traditional teaching center, the Migyur Dorje Center.

Maui Retreats & Hermitage
Vipassana Metta Foundation
(808) 573-3450
email: metta@maui.net
www.maui.net/~metta

Nalandabodhi

Under the direction of the Dzogchen Ponlop Rinpoche, Nalandabodhi was established as a nonprofit organization dedicated to continuing the genuine lineage of Kagyu and Nyingma Tibetan Buddhism within the modern international community. Since Nalandabodhi's inception in 1997, Ponlop Rinpoche has, under the Nalandabodhi umbrella, established main centers and study groups in the United States, Canada, Europe, and Asia.

New Orleans Zen Temple
748 Camp Street
New Orleans, LA 70130
(504) 523-1213
email: aza@gnofn.org

Roshi Robert Livingston, founder and abbot. From the Zen lineage of Roshi Kodo Sawaki and Roshi Taisen Deshimaru. Offers daily *zazen,* quarterly *sesshin,* monthly day of Zen, residency.

New York Insight Meditation Center
P.O. Box 1790
Murray Hill Station, NY 10156
(917) 441-0915
www.nyimc.org

Nonresidential retreats, courses, evening sittings, and other Insight Meditation programs.

Nichiren Buddhist International
29490 Misson Boulevard
Hayward, CA 94544
(510) 690-1222
email: NBIC@nichiren-shu.org
www.nichiren-shu.org

Offers study of the Lotus Sutra and practices of *Nam-myoho-renge-kyo.*

Nipponzan Myohoji
New England Peace Pagoda
100 Cave Hill Road
Leverett, MA 01054
Phone: (413) 367-2202
Fax: (413) 367-9367

NST Myosenji Temple
Nichiren Sho Shu
310 University Boulevard West
Silver Spring, MD 20901-1946
Phone: (301) 593-9397
Fax: (301) 593-6932
http://www.nstmyosenji.org/temple.htm

Pali Text Society
73 Lime Walk
Headington
Oxford OX3 7AD
Phone: (01865) 742125
Fax: +44 1865 750 079
email: pts@palitext.demon.co.uk
www.palitext.demon.co.uk

The society was founded in 1881 by T. W. Rhys Davids "to foster and promote the study of Pali texts." It publishes Pali texts in roman characters, translations in English and ancillary works including dictionaries, concordances, books for students of Pali, and a journal.

Providence Zen Center
Seung San (Korean) lineage
99 Pound Road
Cumberland, RI 02864-1464

Rigpa North America
Sogyal Rinpoche
P.O. Box 607
Santa Cruz, CA 95061-0607

Rochester Zen Center
Rinzai tradition
Philip Kapleau
7 Arnold Park
Rochester, NY 14607
(716) 473-9180

Sakya Center for Buddhist Studies and Meditation (Shakya Sheidrup Ling)
Cambridge, MA

Sakya Monastery of Tibetan Buddhism
Seattle, WA

Nonsectarian in the Tibetan tradition, hosting lamas from all four Tibetan traditions: Sakya, Gelugpa, Kagyu, Nyingma. Offers academic and cultural activities. Principal practice of the monastery is meditation of Bodhisattva Avalokitesvara (Chenrezi). It also holds a Mahakala Puja at the end of each month.

Sakya Phuntsok Ling Center for Tibetan Buddhist Studies and Meditation
Silver Spring, MD

San Francisco Zen Center: Three Locations
www.sfzc.org
Shunryu Suzuki's lineage

City Center
300 Page Street
San Francisco, CA 94102
(415) 863-3136

The City Center offers one-day and weeklong meditation retreats, practice periods, residential training, and a guest student program.

Green Gulch Farm
1601 Shoreline Highway
Sausalito, CA 94965
(415) 383-3134

Offers one-day and weeklong meditation retreats, one- and two-month practice periods, residential farm and work apprenticeship programs, and a guest student program.

Tassajara Zen Mountain Center
39171 Tassajara Road
Carmel Valley, CA 93924
(831) 659-2229

Offers traditional Soto Zen ninety-day training periods and a summer work practice program.

Shambhala International
Trungpa Rinpoche lineage
1084 Tower Road
Halifax, Nova Scotia
(902) 425-2750

Shasta Abbey
Jiyu Kennett's lineage
P.O. Box 199
3612 Summit Drive
Mount Shasta, CA 96067-0199
(916) 926-4208

Sixth Patriarch Zen Center
Berkeley, CA
(888) 786-1762
www.zenhall.org
Zen Master: Hyunoong Sunim

Offers Korean Rinzai Zen, Taoist breathing, meditation; residential training; retreats; weekly Dharma talks.

Society for Buddhist-Christian Studies
Frances Adeney
Louisville Seminary
1044 Alta Vista Rd.
Louisville, KY 40203
fadeney@1pts.edu
www.cssr.org/soc_sbcs.htm

Founded 1987 to provide an ongoing dialogue for those committed to study the Buddhist Christian encounter.

Society for the Study of Chinese Religions
George St. University
Department of Philosophy
Box 4089
Atlanta, GA 30302
email: jhevman2@gsu.edu
www.indiana.edu/@sscr/

Society for the Study of Japanese Religions
email: fordj@wfu.edu
www.wfu.edu/Organizations/ssjr/

An association of scholers dedicated to the study of the religions of Japan, centered at Wake Forest U.

Society for Tantric Studies

Sonoma Mountain Zen Center
6367 Sonoma Mountain Road
Santa Rosa, CA 95404
(707) 545-8105
email: snzc@sirius.com
www.zendo.com/~sonoma

Offers resident training, monthly *sesshins,* guest programs, solo retreats, workshops. Jakusho Kwong, Roshi, is resident teacher and Dharma successor to the Soto Zen lineage of Shunryu Suzuki.

Spirit Rock Meditation Center
Founder: Jack Kornfield
5000 Sir Francis Drake Boulevard
P.O. Box 169
Woodacre, CA
(415) 488-0164
www.spiritrock.org

Offers residential Vipassana retreats, meditation classes, daylong events, family program, teen program, young adult program.

Springwater Center for Meditative Inquiry
Toni Packer, nonsectarian—no longer officially associated with Buddhism
7179 Mill Street
Springwater, NY 14560
(716) 669-2141

Sweetwater Zen Center
2727 Highland Avenue
National City, CA 91950
Phone: (619) 477-0390
Fax: (619) 477-0409
email: sweetwater@swzc.org
www.swzc.org

The new Sweetwater Zen Center led by Anne Seisen Saunders, Sensei is located in National City, near San Diego and offers a program of daily practice, *sesshin*, retreats, and residential training. One of the missions of Sweetwater is to provide a Zen center revealing its practice of wisdom and compassion in the midst of work, family, and social responsibilities.

Theravada Buddhist Meditation
4920 Rose Drive
Westminster, MD 21158
(410) 346-7889
www.carr.org/~imcusa

Meditation in the tradition of Sayagyi U Ba Kim.

Theravada Buddhist Society of America
17450 S. Cabrillo Highway
Half Moon Bay, CA 94019
(650) 726-7604
www.tbsa.org/

Tri-State Dharma
P.O. Box 5378
Cincinnati, OH 45205
Joan Staubach (513) 793-0652
email: tsdharma@TriStateDharma.org

An organization designed to promote the study and practice of Insight Meditation in the Buddhist Theravadin tradition in Ohio, Kentucky, and Indiana. As such, it is actively engaged in facilitating the existing Sangha (community of practitioners) in both study and practice. The organization sponsors retreats and other related activities throughout each calendar year in an effort to bring the teachings to the public.

Tsechen Kunchab Ling
Sakya school
Seat of His Holiness Sakya Trizin
12 Edmunds Lane
Walden, N.Y. 12586

Please send correspondence to:
354 Prelude Drive
Silver Spring, MD 20901
(301) 589-3115
email: info@sakyatemple.org

Unified Buddhist Church, Inc.
Founded by Thich Nhat Hanh
C/O Green Mountain Dharma Center
Ayers Lane, P.O. Box 182
Hartland-Four-Corners, VT 05049
Phone: (802) 436-1103,
Fax: (802) 436-1101
email: MF-Office@plumvillage.org
www.plumvillage.org

Upaya Zen Center
1404 Cerro Gordo Road
Santa Fe, NM 87501
email: upaya@upaya.org
www.upaya.org

Offers Rohatsu *sesshin,* Dogen seminar, and sanctuary programs from one week to three months.

Vajrayana Foundation
2013 Eureka Canyon Road
Corralitos, CA 95076
Phone: (831) 761-6266
Fax: (831) 761-6284

Village Zendo
(212) 340-4656
www.villagezendo.org

Sensei Enkyo O'Hara, resident teacher
Morning and evening *zazen*; *sesshin* and extended retreats.

Zen Center of Los Angeles/Essence Temple
Maezumi's lineage
923 S. Normandie Avenue
Los Angeles, CA 90006
(213) 387-2351
email: zcla@mediaone.net
www.zencenter.org

Zen Center of New York City/Fire Lotus Temple
500 State Street
Brooklyn, NY 11217
(718) 875-8229
www.mro.org/zcnyc
Training center of the Mountains and Rivers Order and Ze Mountain Monastery. Daily *zazen*; Zen arts; workshops; lectures; residential program; monthly *zazen* intensives.

Zen Community of Oregon (ZCO)
Zen Community of Oregon /Great Vow Zen Monastery
P.O. Box 368
Clatskanie, OR 97016
Phone: (866) 446-5416 or (503) 728-0654.
www.zendust.org/community/index.html
Zen practice center based in Portland, Oregon, affiliated with the Soto Zen lineage of Taizan Maezumi Roshi and the Rinzai Zen lineage of Shodo Harada Roshi.

Zen Mountain Monastery (ZMM)
P.O. Box 197PC
South Plank Road
Mt. Tremper, NY 12457
(845) 688-2228
ZMM is a "monastic training center dedicated to providing authentic and traditional, yet distinctly American, Zen training to people of all ages and religious backgrounds." Located in the Catskill Mountains of New York, it covers 230 acres of nature preserve. The main house is over a

hundred years old. Its teachers include John Daido Loori, who is the abbot of the monastery and successor to Hakuyu Taizan Maezumi. Daido Roshi is among the few teachers who are recognized holders of both Rinzai and Soto lineages.

ZMM is built around what it terms the "Eight Gates of Zen": *zazen* (formal seated meditation), Zen study (ancestral lineage and personal study), liturgy (formal services, bowing and chanting), art practice (both traditional Zen and modern forms), body practice (including Tai Chi and everyday activities), Buddhist studies (historical and academic study of Buddhist philosophy), work practice (regular daily chores), and right action (study and practice of the Buddhist precepts). The monastery has a complete offering of retreats and courses, including wilderness skills training, *sesshins,* Zen gardening, *chado* (tea ceremony), Zen archery, canoeing, basics of camping, and classes on death and dying.

Zen Peacemaker Order
(805) 565-7670
www.peacemakercommunity.org

Journals

Bodhi
Quarterly; Tibetan Buddhism, Kagyu and Nyingma schools.
Features the Dharma teachings of Khenpo Tsultrim Gyamtso, Rinpoche, and Dzogchen Ponlop, Rinpoche, as well as providing their teaching schedules and periodic information on the activities and projects of Nalandabodhi. Articles by guest contributors, interviews, Sangha news, poetry, and artwork.

Cybersangha: The Buddhist Alternative Journal
www.santavihara.org/CyberSangha

The Dharma Newsstand
The Dharma Newsstand is an online kiosk for viewing a wide breadth of Buddhist periodicals.
www.dharmanet.org/journals.html

Fearless Mountain Newsletter
Connected to the Thai Forest tradition.
Abhayagiri Buddhist Monastery
16201 Tomki Road
Redwood Valley, CA 95470

Gay Buddhist Fellowship Newsletter
2261 Market Street #422
San Francisco, CA 94114
(415) 974-9878
www.planetaria.net/home/abaki/gbf

Inquiring Mind
Vipassana meditation
P.O. Box 9999
North Berkeley Station
Berkeley, CA 95709

Insight Magazine Online
Insight Meditation Society
www/dharmaorg./insight.htm

Journal of Buddhist Ethics
jbe.gold.ac.uk/faq.html

Journal of the International Association of Buddhist Studies
Scholarly journal of all aspects of Buddhist studies. Published twice yearly.
JIABS
c/o Department of Oriental Languages and Cultures
BFSH2
Lausanne University
CH-1015
Lausanne, Switzerland

Kahawai: A Journal of Women and Zen
Nonsectarian

Living Buddhism
Soka Gakkai
SGI-USA
525 Wilshire Boulevard
Santa Monica, CA 90401

Mandala
Mahayana tradition
125B La Posta Road
Taos, NM
MandalaMagazine.org. Published quarterly in March, June, September, and December.

Mindfulness Bell
Thich Nhat Hanh
P.O. Box 7355
Berkeley, CA 94707

The *Mindfulness Bell,* published three times a year, is the journal of the Order of Interbeing. Each issue includes a Dharma talk by Thich Nhat Hanh, articles by practitioners about their practice, reports on socially engaged work in Vietnam and other outreach projects, and a schedule of upcoming retreats and events. A directory of meditation groups (Sanghas) is available.

Mountain Record
Quarterly
Dharma Communications
Mt. Tremper, NY

Newsletter on International Buddhist Women's Activity

Pacific World
Pure Land
Berkeley

Shambhala Sun
1345 Spruce Street
Boulder, CO 80302-9687
Phone: (902) 422-8404
Fax: (902) 423-2701

Tibet Journal
Quarterly
Features scholarly articles on Tibetan culture.
Managing Editor, the Tibet Journal c/o Library of Tibetan Works & Archives
Gangchen Kyishong
Dharamsala, H.P. 176215, India
Phone: 01892 22467
Fax: 01892 23723

Tricycle: The Buddhist Review
Nonprofit, quarterly educational magazine, available on many newsstands.
92 Vandam Street
New York, NY 10013
www.tricycle.com/

Turning Wheel: Journal of the Buddhist Peace Fellowship
Nondenominational quarterly that publishes material related to peace and social justice. Each issue reflects a season.
Susan Moon, ed.
P.O. Box 4650
Berkeley, CA 94703-9906
(510) 655-6169
bpf@bpf.org

Cyber Communities

Discussion Lists

Buddha-L: Scholarly discussions

Insight-L: Buddhist practice

Tibet-L: Scholarly discussions

Tibetan-Studies-L: Scholarly discussions, no politics

Universal Zendo: Discussion of Zen practice

ZenBuddhism-L: Scholarly discussion of all aspects of Zen Buddhism, including Chinese, Japanese, Korean, and Western

Newsgroups

Alt.philosophy.zen

Alt.religion.buddhism.nichiren

Alt.religion.buddhism.nichiren.shoshu.news

Alt.religion.Buddhism.Tibetan

Alt.zen

Alt.zen+budo

Talk.religion.buddhism

Talk.religion.buddhism.nichiren

Uk.religion.buddhist

Web Sites

There are thousands of Buddhist related Web sites. I am including only a few of the most comprehensive. They will take you to the others.

American Buddhist Center
www.americanbuddhistcenter.org

Buddhanet
www.buddhanet.net
Buddhist information network and magazine.

Buddhism Depot
www.edepot.com/buddha.html
Translates selections from the Dhammapada (Sayings of Buddha). Also has a discussion group.

Buddhism in Canada
buddhismcanada.com
Contains directories of temples and centers by province.

Buddhism Links
www.ncf.carleton.ca/dharma/
Based in Canada, this site lists many links.

Buddhism Meditation/Access to Insight
world.std.com/~metta/index.html
Links to many sites devoted to Buddhist meditation in the Theravada tradition.

Buddhism Pointers or Buddhist Resources File
ccbs.ntu.edu.tw/BRF/
Lists a large number of Buddhist groups and societies, journals, mailing lists, news groups, and other resources.

Buddhist Studies WWW Virtual Library.
www.ciolek.com/WWWVL-Buddhism.html

Dharmanet
www.dharmanet.org
Comprehensive index of Buddhist resources.

Fundamental Buddhism
www.fundamentalbuddhism.com/
Based on the Pali canon, the earliest written records.

Shin Buddhism
www.aloha.net/~rtbloom/shinran/index/html
Based on the Shin/Pure Land traditions.

Soka Gakkai International
sgi-usa.org
Official site for Soka Gakkai, based on the teachings of Nichiren.

Book and Buddhist Supply Sources

The Buddhist Bookstore (Buddhist Churches of America)
1710 Octavia Street
San Francisco, CA 94109
(415) 776-7877
Specializing in Jodo Shinshu/Pure Land Publications
Also Buddhist jewelry, altar supplies, incense, ojuzu (Buddhist beads)

Dharma Crafts
(800) 794-9862
www.dharmacrafts.com
Meditation supplies.

Dharma.shop.com

Four Gates.com
(888) 232-7414
www.fourgates.com
Meditation and yoga supplies, meditation benches, clothing, cushions. Courses, music, jewelry, shrines.

Shasta Abbey Buddhist Supplies
3724 Summit Drive
Mt. Shasta, CA 96967
(800) 653-3315
www.buddhistsupplies.com
Offers altars and altar supplies, statues, meditation cushions and benches; rosaries; scrolls, tapes, cds, and videos; books.

Tibetan Spirit
P.O. Box 1971
Frederick, MD 21702
(888) 327-2890
email: Kftibet@aol.com
www.tibetanspirit.com
Buddhist art and ritual items; hand painted thangkas and metal statues; rugs; jewelry; singing bowls; horns; drums; Tibetan incense.

Wisdom Publications
199 Elm Street
Somerville, MA 02144
(800) 272-4050 (orders)
www.wisdompubs.org
Buddhist books

ZenWorks
P.O. Box 310
Corbett, OR 97019
(866) 446-5416
www.zenworks.org
Handcrafted meditation supplies and statuary.

Institutions Offering Advanced Degrees in Buddhist Studies

Academically Oriented

Columbia University
Harvard University
Indiana University
Princeton University
Stanford University
University of Arizona
University of California at Berkeley
University of California at Los Angeles
University of California at Santa Barbara
University of Chicago
University of Hawaii at Manoa
University of Michigan
University of Pennsylvania
University of Texas at Austin
University of Virginia
University of Washington
University of Wisconsin
Yale University

Practitioner Oriented

Naropa University
2130 Arapahoe Ave.
Boulder, CO 80302
(303) 546-3572
(800) 772-6951
www.naropa.edu

Naropa University offers BA in Religious Studies and MA in Buddhist Studies as well as Master of Divinity.

Texts and Tapes

Abe, Masao. *Zen and Western Thought.* Honolulu: University of Hawaii Press, 1985.

Adam, Enid L. *Religious Community Profiles: The Buddhists in Australia.* Canberra: Australian Government, Publishing Service, 1996.

Aitken, Emma, ed. *Meeting the Buddha: On Pilgrimage in Buddhist India.* New York: Riverhead, 1995.

Aitken, Robert

- *Taking the Path of Zen.* San Francisco: North Point, 1982.
- *The Mind of Clover: Essays in Zen Buddhist Ethics.* San Francisco: North Point, 1984.
- *The Gateless Barrier: The Wu-Men Kuan (Mumonkan).* New York: Farrar, Straus and Giroux, 1991.
- *The Path of Perfection: The Paramitas from a Zen Buddhist Perspective.* New York: Pantheon, 1994.

Akizuki, Ryomin. *New Mahayana: Buddhism for a Post-Modern World.* Trans. James W. Heisig and Paul L. Swanson. Berkeley: Asian Humanities, 1990.

Albanese, Catherine L., ed.

- *The Spirituality of the American Transcendentalists.* Macon, GA: Mercer University Press, 1988.
- *America: Religions and Religion.* 2nd ed. Belmont, CA:m Wadsworth, 1992.

Allwright, Pat. *Basics of Buddhism: Key Principles and How to Practice.* Taplow, UK: Taplow, 1998.

Almond, Philip C. *The British Discovery of Buddhism.* Cambridge: Cambridge University Press, 1988.

Ambedkar, B. R. *The Buddha and His Dhamma*. Bombay: People's Education Society, 1984.

Ames, Van Meter. *Zen and American Thought*. Honolulu: University of Hawaii Press, 1962.

Anderson, Reb.

- *Warm Smiles from Cold Mountains: A Collection of Talks of Zen Meditation*. Berkeley: Rodmell, 1999.
- *Being Upright: Zen Meditation and the Bodhissattva Precepts*. Berkeley, CA: Rodnell, 2001.

Annaud, Jean-Jacques., Becky Johnson, et al. *The Seven Years in Tibet Screen Play and the Story Behind the Film*. New York: Newmarket, 1997.

Aung San Suu Kyi

- *Freedom from Fear*. Ed. Michael Aris. New York: Penguin, 1991.
- *The Voice of Hope*. New York: Seven Stories, 1998.

Avedon, John F. *From the Land of the Lost Continent*. London: Collins, 1969.

Babbitt, Irving, trans. *The Dhammapada*. New York: New Directions, 1965.

Badiner, Allan Hunt. *Dharma Gaia: A Harvest of Essays in Buddhism and Ecology*. Berkeley: Parallax, 1990.

Baker, Richard. *Original Mind: The Practice of Zen in the West*. New York: Riverhead, 1999.

Batchelor, Martine. *Meditation for Life*. Boston: Wisdom, 2001.

Batchelor, Martine, and Kerry Brown, eds. *Buddhism and Ecology*. London: Cassell, 1992.

Batchelor, Stephen

- *The Awakening of the West: The Encounter of Buddhism and Western Culture*. Berkeley: Parallax, 1994.
- *Buddhism Without Beliefs: A Contemporary Guide to Awakening*. New York: Riverhead, 1997.
- *The Tibet Guide*. London and Boston: Wisdom, 1988.

Bays, Jan Chozen. *Jizo Bodhisattva: Modern Healing and Traditional Buddhist Practice*. Boston: Tuttle, 2001.

Becker, Carl. "Japanese Pure Land Buddhism in Christian America." *Buddhist-Christian Studies*" 10 (1990): 143–56.

Bernbaum, Edwin. *The Way to Shambhala*. Berkeley: Shambhala, 1986.

Berrigan, Daniel, and Thich Nhat Hanh. *The Raft Is Not the Shore: Conversations Toward a Buddhist-Christian Awareness.* Boston: Beacon, 1975.

Bethel, Dayle M.

- *Makiguchi the Value Creator: Revolutionary Japanese Educator and Founder of Soka Gakkai.* New York: Weatherhill, 1994.
- *Education for Creative Living: Ideas and Proposals of Tsunesaburo Makiguchi.* Ames: Iowa University Press, 1989.

Bishop, Peter. *The Myth of Shangri-la: Tibet, Travel, Writing and the Western Creation of Sacred Landscape.* Berkeley: University of California Press, 1989.

Blackstone, Kathryn. *Women in the Footsteps of the Buddha: Struggle for Liberation in the Therigatha.* Delhi, India: Curzon, 1998.

Blavatsky, Helena

- *Isis Unveiled.* 2 vols. London, 1887. Pasadena: Theosophical University Press, 1960.
- *The Secret Doctrine.* London: Theosophical University Press, 1888.

Boucher, Sandy

- *Turning the Wheel: American Women Creating the New Buddhism.* Updated and expanded edition. Boston: Beacon, 1993.
- *Opening the Lotus: A Women's Guide to Buddhism.* Boston: Beacon, 1997.

Brazier, David. *Zen Therapy.* London: Constable, 1995.

Brown, Edward Espe. *Tomato Blessings and Radish Teachings.* New York: Riverhead, 1997.

Buddhist Churches of America. *Buddhist Churches of America: A Seventy-Five Year History, 1899–1974.* 2 vols. Chicago: Nobart, 1974.

Butler, Katy. "Encountering the Shadow in Buddhist America." *Common Boundary* 8, no. 3 (1990): 14–22.

Butterfield, Stephen T. *The Double Mirror: A Skeptical Journey in Buddhist Tantra.* Berkeley: North Atlantic, 1994.

Carrithers, Michael. *The Buddha.* Oxford: Oxford University Press, 1983.

Causton, Richard

- *Nichiren Shoshu Buddhism: An Introduction.* London: Rider, 1990.
- *The Buddha in Daily Life: An Introduction to the Buddhism of Nichiren Daishonin.* London: Rider, 1995.

Chadwick, David. *Crooked Cucumber: The Life and Zen Teaching of Shunryu Suzuki.* New York: Broadway, 1999.

Chapple, Christopher Key. *Nonviolence to Animals, Earth, and Self in Asian Ethics*. Albany: State University of New York Press, 1993.

Charters, Ann, ed. *The Portable Beat Reader*. New York: Viking Penguin, 1992.

Chien, Cheng, trans. *Manifestation of the Tathagata: Buddhahood According to the Avatamsaka Sutra*. Boston: Wisdom, 1993.

Chodrun, Pema

- *The Places That Scare Us*. Boston: Shambhala, 2001.
- *The Wisdom of No Escape*. Boston: Shambhala, 1991.

Chodrun, Thubten. *Working with Anger*. Ithaca: Snow Lion, 2001.

Chogyam, Trungpa. *Meditation in Action*. Berkeley: Shambhala, 1969.

Cleary, Thomas

- Trans. *Shobogenzo: Zen Essays by Dogen*. Honolulu: University of Hawaii Press, 1986.
- *Rational Zen: The Mind of Dogen*. Boston: Shambhala, 1993.
- Trans. *The Flower Ornament Scripture: A Translation of the Avatamsaka Sutra*. 3 vols. Boston: Shambhala, 1983–86.
- *Buddhist Yoga: A Comprehensive Course*. Boston: Shambhala, 1995.
- Trans and commentary. *No Barrier: Unlocking the Zen Koan, a New Translation of the Mumonkan*. New York: Bantam, 1993.

Cleary, Thomas, and J. C. Cleary, trans. *The Blue Cliff Record*. Boulder: Prajna, 1978.

Cohen, Andrew

- *Enlightenment Is a Secret*. Corte Madera, CA: Moksha Foundation, 1991.
- *Autobiography of an Awakening*. Corte Madera, CA: Moksha Foundation, 1992.

Coleman, Graham, ed. *A Handbook of Tibetan Culture: A Guide to Tibetan Centres and Resources Throughout the World*. London: Rider, 1993.

Coleman, James William. *The New Buddhism: The Western Transformation of an Ancient Tradition*. New York: Oxford University Press, 2001.

Conze, E.

- *Buddhism, Its Essence and Development*. Oxford: Cassirer, 1960.
- Trans. *Buddhist Scriptures*. Baltimore: Penguin, 1959.

Cox, Harvey. *Turning East: The Promise and Peril of the New Orientalism*. New York: Simon and Schuster, 1977.

Cranston, Sylvia. *HPB: The Extraordinary Life and Influence of Helena Blavatsky: Founder of the Modern Theosophical Movement.* New York: Tarcher/Putnam, 1993.

Davies, Shann, ed. *Tree of Life: Buddhism and Protection of Nature.* Geneva: Buddhist Perception of Nature Project, 1987.

De Bary, Wm. Theodore. *The Buddhist Tradition in India, China, and Japan.* New York: Random House/Modern Library, 1969.

DeFina, Barbara, producer. *Kundun.* Videotape. Touchstone Pictures, 1997.

Dhammapada. John Ross Carter, and Mahinda Palihawadana, trans. New York: Oxford University Press, 1987.

Dockett, Kathleen H. *Resources for Stress Resistance: Parallels in Psychology and Buddhism.* Santa Monica, CA: SGI-USA, 1993.

Dowman, Keith. *The Masters of Mahamudra: Songs and Histories of the Eighty-four Buddhist Siddhas.* New York: State University of New York Press, 1985.

Downing, Michael. *Shoes Outside the Door: Desire, Devotion, and Excess at the San Francisco Zen Center.* Washington, DC: Counterpoint, 2001.

Dresser, Marianne, ed. *Buddhist Women on the Edge: Contemporary Perspectives from the Dharma Frontier.* Berkeley: North Atlantic, 1996.

Dumoulin, Heinrich, and John Maraldo, eds. *The Cultural, Political, and Religious Significance of Buddhism in the Modern World.* New York: Collier Macmillan, 1976.

Ellwood, Robert S.

- *The Eagle and the Rising Sun.* Philadelphia: Westminster, 1974.
- *Alternative Altars: Unconventional and Eastern Spirituality in America.* Chicago: University of Chicago Press, 1979.

Ellwood, Robert S., and Harry B. Partin. *Religious and Spiritual Groups in Modern America.* 2nd ed. Englewood Cliffs, NJ: Prentice Hall, 1988.

Emerick, R. E., trans. *The Khotanese Surangamamasamadhisutra.* London: Oxford University Press, 1970.

Eppsteiner, Fred, ed. *The Path of Compassion: Writings on Socially Engaged Buddhism.* Berkeley: Parallax, 1988.

Epstein, Ron. "Buddhism and Biotechnology." Edited from a Talk Delivered at "Spiritual Dimensions of Our Technological Future," AHIMSA Sixth Annual Conference, International House, University of California at Berkeley, October 3, 1998. www.buddhismtoday.com/english/veg/007-Biotechnology.htm.

Farber, Don, and Rick Fields. *Taking Refuge in L.A.: Life in a Vietnamese Buddhist Temple.* New York: Aperture Foundation, 1987.

Farkas, Mary, ed. *The Zen Eye: A Collection of Zen Talks by Sokei-an.* Tokyo: Weatherhill, 1993.

Fields, Rick. *How the Swans Came to the Lake: A Narrative History of Buddhism in America.* 3rd rev. ed. Boston and London: Shambhala, 1992.

Freemantle, Francesca. *Luminous Emptiness.* Boston: Shambhala, 2001.

Friedman, Lenore. *Meetings with Remarkable Women: Buddhist Teachers in America.* Boston: Shambhala, 1987.

Friedman, Lenore, and Susan Moon, eds. *Being Bodies: Buddhist Women on the Paradox of Enlightenment.* Boston: Shambhala, 1997.

Fujii, Nichidatsu

- *Buddhism for World Peace.* Yumiko Miyazaki, trans. Tokyo: Japan-Bharat Savrodaya Mitrata Sangha, 1980.
- *Beating Celestial Drums.* Yumiko Miyazaki, trans. Los Angeles: Peace, 1982.

Furlong, Monica. *Zen Effects: The Life of Alan Watts.* Woodstock, VT: Skylight Paths, 2001.

Galland, China. *The Bond Between Women: A Journey to Fierce Compassion.* New York: Riverhead, 1998.

Gehlek, Nawang Rimpoche. *Good Life, Good Death: Tibetan Wisdom on Reincarnation.* New York: Riverhead, 2001.

Gilbert, Don

- *Jellyfish Bones.* Oakland, CA: Blue Dragon, 1980.
- *The Upside Down Circle: Zen Laughter.* Nevada City, CA: Blue Dolphin, 1988.

Glassman, Bernard

- *Bearing Witness: A Zen Master's Lessons in Making Peace.* New York: Bell Tower, 1998; Random House, 1999.
- *The Infinite Circle.* Boston: Shambhala, 2002.

Glassman, Bernard, and Rick Fields. *Instructions to the Cook: A Zen Master's Lessons in Living a Life That Matters.* New York: Bell Tower, 1996.

Goddard, Dwight. *A Buddhist Bible.* Boston: Beacon, 1994.

Goldberg, Natalie. *Long Quiet Highway: Waking Up in America.* New York: Bantam, 1993.

Goldstein, Joseph. *The Experience of Insight: A Natural Unfolding.* Santa Cruz: Unity, 1967.

Govinda, Anafarika. *Foundations of Tibetan Mysticism.* London: Rider, 1960.

Green, James, trans. *The Recorded Sayings of Zen Master Joshu.* Boston: Shambhala, 2001.

Gross, Rita

- *Buddhism after Patriarchy: A Feminist History, Analysis, and Reconstruction of Buddhism.* Albany: State University of New York Press, 1987.
- *Soaring and Settling: Buddhist Perspectives on Contemporary Social and Religious Issues.* New York: Continuum, 1998.

Gunaratana, Henepola. *Mindfulness in Plain English.* Boston: Wisdom, 1994.

Gunasekara. V. A. "Ethnic Buddhism and Other Obstacles to the Dhamma in the West." *BuddhaZine.* www.buddhanet.net/bsq14. htm#sec2.

Gunter-Jones, Roger. *Buddhism and the West.* London: Lindsay, 1973.

Habito, Reuben L. F. *Healing Breath: Zen Spirituality for a Wounded Earth.* Maryknoll, NY: Orbis, 1993.

Hakeda, Yoshito S., trans., with commentary. *The Awakening of Faith: Attributed to Asvaghosha.* New York: Columbia University Press, 1967.

Hammon, Phillip, and David MacHacek. *Soka Gakkai in America: Accommodation and Conversion.* Oxford: Oxford University Press, 1999.

Hart, William. *The Art of Living: Vipassana Meditation as Taught by S. N. Goenka.* San Francisco: Harper, 1987.

Harvey, Peter. *An Introduction to Buddhism: Teachings, History, and Practices.* Cambridge: Cambridge University Press, 1990.

Hayward, Jeremy W. *Shifting Worlds Changing Minds: Where the Sciences and Buddhism Meet.* Boston: Shambhala, 1987.

Hayward, Jeremy W., and Francisco J. Varela, eds. *Gentle Bridges: Conversations with the Dalai Lama on the Sciences of the Mind.* Boston and London: Shambhala, 1992.

Henderson, Harold. *Catalyst for Controversy: Paul Carus of Open Court.* Carbondale: Southern Illinois University Press, 1993.

Hill, Michele, ed. *Not Mixing Up Buddhism: Essays on Women and Buddhist Practice.* Fredonia, NY: White Pine, 1986.

Humphreys, Christmas

- *The Development of Buddhism in England.* London: Buddhist Lodge, 1937.

- *Zen Comes West: The Present and Future of Zen Buddhism in Britain.* London: George Allen and Unwin, 1960.
- *Both Sides of the Circle.* London: George Allen and Unwin, 1978.

Hunter, Louise. *Buddhism in Hawaii.* Honolulu: University of Hawaii Press, 1971.

Hurst, Jane. *Nichiren Shoshu Buddhism and the Soka Gakkai in America: The Ethos of a New Religious Movement.* New York: Garland, 1992.

Ikeda, Daisaku

- *Human Revolution.* Vols. 1–5. Tokyo and New York: Weatherhill, 1972–86.
- *Unlocking the Mysteries of Birth and Death: Buddhism in the Contemporary World.* London: Warner, 1995.
- *Dialogue on Life.* Vols. 1 and 2. Tokyo: NSIC, 1995.
- *Faith into Action.* Santa Monica, CA: World Tribune, 1999.
- *For the Sake of Peace: Seven Paths to Global Harmony, a Buddhist Perspective.* Santa Monica, CA: Middleway, 2001.

Itsuki, Hiroyuki. *Tariki: Embracing Despair, Discovering Peace.* New York: Kodansha, 2001.

Jackson, Carl T. *The Oriental Religions and Western Thought.* Westport, CT: Greenwood, 1981.

Jiyu-Kennett, Roshi. *Zen Is Eternal Life.* Mt. Shasta, CA: Village Books, 1987.

Johnson, Kent, and Craig Paulenich, eds. *Beneath a Single Moon: Buddhism in Contemporary American Poetry.* Boston: Shambhala, 1991.

Johnson, Samuel. *Oriental Religions and their Relation to Universal Religion.* 3 vols. Boston: Houghton Mifflin, 1872, 1877, 1885.

Jones, Ken. *The Social Face of Buddhism: An Approach to Social and Political Action.* Boston: Wisdom, 1989.

Kalupahana, David J. *A History of Buddhist Philosophy: Continuities and Discontinuities.* Honolulu: University of Hawaii Press, 1992.

Kapleau, Philip

- *The Three Pillars of Zen.* New York: Anchor, 1980.
- *To Cherish All Life: A Buddhist Case for Becoming Vegetarian.* San Francisco: Harper and Row, 1982.
- *The Zen of Living and Dying: A Practical and Spiritual Guide.* Boston: Shambhala, 1998.
- *Zen: Merging of East and West.* New York: Anchor, 2000.
- *Straight to the Heart of Zen: Eleven Classic Koans & Their Inner Meanings.* Boston: Shambhala, 2001.

Kashima, Tetsuden

- *Buddhism in America: The Social Organization of an Ethnic Religious Institution.* Westport, CT: Greenwood, 1997.
- "The Buddhist Churches of America: Challenges for Change in the 21st Century." *The Pacific World* 6 (1990): 28–49.

Katagiri, Dainin. *Returning to Silence.* Boston: Shambhala, 1988.

Kato, Bunno, Yoshiro Tamura, and Kojiro Miyasaka, trans. *The Threefold Lotus Sutra.* New York: Weatherhill, 1975.

Kawamura, Leslie S., ed. *The Bodhisattva Doctrine in Buddhism.* Waterloo, ON: Canadian Corporation for Studies in Religion, 1981.

Kaye, Les. *Zen at Work.* New York: Three Rivers, 1997.

Kaza, Stephanie, and Kenneth Kraft, eds. *Dharma Rain: Sources of Environmental Buddhism.* Boston: Shambhala, 2000.

Keown, Damien V. *Buddhism and Bioethics.* London: Macmillan, 1992.

Keown, Damien V., Charles S. Prebish, and Wayne R. Husted, eds. *Buddhism and Human Rights.* Surrey, UK: Curzon, 1998.

Kerouac, Jack

- *Dharma Bums.* New York: Penguin, 1991.
- *The Scripture of the Golden Eternity.* San Francisco: City Lights, 1994.
- *Blue Jean Buddha: Voices of Young Buddhists.* Ed. Sumi London. Boston: Wisdom, 2001.

Khema, Ayya. *Being Nobody, Going Nowhere.* Boston and London: Wisdom, 1987.

Khong, Chan. *Learning True Love.* Berkeley, CA: Parallax, 1993.

King, Sallie B. *Buddha Nature.* Albany: State University of New York Press, 1991.

Klein, Anne C. *Meeting the Great Bliss Queen: Buddhists, Feminists, and the Art of the Self.* Boston: Beacon, 1995.

Kornfeld, Jack. *Living Dharma: Teachings of Twelve Buddhist Masters.* Boston: Shambhala, 1996.

Kotler, Arnold, ed. *Engaged Buddhist Reader: Ten Years of Engaged Buddhist Publishing.* Berkeley: Parallax, 1996.

Kraft, Kenneth, ed.

- *Inner Peace, World Peace: Essays on Buddhism and Nonviolence.* Albany: State University of New York Press, 1992.
- *The Wheel of Engaged Buddhism: A New Map of the Path.* New York: Weatherhill, 1999.
- *Zen: Tradition and Transition.* New York: Grove Press, 1988.

Kinsang, Erik Pema, trans. *The Lotus-Born: The Life Story of Padmasambhava, Composed by Yeshe Tsogyal.* Boston: Shambhala, 1993.

Layman, Emma. *Buddhism in America.* Chicago: Nelson Hall, 1976.

Leighton, Taigen Daniel. *Bodhisattva Archetypes: Classic Buddhist Guides to Awakening and their Modern Expression.* New York: Penguin, 1988.

Lhalungpa, Lobsang. *Mahamudra: The Quintessence of Mind and Meditation.* Delhi: Motilal Banarsidass, 2000.

Lin, Irene. "Journey to the Far West: Chinese Buddhism in America." *Amerasia Journal* 22, no. 1 (1996): 107–32.

Linzer, Judith. *Torah and Dharma: Jewish Seekers in Eastern Religions.* Northvale, NJ, and London: Jason Aronson, 1996.

Loori, John

- *The Eight Gates of Zen: Spiritual Training in an American Zen Monastery.* Mt. Tremer, NY: Dharma Communications, 1992.
- *The Heart of Being: Moral and Ethical Teachings of Zen Buddhism.* Boston: Charles E. Tuttle, 1996.

Lopez, Donald S., Jr.

- *Curators of the Buddha.* Chicago: University of Chicago Press, 1995.
- *The Story of Buddhism: A Concise Guide to its History and Teachings.* San Francisco: HarperCollins, 2001.
- *Prisoners of Shangri-La: Tibetan Buddhism and the West.* Chicago: University of Chicago Press, 1998.

Lorie, Peter, and Hillary Foakes, eds. *The Buddhist Directory: The Total Buddhist Resource Guide.* Boston: Tuttle, 1997.

Macy, Joanna

- *Despair and Empowerment in the Nuclear Age.* Philadelphia: New Society, 1983.
- *Thinking Like a Mountain: Towards a Council of All Beings,* with John Seed, Arne Naess, and Pat Fleming. Gabriola Island, BC: New Society, 1988.
- *Mutual Causality in Buddhism and General System Theory: The Dharma of Natural Systems.* Albany State University of New York Press, 1991.
- *World as Lover, World as Self.* Berkeley, CA: Parallax, 1991.
- *Widening Circles: A Memoir.* Gabriola Island, BC: New Society, 2000.

Maezumi, Taizen. *The Way of Everyday Life: Zen Master Dogen's Genjokoan with Commentary.* Los Angeles: Center, 1978.

Martin, Julia, ed. *Ecological Responsibility: A Dialogue with Buddhism.* Sambhota Series V. Delhi: Sri Satguru, 1997.

Matsungaga, Alicia. *The Buddhist Philosophy of Assimilation.* Rutland, VT: Tuttle, 1969.

Matthiessen, Peter. *Nine-Headed Dragon River: Zen Journals.* Boston: Shambhala, 1987.

Mettraux, Donald

- *The History and Theology of Soka Gakkai: A Japanese New Religion.* Lewiston, NY: Edwin Mellen, 1988.
- *The Lotus and the Maple Leaf: The Soka Gakkai Buddhist Movement in Canada.* Lewiston, NY: University Press of America, 1996.

Mills, Charles D. B. *The Indian Saint: Or, Buddha and Buddhism.* Northampton, MA: Journal and Free Press, 1876.

Mitchell, Donald W. *Buddhism: Introducing the Buddhist Experience.* New York: Oxford University Press, 2002.

Montgomery, Daniel B. *Fire in the Lotus: The Dynamic Buddhism of Nichiren.* London: Thorsons, 1991.

Moore, Dinty W. *The Accidental Buddhist: Mindfulness, Enlightenment, and Sitting Still.* Chapel Hill: Algonquin, 1997.

Morgante, Amy, ed. *Buddhist Perspectives on the Earth Charter.* Boston: Boston Research Center for the 21st Century, 1997.

Morreale, Don, ed.

- *Buddhist America.* Santa Fe: John Muir, 1988.
- *The Complete Guide to Buddhist America.* Boston: Shambhala, 1998.

Mullen, Glenn H. *The Fourteen Dalai Lamas: A Sacred Legacy of Reincarnation.* Santa Fe: Clear Light, 2001.

Mullin, Blenn. *Death and Dying: The Tibetan Perspective.* London: Arkana, 1986.

Nagao, Gadjin. *Madhyamika and Yogacara: A Study of Mahayana Philosophies.* Trans. and ed. L. S. Kawamura. Albany: State University of New York Press, 1991.

Needleman, Jacob. *The New Religions.* New York: E. P. Dutton, 1977.

Nhat Hanh, Thich.

- *Anger: Wisdom for Cooling the Flames.* New York: Riverhead, 2001.
- *Being Peace.* Berkeley, CA: Parallax, 1987.
- *Peace Is Every Step.* Berkeley, CA: Parallax, 1991.
- *Touching Peace.* Berkeley, CA: Parallax, 1992.

- *Love in Action: Writings on Nonviolent Social Change*. Berkeley, CA: Parallax, 1993.
- *Call Me by My True Names*. Berkeley, CA: Parallax, 1993.
- *Interbeing*. Berkeley, CA: Parallax, 1998.
- *For a Future to Be Possible: Commentaries on the Five Wonderful Precepts*. Berkeley: Parallax, 1993.

Nordstrom, Lou Mitsune, ed. *Namu Dai Bosa: A Transmission of Zen Buddhism to America*. New York: The Zen Studies Society, 1976.

Numrich, Paul. *Old Wisdom in the New World: Americanization in Two Theravada Buddhist Temples*. Knoxville: University of Tennessee Press, 1996.

O'Halloran, Maura. *Pure Heart, Enlightened Mind*. New York: Riverhead, 1994.

Olcott, Henry S. *Buddhist Catechism, According to the Canon of the Southern Church*. Boston: Estes and Lauriat, 1885.

Packer, Toni

- *What Is Meditative Inquiry?* Springwater, NY: Springwater Center, 1988.
- *The Work of This Moment*. Boston: Shambhala, 1990.

Pallis, Marco. *A Buddhist Spectrum*. New York: Seabury, 1981.

Paul, Diana. *Women in Buddhism: Images of the Feminine in Mahayana Buddhism*. Berkeley: University of California Press, 1985.

Payutto, P. A. "Buddhist Economics: A Middle Way for the Market Place." 205.180.85.40/w/pc.cgi?mid=11129&sid=7271.

Peck, L. Adams (Elizabeth Barrington). *The Story of Oriental Philosophy*. New York: New Home Library, 1928.

Peiris, William. *The Western Contribution to Buddhism*. Delhi: Motilal Banarsidass, 1973.

Piyananda, Walpola. *Saffron Days in L.A.: Tales of a Buddhist Monk in America*. Boston: Shambhala, 2001.

Prebish, Charles S.

- *American Buddhism*. North Scituate, MA: Duxbury, 1979.
- *Luminous Passage: The Practice and Study of Buddhism in America*. Berkeley and Los Angeles: University of California Press, 1999.
- "Ethics and Integration in American Buddhism." *Journal of Buddhist Ethics* 2 (1995): 125–39.

Prebish, Charles S., and Kenneth K. Tanaka, eds. *The Faces of Buddhism in America*. Berkeley: University of California Press, 1998.

Prothero, Stephen. *The White Buddhist: The Asian Odyssey of Henry Steele Olcott*. Bloomington: Indiana University Press, 1996.

Queen, Christopher S., ed. *Engaged Buddhism in the West*. Boston: Wisdom, 2000.

Queen, Christopher S., and Sallie B. King, eds. *Engaged Buddhism: Buddhist Liberation Movements in Asia*. Albany: State University of New York Press, 1996.

Rahula, Wapola

- *What the Buddha Taught*. Bedford: Gordon Fraser, 1959.
- *The Heritage of the Bhikkhu*. New York: Grove, 1974.

Rapaport, Al, and Brian D. Hotchkiss, eds. *Buddhism in America: Proceedings of the First Buddhism in America Conference*. Rutland, VT: Tuttle, 1998.

Rawlinson, Andrew. *The Book of Enlightened Masters: Western Teachers in Eastern Traditions*. Chicago and LaSalle: Open Court, 1997.

Ray, Reginald. *Secret of the Vajra World: The Tantric Buddhism of Tibet*. Boston: Shambhala, 2001.

Reps, Paul, and Nyogen Senzaki. *Zen Flesh Zen Bones: A Collection of Zen and Pre-Zen Writings*. Garden City, NY: Doubleday Anchor.

Ricard, Matthieu, and Trinh Xuan Thuan. *The Quantum and the Lotus: A Journey to the Frontiers Where Science and Buddhism Meet*. New York: Crown, 2001.

Rockefeller, Steven C., and John C. Elder. *Spirit and Nature: Why the Environment Is a Religious Issue*. Boston: Beacon, 1992.

Sangharakshita

- *New Currents in Western Buddhism*. Glasgow: Windhorse, 1990.
- *The Eternal Legacy: An Introduction to the Canonical Literature of Buddhism*. London: Tharpa, 1985.

Sargent, Jiho. *Asking About Zen: 108 Answers*. New York: Weatherhill, 2001.

Sasaki, Ruth Fuller, Yoshitaka Iriya, and Dana R. Fraser, trans. *A Man of Zen: The Recorded Sayings of Layman P'ang*. New York: Weatherhill, 1971.

Schell, Orville. *Virtual Tibet: Searching for Shangri-La from the Himalayas to Hollywood*. New York: Metropolitan Books/Henry Holt, 2000.

Schneider, David. *Street Zen: The Life and Works of Issan Dorsey*. Boston: Shambhala, 1997.

Schumacher, E. F. *Small Is Beautiful: Economics as if People Mattered*. New York: Harper and Row, 1975.

Schumacher, Michael. *Dharma Lion: A Biography of Allen Ginsberg.* New York: St. Martin's, 1992.

Seager, Richard Hughes

- *Buddhism in America.* Columbia Contemporary Religious Series. New York: Columbia University Press, 1999.
- *The World's Parliament of Religions: The East/West Encounter, Chicago, 1893.* Bloomington: Indiana University Press, 1995.

Seed, John, Joanna Macy, Pat Fleming, and Arne Naess. *Thinking Like a Mountain: Towards a Council of All Beings.* Philadelphia: New Society, 1988.

Seuss, D. *The Lorax.* New York: Random House, 1971.

Shainberg, Lawrence. *Ambivalent Zen.* New York: Pantheon, 1995.

Shaw, Miranda. *Passionate Enlightenment: Women in Tibetan Buddhism.* Princeton: Princeton University Press, 1994.

Sherrill, Martha. *The Buddha from Brooklyn: A Tale of Spiritual Seduction.* New York: Vintage, 2000.

Shibayama, Zenkei. *Zen Comments on the Mumonkan.* Trans. Sumiko Kudo. New York: Harper and Row, 1974.

Sidor, Ellen S., ed. *A Gathering Spirit: Women Teaching in American Buddhism.* Cumberland, RI: Primary Point, 1987.

Sivaraksa, Sulak

- *Seeds of Peace: A Buddhist Vision of Renewing Society.* Berkeley, CA: Parallax, 1998.
- *Loyalty Demands Dissent: Autobiography of an Engaged Buddhist.* Berkeley, CA: Parallax, 1998.

Sizemore, Russell F., and Donald K. Swearer, eds. *Ethics, Wealth and Salvation: A Study in Buddhist Social Ethics.* Columbia: University of South Carolina Press, 1990.

Smith, Vincent A. *Asoka: The Buddhist Emperor of India.* Delhi: S. Chand and Co., 1964.

Snelgrove, David. *Indo-Tibetan Buddhism.* Boston: Shambhala, 1987.

Snelling, John. *The Buddhist Handbook: The Complete Guide to Buddhist Schools, Teaching, Practice, and History.* Rochester, VT: Inner Traditions, 1991.

Snow, David A. *Shakubuku: A Study of the Nichiren Shoshu Buddhist Movement in America, 1960–1975.* New York: Garland, 1993.

Snyder, Gary

- *Turtle Island.* New York: New Directions, 1974.

- *The Real Work: Interviews and Talk, 1964–79.* Ed. W. Scott McLean. New York: New Directions, 1980.
- *The Practice of the Wild.* San Francisco: North Point, 1990.
- *No Nature: New and Selected Poems.* New York: Pantheon, 1992.

Sogyal, Rinpoche. *The Tibetan Book of Living and Dying.* San Francisco: HarperCollins, 1993.

Storlie, Erik Fraser. *Nothing on My Mind: Berkeley, LSD, Two Zen Masters, and a Life on the Dharma Trail.* Boston: Shambhala, 1996.

Subhuti, Dharmacari (Alex Kennedy)

- *Buddhism for Today: A Portrait of a New Buddhist Movement.* 2nd ed. Glasgow: Windhorse, 1988.
- *Sangharakshita, A New Voice in the Buddhist Tradition.* Birmingham: Windhorse, 1994.

Surya Das, Lama. *Awakening the Buddha Within: Tibetan Wisdom for the Western World.* New York: Broadway, 1999.

Sutta-Nipata. Trans. V. Fausboll. Delhi, India: Motalil Banarsidass, 1968.

Suzuki, Daisetz Teitaro. *An Introduction to Zen Buddhism.* New York: Grove Weidenfeld. 1964.

Suzuki, Shunryu

- *Zen Mind, Beginner's Mind.* New York: Weatherhill, 1970.
- *Branching Streams Flow in the Darkness: Zen Talks on the Sandokai.* Berkeley: University of California Press, 1999.

Swearer, Donald K. *Buddhism in Transition.* Philadelphia: Westminster, 1970.

Swick, David. *Thunder and Ocean: Shambhala and Buddhism in Nova Scotia.* Lawrencetown Beach, Nova Scotia: Pottersfield, 1996.

Tachibana, S. *The Ethics of Buddhism.* London: Curzon, 1981.

Tamney, Joseph B. *American Society in the Buddhist Mirror.* New York: Garland, 1992.

Tanahashi, Kazuaki, ed and trans. *Moon in a Dewdrop: Writings of Master Dogen.* New York: Farrar, Straus and Giroux, Northpoint, 1985.

Tanaka, Kenneth K. *Ocean: An Introduction to Jodo Shinshu Buddhism in America.* Berkeley, CA: Wisdom Ocean, 1997.

Tanaka, Kenneth K., and Eisho Nasu, eds. *Engaged Pure Land Buddhism: The Challenges Facing Jodo Shinshu in the Contemporary World.* Berkeley, CA: Wisdom Ocean, 1998.

Tendzin, Osel. *Buddhism in the Palm of Your Hand.* Boston: Shambhala, 1982.

Tenzin, Gyatso, Dalai Lama XIV

- *Answers: Discussions with Western Buddhists*. Trans. and ed. Jose Cabezon. Ithaca: Snow Lion, 2001.
- *Ethics for the New Millennium*. New York: Riverhead, 1999.
- *Kindness, Clarity, and Insight*. Ed. J. Hopkins and E. Nappers. Ithaca: Snow Lion, 1984.

Tenzin, Gyatso, and Jean-Claude Carriere. *Violence and Compassion*. New York: Doubleday, 1996.

Thera, Nyanaponika. *The Heart of Buddhist Meditation*. London: Rider, 1983.

Thurman, Robert. *Inner Revolution: Life, Liberty, and the Pursuit of Real Happiness*. New York: Riverhead, 1998.

Titmuss, Christopher. *The Green Buddha*. Totnes, UK: Insight, 1995.

Tonkinson, Carole, ed. *Big Sky Mind: Buddhism and the Beat Generation*. New York: Riverhead, 1995.

Trungpa, Chogyam

- *Born in Tibet*. Rev. ed. Boulder: Prajna, 1981.
- *Cutting Through Spiritual Materialism*. Berkeley, CA: Shambhala, 1973.
- *The Myth of Freedom and the Way of Meditation*. Boulder: Shambhala, 1976.

Tsomo, Karma Lekshe, ed.

- *Sakyadhita: Daughters of the Buddha*. Ithaca: Snow Lion, 1989.
- *Buddhism Through American Women's Eyes*. Ithaca: Snow Lion, 1995.

Tuck, Andrew. *Comparative Philosophy and the Philosophy of Scholarship: Western Interpretations of Nagarjuna*. New York: Oxford University Press, 1990.

Tuck, Donald. *Buddhist Churches of America: Jodo Shinshu*. Lewiston, NY: Edwin Mellen, 1998.

Tucker, Evelyn, and Duncan Ryuken Williams, eds. *Buddhism and Ecology: The Interconnection of Dharma and Deeds*. Cambridge, MA: Harvard Center for the Study of World Religions, 1998.

Tweed, Thomas A. *The American Encounter with Buddhism, 1844–1912: Victorian Culture and the Limits of Dissent*. Chapel Hill: University of North Carolina Press, 1992.

Tweed, Thomas A., and Stephen Prothero. *Asian Religions in America: A Documentary History*. New York: Oxford University Press, 1999.

Tworkov, Helen. *Zen in America: Five Teachers and the Search for an American Buddhism*. New York: Kodansha International, 1989.

Unno, Taitetsu. *River of Fire, River of Water*. New York: Doubleday, 1998.

Van Biema, David. "Buddhism in America." *Time*, October 13, 1997.

Van de Wetering, Janwillem: *Afterzen: Experiences of a Zen Student Out on His Ear*. New York: St. Martin's, 1999.

Van Esterik, Penny. *Taking Refuge: Lao Buddhists in North America*. Tempe: Program for Southeast Asian Studies, Arizona State University, 1992.

Verluis, Arthur. *American Transcendentalism and Asian Religions*. New York: Oxford University Press, 1993.

Vessantara, Dharmachari. *The Friends of the Western Buddhist Order*. Glasgow: Windhorse, 1988.

Victoria, Brian. *Zen at War*. New York: Weatherhill, 1997.

Watson, Burton

- Trans. *The Vimalakirti Sutra*. New York: Columbia University Press, 1996.
- Trans. *The Zen Teachings of Master Lin-Chi*. New York: Columbia University Press, 1999.

Watson, Gay, Stephen Batchelor, and Guy Claxton. *Psychology of Awakening: Buddhism, Science, and Our Day-to-Day Lives*. York Beach, ME: Samuel Weiser, 2000.

Watts, Alan. *Beat Zen, Square Zen, and Zen*. Rev. ed. San Francisco: City Lights, 1959.

Watts, Jon, Alan Senauke, and Santikaro Bhikku. *Entering the Realm of Reality: Towards Dhammic Societies*. Bangkok: International Network of Engaged Buddhists, 1997.

Welwood, John, ed. *The Awakening of the Heart*. Boulder and London: Shambhala, 1983.

Whitmyer, Claud, ed. *Mindfulness and Meaningful Work: Explorations in Right Livelihood*. Berkeley, CA: Parallax, 1994.

Williams, Duncan Ryuken, and Christopher S. Queen, eds. *American Buddhism: Methods and Findings in Recent Scholarship*. Surrey, UK: Curzon, 1999.

Williams, George M. *Freedom and Influence: The Role of Religion in American Society*. Santa Monica, CA: World Tribune, 1985.

Williams, Paul. *Mahayana Buddhism: The Doctrinal Foundations*. London: Routledge, 1989.

Wilson, Martin. *Rebirth and Western Buddhism*. London: Wisdom, 1987.

Yamada, Koun. *Gateless Gate*. Los Angeles: Center, 1979.
Yampolsky, Philip. *The Platform Sutra of the Sixth Patriarch*. New York: Columbia University Press, 1967.
Yamplosky, Philip B., ed. *Selected Writings of Nichiren*. New York: Columbia University Press, 1990.
Zimmer, Heinrich. *Philosophies of India*. London: Routledge and Kegan Paul, 1969.

Index

About the Author

Diane Morgan teaches religion and philosophy at Wilson College in Chambersburg, Pennsylvania. She is the author of over a dozen books, including Best Guide to Eastern Philosophy and Religion (2001).